The
WHO'S WHO
of
Children's
Literature

(*overleaf*) Billy Bunter, the immortal fat boy of Frank Richards' Greyfriars School, created in the popular boys' weekly *The Magnet* in 1908 and probably the most famous and widely-discussed fictional school in English literature. Drawn by veteran illustrator C. H. Chapman, who has been depicting Bunter for nearly 60 years

(From an original drawing in the Editor's collection. Reproduced by permission of the artist)

The WHO'S WHO of Children's Literature

Compiled and edited
by Brian Doyle

HUGH EVELYN LONDON

First published in 1968 by
Hugh Evelyn Limited, c
9 Fitzroy Square, London W1
© 1968, Brian Doyle
S.B.N. 238. 78812. 1
Designed by Sheila Sherwen
Printed and bound in Great Britain by
The Camelot Press, London and Southampton

Contents

List of Illustrations

Sources of Illustrations

The author and publisher wish to acknowledge the sources of the illustrations and to thank the following for permission to reproduce them:

George Allen & Unwin Ltd, plate 13; Associated British Pictures Corporation, plate 31; Ernest Benn Ltd, plates 68, 87, 99, 100; A. & C. Black Ltd, plates 91a, 91b; Blackie & Son Ltd, plate 86; The Boy's Own Annual, plate 47; The Brockhampton Press, plates 40, 84; Jonathan Cape Ltd, plate 70; Cassell & Co., plates 4, 12, 33, 48, 49; Chapman & Hall Ltd, plate 92; Chatto & Windus Ltd, plate 97; William Collins Sons & Co. Ltd, plates 15, 16, 80, 82; J. M. Dent & Sons Ltd, plates 24, 25, 34, 85, 89, 90, 103; Walt Disney Productions Ltd, plate 38; Eyre & Spottiswoode Ltd, plate 35; P. R. Gawthorne Ltd, plate 20; Gillman & Soame Ltd, Oxford, plate 73; Ginn & Co., Boston & New York, plate 26; Harper & Row Publishers Inc., plate 2; Heirloom Library, plates 11, 36; Hodder & Stoughton Ltd, plates 14, 17, 41, 42, 43, 45, 46; Macmillan & Co. Ltd, plates 7, 8, 10, 27, 29, 30; The Macmillan Company, New York, plate 6; Methuen & Co. Ltd, plates 75, 77, 102, 104; M-G-M Pictures, plate 37; John Murray Ltd, plate 98; The Hamlyn Group (George Newnes Books), plates 32, 50, 79, 81, 83; Oxford University Press, plates 39, 71, 74, 76, 78; Paramount Film Service Ltd, plates 23, 44; Radio Times Hulton Picture Library, plates 51–66, 72; Renown Productions, plate 28; RKO Radio Pictures/Pathé, plate 22; George Routledge & Sons, plates 1, 60, 101; Raphael Tuck & Sons Ltd, plates 18, 19; Ward, Lock & Co. Ltd, plate 3; Frederick Warne & Co. Ltd, plates 67, 69, 95, 96; United Artists Corporation Ltd, plate 5; plate 90, © The World Publishing Company; illustration by Willy Pogany (plate 21) from the book *Alice's Adventures in Wonderland* by Lewis Carroll; © 1929, by E. P. Dutton & Co., Inc. Renewal, ©, 1957 by Mrs Willy Pogany; reproduced by permission of E. P. Dutton & Co., Inc.

Introduction

The Who's Who of Children's Literature will, I hope, fill a gap that has long seemed evident in the field of reference material concerning this important and influential branch of literature.

Until now, if anyone has required basic information about a certain writer or illustrator of children's books, he has had to refer to numerous books, many of which are now rare and difficult to locate. Again, several otherwise notable histories of children's literature do not even mention many of its most popular and famous contributors. Names such as Enid Blyton, Richmal Crompton, W. E. Johns, L. Frank Baum and Charles Hamilton ('Frank Richards') spring to mind. Yet these writers (and many more) are leading 'best-sellers' with children in many parts of the world and the books they write and the characters they create play a not insignificant part in the lives of their young readers. This *Who's Who* contains the names of many of these widely-read writers, as well as most of those 'approved' authors and illustrators you would expect to find – with a few unexpected names included too (who would have suspected, for example, that Bram Stoker, world-famed for his *Dracula* horror story, also wrote a book of children's stories?).

While the *Who's Who* is a guide to the most notable authors and illustrators of children's books, from the early nineteenth century to the present day, some early classics have also been included. It is arranged alphabetically in two sections.

The selection has been limited to approximately 300 names since, if complete thoroughness had been aimed at, the work would have taken up several volumes. Editorial emphasis has been placed on those English-language authors, both British and American, who constitute the heritage of juvenile literature. Some European authors who through translation of their work have found a place among the English classics of children's literature have also been included. I have tried to present a handy reference-guide which I hope can be read and enjoyed for pleasure, as well as consulted for facts. I trust it may prove helpful to librarians, teachers, parents, researchers, journalists, and all who have to do with children and their reading. The book may well provide some nostalgic browsing for everyone who has ever read a children's book and revive a few pleasant memories. If it sends them back to the juvenile bookshelf to renew acquaintance with the heroes and heroines (to say nothing of the villains) of their youth, so much the better. The best children's stories can be read and enjoyed by any age. Today's young readers may welcome the opportunity to learn something about their current favourite author or artist, too.

In short, if ever a child – of today or yesterday – had a favourite writer or illustrator, then there is a very good chance that he or she will be found here. The authors, it should be noted, are all writers of fiction in this field; juvenile non-fiction is another subject entirely and is not covered here, though if an author has produced notable factual books in addition to his stories, they are naturally mentioned.

But, of course, the best way to discover the scope of the work is to skim through the entries.

Acknowledgements for the various illustrations and portraits used in the book can be found on page viii and mention of some books consulted are in the bibliographical section. I should like to add a word of thanks to the staff of the British Film Institute for their help in selecting suitable film stills and for the film companies concerned for their co-operation in giving their permission for these to be used. Thanks, too, to Mr C. H. Chapman, veteran *Magnet* illustrator, for allowing me to reproduce the composite picture of Billy Bunter as a frontispiece; also, to Hugh Owen, of Dorset, for his assistance in compiling the entries on Bridges, Everett-Green, Gilson and Upton, and to John Rolph, for his editorial help and suggestions. Certain entries (chiefly concerning authors and illustrators of old boys' papers and magazines) originally appeared, in a slightly different form, in my earlier publication *The Who's Who of Boys' Writers and Illustrators* in 1964; some of these entries were compiled from the original researches of the indefatigable contributors to the *Collector's Digest* magazine, notably W. O. G. Lofts, Leonard and Josie Packman, Robert Blythe, Frank Vernon Lay, Walter Webb, Derek Adley, Leonard Allen, the late Herbert Leckenby and editor Eric Fayne. Grateful acknowledgements to them all. Finally, a heartfelt word of thanks to my long-suffering publishers for their patience, understanding and encouragement while waiting more than three years for the eventual and long-delayed delivery of the finished manuscript.

It only remains for me to say that the preparation of the *Who's Who* has been a labour of love. I hope very much that readers will receive the same pleasure and satisfaction when referring to it, as I did during its compilation.

BRIAN DOYLE

Putney,
London.
March 1968.

For Pandora and Tarquin
who have yet to discover many
of the treasures mentioned
in this book

The Authors

Adair, Cecil

See: Everett-Green, Evelyn

Aesop

Definite facts relating to the life of Aesop, whose name will for ever be associated with the art of the fable, are notable for their absence. There are several different theories surrounding his birthplace, career and death, and no one version can be derided as wrong, as none can be hailed as completely authentic. The commonly accepted story, however, is that Aesop was born a slave in the Greek island of Samos about the year 620 B.C. He was owned by two masters in succession, who both lived in Samos and who were called Xanthus and Iadmon. The latter eventually granted Aesop his freedom as a reward for his wit, learning – and storytelling, at which he had proved himself a master. Aesop became interested in public affairs and travelled widely, telling stories and fables wherever he went, many of them thinly disguising political references and opinions. When, at length, the ex-slave arrived at Sardis, the capital of Lydia, his fame had preceded him and he was at once accepted at the court of Croesus, where he quickly became a firm favourite. Croesus invited Aesop to work for him on diplomatic missions throughout Greece. Aesop proved himself a fine ambassador and frequently smoothed out arguments and political differences by telling his entertaining and wise fables – brief moral tales featuring animals or inanimate objects. At Athens, for example, he warned the people – by telling of *The Frogs Desiring a King* – that the known rule and tyranny of Pisistratus might well be preferable to that of someone they did not know and which could be ten times worse. Eventually – around 560 B.C. – Aesop met his death. On a diplomatic mission to Delphi, he had a disagreement over money matters. The enraged Delphians accused him of impiety and brought him to trial. One story says that Aesop made one last attempt to save his life by appealing to the Delphian reverence for the laws of hospitality by re-telling the fable of *The Eagle and the Beetle*. But to no avail. Aesop was found guilty and executed – hurled to his death from a high precipice outside the city. The cruel death of Aesop did not go unavenged.

The people of Delphi were inflicted with a series of calamities until they made public reparation of their crime. The well-known adage, 'The blood of Aesop', later warned that a murdered man's blood would always be avenged.

Aesop's fame did not die with him. A statue was erected to his memory at Athens and was the work of Lysippus, a famous Greek sculptor. Aesop's fables lived on too. Later writers of the ancient world (notably the Greek Babrius and the Roman Phaedrus) made written collections of Aesop's fables, also adding others from other sources. A particularly comprehensive collection was set down by Demetrius Phalereus of Athens about three centuries after Aesop's death. Translated into Latin in the first and third centuries A.D., the Aesop fables were later used as textbooks in schools and subsequently translated again into many languages. They have been in English print ever since Caxton translated them from French in 1484. Every age has changed and adapted the stories, but they have always retained their original and memorable morals. Many phrases from them, such as 'sour grapes' or 'a wolf in sheep's clothing', have become part of everyday conversation. And, after twenty-five centuries, the fables of Aesop are as instructive and entertaining as ever.

Ainsworth, Ruth

Born in Manchester, 1908. Published two books of poetry for children, *All Different* and *The Evening Listens*, before becoming associated with the BBC's radio programme 'Listen With Mother', for which she wrote several stories, some of them about her popular character, Rufty Tufty the Golliwog, which she later collected and augmented into such books as: *Listen With Mother Tales, Rufty Tufty the Golliwog*, (1952), *Charles Stories, More About Charles, Rufty Tufty at the Seaside, Rufty Tufty Goes Camping, Rufty Tufty Runs Away, Rufty Tufty Flies High, Rufty Tufty's Island, Rufty Tufty and Hattie, Rufty Tufty Makes a House, The Snow Bear, Cherry Stones, Far-Away Children, The Wolf Who Was Sorry* and *The Ten Tales of Shellover*, etc. Also two books of puppet plays: *Nine Drummers Drumming* and *The Little Mushrooms*; and, for schools, the *Look Ahead* Readers, etc. She lives in Northumberland.

Ainsworth, William Harrison

Born in Manchester in 1805, the son of a solicitor. He was intended for the legal profession, but wasn't enthusiastic about following in his father's footsteps. When he went to London to finish his law studies he became acquainted with literary and dramatic circles and subsequently worked with a publishing firm. Later he took up writing and journalistic work. In 1834 came his first successful novel, *Rookwood,* which had a highly-romanticised highwayman, Dick Turpin, as its leading figure. Around forty more novels later came from his prolific pen, usually with well-known historical events and notabilities as their theme. Some of the most popular were: *Crichton* (1837), *Jack Sheppard* (1839), *The Tower of London* (1840), *Old St Paul's* (1841), *Guy Fawkes* (1841), *The Miser's Daughter* (1842), *Windsor Castle* (1843), *The Lancashire Witches* (1849) and *The Star Chamber* (1854). Probably the best of Ainsworth's novels is *Old St Paul's,* which has life in London from April 1665 to September 1666 as its basis – a period covering both the Great Plague and the Great Fire. His great descriptive flair brought both events graphically to life. He died in 1882.

Alcott, Louisa May

Born in Pennsylvania, USA, in 1832, the daughter of Amos Bronson Alcott, the philosopher and educationalist. She had three sisters – one older, Anna, and two younger, Elizabeth and May. Her father lived – and made his family live – a strict life, with plain food and no meat to eat. He often filled his house with people he took pity on, when he could scarcely afford to keep his own wife and daughters. Louisa attended many different schools until she was fifteen, when she taught in a small school herself, to earn money to help the household expenses. She wrote some stories about birds and flowers, which a publisher saw and liked. He published them in a small volume called *Flower Fables* – Louisa's first book (1852). Soon afterwards she went to Boston where she taught again, took in sewing, and wrote numerous melodramatic pot-boilers for second-rate magazines. It all helped the family finances. The turning point in her writing career came in 1863, when she published a book called *Hospital Sketches,* based on her own experiences as a nurse with the army during the American Civil War. It sold well and was favourably reviewed. Her first novel, *Moods* (1864), did not excite much interest, though it was praised by a young book critic named Henry James. In 1867 she was asked by her publisher to write a girl's book; around the same time she was invited to become editor of a magazine called *Merry's Museum*. She had often thought of writing a book about her own family ('the pathetic family' as she often called it) and now began to write the first chapters of what was to become *Little Women*. Chapters appeared, in shortened form, in *Merry's Museum* and were well received, so Louisa set about writing her book in earnest. It appeared in 1868, with illustrations by her younger sister, May Alcott. It was an immediate success and to this day is probably the most popular and widely-read book ever written for girls. Based on many real-life incidents concerning Louisa herself, and her sisters and parents, the book is full of charm, humour and sentiment. A sequel was inevitable and followed in 1869: *Good Wives* (in the USA it was called, simply, *Little Women, Part Two*). The following year came *An Old-Fashioned Girl*, based on Louisa's own experiences of earning her living, and in 1871 came *Little Men*, about the later years of the now-famous March family. *Eight Cousins* (1874) and its sequel *Rose in Bloom* (1876) tell of a rather larger family. *Under the Lilacs* (1878) and *Jack and Jill* (1880) appeared as serials in *St Nicholas*, the former about a homeless little boy and the latter of a little girl invalid and the ways in which her friends cheered her up until her convalescence was over. The last of the books about the March family, *Jo's Boys*, appeared in 1886. Other books included: *Work* (1873), *Silver Pitchers* (1876), *A Modern Mephistopheles* (1877), *Aunt Jo's Scrap-Bag* in six volumes (1872–82), *Proverb Stories* (1882), *Spinning Wheel Stories* (1884), *Lulu's Library* in three volumes (1886–89) and *A Garland for Girls* (1888). But it is on *Little Women* that her fame rests and it is a sign of its universal appeal that it has been translated into nearly twenty languages. Louisa May Alcott died, two days after her father, in 1888.

Alger, Horatio

Born on 13th January 1834, in Revere, Massachusetts, the son of a clergyman, and educated at Gates Academy and Harvard

College. He also studied at Harvard Divinity School, since his father wanted him to follow in his footsteps and enter the church. But he rebelled against the idea eventually and, with the help of a small legacy, went to live in Paris. He returned to America in 1864 and became pastor of the Unitarian Church in Brewster, Massachusetts. Two years later he became restless again and left for New York, where he began writing in earnest (he had already published two or three mediocre novels). He contributed stories to *Student and Schoolmate* and the magazine's editor, W. T. Adams ('Oliver Optic'), introduced him to the literary life of the city. His first book for boys, *Ragged Dick*, appeared in 1867 and set the pattern for the rest of his many stories, which almost invariably told of the rise of a poor boy from rags to riches and success. His heroes were usually shoe-blacks, newsboys, match-sellers, farm-boys or street-musicians and always managed to triumph over their trials and win through smiling and on top at the end. Around the time *Ragged Dick* was published, Alger became associated closely with the Newsboys' Lodging House in New York, devoting much time, money and interest to its well-being – and that of its inmates. He served on charity committees, worked on commissions specially set up to improve living and working conditions of young people in New York – and was instrumental in getting a law passed which forbade cruelty to children. All the while he was helping and encouraging the boys who slept at the Newsboys' Lodging House and spotlighting their difficulties in his books. He often wrote a series of stories under a collective title, e.g. *The Ragged Dick Series* (1867), *The Luck and Pluck Series* (1869) and *The Tattered Tom Series* (1871). He wrote more than 100 titles, typical ones including: *Ben the Luggage Boy* (1870), *From Canal Boy to President* (1881), *From Farm Boy to Senator* (1882) and *A New York Boy* (1898). All preached, though in a kindly and entertaining way, that goodness and cheerfulness lead inevitably to riches and success. His books sold over twenty million copies and his name – and the names of many of his popular fictional heroes – became household words. He was, without doubt, one of the most widely-read and influential juvenile writers of the latter half of the nineteenth century in America. The 'Horatio Alger Awards' are presented each year by the American Schools and Colleges Association to those Americans who, they consider, have risen to success and fortune despite early handicaps. He died at South Natick, Massachusetts, on 18th July 1899.

Allen, Agnes

Born London and educated at James Allen's Girls' School, Dulwich, and Redhill School of Art. Author of several children's historical surveys of 'everyday' subjects, e.g. clothes, homes, books, etc. Published her first book, *The Story of the Village*, in 1947, and subsequent books include: *The Story of Painting*, *The Story of Your Home* (winner of the Carnegie Medal in 1949), *The Story of Parliament*, *The Story of the Book*, *The Story of the Highway*, *The Story of Clothes*, *The Story of Michaelangelo*, *The Story of Archaeology*, *The Story of Sculpture*, *Living Long Ago*, *Living in the Middle Ages*, *Living Under the Tudors and Stuarts* and *Life in Britain Since 1700*. Most of the books were illustrated by Miss Allen in conjunction with her husband, Jack Allen. Died in 1959.

'A. L. O. E.'

See: Tucker, Charlotte Maria.

Andersen, Hans Christian

Born in 1805 in Odense, Denmark, the son of a poor shoemaker and a washerwoman. His father was self-educated and read his shelf of classics aloud to young Hans, who was by nature a dreamer, a romantic yearner after things he could not yet understand. He avoided school when he could and spent hours making puppets and a puppet-theatre, dressing his creations and finally presenting his own versions of the stories his father told him. He was particularly fascinated by Shakespeare and soon developed an overriding ambition to become a great actor. But Hans' friends laughed at his grand ambitions; he was rather ugly, awkward and – apart from his reading – almost completely uneducated. But Hans was undeterred and at fourteen he left home and set off for Copenhagen to seek his fortune. He tried singing, ballet-dancing, acting and reciting – but failed dismally at all. Eventually, through the good offices of a friend at the Royal Theatre, King Friedrich VI arranged for him to go to school at public expense and he studied at Slagelse and Elsinore. All this time Hans had been writing stories and plays, but without any success. On his return to Copenhagen, after his education was finished, he continued writing until, in 1829, his first book appeared. It was a fantasy called *A Walking trip from Holmens Kanal to the East Point of Amger* and was well received. In that same year his first fairy tale, *The Snow Maiden*, appeared in a Copenhagen daily newspaper. In 1830 came his *Collected Poems*. Then Hans set off on a lengthy tour of the Continent, putting part of his trip into a book called *Travel Silhouettes*. In 1835 came his first novel *The Improvisator*. That same year he published a small paper-bound volume containing four more fairy stories – or 'trifles', as he called them. The stories were *The Tinder Box*, *Big Claus and Little Claus*, *The Princess and the Pea* and *Little Ida's Flowers*. In 1838 the King granted Hans a pension, which made him independent. He wrote more and more fairy stories (as well as plays and other books, which he regarded as much more important than his children's tales) and their fame spread throughout the world, as well as throughout Denmark. His most famous story was (and is) perhaps *The Ugly Duckling*, which reflected Hans Christian Andersen's own troubled life. Among his other celebrated tales are *The Little Mermaid*, *Thumbelina*, *The Swineherd*, *The Emperor's New Clothes*, *The Constant Tin Soldier*, *The Nightingale* and *The Little Match-Girl*. In 1846 Andersen's fairy tales were first translated into English by Mary Howitt, who called the book *Wonderful Stories for Children*. The following year she also translated Andersen's *The Story of My Life*; it was dedicated to Jenny Lind, the famous singer, whose great friendship with Andersen lasted until his death in 1875. Today, his wise and touching stories are as popular as they have ever been.

Anstey, F.

Real name: Thomas Anstey Guthrie. Born on 8th August 1856 in London, the son of a tailor, and educated at a preparatory school in Surbiton, King's College School, Wimbledon, London, and Trinity Hall, Cambridge, where he studied law, being called to the Bar in 1881. He turned to full-time writing, however, upon the immediate success of his famous humorous school novel *Vice Versa*, published the following year, 1882. This, one of the funniest and most entertaining school stories ever written, told of a pompous father who, magically and accidentally, exchanges bodies with his schoolboy son, Dick Bultitude. It has never been out of print since its publication. From 1877 until 1930 Anstey was on the staff of *Punch*, to which he contributed a column called 'Voces Populi'. His later fantasy novels (read by all ages) include *The Tinted Venus* (1885), *A Fallen Idol* (1886), *Tourmalin's Time Cheques* (1891), *The Talking Horse* (1892) and *The Brass Bottle* (1900). He published three books for children: *Paleface and Redskin, and Other Stories for Boys and Girls* (1898), *Only Toys* (1903) and *In Brief Authority* (1915), in which an ordinary family is suddenly transported to a fairy world. The 'F' in his pen-name was due to an early misprint and should have been a 'T'; Anstey decided that the 'F' brought him luck, so it stayed. He died on 10th March 1934.

Armstrong, Richard

Born 1903, in Northumberland, the son of a blacksmith. He left school at thirteen and worked for three years in a large steelworks on Tyneside, progressing from errand-boy, greaser and labourer to crane-driver. Following the First World War he became an apprentice in the Merchant Navy, subsequently serving for seventeen years in tramp steamers, liners, colliers and oil tankers all over the world. He was later to draw heavily upon his experiences in both steel-works and Merchant Navy for many of his books for boys. The first of these, *The Mystery of Obadiah*, was published in 1943 and set amidst the Northumbrian moors and Tyneside factories he knew so well. The story told of three boys who turned amateur detectives and tracked down a mysterious burglar after a patient pursuit culminating in a disused mine. It was followed in 1946 by a sequel, *Sabotage at the Forge*, set mainly in a Tyneside steel-works. *Sea Change* (1948) described graphically and sympathetically the experiences of a Merchant Navy apprentice on a return voyage to Barbados; it gave a superb picture of what life at sea, stripped of its conventional glamour, can really be like. Armstrong drew largely upon his own memories to re-create the story of how a boy can gradually become a man in a few short weeks. This was the first 'boys' story', as such, to be awarded the Carnegie Medal as the Best Children's Book of the Year. Armstrong's subsequent titles – many of them again featuring young Merchant Navy heroes – include: *The Whinstone Drift* (1951), *Danger Rock* (1955), *The Lost Ship* (1956), *No Time for Tankers* (1958), *The Lame Duck* (1959), *Horseshoe Reef* (1960), *Out of the Shallows* (1961), *Trial Trip* (1962), *Island Odyssey* (1963), *The Big Sea* (1964), *The Secret Sea* (1966), *Greenhorn* (1966), *The Mutineers* (1968) and the first two volumes of a three-part *History of Seafaring* (1967–68). *Grace Darling* (1965) was a factual book on a famous maritime heroine. Richard Armstrong has also written several successful adult novels.

Asbjörnsen, Peter Christian

Born in 1812, in Christiania, Norway. While still at school he met and formed a life-long friendship with Jörgen Moe (who later became a lyric poet and Bishop of Christiansand). Whilst still in their teens, the two friends developed an intense interest in the collection of local folk tales and fairy stories. Their interest became a passion and they collected hundreds of traditional tales during their fishing and walking tours in the mountains, valleys and pastures of their native Norway. Asbjörnsen became a professional zoologist but this did not hinder his study and gathering of the Norwegian folk tale. Whilst searching for specimens, he would visit isolated areas of his country where storytelling was still the prime form of entertainment – and thereby add new stories to his collection. Moe devoted his holidays to similar pursuits and the inseparable friends spent what was left of their spare time in writing down on paper the tales they had so painstakingly collected. In 1838 Asbjörnsen first announced some of the results of his and Moe's researches, and published some of the first stories, in a Norwegian children's publication called *Nor*. In 1843–44 came *Norwegian Folk and Fairy Tales*, collected and edited by Asbjörnsen and Moe. It became widely popular and was followed in 1845 and 1848 by two collections of stories about the nymphs or sirens which haunt the woods and mountains of Norway; these were written by Asbjörnsen alone. He later published a further selection of

Norwegian folk and fairy tales in 1871. From the earlier collections, the British scholar and traveller, Sir George Webbe Dasent, translated his *Popular Tales from the Norse* in 1859, bringing the Norwegian stories to a wider readership. This work was not meant primarily for children, but Dasent's *Selections from Popular Tales of the Norse*, published in 1862, was. In 1874 came Dasent's further translated selection from Asbjörnsen and Moe, *Tales from the Fjeld*. Among the first collection of Tales was one called *East of the Sun and West of the Moon*, which has given its name as title to many subsequent translated collections of Norwegian folk and fairy tales, and which is probably Asbjörnsen's and Moe's most popular story. Other famous stories in their collections include *The Three Billy Goats*, *The Princess on the Glass Mountain*, *The Giant Who Had No Heart*, *Peter Gynt* and *The Pancake*. The main elements of these tales are rarely gauzy-winged fairies, but rough-humoured giants, trolls, witches, hags, animals (usually talking ones) and magical objects. They have certain affinities with the tales of the Brothers Grimm and are certainly as entertaining, and many of them conjure up the majesty and enchantment of the Norwegian scene as no other stories have done. Peter Asbjörnsen died in 1885, surviving his friend and fellow-scholar, Jörgen Moe, by three years.

Ashford, Daisy

Born at Petersham, Surrey, in 1881, and educated at The Priory, Haywards Heath, Sussex. At the age of nine she wrote a 'novel' called *The Young Visiters*, among many other stories, which was put away in a drawer and forgotten. Miss Ashford 'gave up' serious writing at the age of fifteen, when she began to sit for school examinations. Then, in 1919 – an adult woman of thirty-eight – she happened to come across her childhood novel, handwritten in a small, maroon-coloured notebook, and sent it to a friend who was ill, in the hope of cheering her up. The friend was charmed with *The Young Visiters* and sent it to Frank Swinnerton who, in turn, strongly recommended it to Chatto and Windus. It was published that same year, 1919, with an introduction written by James Barrie (and many people concluded that Barrie wrote the book himself, as a jest!). From that year to this it has never been out of print. Though not truly a children's book, *The Young Visiters* is enjoyed by them – and relished even more by adults, chiefly because of the mixture of innocence and worldly knowledge which the youthful Daisy used in telling her highly-amusing story about such memorable characters as Mr Salteena, Ethel Monticue, the Earl of Clincham, Procurio and Bernard Clark. No small attraction of this would-be sophisticated picture of life in Victorian high society is its mis-spelling and mis-punctuation – the former failing perpetuated even in the book's title! After a collection of further juvenile writings – *Daisy Ashford: Her Book* – Miss Ashford contributed nothing to the world of letters. Soon after her name became a household one she married James Patrick Devlin, took up market gardening and lived in Norwich. She had two sons and two daughters. In 1965 a new selection, taken mainly from *Daisy Ashford: Her Book* and written by both Daisy and her younger sister, Angela, was published under the title *Love and Marriage*. In 1966 came a further story from the same volume, titled *Where Love Lies Deepest*.

Atkinson, Mary Evelyn

Born at Highgate, London, 1899. Educated privately and at Leeson House, Langton Matravers, Dorset. Author of novels for boys and girls, with the emphasis on family adventure. Her first fourteen books featured the engaging and believable Lockett family – Jane, Bill and Oliver – though often introducing added semi-regular characters too. Her first book about them was *August Adventure* (1936), which was followed by a whole series at the rate of one a year: *Mystery Manor* (1937), *The Compass Points North* (1938), *Smugglers' Gap* (1939), *Going Gangster* (1940), *Crusoe Island* (1941), *Challenge to Adventure* (1942), *The Monster of Widgeon Weir* (1943), *The Nest of the Scarecrow* (1944), *Problem Party* (1945), *Chimney Cottage* (1946), *The House on the Moor* (1947), *The Thirteenth Adventure* (1948) and *Steeple Folly* (1949). In 1951 M. E. Atkinson introduced a new family – young Fricka Hammond and her cousins Adrian, Hugo and Katharine (better-known as 'Sugar'). This first book about them was *Castaway Camp*, and was followed by *Hunter's Moon, Unexpected Adventure* and *Riders and Raids*. In recent years Miss Atkinson has concentrated on the girls' pony story – *Horseshoes and Handlebars* being one of several typical titles. Although her earlier novels are probably her best, Miss Atkinson can always be relied upon for a good, fast-moving tale with plenty of first-class character-drawing. She has also written many one-act plays for women. Today she lives in Somerset.

Avery, Gillian

Born in 1926, in Redhill, Surrey, and educated at Dunottar School, Reigate, Surrey. On leaving school she became a junior reporter on the *Surrey Mirror* for two years. In 1949 she was appointed assistant illustrations editor on the *Oxford Junior Encyclopaedia* and held this post until 1954. She married A. O. J. Cockshut in 1952; he was at that time a Fellow of Balliol College, Oxford, and it was largely through him that Miss Avery developed her deep interest in Victorian literature and Victorian life – an interest which is reflected in every book she has written. Her first children's book, *The Warden's Niece*, was published in 1957 and was set in Victorian Oxford. In this, as in her subsequent children's novels, Miss Avery managed to convey what must surely be an authentic and atmospheric background of late-Victorian life and society, as well as a group of the most realistic and believable fictional children (often reminiscent of E. Nesbit's, in fact – and praise could come no higher!). Her subsequent stories include: *Trespassers at Charlcote* (1958), *James Without Thomas* (1959), *The Elephant War* (1960), *To Tame a Sister* (1961), *The Greatest Gresham* (1962), *The Peacock House* (1963), *The Italian Spring* (1964) and *The Call of the Valley* (1966). She has also compiled five anthologies: *The Sapphire Treasury* (1959), a selection of Victorian stories; *In the Window Seat* (1962), a further collection of Victorian tales; *Unforgettable Journeys* (1965), comprising thirty-five fictional and factual journeys made by young people; *School Remembered* (1967) and *The Hole in the Wall* (1968), a selection of Georgian and Victorian stories for children. In 1961 Miss Avery wrote a short biographical and bibliographical study of a well-known Victorian children's writer, *Mrs Ewing*, and in 1965 came *Nineteenth Century Children*, which dealt with heroes and heroines in English children's stories from 1780 to 1900. As well as writing 'Victorian' children's novels, Gillian Avery's chief

13

literary aim is reviving interest in outstanding examples of children's stories published in Victorian times and, if possible, getting them reprinted for the benefit of modern readers. She began doing this in 1967 by editing a series of 'Gollancz Revivals' of old children's books, including titles by Mrs Ewing, Lang, Yonge and Farrow. She lives in Manchester.

Avery, Harold

Born in 1867 at Redditch, Worcestershire, the son of a local Justice of the Peace, William Avery. Educated at Dunheved College, Launceston, the Midland Collegiate School, Birmingham, New College, Eastbourne, and, finally, at a large day-school in Dresden, Germany. Served in the Worcestershire Regiment during the First World War. Began writing stories as a small boy and, for a time during his early schooldays, organised and edited a handwritten 'magazine', which circulated among his relatives and friends. His first short stories appeared in the boys' magazine *Young England* in the early 1890s and he subsequently wrote many short stories, chiefly on public school life, which appeared in a variety of boys' papers and magazines, including *Boy's Own Paper* and *The Captain*. His first book comprised a collection of short school stories, *The School's Honour* (1894). It was his very popular public school serial *The Triple Alliance* – serialised in *Boy's Own Paper* in 1896 and published in book form the following year – which really established him as one of the foremost authors of this then-popular type of boys' story. Numerous school stories flowed from his pen for the next forty years, typical titles including: *The Dormitory Flag, The Cock House Cup, Won for the School, Chums at Charlhurst, Mobsley's Mohicans, Frank's First Term, Between Two Schools, Not Cricket!, Play the Game* and *Heads or Tails*. He also wrote children's stories and adventure yarns, as well as adult novels such as *A Week at the Sea, Every Dog His Day* and *Thumbs Up*. He was a keen sportsman, excelling particularly at hockey. He lived much of his life in Evesham, Worcestershire, and died there in 1943.

Awdry, Rev. Wilbert Vere

Born at Ampfield, near Romsey, Hampshire, 1911, and educated at Dauntsey's and St Peter's Hall, Oxford. Rector of Elsworth and Knapwell, Cambridgeshire, 1946–53; Rural Dean of Bourn, 1950–53; Vicar of Emneth, Wisbech, 1953–1965. Secretary of the Diocesan Children's Council from 1956. In 1945 he published a little book called *The Three Railway Engines*, illustrated by John Kenney and featuring a trio of endearing, animated engines who could think and talk to one another. Its popularity prompted another similar book, *Thomas the Tank Engine*, and then another – until today there are over twenty of them. Typical later titles are *James the Red Engine*, *The Troublesome Engines*, *Henry the Green Engine*, *Toby the Tram Engine*, *The Twin Engines* and *Gordon the Big Engine*. The series is now illustrated by John Kenney, C. Reginald Dalby, and Gunvor and Peter Edwards. For his railway series – which has sold nearly 3 million copies – the Rev. Awdry created an imaginary island called Sodor on which he planned the Fat Controller's Railway System (though, more recently, a Thin Controller has arrived on the scene too). Sodor Island is between the Isle of Man and the West Coast of England, with connections to the mainland by rail. In addition to the series of books, there is also a specially-drawn map of Sodor (showing exactly where the engines have had all their adventures, etc.), press-out model books, and gramophone records. The Rev. Awdry's other books include *Belinda the Beetle* and *Our Child Begins to Pray*. He lives at Stroud, Glouccstershire.

Baden-Powell, Lord Robert

Born 1857, in London, and educated at Charterhouse. Served for twenty-two years in the 13th Hussar Regiment, also commanding the 5th Dragoon Guards. The distinguished soldier first won fame for his part in the defence of Mafeking during the Boer War. It was as the founder of the Boy Scout movement – and of the popular magazine *The Scout* – that most young people came to know and respect him. He founded the Boy Scouts in 1908, after writing his famous book *Scouting for Boys* in the same year (it originally appeared in six fortnightly parts). These first booklets were extremely successful and letters poured into the publishers' offices from interested readers who wanted to know more – and *do* more – about Scouting. 'B-P', as Chief Scout, launched *The Scout* (in conjunction with C. Arthur Pearson Ltd)

15

in April 1908; the first article was *How I Started Scouting* by Lord Baden-Powell himself and he continued to contribute articles throughout the rest of his life. He founded the Girl Guide Movement in 1910. He wrote many books and pamphlets on Scouting, Roving and Guiding (and not forgetting Wolf Cubbing), including *Rovering to Success, Girl Guiding, The Wolf Cubs' Handbook, Indian Memories* and *An Old Wolf's Favourites*, as well as various works on his military experiences. He died in 1941.

Bagnold, Enid

Educated at Godalming and Paris and also studied painting. During the First World War she served as a V.A.D. and later wrote her first book, *A Diary Without Dates* (1917), about her experiences. Later she joined the First Aid Nursing Yeomanry, was attached to the French army and wrote her second book about that period, *The Happy Foreigner* (1920). In 1920 she also married Sir Roderick Jones, the Chairman of Reuter's News Agency. As well as her other adult novels and plays, she wrote two durable children's books. *Alice and Thomas and Jane* was published in 1935 and illustrated by the author with the help of her eight-year-old daughter, Laurian Jones. It is a happy family story about the three small children of the title who live at Rottingdean in Sussex and have adventures. Five years later, in 1930, came the very popular *National Velvet* (also illustrated by Laurian Jones, by then aged thirteen). The 'National' of the title was the Grand National horse-race, and 'Velvet' the name of the fourteen-year-old heroine who, in the space of a year, became an heiress, bought a horse for a shilling and won the Grand National on that same horse, who was called The Piebald. In 1946 Miss Bagnold wrote the story as a stage play too. Earlier, in 1944, it was produced as a successful motion picture.

Ballantyne, Robert Michael

Born on 24th April 1825, in Edinburgh, a nephew of James Ballantyne, the editor and publisher of Sir Walter Scott's works, and a brother of James Robert Ballantyne, the Orientalist and translator of Hindu philosophical works. At sixteen he joined the Hudson Bay Fur Company as a clerk and spent six years in

Canada fur-trading with the Red Indians and others. It was a tough, adventurous life which was to stand him in good stead when he came to write his adventure stories. His long letters home to his mother in Scotland gave him his first taste for writing and were written to offset his recurring home-sickness. On his return to Edinburgh in 1847 he worked for the printing and publishing firm of Thomas Constable, and in 1848 he published his first book, a record of his experiences and everyday adventures with the Hudson Bay Company, *Hudson's Bay or, Life in the Wilds of North America*. It was quite a success, but Ballantyne waited another eight years before attempting a further book. Then, a member of the Nelson publishing firm suggested he wrote a boys' adventure story for them. The result was *Snowflakes and Sunbeams, or the Young Fur-Traders*, published in 1856. It was subsequently best-known under the latter part of the title and became a best-seller. In 1857 came *Ungava*, also set in the snow-covered Canada Ballantyne knew so well, and in 1858 his most famous story, *The Coral Island*. It told of the shipwreck upon a South Sea Island of three young boys, Ralph, Jack and Peterkin, possessing between them only a telescope and an axe. It was an immediate best-seller and has never been out of print since. A minor error Ballantyne made (in connection with a coconut) in *The Coral Island* made him resolve never to write again about things of which he had not himself had first-hand knowledge or personal experience. He kept his resolution to the best of his ability and tried to ensure that his later stories were authentic. For example, he visited Algiers especially before writing *The Pirate City* (1874), spent two weeks on the North Sea with deep-sea fishermen for *The Young Trawler* (1884), travelled through the London streets on a fire-engine for *Fighting the Flames* (1867), lived for three weeks in the Bell Rock lighthouse for *The Lighthouse* (1865), ventured out with the Ramsgate lifeboat for *The Lifeboat* (1864), descended into Cornish tin-mines for *Deep Down* (1868), worked on the railway for *The Iron Horse* (1871) and in the Post Office for *Post Haste* (1880); and for *Erling the Bold: A Tale of the Norse Sea-Kings* (1869) he even learned the Norse language and also visited Iceland. Favourites among Ballantyne's other books are *Martin Rattler* (1858), set in the jungles of Brazil, *The Dog Crusoe* (1861) and *The Gorilla Hunters* (1861). His other titles include: *The World of Ice* (1860),

The Golden Dream (1861), *The Red Eric* (1861), *The Wild Man of the West* (1863), *Shifting Winds* (1866), *Silver Lake* (1867), *Away in the Wilderness* (1869), *Black Ivory* (1873), *Under the Waves* (1876), *Rivers of Ice* (1876), *The Settler and the Savage* (1877), *The Red Man's Revenge* (1880), *Philosopher Jack* (1880), *The Giant of the North* (1882), *The Madman and the Pirate* (1883), *The Battery and the Boiler* (1883), *Dusty Diamonds* (1884), *Twice Bought* (1885), *Red Rooney* (1886), *The Middy of the Moors* (1888) and *The Walrus Hunters* (1893). Between 1863 and 1886 *Ballantyne's Miscellany* was published and comprised eighteen small, pocket-sized adventure volumes by Ballantyne. He was one of the first – and most prolific – writers producing books specially for boys and his popularity was immense. His stories had a two-fold purpose – to entertain and to instruct. But the instruction was painless and the entertainment was there in full and exciting measure, so youthful readers took it all in their stride, swallowing each 'new Ballantyne' whole as soon as it came out. Altogether he wrote over eighty books in less than forty years. Several of his stories were serialised in various popular boys' papers too, including the *Boy's Own Paper*. He was an accomplished artist (he exhibited at the Royal Scottish Academy) and occasionally illustrated his own stories. More often, he supplied the illustrator with detailed sketches of how he wanted a scene to appear. In his later years Ballantyne made his home at Harrow, near London. Failing health, caused through overwork, took him to Italy and he died in Rome on 8th February 1894.

Bannerman, Helen Brodie Cowan

Born in Edinburgh, Scotland, in 1863, where she spent part of her childhood. She was the daughter of an army chaplain who was stationed in many parts of the British Empire and always took his large family with him. At the age of two she was taken to Madeira and stayed there for ten years. After studies in Germany, and several more years of travel, Helen married an army doctor and spent thirty years of her married life in India, where her husband worked to combat the plague in Madras and Bombay. In 1899, when she was returning to her husband's army station after leaving her two small daughters to be educated

1 J. D. Watson (*c* 1890)   2 Louis Rhead (1900)

3 A. E. Jackson (*c* 1920)   4 Walter Paget (1905)

Robinson Crusoe as seen by different illustrators

5 Dan O'Herlihy in the title-role of Luis Bunuel's film version in 1953

6 Federico Castellon (1962)

Robinson Crusoe as seen by different illustrators

in Scotland, and heart-broken by the long separation from them she would have to endure, she wrote and illustrated a tiny coloured book and called it *The Story of Little Black Sambo*, partly to amuse her daughters (to whom she intended sending it) and partly to comfort herself. Her children – and their friends – loved it so much that the author was encouraged to send it to a publisher in London. E. V. Lucas saw it, strongly recommended it and it was duly published that same year – 1899. (The following year it appeared in America.) It was presented in a minute 5 in. × 4½ in. format, with a coloured illustration facing each page of text. It caused no immediate sensation, but gradually children who read it – and had it read to them – took it to their hearts, and before long *Little Black Sambo* was a household name in both Britain and the United States. The amusing story of a little black boy, his new clothes and his incident-packed walk through the jungle, where he encounters fierce tigers and finally returns home to eat 169 pancakes (because he was so hungry), has a simple humour and charm and each incident is graphically illustrated so that the youngest child can appreciate it. Following this unexpected but pleasing success, Helen Bannerman published several similar little books and, though they enjoyed minor successes, none caught on as spectacularly as that original *Little Black Sambo*, which is today constantly in print in many countries. The other titles include: *Little Black Mingo* (1901), *Little Black Quibba* (1902), *Little Kettle-Head* (1904), *Pat and the Spider* (1905), *The Teasing Monkey* (1907), *Little Black Quasha* (1908) and *Little Black Bobtail* (1909). In 1936 her American publisher called on Mrs Bannerman in her Edinburgh home to ask her to write another story about Little Black Sambo. She was at first reluctant – but finally relented. The result was the penultimate volume of the series, *Sambo and the Twins* (1937). In 1965 a final story, *Little White Squibba*, was published posthumously. Helen Bannerman had two sons and two daughters. She died on 13th October 1946, in her native Edinburgh.

Barne, Kitty

Wrote more than twenty books for children. Many reflected her life-long love of music. She studied at the Royal College of

Music and was prominent in the musical activities of the Girl Guides Association. She began writing for children in 1935 with *The Easter Holidays* (later re-published in 1955 as *The Secret of the Sandhills*), but her first big success was in 1938 with *She Shall Have Music*, a deeply-felt story about a little girl who wanted to be a concert pianist – and succeeded. Music again played a large part in her next book, *Musical Honours* (1939), about a family of ambitious and musically gifted children. It was also touched on in *Family Footlights* (1939). At the beginning of the Second World War, Kitty Barne was a member of the Women's Voluntary Service and, in this capacity, was one of those responsible for the reception of wartime child-evacuees to Sussex. *Visitors from London* (1940) was the result of this experience. The book was awarded the Carnegie Medal as the best children's publication of the year. It told the story of a large group of London cockney children evacuated to a Sussex farm and the effects of their stay on themselves and on the children and adults who took them in. At the time it was published, intensely topical, the book was also observant, gay, humorous and touching. Other stories with a wartime background followed, including *We'll Meet in England* (1942), about a Norwegian family escaping from the Nazi occupation, and *In the Same Boat* (1945), basically a thriller but also posing the problems of international relations. Another musical story was *Barbie*, this time about a girl-violinist. Other children's novels include: *Dusty's Windmill* (1949), *Three and a Pigeon*, *Tann's Boarders* and *Admiral's Walk*. Miss Barne's love for animals produced *Roly's Dogs* and *Bracken, My Dog*, and two delightful true pony stories, *Rosina Copper* (1954) and *Rosina and Son* (1956). Her non-fiction books include *Introducing Mozart*, *Introducing Schubert*, *Introducing Handel* and *Introducing Beethoven*, *Listening to the Orchestra* and *Elizabeth Fry*, a biography. Kitty Barne was married to Eric Streatfeild and was the sister-in-law of another popular children's writer, Noel Streatfeild. She was also the sister-in-law of Ruth Gervis, illustrator of many children's books, including several by Miss Barne. She died in 1957.

Barrie, Sir James Matthew, Bart., O.M.

Born in 1860 in Kirriemuir, Angus, near Dundee, the son of a weaver. He was educated at Glasgow Academy, Dumfries

7 E. G. Thomson's cover design for Lewis Carroll's *The Nursery 'Alice'* (1890)

Alice as seen by different illustrators

8 Sir John Tenniel (1865)

9 Mervyn Peake (1954)

10 Lewis Carroll (1863)

11 Philip Gough (*c* 1950)   12 Charles Robinson (1910)

13 George Soper (1911)

14 Gwynedd M. Hudson (1922)   15 G. W. Backhouse (*c* 1940s)

16 A. H. Watson (1939)   17 A. E. Jackson (1915)

Alice as seen by different illustrators

18 A. L. Bowley (1921)   19 Mabel Lucie Attwell (1910)

20 Rene Cloke (1943)   21 Willy Pogany (1929)

22 and 23 *Alice in Wonderland* has been filmed at least half a dozen times. Above is a scene from the RKO/Pathé silent version made in 1927, with Ruth Gilbert as Alice. Below is Charlotte Henry in the 1933 Paramount production, which included in its star-packed cast Gary Cooper as the White Knight, Cary Grant as the Mock Turtle and W. C. Fields as an irascible Humpty Dumpty

Academy and Edinburgh University. After working as a journalist in Nottingham he went to London and wrote for various newspapers and magazines there. After the success of several published novels, including *The Little Minister* (1891), *Margaret Ogilvie* (1896), *Sentimental Tommy* (1896) and its sequel *Tommy and Grizel*, he turned to writing plays and achieved great success with *Walker, London* (1892), the stage version of *The Little Minister* (1898), *Quality Street* (1901) and *The Admirable Crichton* (1902). In 1904 came his greatest work – and one of the most famous children's stories ever written – *Peter Pan*. This original play version was first produced at the Duke of York's Theatre, London, on 27th December 1904, with Nina Boucicault as Peter and Gerald du Maurier as Captain Hook. Peter Pan was created by Barrie whilst telling stories to a group of small boys in Kensington Gardens. At first, Barrie visualised him as a baby, in a section of his book *The Little White Bird* (1902). This section was later re-published separately under the title *Peter Pan in Kensington Gardens*, with superb pictures by Arthur Rackham (1906). Peter Pan, 'the boy who wouldn't grow up', is the centre-piece of a play which combines fairy-tale magic with bloodthirsty pirates and redskins. The play has been produced in London and the Provinces almost every year since that first memorable occasion and its immortality is underlined by the beautiful statue of Peter Pan which stands in Kensington Gardens, London. The actual play was not published until 1928, but in 1911 Barrie wrote the story as a children's book called *Peter and Wendy* (*Peter Pan and Wendy* in later editions). Subsequently the story was 'retold' (with Barrie's approval) by such people as Daniel O'Connor, May Byron and Eleanor Graham, with a variety of illustrators. Among the latter have been Alice B. Woodward, Mabel Lucie Attwell, Nora S. Unwin, F. D. Bedford, Gwynedd M. Hudson and Edward Ardizzone. Barrie's additional scene or epilogue to the play of *Peter Pan*, *An Afterthought* (or *When Wendy Grew Up*), performed only once on the stage (in 1908), was published in book form for the first time in 1957; the characters are Peter, the grown-up Wendy, and her daughter. In 1929 Barrie made a gift of all rights and royalties in *Peter Pan* to the Great Ormond Street Hospital for Sick Children. Barrie wrote little else for children after *Peter Pan*. *A Kiss for Cinderella* was an enchanting children's Christmas play, and one or two short stories appeared in various publications. But there was nothing further for children in the same incomparable category as *Peter Pan*. Barrie died in 1937.

Batten, Harold Mortimer

Born 1888, in Singapore, and educated at Oakham School, where he was a brilliant rugby football player, subsequently representing Bradford and Northampton. In his early twenties he travelled throughout Canada working as prospector, forest-ranger and surveyor. Later, he turned to fur-trapping and running a motor-boat service on the Mattagami River. He served in the First World War as a motor-cyclist, later fighting with the French Army (and being awarded the Croix de Guerre), finally transferring to the Royal Air Force. Began writing profession-ally around 1912, contributing to such boys' papers as *The Captain*, *Chums* and *Boy's Own Paper* and to adult publications including *Blackwood's*, *Chambers'*, *The Field* and *Illustrated London News*. He won a high reputation as a writer on natural history and his numerous stories and articles on wild animals became very popular; he wrote many books on the subject, including *Tales of the Wild*, *The Romantic Story of the Countryside*, *Prints from Many Trails*, *Tracks and Tracking* and *Starlight*. He became a frequent and popular broadcaster on BBC radio from the early 1920s.

Baum, Lyman Frank

Born in Chittenango, New York, on 15th May 1856, and educated in Syracuse. Worked as a newspaper reporter in New York, then managed several theatres, also acting and seeing four of his own plays produced (two of them were *The Maid of Arran* and *The Queen of Killarney*). He left the theatre in his late twenties to raise fancy poultry and his first published book was *The Book of Hamburgs* (a textbook on chickens) in 1886. He also joined forces with a friend to manufacture a new brand of axle-grease called 'Baum's Castorine'. He next went to Aberdeen, South Dakota, and opened 'Baum's Bazaar', a general store, which he sold a few years later in order to publish and edit Aberdeen's weekly newspaper, *The Saturday Pioneer*. In 1891, after the paper had gone bankrupt, Baum went to Chicago as a crockery salesman and newspaper reporter and, in 1897, founded a national association of shop window-dressers, also publishing and editing *The Shop Window*, a trade magazine for dry goods merchants and window-dressers. That same year – 1897 – he combined with a young and almost unknown artist named Maxfield Parrish to publish his first children's book, *Mother Goose in Prose*; the last story in the book introduced a little farm girl named Dorothy. In 1899, Baum wrote *Father Goose: His Book*, a collection of humorous rhymes for children, illustrated by a Chicago newspaper artist friend, William Wallace Denslow. But Baum had not entirely forsaken his dry goods trade to write children's books – in 1900 he wrote *The Art of Decorating Dry Goods Windows*. Also in 1900 – and what could be in greater contrast! – came the immortal *The Wonderful Wizard of Oz*, again illustrated by Denslow. In the story a cyclone carries the little Kansas farm girl Dorothy (already introduced in *Mother Goose in Prose*) and her inseparable dog Toto to the magical land of Oz, where she meets a Scarecrow, a Tin Man, a Cowardly Lion, witches (good and bad), the 'Wizard' and many other strange characters, has memorable adventures and is finally carried back home, safe and sound. The book was a huge success and soon became America's favourite children's fantasy. Baum wrote other children's books over the next four years, including *A New Wonderland* (1900), *Dot and Tot of Merryland* (1901), *American Fairy Tales* (1901), *The Master Key* (1901), *The Life and Adventures of Santa Claus* (1902) and *The Enchanted Island of Yew* (1902), but the reading public of America wanted more of Oz – and wrote telling Baum and his publishers so. Baum wasn't enthusiastic about reviving Oz but, in 1904, he gave in and published *The Marvellous Land of Oz* (illustrated by John R. Neil, as are all subsequent Oz books by Baum). This time the young hero was called Tip, and also featured were the Scarecrow and the Tin Woodman, with such new characters as Jack Pumpkinhead, the Saw-Horse and the Woggle Bug. From then on, Baum continued to produce Oz books – fourteen altogether – as well as his many other children's stories. Titles include: *Ozma of Oz* (1906), *Dorothy and the Wizard in Oz* (1908), *The Road to Oz* (1909), *The Emerald City of Oz* (1910), *The Patchwork Girl of Oz* (1913), *Tik-Tok of Oz* (1914),

The Scarecrow of Oz (1915), *Rinkitink in Oz* (1916), *The Lost Princess of Oz* (1917), *The Tin Woodman of Oz* (1918), *The Magic of Oz* (1919) and *Glinda of Oz* (1920). Other children's fantasy stories by Baum included: *Queen Zixi of Ix* (1905), *The Woggle-Bug Book* (1905), *John Dough and the Cherub* (1906), *The Sea Fairies* (1911) and *Sky Island* (1912). He also wrote under several pseudonyms: as 'Laura Bancroft' he wrote *Twinkle and Chubbins* (1911) and *Policeman Bluejay* (1906) (later re-issued as *Babes in Birdland* under Baum's own name); as 'Floyd Akens' he wrote many books for boys and as 'Edith Van Dyne' many for girls. He contributed several titles to such series as *Boy Fortune Hunter*, *Sam Steele*, *Aunt Jane*, *Daring Twins* and *Flying Girls*. As 'Schuyler Stanton' he wrote several adult novels, including *The Fate of a Clown* (1905). In 1902, Baum returned to the theatre world he had known so well to write the book and lyrics for a musical comedy based on *The Wizard of Oz*. It opened in Chicago, was a tremendous success and moved on to New York, where it ran for eighteen months to capacity houses. The first Oz book by Baum has also been made into motion pictures no less than three times – two silent and the impressive colour musical starring Judy Garland in 1939. L. Frank Baum – 'the Royal Historian of Oz' as he sometimes described himself wryly – died in Hollywood (where he had spent the last years of his life) on 6th May 1919, at the age of sixty-three. After his death no less than twenty-six further Oz books were published, making a grand total of forty; Ruth Plumly Thompson wrote nineteen, John R. Neil (Baum's illustrator) wrote three, Jack Snow two, Rachel Cosgrove and Colonel Frank Baum (Baum's son) one each. The series finished (apparently) in 1951. Between them, the forty Oz books have sold well over seven million copies throughout the world.

'B. B.'

See: Watkins-Pitchford, D. J.

Beck, Christopher

See: Bridges, T. C.

Beaman, S. G. Hulme

Creator and illustrator of 'Toytown' with all its enchanting characters, including Larry the Lamb, Dennis the Dachshund, Mr Growser, Ernest the Policeman, the Mayor, the Magician, the Inventor, Mrs Goose, Letitia the Lamb, Mr Noah, *et al.* Hulme Beaman made his first mark as an illustrator of originality in 1926 with *The Seven Voyages of Sinbad the Sailor*. In 1928 came the first of his Toytown books, *Tales of Toytown*, followed by *Stories from Toytown*. They were reasonably successful, but it was the brilliantly produced and performed Children's Hour plays based on the stories and broadcast in the BBC's radio programmes in the early 1930s that really caused them to catch on so tremendously with young audiences. The hand-picked casts were headed by Derek McCulloch ('Uncle Mac'), Head of BBC Children's Hour, who played Larry the Lamb as well as narrating the plays, which were soon being written especially for radio by Hulme Beaman. Altogether he wrote over twenty-five stories and radio plays about the Toytown characters, who retained their popularity with the listening children (and their parents!) for over thirty years. The radio versions were still being broadcast when the BBC Children's Hour ended in 1964 and can now often be heard in that programme's successor, 'Story Time'. A series of Toytown stories in book form began publication in 1957 and ran to many volumes – all fully illustrated in colour by Kenneth Lovell. S. G. Hulme Beaman wrote and illustrated other children's books, including *The Adventures of John Trusty*, and also illustrated such other stories as Stevenson's macabre *Dr Jekyll and Mr Hyde* – a contrast indeed to Toytown! His drawings were unmistakable, with their three-dimensional, seemingly wooden, jointed characters, and have since had many imitators. But Hulme Beaman – and Toytown – were unique.

Bell, Robert Stanley Warren

Born in 1871, the eldest son of the Rev. G. E. Bell, Vicar of Henley-in-Arden, Warwickshire, and educated at St John's College, Leatherhead. He was originally intended for a legal career but his inclinations were towards writing and he eventually gave up reading for the Bar. He became a master at a private school, writing his first (adult) novel in his spare time. This was *The Cub in Love* (1897). The year before, he had begun his long association with boys' literature in general and boys' papers in particular by contributing a public school serial, *The Boys of Daneleigh College*, to Newnes' *British Boys* magazine; it appeared under the pen-name of 'Hawkesley Brett'. In 1899, at the age of twenty-eight, he joined George Newnes Limited as founder and first editor of *The Captain*, a high-quality, monthly boys' magazine which specialised in public school stories and subsequently won special fame for publishing P. G. Wodehouse's early school stories. For over ten years Bell was the original 'Old Fag' (the editor's pseudonym) and also contributed ten serials and numerous short stories. His school tales were usually about Greyhouse, though he also wrote about Claverdon School too. Most of his serials subsequently appeared in book form. His titles include: *Tales of Greyhouse* (1901), *J. O. Jones* (1903), *Jim Mortimer* (1908), *Black Evans* (1912), *Mystery of Markham* (1913), *Dormitory Eight* (1914), *Smith's Week* (1915), *Greyhouse Days* (1918) and *The Three Prefects* (1918). He also wrote several adult novels. Bell resigned from *The Captain* in 1910 to write primarily for the theatre. The following year saw the successful production of his comedy *A Companion for George* in the West End. After war service with the RFC and RAF he settled down at Westcliff-on-Sea, Essex, and resumed his writing. He died on 26th September 1921. His brother was the popular novelist John Keble Bell, who was best known as 'Keble Howard'.

Belloc, Hilaire

Born in Paris in 1870, the son of a Frenchman and an English-woman. Four of his great-uncles were generals under Napoleon and Belloc himself served for a time in the French artillery. He was educated at the Oratory School, Birmingham, and at Oxford University. His first book, *Verses and Sonnets*, was published in 1895, and the following year came *The Bad Child's Book of Beasts*, a book of nonsense verses. Later came more volumes of nonsense verses: *More Beasts for Worse Children* (1897), *Cautionary Tales for Children* (1908), *New Cautionary Tales* (1930), *More Peers* and *Ladies and Gentlemen* (the last two not so suitable for children, perhaps, as the others). These popular nonsense verses include such titles as 'Jim, who ran away from his Nurse and was eaten by a lion', 'Henry King, who chewed bits of String, and was early cut off in Dreadful Agonies' and 'Sarah Bing, who could not read and was tossed into a hedge by a Bull', and such pithy descriptions of animals as 'The Hippopotamus: I shoot the Hippopotamus with bullets made of platinum, Because if I use leaden ones his hide is sure to flatten 'em.' Joseph Hilaire Peter Belloc (to give him his full name) was one of the most versatile writers ever. He was poet, historian, traveller, essayist, novelist and biographer – and it is as an historian that he will probably be best remembered. He published biographies of Napoleon, Danton, Robespierre, Cromwell, Richelieu, Charles I and William the Conqueror, as well as a *History of England*. He also wrote several novels, travel books and collections of essays and, in all, wrote over 100 diverse books. From 1906–10 he was Liberal M.P. for South Salford, and from 1911–13 was Head of the English Department of the East London College. He was well known as a devout Catholic and in 1934 the Pope conferred on him the rank of Knight Commander of the Order of St Gregory the Great. He also received honorary degrees from Glasgow and Dublin Universities. He died in 1953.

Bemelmans, Ludwig

Born 27th April 1898, in Meran, Austrian Tyrol, and educated in Regensburg and Rothenburg, Bavaria. He went to New York in 1914, becoming an American citizen in 1918. He once wrote that when he sailed from Rotterdam for America, at the age of sixteen, he supplied himself with two pistols and plenty of ammunition to protect himself from the Indians. One of his favourite authors was James Fenimore Cooper and he half expected to find Red Indians waiting to attack him on the outskirts of New York City. In New York he worked as a waiter in various restaurants and hotels, then served with the United States Army during the First World War. After more restaurant service he became a restaurant proprietor himself. He told something of his early career in the foregoing jobs in such books as *My War With the United States* (1937) and *Life Class* (1938).

27

His other adult books include *Hotel Splendide*, *The Donkey Inside* and *Dirty Eddie*. Bemelmans began writing and illustrating his enchanting children's books in 1934 with *Hansi*, the story of a small boy's winter holiday in the Tyrolean mountains. Other early books included *The Golden Basket* (1935), *Castle Number Nine* (1936) and *Quito Express* (1937). In 1937 too he illustrated Munro Leaf's book *Noodle* (the dachshund). In 1939 came the first of his splendid picture-books about *Madeline* (named after his own wife, Madeline Freund, whom he married in 1935). Madeline was the smartest of twelve schoolgirls who lived in an old house in Paris. Large-scale, colourful and witty paintings and drawings tell the story exuberantly and the text too is just right (first publication of *Madeline* in Britain was in 1954). Subsequent books in the series include *Madeline's Rescue* (1954), (winner of the Caldecott Medal), *Madeline and the Bad Hat* (1958), *Madeline and the Gypsies* (1961) and *Madeline in London* (1962). In addition to his books, Bemelmans has contributed to many American and European magazines. He has travelled widely, but makes his home in New York City.

Bevan, Tom

Born 1868, in Risca, Monmouthshire, and educated at Sir Thomas Rich's School, Gloucester, and St Paul's College, Cheltenham. Originally a schoolmaster, he later became educational editor for Sampson Low and Marston, the publishers, holding this post from 1917 until 1931. Wrote many stirring adventure and historical stories for boys, including several serials for such boys' publications as the *Boy's Own Paper*. His books include: *The Chancellor's Spy*, *The Grey Fox of Holland*, *The Heroic Impostor*, *Young Lion-Heart*, *Held by Rebels* and *The Jungle Spies*; also *The Tom Bevan Omnibus*. He additionally published a series of handbooks on English History for students. He lived in Ringwood, Hampshire, for some years and died around the late 'thirties.

Bianco, Margery Williams

Born London, 22nd July 1881. Published several novels during the early part of the century, including *The Late Returning*

(1902); also a short book about Paris. Then, in 1922, came her first book for children, *The Velveteen Rabbit*, illustrated by William Nicholson. It was a story about nursery toys and about one rather dilapidated velveteen rabbit who meant a great deal to his small owner; it was also a tale based on the premise that toys often come to life if they are loved enough. The story and the pictures were enchanting, and the book became a minor classic, both in Britain and America. Mrs Bianco – who was married to Francisco Bianco, a dealer in rare books and manuscripts – wrote several more books about the world of nursery toys, including *Poor Cecco* (1925), about a wooden toy dog, and illustrated by Arthur Rackham; *The Little Wooden Doll* (1925), illustrated by Pamela Bianco, the author's teenage daughter; *The Skin Horse*, also illustrated by Pamela Bianco; and *The Adventures of Andy* (1927). Other children's books include: *Street of Little Shops, The Apple Tree, Franzi and Gizi, Good Friends, Winterhound, Other People's Houses, All About Pets, Bright Morning* and (with James Cloyd Bowman) *Tales from a Finnish Tupa*. Margery Bianco enjoyed travelling and visited France and Italy. She died in 1944.

Bird, Maria

Writer of the popular 'Andy Pandy' TV stories and books. Andy Pandy, the little clown, and his friends, Teddy Bear and rag-doll Looby Loo, made their first appearance in 'Watch with Mother' on BBC television in 1950, and although only thirty films exist they are shown regularly in Britain and several countries abroad. The TV programmes are produced by Freda Lingstrom and the songs are sung by Gladys Whitred. Maria Bird also writes the music, as well as telling the story in the TV productions. She has also published nearly thirty Andy Pandy books (illustrated by Matvyn Wright), contributes to the *Andy Pandy Annual*, etc. and has also published a book about another set of her popular TV characters, 'The Woodentops'.

Blake, Wilton

See: Parry, D. H.

Blyth, Harry

Born 1852, in Scotland. Creator of the immortal fictional detective, Sexton Blake, whose adventures have been followed avidly by boys (and their parents) for over seventy years. Blyth began his writing career as a journalist in Glasgow, subsequently running his own paper *Chiel* (sub-titled 'The Scottish Punch') for several years. A series of crime articles he wrote for the Sunday *People* caught the eye of Alfred Harmsworth (later Lord Northcliffe and founder of the Amalgamated Press), who commissioned him to write a number of detective stories for his new boys' paper *The Marvel*. Blyth hit on the name of Sexton Blake for his star detective and the first story featuring the character appeared in No. 6 of *The Marvel* in December 1893. It was called *The Missing Millionaire* and the sequel, *A Christmas Crime*, appeared the following week. The author's name was given as 'HAL MEREDITH', one of Blyth's many pen-names. He received the princely sum of £9. 9s. 0d. for the first story and the full copyright for this subsequently world-famous character. Other writers of the Blake saga later added such new characters as Tinker, the detective's young assistant, and Pedro, his faithful bloodhound. Blyth contributed prolifically to many other boys' papers and magazines. One of his writing idiosyncrasies was to begin a story almost invariably with the spoken word. He died of typhoid fever in February 1898.

Blyton, Enid Mary

Born *c.* 1900, in Dulwich, London. Originally intended to make music her career, becoming an accomplished pianist and singer at an early age. She had always loved writing, however, and her first published work was a poem in one of Arthur Mee's children's magazines, which appeared when she was fourteen. A second poem later appeared in *Nash's Magazine*. At eighteen, when she was preparing to sit for her L.R.A.M. examination and enter the Guildhall School of Music in London, she decided to become a schoolteacher instead. The decision was hastened when she taught at Sunday School for a period and realised how much pleasure and satisfaction she found in teaching children and telling them stories. She wished to specialise in kindergarten work and studied for three years at a Froebel

Institute. She subsequently entered the field of educational journalism and became Editor of *Modern Teaching*, Associate Editor of *Pictorial Knowledge* and part-author of *Two Years in the Infants' School*. In 1923 she published her first book, *Real Fairies*, a collection of her own children's verses. Around this period she was also contributing verses to *Punch*. She continued with her educational work and editing until the mid-'thirties, when she began writing children's stories prolifically. Soon she was writing and editing her own young children's magazine, *Sunny Stories*, which was very successful and contained many serials and stories later to be published in book form. Among her earliest children's books were *The Adventures of the Wishing Chair* (1937), *The Enchanted Wood* (1939), *Naughty Amelia Jane* (1939), *Mr Meddle's Mischief* (1940), *The Naughtiest Girl in the School* (1940), *The Adventures of Mr Pinkwhistle* (1941), *Hello, Mr Twiddle!* (1941), *The Adventurous Four* (1941), *Circus Days Again* (1942) and *The Magic Faraway Tree* (1943). Since those early days, Enid Blyton has become a phenomenon, a legend – and sometimes a controversial figure – in the world of children's books. She is undoubtedly the most prolific and popular children's author of all time. She has published around 400 books, of which over 200 are constantly in print, since the demand for her titles never slackens. Among her 'series' of books about popular characters are those featuring The Famous Five, The Secret Seven, Mr Galliano's Circus, The Wishing Chair, St Clare's, Malory Towers, The Magic Faraway Tree, Mr Pinkwhistle, Mr Meddle, Mr Twiddle, The Naughtiest Girl in the School, Naughty Amelia Jane, The Three Golliwogs, Mary Mouse, Josie, Click and Bun, Dame Slap and Her School, Noddy, Brer Rabbit, and The Six Cousins. Other series are the 'Adventure', 'Mystery', 'Secret' and 'Family' titles. All in addition to an enormous list of story-collections, nature-study books, religious subjects, etc. Miss Blyton caters for all ages and tastes of juvenile readers and, as she once said, likes to 'take a child by the hand when he is three and walk with him all his childhood days'. She has also written over 200 'readers' for schools. Her sales are vast: the 'Noddy' books have sold more than eleven million to date and the 'Famous Five' titles total a sale of around three million in British editions alone. Miss Blyton has about twenty-five British publishers and around forty foreign ones. Her books are translated into practically every known language throughout the world, including Russian, and not forgetting Swahili, Hebrew, Indonesian, Tamil and Fijian. According to recently published official statistics, Enid Blyton comes third in the list of Britain's most-translated authors, being beaten only by Agatha Christie and William Shakespeare! In world-order she came twelfth with 399 translations of her works being published throughout the world – ahead of such writers as Dickens, Hans Andersen, Twain, Zola and Somerset Maugham. Enid Blyton has also written the successful London stage Christmas play *Noddy in Toyland*, another play for older children, based on her 'Famous Five' books, and several films for the Children's Film Foundation. For several years she wrote and edited her own *Enid Blyton's Magazine*. She generously devotes much of her time to helping charitable organisations, particularly those benefiting children and animals, and has formed several 'Clubs' for her readers to join and help these organisations too. Certain educationalists, teachers and librarians tend to frown on Enid Blyton's stories, saying they are trivial, indifferently written and unimaginative, among other things. Some public libraries in Britain have actually banned Blyton books from their shelves. This is no place to enter into the controversy. Children of all ages read – and enjoy – Enid Blyton's books all over the world, and the pleasure she brings them is reflected in the hundreds of spontaneously written letters she receives every week from children. Enid Blyton was married to the late Kenneth Darrell Waters, a retired surgeon who died in 1967, and has two grown-up daughters, Gillian and Imogen. The family home is at 'Green Hedges' (an address well known to readers of Miss Blyton's numerous editorial chats and forewords), a beautiful country house in Beaconsfield, Buckinghamshire.

Bond, Michael

Born Newbury, Berkshire, 1926, and educated at Presentation College, Reading. Former BBC TV cameraman. Author of the popular 'Paddington the Bear' books, the first of which, *A Bear Called Paddington*, appeared in 1958. Successors were *More About Paddington* (1959), *Paddington Helps Out* (1960), *Paddington Abroad* (1961), *Paddington at Large* (1962), *Paddington Marches On*

(1964) and *Paddington at Work* (1966). Paddington is originally found – a very small bear – all alone on Paddington Station, complete with a label round his neck reading 'Please take care of this Bear' and his luggage: a half-eaten jar of marmalade and a photograph of his Aunt Lucy, whom he has left behind in 'Darkest Peru'. The Brown family took him in – and after that adventures followed, fast, furious and funny. The 'Paddington' books are popular abroad too and have been translated into several languages, including Swedish, Danish and Dutch. *The Adventures of Paddington* (1965) is a 'de luxe' edition of the first two titles. In 1967 Bond introduced a new character – an orphan mouse – in *Here Comes Thursday*. It was followed by *Thursday Rides Again* (1968). Michael Bond has also written many radio and TV plays, as well as articles and short stories for national newspapers and magazines.

Boston, Lucy M.

Born in 1892 in Southport, Lancashire, and educated at Downs School, Seaford, Sussex, at a Quaker school in Surrey, a Paris finishing-school and Somerville College, Oxford. On leaving Oxford she trained to be a nurse at St Thomas's Hospital, London, then found herself nursing wounded soldiers at a French hospital during the First World War. She married in 1917 and lived in Cheshire, devoting much time to her favourite pastimes of writing poetry and painting. When her marriage ended in 1935 she left England and lived in Europe, frequenting art galleries, painters' studios and concert halls. She returned to England in 1939, settling down at the Manor House, Hemingford Grey, near Cambridge. This was the house that was to play such an important role in her later books. In 1954 – when she was over sixty – she published her first book, *Yew Hall*, her only adult novel. Also in 1954 came her first children's book, *The Children of Green Knowe*. Green Knowe is the strange, haunted old house near Cambridge, with its huge garden and the river near by, to which a small boy, Tolly, goes to stay with his great-grandmother. As he explores the house and gardens he comes to see and play with the ghosts of his child ancestors who had once lived in the house. And in the evenings his great-grandmother, Mrs Oldknow, tells him stories of the children of the

33

past. The story has great beauty, atmosphere and excitement and was welcomed by reviewers and discerning young readers. A series of stories set in the memorable Green Knowe followed: *The Chimneys of Green Knowe* (1958), *The River at Green Knowe* (1959), *A Stranger at Green Knowe* (1961) – which was awarded the Carnegie Medal as the Best Children's Book of the Year – and *An Enemy at Green Knowe* (1964). In 1965 came a different type of story, *The Castle of Yew* – though it was still set in the garden of Green Knowe. It told of the adventures of two boys who shrank to the size of 'Tom Thumb' and entered miniature castles cut from yew bushes, ingeniously fighting off attacks by such creatures as a cat, a moorhen and a squirrel. Slighter than the actual Green Knowe series and intended for younger readers, the story is amusing and deftly told. *The Sea-Egg* was another haunting fantasy published in 1967. So, though she did not begin her new career as a children's writer until she was more than sixty, Mrs Boston has created a whole new and haunting legend, based around the old house called Green Knowe. All illustrated, incidentally, by her talented artist son, Peter Boston. And she still lives at the Manor House, Hemingford Grey – the Green Knowe of her books.

Bowen, Olwen

Author of a series of humorous animal stories, published in Britain in the 1930s, which were very popular at the time. Her most engaging character was 'Hepzibah Hen', whose adventures were broadcast in the early BBC radio Children's Hour. Her books included: *Hepzibah Hen, Hepzibah Again, Young Yap, Beetles and Things, Taddy Tadpole, Runaway Rabbit, Mr Quill's Animal Shop* and *The Great Black Rock*. A *Hepzibah Omnibus*, containing the first four titles, was published (with a glowing foreword by Clemence Dane) in 1936. Miss Bowen had the advantage of being illustrated by the two foremost animal artists in Britain at that period – L. R. Brightwell and Harry Rountree.

Boylston, Helen Dore

Born 1895, in Portsmouth, New Hampshire, USA. Her ambition from early childhood was to become a nurse and, immediately upon her graduation from Massachusetts General Hospital in 1916, she went to France as a volunteer with the Harvard Medical Unit, doing active nursing throughout the rest of the First World War. Many of her later nursing stories were based on her own practical experiences. She was largely responsible for the flood of 'career novels' for young people which began to appear during the late 1930s, continuing into the 1950s, with the publication of her 'Sue Barton' and 'Carol' books. *Sue Barton: Student Nurse* was published in America in 1936 (appearing in Britain three years later) and was followed by a series of sequels, tracing the nursing career of the heroine, from raw probationer in a great American hospital to the heights of the profession. Typical subsequent titles include: *Sue Barton: Senior Nurse*, *Sue Barton: Superintendent Nurse*, *Sue Barton: Rural Nurse* and *Sue Barton: Visiting Nurse*. Miss Boylston also wrote the popular 'Carol' series, about a young actress and her career in the theatre, etc. The first title was *Carol Goes on the Stage*.

Brabourne, Lord

See: Knatchbull-Hugessen, E. H.

Brazil, Angela

Born in Preston, Lancashire, on 30th November 1868, the daughter of a cotton manufacturer, and educated at Manchester High School and Ellerslie College, where she was head girl. Subsequently she was a fellow-student of Baroness Orczy (creator of the popular 'Scarlet Pimpernel') at an art school. After the death of her father she travelled in Europe and the Middle East with her mother. She began writing at the age of thirty-six and was a forerunner of the extremely popular girls' school story *genre*, which really began with the tremendous success of her first few books. Her first hit was *The Fortunes of Philippa* in 1906, which was loosely based on her mother's story. Over the next forty years she published over fifty stories of schoolgirl life which were easy to read and reasonably true to life. She was the first writer to specialise in girls' public school tales and one might perhaps call her the feminine equivalent of Talbot Baines Reed. Some of her other typical titles are: *The*

Manor House School (1911), *A Pair of Schoolgirls* (1912), *The School by the Sea* (1914), *A Patriotic Schoolgirl* (1918), *Captain Peggie* (1924), *An Exciting Term* (1936), *The New School at Scarsdale* (1940) and *The School on the Loch* (1946). In 1935 she wrote her autiobiography, *My Own Schooldays*. Her name, incidentally, has the accent on the first syllable. Died 13th March 1947.

Brent-Dyer, Elinor Mary

Born in South Shields and educated privately in Leeds. Famous for her long series of girls' school stories set in the Chalet School, high in the Austrian Tyrol, near Innsbruck. The first book, *The School at the Chalet*, appeared in 1925 and, up to 1967, a further fifty-six titles had been published. The fiftieth in the series, *The Chalet School Reunion*, appeared in 1963, and in the story practically all the leading characters over the years turned up to reminisce and bring the readers up to date with their careers and family histories. Miss Brent-Dyer has also written other girls' series about La Rochelle and Chudleigh Hold Schools as well as other girls' and children's stories and school geography readers.

Brereton, Captain Frederick Sadleir

Born in 1872 and was a relative of G. A. Henty, in whose steps he followed as a popular writer of boys' adventure and historical stories. He served in the British Army for many years and saw action in most parts of the world. He always undertook careful research before starting a new book, ensuring that the facts and atmosphere of the story, whether it be the Conquest of Mexico or the Boer War, were as authentic as possible. He was one of the most widely read boys' writers during the first twenty years of the century and his stories were translated into several languages. Though the majority of his books appeared under his name with the prefixed rank of 'Captain', he later became a Lieutenant Colonel and some stories carried this rank in later years and editions. One of his first books was *With Rifle and Bayonet: A Story of the Boer War*, published in 1900. Later notable stories were *Under the Spangled Banner: A Tale of the Spanish–American War* (1903), *With Wolseley to Kumasi: A Tale of the*

24 S. Van Abbé (1949)

25 Louis Rhead (*c* 1920)

26 Hugh Thomson (1918)

27 E. J. Sullivan (1896)

'The Fight' between Tom and Slogger Williams, from Thomas Hughes'
Tom Brown's Schooldays, seen by different artists

28 Robert Newton as Dr Arnold, John Charlesworth as East, John
Howard Davies as Tom and John Forrest as Flashman in Renown's screen
version of *Tom Brown's Schooldays* in 1951. Earlier films were made in 1916
and 1940

29 Arthur Hughes (1889)

30 J. Macfarlane (1916)

31 The first film of Richmal Crompton's popular *Just William* was made by Associated British in 1939 and starred Dicky Lupino (as William) with Norman Robinson, Peter Miles and Roddy McDowall as the mischievous 'Outlaws'. Two later pictures (with William Graham in the lead) were produced in 1947 and 1948

32 William, as readers of the 30-odd books in the series know him – depicted by Thomas Henry, his illustrator for 40 years. Henry illustrated the stories from the beginning, in 1920, but did not meet author Richmal Crompton personally until 1954!

Robert Louis Stevenson's
blood-curdling but likeable
Long John Silver, from
Treasure Island – perhaps the
greatest adventure story of
them all – as portrayed by
different illustrators

33 Above left: Walter Paget
(1899)

34 Above right: S. Van Abbé
(1948)

35 Right: Mervyn Peake
(1949)

36 Above: Werner Stein
(c 1950)

37 and 38 *Treasure Island* has
been filmed several times.
M-G-M's version in 1934
starred Wallace Beery as Long
John Silver (above) with
Jackie Cooper as young Jim
Hawkins. The Walt Disney
production, made in Britain in
1950, had the memorable, eye-
rolling Robert Newton
(right) as the one-legged pirate,
with Bobby Driscoll as Jim

39 Rowland Hilder's striking portrayal of Long John Silver (1929)

First Ashanti War (1908), *How Canada Was Won: A Tale of Wolfe and Quebec* (1909), *Under Haig in Flanders* (1917), *The Armoured Car Scouts* (1917) and *With the Allies to the Rhine* (1919). He wrote over fifty boys' books altogether and also contributed to various boys' magazines and annuals. He died in 1957.

Bridges, Thomas Charles

Born 1868, in France, the son of a clergyman, and educated at Marlborough College. At eighteen went to Florida to work on an orange plantation. After much hard work and many adventures he returned to England in 1894 almost penniless and decided to try his hand at writing. His first two articles (on fishing in Florida) appeared in *The Field*, then, after contributing many free-lance articles to various magazines, including *Answers*, he joined the staff of the latter as a sub-editor. He resigned after four years to return to free-lance writing, contributing his first boys' story to a juvenile magazine around 1902. This was a serial in *Boys' Realm* called 'Paddy Leary's Schooldays', the adventures of an Australian boy at an English public school. It was so popular that he wrote two further long sequels and several short stories about the same characters. He became a prolific contributor to many other boys' papers, including *Chums, Union Jack, Scout,* etc. His first boys' book, *The Squirrel,* was published in 1907, followed by more than sixty others. Titles include: *A Fight for Fortune* (1915), *On Land and Sea at the Dardanelles* (1915), *With Beatty in the North Sea* (1917), *Martin Crusoe* (1920), *Men of the Mist* (1923), *The City of No Escape* (1925), *Sons of the Air* (1929), *Dead Man's Gold* (1936) and *The Death Star* (1940). Under the pseudonym 'CHRISTOPHER BECK', he wrote many more titles, including: *Stronghand Saxon* (1910), *The Crimson Aeroplane* (1913), *Sons of the Sea* (1914), *The Brigand of the Air* (1920) and *The People of the Chasm* (1923). His other pen-names include 'MARTIN SHAW' and 'JOHN STANTON'. He also wrote several books of non-fiction, including: *The Book of Invention* (1925), *The Book of the Sea* (1927), *Heroes of Modern Adventure* (with Hessel Tiltman) (1927), *The Romance of Buried Treasure* (1931), etc. Bridges lived on Dartmoor for several years, later passing his final years in Torquay, Devon. He died in June 1944.

Brooks, Edwy Searles

Born on 11th November 1889, at Hackney, London, the son of a Congregational minister, and educated at Banham Grammar School, Norfolk. Best known for his creation of 'St Frank's School', which he wrote about in numerous stories in the popular boys' paper, *The Nelson Lee Library*, between 1917 and 1933. He also wrote many stories about detective Nelson Lee and his boy assistant, Nipper, for that paper, as well as others featuring Sexton Blake and other characters. He also 'stood in' for Frank Richards (Charles Hamilton) and wrote several tales of Greyfriars School for *The Magnet*, etc. Used a large number of pseudonyms, including 'REGINALD BROWNE' and 'EDWARD THORNTON', under which names he wrote humorous school stories. As 'BERKELEY GRAY' he wrote adult thrillers featuring adventurer Norman Conquest and as 'VICTOR GUNN' wrote about Superintendent Ironsides of Scotland Yard in another series of books. He died in December 1965.

Brown, Pamela

Born at Colchester, Essex, in 1924, and educated at Colchester County High School, Brecon County School, and the Royal Academy of Dramatic Art. She began her first book, *The Swish of the Curtain*, while a schoolgirl of fourteen, starting it with a friend, then, going to South Wales on the outbreak of the Second World War, finishing it there alone in about six months. It was based to some extent on the experiences of herself and her friends while putting on amateur dramatic productions in her home town of Colchester. The first publishers to whom she sent it accepted it (on the condition that she cut some of it) and it was duly published in 1941, when Miss Brown was sixteen. Around the same time it was also serialised on the BBC Children's Hour programme and gained tremendous popularity. *The Swish of the Curtain* told the story of the Blue Door Theatre at Fenchester and its youthful company of actors and actresses (also their own producers, composers, designers, dressers and stage-hands). It breathed the spirit of the theatre and was full of vivid characterisation and incident. With the money she made from this book Pamela Brown went to

R.A.D.A. and trained for the stage herself. She subsequently appeared as a professional actress under the name Mela Brown (to avoid confusion with another well-known actress with her own name). In 1945 she published a sequel to her first story called *Maddy Alone*; later came three further 'Blue Door' books: *Golden Pavements* (1947), *Blue Door Venture* (1949) and *Maddy Again* (1956). Her other children's novels include: *To Be a Ballerina* (1950), *Family Playbill* (1951), *The Television Twins* (1952), *Harlequin Corner* (1953), *The Windmill Family* (1954), *Back-Stage Portrait* (1957), *Showboat Summer* (1957), *Understudy* (1958), *First House* (1959), *The Bridesmaids* (1956), *As Far as Singapore* (1959) and *The Other Side of the Street* (1965); also a fictionalised biography of Louisa M. Alcott, *Louisa* (1955). From 1950–55, Pamela Brown was a leading BBC Children's Television producer, being responsible for the production of many successful TV plays and serials. She produced for Scottish TV, 1957–58. She lives in London with her husband and two daughters.

Browne, Frances

Born 16th January 1816, at Stranorlar, Donegal, Ireland, where her father was the village postmaster. She was seventh in a family of twelve children and was blind from birth. Her brothers and sisters taught her stories, many of them legendary Irish folk and fairy tales, and she loved them so much that she soon began inventing stories of her own to re-tell to her family. She also wrote poetry while still a young child. In 1847 she and a sister moved to Edinburgh, Scotland, and in 1852 they settled down in London. It was here that Frances Browne took up writing seriously and managed to make a living by it. She published several modestly successful novels, but in 1856 she turned to writing children's stories and that Christmas (though dated 1857) she published *Granny's Wonderful Chair and Its Tales of Fairy Times*. This enchanting book consists of several stories of fairyland, told by a magic chair to a small girl. It contains some vivid pieces of descriptive writing – even more admirable when it is recalled that the author was blind and had seen none of the things she was writing about. The original edition had illustrations by Kenny Meadows. Though successful, *Granny's Wonderful Chair* did not really achieve any great plaudits on its first appearance and, indeed, was not reprinted for more than twenty years. Several more children's stories followed, including *Our Uncle the Traveller* (1859) and *The Young Foresters* (1860), but scarcely any more stories of fairyland. Instead, Frances Browne concentrated upon historical books, also publishing more 'straight' novels and books of verse. Little else is known about her life and the exact date of her death is uncertain; it was most probably 1879.

Browne, Reginald

See: Brooks, E. S.

Brunhoff, Jean de

Born in France in 1899 and educated at the École Alsacienne, Paris. Creator of the immortal 'Babar the Elephant' picture-books for young children. Wrote and illustrated the first story, *The Story of Babar the Little Elephant*, in 1931 in France, where it was first published. 'In the Great Forest a little elephant was born. His name was Babar.' And with these opening words began the saga of Babar, lasting over six further books (and continued by Brunhoff's son in another four). *The Story of Babar* was first published in Britain in 1934, and in America the previous year. Subsequent titles included: *Babar's Travels* (1932 France, 1935 Britain), *Babar the King* (1933 France, 1936 Britain), *Babar's Friend Zephir* (1936 France, 1937 Britain), *Babar at Home* (1938 both France and Britain), *Babar and Father Christmas* (1940 Britain, 1941 France), and *Babar's ABC* (1935 France, 1949 Britain). A. A. Milne wrote a special Introduction to the first translation of the first Babar book in 1934. The original format of the books (both in France and Britain) was very large; in more recent editions they have been cut down to a smaller and more manageable size. The huge, detail-packed coloured drawings of Babar's adventures appeal enormously to the young child, who can spend ten minutes gazing at each one at a time. The last few titles were published posthumously as Jean de Brunhoff died in 1937. His son Laurent continued the stories after the Second World War.

Brunhoff, Laurent de

Son of Jean de Brunhoff, creator of the famous 'Babar the Elephant' picture-books. Writer-artist Laurent took over from his father (who had died in 1937) soon after the end of the Second World War, in 1947, when he published *Babar and That Rascal Arthur* in France. In a style incredibly similar to his father's he continued the saga of Babar, to the huge delight of children (and their parents) everywhere. This first book appeared in Britain in 1948, and was followed by *Picnic at Babar's* (1950), *Babar's Visit to Bird Island* (1952) and *Babar's Castle* (1962). *Babar's French Lessons* (1965) was a simple and colourful introduction to the French language. In 1965 too came another picture-book about an entirely new character, *Serafina the Giraffe*, followed in 1967 by *Serafina's Lucky Find*, and in 1968 by *Captain Serafina*.

Buckeridge, Anthony Malcolm

Born in London, 1912, and educated at Seaford College, Sussex, and University College, London. Became a schoolmaster and taught for many years at a boys' preparatory school, also writing various stories and articles in his spare time. His famous schoolboy character 'Jennings' was born when Buckeridge used to tell his pupils stories, both in the classroom and at bedtime before 'lights out'. His listeners begged for more stories about Jennings and before long the character 'took over' and all Buckeridge had to do was invent a plausible situation, then imagine how that remarkable schoolboy would behave in the circumstances. In 1948 he wrote a series of radio plays for BBC Children's Hour about Jennings and Darbishire and their friends at Linbury Court School. The series achieved enormous success and was later voted the most popular programme of the year by young listeners. From then on Jennings became a regular and popular feature of BBC Children's Hour, subsequently appearing in a BBC Television series too. In 1950 came *Jennings Goes to School*, the first in the long and best-selling series of books about Jennings. Subsequent titles, published at the rate of around one a year, include: *Jennings Follows a Clue*, *Jennings' Little Hut*, *Jennings and Darbishire*, *Jennings' Diary*, *According to Jennings*, *Our Friend Jennings*, *Thanks to Jennings, Take Jennings For Instance, Jennings as Usual, The Trouble With Jennings, Just Like Jennings, Leave It to Jennings, Jennings, of Course, Especially Jennings, A Bookful of Jennings* and *Jennings Abounding.* The stories are full of humour and slapstick incident, easy to read and among the most popular juvenile books on the market today. Buckeridge obviously knows small boys and their ways thoroughly, and probably based some of his characters on pupils he has known during his career as a school-master. The day-to-day life described in the books has the authentic touch and the episodes are usually genuinely funny. By now, Jennings has joined Tom Brown and Billy Bunter as the most famous schoolboys in fiction. Well over a million copies of the Jennings books have been sold in English-speaking coun-tries alone and they have also been translated into such langu-ages as French, German, Dutch, Norwegian, Swedish, Danish and Modern Hebrew. In other countries, Jennings is known under different names: in Germany he is 'Fredy', in Norway 'Stompa' (here he is also the hero of several films) and in France he is famous as 'Bennett' (a recent title published in France won an award as Best Children's Book of the Year). In Britain, over eighty radio and TV plays have been broadcast about him. Anthony Buckeridge has also written a series of four books about another energetic schoolboy named Rex Milligan. *Rex Milligan's Busy Term, Rex Milligan Raises the Roof, Rex Milligan Reporting* and *Rex Milligan Holds Forth*; also a humor-ous family story, *A Funny Thing Happened.* He has also edited and compiled three anthologies: *Stories for Boys* (1957), *In and Out of School* (school stories by various writers) (1958), and *Stories for Boys: 2* (1965). He is married with one son and one daughter and lives in Kent.

Burgess, Thornton Waldo

Born in Sandwich, Massachusetts, USA, on 14th January 1874. After a year at a commercial college in Boston, he worked as a cashier and assistant book-keeper in a shoe shop. In 1895 he went to Springfield, Massachusetts, and took a job as office boy with the Phelps Publishing Company. He soon became a reporter for a weekly magazine published by the firm, also writing for various farming papers and for *Country Life in*

America. Phelps also published *Good Housekeeping* and from 1904–11 Burgess was associate editor. During this period he wrote the first of his *Old Mother West Wind* stories and sent them in letters to his five-year-old son who was away from home. Some of the tales were published by *Good Housekeeping*, and in 1910 the first of the *Old Mother West Wind* series appeared in book form. They ran to eight volumes eventually, appearing between 1910 and 1918, and comprised amusing little nature stories, explaining such queries as 'When Mr Moose lost his horns', 'Why Miner the Mole lives underground', 'Where Mr Quack got his webbed feet', and so on. These stories were followed by the *Bedtime Story* series, running to some twenty volumes and appearing between 1913 and 1919. Typical titles included: *The Adventures of Old Mr Toad*, *The Adventures of Buster Bear*, *The Adventures of Jerry Muskrat* and *The Adventures of Peter Cottontail*. Later came the *Green Meadow* series (four volumes, 1918–20), the *Green Forest* series (four volumes, 1921–23), *Tales from the Story Teller's House* (1937), *While the Story Log Burns* (1938), *The Dear Old Briar Patch* (1947), *Bedtime Stories* (1959) and many others. All his books have been illustrated by Harrison Cady. In 1912 Burgess began the daily nature stories for the *Herald Tribune* syndicate – and was still writing them forty-five years later. In 1960 he published his autobiography, *Now I Remember*. He also wrote many books for Boy Scouts and always took a keen interest in the Scouting movement. Northwestern University awarded him an Honorary Litt. D. in 1938. He died, at the age of ninety-one, on 5th June 1965.

Burnett, Frances Eliza Hodgson

Born 24th November 1849, in Manchester, the daughter of a hardware dealer. Her father died when Frances was only four, leaving her mother with five children and little money to bring them up on. Frances loved making up stories and, as a school-child in Manchester, wrote many poems and novelettes. In 1865 the family emigrated to America, at an uncle's invitation, and they lived in a log-cabin in Knoxville, Tennessee. Still facing poverty – but at least now in a healthy, 'wide-open-spaces' environment as a contrast to the grimy, wet Manchester of 100 years ago – Frances decided to try some of her stories on magazine editors. In later years, she said that she was lucky enough never to have had a manuscript rejected, and all these early efforts were, indeed, published in various magazines. In 1876 her first novel, *That Lass o' Lowrie's*, telling of life among the Manchester poor, and written from experience, was an immediate success and heralded some forty subsequent novels she was to publish. In 1873 she married Dr Swan Burnett and had two sons – Lionel, born in 1874, and Vivian in 1876. In 1877 the family moved to Washington and Frances began to write a few children's stories for *St Nicholas*, the famous American children's magazine. Probably the best-known of these early short children's tales is the somewhat over-sentimental *Editha's Burglar* (1881), about a little girl who persuades a tough burglar to carry out his raid quietly without waking her mother! Her most famous book, *Little Lord Fauntleroy*, was originally serialised in *St Nicholas* in 1885 and published in book form in 1886. It became an immediate best-seller and two years later was produced as a stage play, with Vera Beringer (one of Lewis Carroll's child friends) in the title role, and was a tremendous success. King Edward VII was reported to have enjoyed the play very much and to have insisted on Miss Beringer being presented to him after the performance. The 'Little Lord Fauntleroy' of the title was American-born Cedric Errol who, at seven, finds he is heir to his English grandfather, the embittered old Earl of Dorincourt. Cedric travels to England with 'Dearest', his mother, and eventually wins the heart of the Earl with his fine virtues. Some readers (especially boys) found the hero a prig, with his velvet suit, lace collar and long curls – a costume which caught on in almost as big a way as the book, much to the disgust of the aforementioned small boys! Reginald Birch's original illustrations to the story were based on photographs of the author's young son, Vivian, in the outfit, which was not, incidentally, created by Mrs Burnett but was fairly common dress in England. The rags-to-riches theme has always been a favourite one in children's literature and this famous tale is a supreme example. It was once described as 'the best version of the Cinderella story in modern idiom that exists'. Mrs Burnett's next story was *Sara Crewe; or, What Happened at Miss Minchin's*, serialised in *St Nicholas* in 1887 and published in book form the following year. In 1902 she dramatised the story into a stage play which was almost as popular as *Little Lord Fauntleroy*; so successful, in fact, that she was persuaded to re-write the story, basing the new version upon the play and including characters not in the original book. This final version appeared in 1905, under the play's title, *A Little Princess*. It is the Cinderella story again, about a pupil at boarding-school who is transformed from favoured heiress to drudge, on her father's death – and then, eventually, back into favourable circumstances once again. In 1888, the year in which *Sara Crewe* originally appeared as a book, Mrs Burnett moved to England with her two sons and lived at Maytham Hall in Rolvenden, Kent, for twelve years. She returned to live in Long Island, New York, in 1901 (having been divorced from Swan Burnett in 1898), but still visited England from time to time. She wrote many other books, for both adults and children, and those for the latter included *Little St Elizabeth and Other Stories* (1890) which contained many of her short tales for *St Nicholas*, *The One I Knew the Best of All* (1893), describing her early life, *The Captain's Youngest and Other Stories* (1894), *The Two Little Pilgrims' Progress* (1895), *The Land of the Blue Flower* (1909) and *The Secret Garden* (1911). This last is perhaps the one children's book of Mrs Burnett's likely to live on long after the others. Its heroine, Mary, is plain and ill-tempered as well as orphaned and neglected. At the huge house where she is sent to live she finds a 'secret garden' and makes friends with two boys, Colin and Dickon. Together, the children tend the garden and make it bloom once again, at the same time, and without realising it, causing themselves to grow and bloom too. The story has an enchanting setting, wonderful descriptions and a deep knowledge of child psychology. Frances Hodgson Burnett's second marriage, to Stephen Townshend, lasted only a short time. She died in America, on 29th October 1924.

Burton, Hester

Born in Suffolk, the daughter of a doctor, she was educated at Headington School, Oxford, and read English at St Anne's College, Oxford. She has edited such works as

Coleridge and the Wordsworths and *Tennyson* for the Oxford Sheldonian Series. Wrote her first children's book, *The Great Gale*, in 1960 – a dramatic and exciting story set among the great floods in Britain in 1953. In 1962 came *Castors Away!*, a drama set in the days of Trafalgar. The following year she was awarded the 1963 Carnegie Medal for *Time of Trial*, the story of a nineteenth-century social reformer and his family, particularly his daughter, Margaret. Earlier, in 1959, she edited a book of short stories for older children: *Her First Ball. No Beat of Drum* (1966) was set in England and Tasmania in the 1830s. She has also worked as an assistant editor in the revision of the *Oxford Junior Encyclopaedia*. Hester Burton was a schoolteacher for a time and during this period gained a useful knowledge of what children and teenagers look for in their reading. She is married to an Oxford don and has three daughters.

Cannan, Joanna

See: Pullein-Thompson.

Carroll, Lewis

Real name: Charles Lutwidge Dodgson. Born 27th January 1832, at Daresbury, near Warrington, Cheshire, where his father was vicar (and later became Archdeacon of Richmond, Yorkshire). Educated at Richmond Grammar School (Yorkshire), Rugby, and Christ Church, Oxford University, where he began his studies in January 1851. He had a distinguished career at Oxford, gaining the Boulter Scholarship in 1851, and the following year winning First Class Honours in Mathematics and Second Class in Classical Moderations; later he became both B.A. and M.A. He was elected Senior Student (equivalent to Fellow) of Christ Church, and also Lecturer, in 1855. He lived and worked at Christ Church for the rest of his life. In 1861 he was ordained a deacon but did not undertake parochial work, since he preferred his work at Oxford. His first published work appeared in *Hall's Oxonian Advertiser* in the Summer of 1854 – two sets of serious verses. Other items appeared in such periodicals as *The Train, Comic Times, The Whitby Gazette* and *College Rhymes*. For his work in *The Train* he created his famous pseudonym 'Lewis Carroll' by translating Charles Lutwidge into Latin as Carolus Ludovicus, reversing them and re-translating as Lewis Carroll. The first time he used the pen-name was under his long poem *The Path of Roses* in 1861. During all his adult life Carroll (as we may call him for convenience's sake) had made most of his friends among children and, almost exclusively, among little girls. He was a shy man (his stammer probably had something to do with this) and he found that he lost it completely when chatting freely with small girls, whom he adored. On the Fourth of July 1862 there occurred a river trip and picnic on the Thames which was the genesis of the most famous children's book ever written in any language. Lewis Carroll and a friend, Robinson Duckworth, took the three small daughters of Henry Liddell, Dean of Christ Church, up-river and, during the trip, Carroll began to tell them the story of *Alice's Adventures Underground*, making it up as he went along. The three Liddell sisters were named Lorina, Alice and Edith – and his favourite was nine-year-old Alice. At the end of the day, Alice asked Carroll if he would write Alice's adventures out for her – and by the end of the year he had begun the task, finishing it the following February. He drew pictures to illustrate a special neatly-handwritten and bound copy which he presented to Alice Liddell early in 1863. Several people saw the story – including Henry Kingsley (brother of Charles) and George MacDonald – and urged Carroll to publish it. He eventually revised the story, wrote additional chapters and polished it generally, and it was first published, with John Tenniel's incomparable illustrations, in July 1865 – three years after the first telling of the story on that river picnic. Tenniel was dissatisfied with the printing of his pictures in this first edition of *Alice's Adventures in Wonderland* (as it was now called) and Carroll recalled most of the copies (the little more than a dozen copies which survived are today collectors' rarities). In December 1865 (though dated 1866), Macmillan's issued the second edition of the book, which Tenniel approved. Though early reviewers gave the book a mixed reception it sold well and has never been out of print since. In December, 1871 (dated 1872) came *Through the Looking-Glass and What Alice Found There*, again illustrated by Tenniel, and even more successful than *Alice*. These two stories marked a turning-point in children's literature generally, which until then had been packed with sombre moral overtones, religious teachings and gloomy, sin-obsessed heroes and heroines. 'The work was a revolution in its sphere', wrote Harvey Darton in *Children's Books in England* (1932). He was right. By the end of the nineteenth century the two 'Alice' books had passed into immortality and their characters and their sayings become household words. Lewis Carroll's chief fame rests on the 'Alice' books, but had he never written a word his name would have gone down in British – indeed world – photographic history. He has been described as 'the nineteenth century's most outstanding child photographer' and was also a fine amateur adult portraitist. He wrote many other books, chiefly mathematical treatises, puzzles, games and exercises in logic, but never again reached the magical heights of 'Alice'. In 1876 he published a long nonsense poem, *The Hunting of the Snark*; in 1883 came *Rhyme? And Reason?*, humorous verses and puzzles; and 1885 saw the appearance of *A Tangled Tale*, an attempt to interest children in mathematics. *Sylvie and Bruno* was published in 1889, and its sequel *Sylvie and Bruno Concluded* in 1893, both illustrated by Harry Furniss. Determined to be different from *Alice* in his latest children's story, Carroll produced what has been called 'one of the most interesting failures in English literature.' Basically the story of two fairy children who journey through Elfland and Dogland, the book is apt to preach, is laboriously told for much of its length and is frequently reminiscent of a routine adult novel of the period. It has compensations, such as some of the characters the children encounter on their travels, and some amusing nonsense verse, but it was not, as everyone sadly agreed, another *Alice*. The germ of the idea for the tale, incidentally, was a short story, *Bruno's Revenge*, which Carroll wrote for *Aunt Judy's Magazine* in 1867. A facsimile of Carroll's original 'Alice' story, *Alice's Adventures Underground*, was published, with his own illustrations, in 1886. Towards the end of his life he was fascinated by mathematical games and puzzles even more than ever and his last book, Part One of *Symbolic Logic*, appeared in 1896. He suffered from recurring ill-health in his later years and, visiting his sisters in their house, 'The Chestnuts', in Guildford, Surrey, for Christmas 1897, he caught a feverish cold which turned to bronchitis. He died there on 14th January 1898 and is buried in the Old Cemetery in Guildford. Throughout his writing career, 'C. L. Dodgson' and 'Lewis Carroll' had enjoyed virtually different careers – though few will disagree that it is the latter name which will live on. One amusing anecdote is told in this respect: like everyone else who read it Queen Victoria was captivated by *Alice's Adventures in Wonderland* and soon after its publication in 1865 she sent for Lewis Carroll and, at the end of their chat, asked him to be sure to send her a copy of his next book. He obeyed the royal command but must have disappointed Her late Majesty – the book she received was a complex work on higher mathematics by an Oxford don named Charles Lutwidge Dodgson. . . !

Charlesworth, Marie Louisa

Born on 1st October 1819, in the rectory at Little Blakenham, Suffolk, the daughter of the Reverend John Charlesworth, at that time rector of the tiny parish of Flowton, later becoming curate-in-charge of the parish of Little Blakenham. Her parents were both tireless workers in the cause of the Church and were very active in helping the local poor and needy. When Maria was a small child the family moved to nearby Ipswich, where the Rev. Charlesworth took up a new church appointment, and it was there that she grew up and was educated. After a spell at Bramford, near Ipswich, the family moved to London, where the Rev. Charlesworth had charge of a small parish near St Paul's Cathedral. The London air did not agree with Maria, so used to the country winds of Suffolk, and in time she became ill and, eventually, an invalid, confined to her room. Like her parents she had devoted her life to helping and ministering to the poor and needy and encouraging them to worship. Now she took up her pen and wrote a semi-autobiographical work called *The Female Visitor to the Poor*, published in the early 1850s. Then, in 1854, came her most famous book, *Ministering Children*, which was an unashamedly didactic and moral work of over 400 pages, telling numerous episodes about little children and the way in which they went out of their way to help poor, sick and unhappy people. The author's aim, in 'training the sympathies of children by personal intercourse with want and sorrow', was to induce youthful readers to emulate the tiny paragons in the stories and devote their time, and indeed their lives, to performing kind deeds for those less fortunate than themselves. It rapidly became a best-seller of the latter half of the nineteenth century and, in its first thirty-five years, sold 170,000 copies in England alone, besides many editions published in America, France, Germany, Sweden, etc. A sequel appeared in 1862, titled, appropriately enough, *Ministering Children; A Sequel*, and among her other titles (which totalled seventeen) were: *Sunday Afternoons in the Nursery*, *The Old Looking-Glass*, *The Broken Looking-Glass*, *Oliver of the Mill* and *England's Yeomen*. She later moved to Nutfield, Surrey, on her father's death, and worked for the poor there and in other places, including Bermondsey, in London, where she established a Mission and a ragged school. She died on 16th October 1880 and is buried in Nutfield churchyard.

Chaundler, Christine

Born Biggleswade, Bedfordshire. Author of numerous girls' school stories and other children's books. Typical school story titles are: *The Thirteenth Orphan*, *Reforming the Fourth* and *Sally Sticks it Out*. Was at her peak of popularity during the 1920s and 1930s, when she rivalled such similar girls' writers as Angela Brazil, Elinor Brent-Dyer and Dorita Fairlie Bruce. She was sub-editor of *Little Folks*, 1914–17, and editor of juvenile books for James Nisbet and Company, 1919–22. She reviewed children's books for *The Quiver* for a period beginning in 1933. In 1937 she wrote a writer's guide to the juvenile market called *The Children's Author*. She also wrote a book of verse for children entitled *The Golden Years* and a collection of stories, *The Children's Story Hour*. Has contributed girls' stories and children's tales to many annuals, papers, magazines, etc., and articles to adult magazines such as *Child Education* and *The Quiver*. In more recent years Miss Chaundler has published a series of informative books for the younger child, including: *A Year Book of Customs*, *A Year Book of Folk Lore*, *A Year Book of Legends*, *A Year Book of Saints*, *A Year Book of the Stars* and (for older readers) *Everyman's Book of Legends*.

Church, Richard

Born London, 26th March 1893, and educated at Dulwich Hamlet School. Published his first book of poems, *Flood of Life*, in 1917, since when he has produced well over fifty books of verse and prose and is today one of Britain's most distinguished poets, novelists and literary critics. He worked as a civil servant for nearly twenty-five years. Published his *Collected Poems* in 1948, and in 1957 his *The Inheritors* won the Foyle Poetry Prize. His most famous novel is *The Porch* (1937). In 1955 came his widely praised volume of early autobiography *Over the Bridge*, followed two years later by its successor, *The Golden Sovereign*; the former won the *Sunday Times* Gold Medal and £1,000 Prize. The first of his books for children, *A Squirrel Called Rufus*, appeared in 1941 and told of a war between red and grey squirrels in a wood, with deeper meanings hidden beneath the surface. In 1954 came *Dog Toby*, a graphic picture of three children and their dog involved in frontier war tensions in Central Europe. *The Cave*, an unusual story of a group of boys lost in an underground limestone cave – and of the subtle character changes they undergo as a result of their experiences – appeared in 1950. A sequel, featuring the same boys, was published in 1958 and entitled *Down River*. This had a search for Roman relics as its basis, but soon developed into a crooks *v.* boys tussle and, though excellently written and presented, like all Church's children's books, is probably the least impressive of them. It is a fine quartet of children's books and *The Cave*, with its impressive picture of boys and the problems of leadership, is almost a classic of its kind. Richard Church is a C.B.E. and a Fellow of the Royal Society of Literature. He lives in a picturesque converted oasthouse near Cranbrook, in Kent.

Clare, Helen

See: Clarke, Pauline

Clarke, Pauline

Born in Nottinghamshire and educated at Somerville College, Oxford, where she gained her M.A. degree in English. After becoming a journalist and working on a children's magazine for a time she went to stay with an artist-friend, Cecil Leslie, to help look after the house and garden – to say nothing of the several Pekinese dogs kept as pets! She decided to write a story, for her friend to illustrate, also incorporating the dogs. The book, entitled *The Pekinese Princess*, was published in 1948 and could be described as Chinese fairy-tale. It was, as intended, illustrated by Cecil Leslie, who has illustrated many of Miss Clarke's subsequent books. Her later stories include: *The White Elephant* (1952), *Smith's Hoard* (1955) (reprinted as *The Golden Collar* in 1967), *The Boy With the Erpingham Hood* (1956), *Torolov the Fatherless* (1958), *The Robin Hooders* (1960), and *Keep the Pot Boiling* (1961). In 1962 Miss Clarke was awarded the Carnegie Medal for the Best Children's Book of the Year – *The Twelve and the Genii*. This was a beautifully evoked story of a group of modern children who find the dozen wooden soldiers that were once the favourite toys of the Brontë family. The soldiers come alive and explain that an American collector wants to buy them and take them back to America. With the children's help they escape and return to Haworth, the Brontës' home in Yorkshire. Pauline Clarke has also written a series of stories for younger children, including: *James the Policeman* (1957), *James and the Robbers* (1959), *James and the Smugglers* (1961), *James and the Black Van* (1963), *The Bonfire Party* (1966) and *Sarday the Sailor* (1968). In 1964 came a colourful alphabet book, *Crowds of Creatures*. Under the pseudonym of 'HELEN CLARE' Miss Clarke has written several more children's books; the first, in 1953, was centred around the Arthurian legends but set in modern times and titled *Merlin's Magic*. A story about a girl awaiting her summer holiday was *Seven White Pebbles* (1956). But her best-known books, written under this name, are the series about a small girl who regularly becomes tiny enough to enter her own doll's-house and have adventures with her dolls and toy animals. Titles include: *Five Dolls in a House* (1953), *Five Dolls and the Monkey* (1956), *Five Dolls in the Snow* (1957), *Five Dolls and their Friends* (1959) and *Five Dolls and the Duke* (1963). All these stories were reprinted in two omnibus volumes – *Five Dolls in a House and Other Stories* and *Five Dolls and Their Friends and Other Stories* – in 1967. She lives at Blakeney, on the north Norfolk coast.

Cleaver, Hylton

Born 1891 and educated at St Paul's School, London. As a boy his favourite magazine was the celebrated *Captain*, and when he was twenty-two he decided to try his hand at writing a school story for it. 'The Red Rag', as it was called, was immediately accepted, appearing in 1913. He quickly became one of the most popular school story writers in Britain, with a huge following. Most of his tales were about Harley or Greyminster and some were based loosely upon his own schooldays at St Paul's, where a rather eccentric and much-loved master named Elam served as a model for his most amusing and memorable creation, Mr Dennett, a housemaster at Greyminster. Cleaver wrote many serials for such boys' magazines as *Boy's Own Paper*, *Chums* and *The Captain*, as well as numerous short stories and over twenty hard-cover school stories. His first book was *Roscoe Makes Good* (1921), and other typical titles were *The Short Term at Greyminster*, *The Harley First Eleven*, *A House Divided*, *Captain for a Day* and *The School That Couldn't Sleep*. He also published adult novels, sporting books and an autobiography, and had several stage plays produced. He served in the army during the First World War and wrote several school stories in long-hand while in the trenches, all of which appeared in *The Captain*. He was later a sports writer for the London *Evening Standard* for more than twenty years (late 1930s until 1960), covering mainly rugby, riding and rowing. He died in London in 1961.

Clifford, Martin

See: Hamilton, Charles

Coatsworth, Elizabeth

Born Buffalo, New York, 1893. Educated privately and, after graduation from Vassar, gained her M.A. at Columbia University. Travelled widely throughout the United States, Mexico, Europe, Egypt and the Orient. After publishing three volumes of poetry in the 'twenties she won the 1930 Newbery Award in America for her children's book *The Cat Who Went to Heaven*, a beautifully written and illustrated (by Lynd Ward) book, telling a sad little tale about a poor artist, a humble cat and a Buddhist miracle. Her first period story, *Away Goes Sally* (1934), told of the migration of young Sally's aunts and uncles from Massachusetts to Maine in a little house on runners. Four further books about Sally followed, telling of her experiences as she grew up. They include *Five Bushel Farm* and *Fair American*. In 1938 came *Alice-all-by-Herself*, about a little girl who lives in Maine on the sea-coast in an eighteenth-century house. Miss Coatsworth's other titles for children include: *The Cat and the Captain* (1930), *The Golden Horseshoe* (1936), *Here I Stay* (1938), *The Littlest House* (1940), *The Enchanted* (1951) and *Horses, Dogs and Cats* (1957). Another book, of poems, was *Summer Green* (1948), and there are fine poems scattered through her prose books too.

Cockton, Henry

Born 1807, in London. Is remembered almost entirely for his long book *Valentine Vox the Ventriloquist* (1840), which was the forerunner of every other story of ventriloquism ever published – and many have appeared in the realms of children's literature since then. Cockton performed a similar service for sleepwalkers in humorous stories when his *Sylvester Sound the Somnambulist* was published soon after *Vox*; children's stories have had their fair share of these nocturnal ramblers too. Cockton died in 1852, without realising just what he had started . . .

Coke, Desmond

Born London, 5th July 1879, the son of Major-General Talbot Coke. Educated at Shrewsbury School, where he became Captain and also edited *The Salopian*, the school magazine. Later, at Oxford, he edited *Isis*. While still at Oxford he wrote a 'burlesque' school novel called *Sandford of Merton*, which was published in 1903 under the pseudonym 'BELINDA BLINDERS'. In 1906 came his now-classic story of life at Shrewsbury, *The Bending of a Twig*. During this period Coke was a schoolmaster himself, at Clayesmore, where he remained for six years. His later school stories – first-class ones, full of outstanding character studies – included *The House Prefect* (1907) *The School Across the Road* (1909) and *The Worst House at Sherborough* (1913). Three more novels of public school life, aimed rather more at adult readers than boys, were: *Wilson's* (1911), *The Worm* (1927) and *Stanton* (1931). *The Chaps of Harton* (1913) was another school story burlesque and *Youth, Youth. . . !*, a collection of perceptive short school stories. Coke also wrote several adult novels. He was a noted collector of English paintings and antiques and presented his unique collection of 18th-century silhouettes on ivory, glass and plaster to the Victoria and Albert Museum in 1923. He served as Captain and Adjutant with the Royal North Lancashire Regiment in 1914–17 and saw active service in France. He died in the 1940s.

Collingwood, Harry

Real name: W. J. C. Lancaster. Born 1851 at Weymouth, Dorset. He was a distinguished student at the Royal Naval College, Greenwich, carrying off many prizes, and on completion of his studies there joined the Royal Navy. Defective eyesight compelled him to retire from the navy, however, and he became a civil engineer, specialising in sea and harbour work and hydrography. In the course of both careers he saw many countries and so, when he began to write his popular adventure stories for boys, he had personal knowledge of the places and peoples he described so graphically. His first boys' book, *The Secret of the Sands*, appeared in 1879 and he produced numerous other titles over the following forty years. His stories were mainly sea adventures, but he also wrote several flying tales too. Typical titles include: *The Pirate Island, The Log of the 'Flying Fish', Congo Rovers, A Middy in Command, With Airship and Submarine, A Middy of the Slave Squadron, A Chinese Command, Two Gallant Sons of Devon, The Adventures of Dick Maitland, A Strange Cruise, Across the Spanish Main, In the Grip of Anarchists* and *The Strange Adventures of Eric Blackburn*. He was a keen follower of sport and excelled at swimming, rifle-shooting and horse-riding; he was also an enthusiastic yachtsman. He died in the 1920s.

Collodi, Carlo

Real name: Carlo Lorenzini. He adopted the name 'Collodi' after his mother's birthplace, a small village in Tuscany, Northern Italy. Born in Florence on 24th November 1826, the son of a cook and a domestic servant. He had a rough, tough upbringing, often running wild in the streets of Florence. He was educated there and, on leaving school, entered a seminary to study for the priesthood. He found he was not really suited for the life, however, and in 1846 began writing for various local newspapers. On the outbreak of war against the Hapsburg Empire (which at that time ruled Tuscany) in 1848, he joined the Tuscan volunteers, and, on returning to Florence the following year, took up journalism as a career. He started a small newspaper of his own, *Il Lampione*, which concentrated on the lighter side of life but which had serious meaning behind the humour. After a while the government closed this paper, but in 1853 he founded a theatrical journal called *La Scarrammucia* for which he wrote many dramatic criticisms. He also wrote several books between 1850 and 1859 on a wide variety of subjects – travel, local Italian industries, humour, novels, and also a work on his beloved Florence. On the outbreak of the Italian-Austrian war in 1859 he joined a cavalry regiment and fought on the plains of Lombardy. Back in Florence in 1860 he became a government official, becoming particularly interested in administrating educational reforms, and he did much good work in this field. When he was over fifty he was asked to translate three of Perrault's fairy tales from the French. They were so successful that he was invited to write something of his own for children. Being an education-alist, he produced a school textbook of an entirely new kind – one which could amuse and entertain pupils as well as instruct them. This was a new version of *Gianetto* by Parravicini and re-titled *Giannettino* (1876) by Collodi. *Geographia di Giannettino* followed in 1877 and other educational books continued the series. In 1881 Collodi decided to try something different and wrote a story about a little wooden puppet named Pinocchio ... Hearing that a friend had just been appointed editor of a new children's paper called *The Children's Journal* in Rome, he sent the story along, telling him to do what he liked with 'this bit of foolishness'. This very first adventure of Pinocchio appeared in the next issue of the paper, on 7th July 1881, and youthful Italian readers demanded more. Collodi wrote more episodes as and when he thought of them and had the time. In 1883 *The Adventures of Pinocchio* appeared in book form and before long a million copies had been sold in Italy alone. The book's original English translation was by M. A. Murray and was published in both Britain and America in 1892. This incident-packed story of a wooden puppet which, coming to life whilst being made by a kind old carpenter, sets off on a series of bizarre adventures is fast-moving and exciting. The sugar also coats a few morals (Pinocchio lies and his nose grows longer, he chooses a lazy life and is turned into a donkey, and so on) but this aspect is by no means overdone. *Pinocchio* is certainly the best puppet story ever written and probably the best children's book to have come from Italy. Walt Disney's full-length colour cartoon film version in 1940 introduced Pinocchio to an even wider audience. Collodi contributed other stories to Italian children's papers and books (one of the best being a long short-story called *Pip, or The Little Rose-Coloured Monkey*) but nothing ever approached the success of *Pinocchio*. Collodi never married or had any children of his own. He died on 26th October 1890, and today there are small memorials in Florence and Collodi to honour the memory of the creator of the immortal little *Pinocchio*.

Colwell, Eileen H.

Born in Yorkshire, the daughter of a Methodist Minister. Studied for her Fellowship of the Library Association at University College, London, gaining this distinction in 1924. After working for two years at Bolton Public Library she went to Hendon, in North London, in 1926, to found a library service especially for children. Under her guidance and direction Hendon was, in a few short years, to have perhaps the finest children's libraries in Britain. Today Miss Colwell controls a number of children's public libraries in the Hendon area, and also around fifty local school libraries. In 1937 she was instrumental in founding the Association of Children's Librarians and worked as its first secretary. Since its origination in 1936 she has been a member of the committee which chooses the annual Carnegie Medal, awarded to the Best Children's Book of the Year, and is also a member of the Hans Andersen Medal jury. She is chairman of an international committee on children's library work and has travelled to many countries to observe libraries there. She is probably one of the world's foremost authorities on children's libraries and books and has lectured on the subject to organisations and colleges all over the world. She has written numerous articles on children's books and storytelling for various publications and her first book was *How I Became a Librarian* (1956). In 1961 she published a 'Bodley Head Monograph' book on *Eleanor Farjeon* and the following year edited a collection of stories for the 'under-fives', specially published by Puffin Books and titled *Tell Me a Story*. In 1963 came *Storyteller's Choice*, a collection of twenty stories she has told successfully to children over the years; the book also included notes on the art of storytelling in general and on how to tell each story included in the book. *Tell Me Another Story*, a Puffin collection for children aged from four to six, came in 1964, and the following year *A Second Storyteller's Choice*, on the same lines as her 1963 book. *Time for a Story* (1966) was another Puffin collection, and *A Hallowe'en Acorn* (1966), an anthology of appropriately ghostly tales. *The Youngest Storybook* appeared in 1967.

Conquest, Owen

See: Hamilton, Charles

Coolidge, Susan

Real name: Sarah Chauncey Woolsey. Born 29th January 1835, in Cleveland, Ohio, USA, and educated at private schools there. Wrote her first book, *A New Year's Bargain*, in 1871; it was a story in which two children receive a story and gift from each of the months in the year. It was followed in 1872 by what was to be her most famous book and the first of a series: *What Katy Did*. Katy is a headstrong, good-hearted young American girl and the book tells of her escapades and those of her family. Other books in this series, in which the leading characters grow from childhood to marriage, are: *What Katy Did at School* (1873), *What Katy Did Next* (1886), *Clover* (1888) and *In the High Valley* (1891). The stories have much of the warmth and naturalness of those by Louisa M. Alcott. Other children's stories (mainly intended for girls) include: *Mischief's Thanksgiving* (1874), *Eyebright* (1879), *Cross Patch* (1881), *A Little Country Girl* (1885) and *Just Sixteen* (1889). She also wrote three volumes of verse – *Verses* (1880), *A Few More Verses* (1889) and *Last Verses* (1906) – a history of Philadelphia, and edited the letters of Fanny Burney (1880) and those of Jane Austen (1892). She died on 9th April 1905.

Cooper, James Fenimore

Born 15th September 1789, in Burlington, New Jersey, USA, the son of William Cooper, a prosperous land agent who moved the family to the shores of Otsego Lake, in central New York State, and established Cooperstown; he later became a judge and a Member of Congress. Young James Cooper (he added his mother's family name 'Fenimore' soon after his writing career had begun) spent his boyhood around Otsego Lake, learning about frontier and wild life – knowledge he was later to put to good use in his novels. He was educated at a small local school, at Albany, N.Y., and at Yale, from where he was dismissed following a youthful escapade. He later enlisted as a merchant seaman before serving for three years as a midshipman in the U.S. Navy, chiefly being occupied in patrolling the Great Lakes. In 1811 he resigned his commission to marry and settle down to the life of a country gentleman. In 1820 he published his first novel, *Precaution*, which he wrote to justify a light-hearted claim to his wife that he could write a better novel than the English one she was currently reading. It was a competent novel of manners and aroused little comment. *The Spy*, which followed in 1821, however, became a best-seller and it was on the strength of this that Cooper decided to devote himself to full-time writing. *The Spy* was a mixture of adventure, espionage and romance. In 1823 came the first of the 'Leatherstocking Tales', *The Pioneers*. It was the first in order of writing but not of narrative. The rest of the series of five 'Leatherstocking' novels are, in order of publication:

The Last of the Mohicans (1826), *The Prairie* (1827), *The Path-finder* (1840) and *The Deerslayer* (1841). For the fullest effect they should be read in correct narrative sequence, following the hero from youth to old age, in this order: *The Deerslayer*, *The Last of the Mohicans*, *The Pathfinder*, *The Pioneers* and, finally, *The Prairie*. The hero is an American hunter who spends his life among the Red Indians and undergoes many adventures. His actual name is Natty Bumppo, but he is also known variously as 'Leatherstocking', 'Pathfinder', 'Deerslayer' and 'Hawkeye'. The sequence of five novels – for which Cooper is best known – was skilfully abridged and edited by Allan Nevins in 1954 and published under the general title *The Leatherstocking Saga* (Pantheon Books, New York). It is worth noting, perhaps, that the *Cambridge History of American Literature* has described 'Leatherstocking' as 'the most memorable character American fiction has given to the world'. *The Pilot* (1822) was an excellent sea story. From 1826 to 1833 Cooper travelled abroad, officially as U.S. Consul in Lyons. In 1839 came his *History of the Navy in the United States*. Later he returned to Cooperstown, where he wrote many more novels, satirical and other works, and a supplementary volume to his Naval history, spotlighting American naval officers and their lives. But these works never reached the wide popularity of his earlier novels. Sometimes called 'the American Walter Scott', James Fenimore Cooper was the first American author to win international fame. He died in Cooperstown on 14th September 1851.

Coppard, Alfred Edgar

Born 4th January 1878, at Folkestone, Kent, the son of a tailor, and educated in Brighton. When he was only nine he worked as a shop-boy in Whitechapel, London, then became an office-boy back again in Brighton. He was largely self-educated and also a fine athlete, at one time competing as a professional sprinter. Later he became an accountant at Oxford and around this time began writing. In 1919 he gave up his full-time job to devote himself entirely to writing prose and poetry, and underwent extreme poverty for about two years. His first book was *Adam and Eve and Pinch Me* in 1921, followed by further collections of his entertaining short stories, interspersed with several volumes of poetry, his *Collected Poems* appeared in 1928 and the first part of an autobiography, *It's Me, O Lord!*, in 1957. In 1930 came his one book for children, *Pink Furniture*, which quickly became a minor classic of its time. This 'Tale for Lovely Children with Noble Natures' was the story of little Toby Tottel's quest for the Land of Pink Furniture and his adventures with many strange creatures and characters on the way. Essentially a nonsense fantasy it is also liberally scattered with verses and songs. Coppard died on 13th January 1957.

Corbett, Harry

Born in Yorkshire. Originally studied as an electrical engineer and is an Associate Member of the Institute of Electrical Engineers. The turning-point in his career came in 1948 when he bought a Teddy Bear puppet in a novelty shop on Blackpool's North Pier, with the idea of amusing his three-year-old son, David. With the glove-puppet he worked up various stories and routines to entertain David and, in time, his adult friends at parties and shows. In 1952 he was seen doing one of his 'Teddy Bear routines' in Yorkshire by a BBC television producer, who at once saw the possibilities and booked Corbett for BBC Television Children's Hour. The first show was an instant success and Eric Fawcett, the producer, suggested that a distinctive name should be given to the bear, and 'Sooty' was born (chiefly as a result of his black ears and nose). His dog friend 'Sweep' followed soon afterwards. Harry Corbett, manipulator and chief script-writer, has been appearing on Children's TV programmes with 'Sooty' and 'Sweep' regularly since 1952 and has made several guest appearances in adult TV shows. His TV films are shown extensively throughout the world (including America) and a London Christmas stage show is now a regular occurrence. 'Sooty' now features in his own yearly Annual, other books about his adventures, children's comics and newspaper strips, and is one of today's most popular characters with young readers and audiences.

Cox, Jack

Born 1915, in Worsley, Lancashire, and educated at Eccles

Grammar School and Manchester University, where he gained his M.A. degree. He also studied at the Institute of International Relations in Geneva. He was originally a schoolmaster but gave up teaching in 1937 to join the staff of the *Manchester Guardian* (previously he had worked for the *Daily Mail* during University vacation). During the Second World War he served as an officer in the Royal Engineers. In 1946 he became editor of the famous *Boy's Own Paper*, a position he held successfully until the end of 1966 when the magazine was about to cease publication. He has written and/or edited many books for boys, many of them dealing with outdoor activities such as camping, scouting, hiking, climbing, etc., on which he is an acknowledged authority. His books in this field are widely used in the training of youth leaders and teachers and he was instrumental in the launching of the Duke of Edinburgh's Award scheme. He lectures and gives talks on scouting and other open-air pursuits all over Britain and writes regularly for national newspapers, including football articles for the *Sunday Times*. His non-fiction titles include: *Camping for All* (1953), *The Outdoor Book* (1954), *Camp and Trek* (1956), *Boy's Own Book of Hobbies* (1958), *Outdoor Hobbies* (1960), *Fun with Radio*, *Fun with Electronics* (in collaboration with Gilbert Davey) (1962), etc. For many years he edited the *Boy's Own Companion*, an annual compilation containing 'the best of the *B.O.P.*', and, more recently, the *Boy's Own Annual*. He has also written several adventure stories for boys, including a series about an enterprising hero known as 'Skipper'; titles include: *Dangerous Waters* (1957), *Calamity Camp* (1958) and *Eagle Mountain* (1960). He has written many scripts and programmes for TV and radio, also appearing regularly in these mediums. Jack Cox is today general editor of several publications issued by Purnell's, as well as editor of the *Boy's Own Annual*, which still continues as a yearly book. He has three sons and lives at Northwood, Middlesex (he also has a cottage in North Wales).

Cradock, Mrs H. C.

Author of the colourful picture story books about *Josephine and Her Dolls* (the first of the series, published in 1915), which were charmingly illustrated by Honor C. Appleton. Other titles in the series, which ended in 1939, included *Josephine Keeps House*, *Josephine's Birthday*, *Josephine Keeps School*, *Josephine's Christmas Party*, *Josephine Goes Shopping*, *Josephine at the Seaside*, *Josephine*, *John and the Puppy*, *Josephine Goes Travelling* and *Josephine's Pantomime*. The simply-told stories related the nursery adventures of the little girl Josephine (and sometimes her friend, John) and her dolls and toy animals, who included Quacky-Jack the sailor duck, Big Teddy and Little Teddy, the Dutch Doll, the Japanese Dolls, Dora and Dorothy Doll, and Granny, the old lady doll. The books were originally published in a spacious quarto format but have recently been reissued in a smaller size.

Craik, Mrs

See: Mulock, D. M.

Crockett, Samuel Rutherford

Born 24th September 1860, at Little Duchrae, Balmaghie, Kirkcudbrightshire, Scotland, and educated at Cowper's School, Castle Douglas, and Edinburgh University. He began his studies at the latter when only sixteen and kept himself there chiefly by journalism in his spare time. He gained his degree in 1879 and, after three years as a private tutor travelling in Germany, Switzerland and Italy, he decided to enter the church and studied at New College, Edinburgh, from 1882–86, when he became minister of the Free Church at Penicuik, just outside Edinburgh. In 1886 he published a book of poems, *Dulce Cor*. His first volume of collected stories and sketches, *The Stickit Minister*, appeared in 1893 and was an instant success, and he soon became a leading writer in what was known as 'the Kailyard school' of writing, which dealt mainly with sentimental pictures of life in Scottish villages. The following year came two novels – *The Lilac Sunbonnet* and *The Raiders*. The latter story set a pattern which the majority of Crockett's subsequent novels followed over the years and was an exciting, romantic, historical adventure. In 1897 came his first children's book, *Sir Toady Lion*. This had a small Scottish boy as its hero ('Toady Lion' being his own first attempt at pronouncing the name of his hero, Richard Coeur-de-Lion) and was based on Crockett's own childhood adventures around Threave Castle, when he used to lead an army of boys against a similar group from a rival school. The same situation exists in *Sir Toady Lion*. The same character's exploits are continued in a sequel, *Sir Toady Crusoe* (1905). Both books put over amusingly and realistically the world of small boys at play, though they do tend to over-sentimentality at times. Both stories are superbly illustrated, in their original editions, by Gordon Browne. Two further children's books were *Sweetheart Travellers* (1895) and *Sweethearts at Home* (1912), but both are sentimental in the extreme. Crockett wrote nearly fifty books (including thirty in his last ten years) and among them might be mentioned one outstanding example of his romantic adventures – *The Black Douglas* (1899). One of Crockett's greatest admirers was Robert Louis Stevenson, who dedicated one of his best-known poems to him. Crockett died at Avignon on 21st April 1914.

Crompton, Richmal

Real name: Richmal Crompton Lamburn. Born on 15th November 1890, in Bury, Lancashire, the second daughter of the Rev. E. J. S. Lamburn, an English master at Bury Grammar School. Her unusual christian name, Richmal, has been in the family, on her mother's side, since the early 1700s; her second christian name comes from a grandmother who married a John Crompton. Educated at St Elphin's School and Royal Holloway College. She gained a Bachelor of Arts degree (Classics, 2nd class honours) from London University and decided upon teaching as a career. By 1920 she was Senior Classical Mistress at Bromley High School for Girls. Between terms she wrote occasional short stories, including some featuring children. Among her stories was one about a quartet of energetic small boys named William, Ginger, Douglas and Henry; the editor of *Home Magazine* accepted it and asked for more. Several further stories about schoolboy William Brown and his friends – and enemies – appeared in this publication, later transferring to the popular *Happy Magazine*. They eventually proved so popular with readers of all ages that

Newnes published a collection of the tales in May 1922, under the title *Just William*. *More William* followed later the same year and *William Again* in 1923. By 1924 *William the Fourth* was out, and Miss Crompton's headmistress was urging her to give up her popular writing in favour of an academic career. On the other hand, her publishers were advising her to give up teaching and become a full-time writer. A sudden attack of polio practically forced the decision out of her hands. She resigned from her school and concentrated on full-time authorship, and 'William' continued his triumphant career. Originally the character was based on Miss Crompton's mischievous younger brother; then, later, a nephew served as a model. Eventually, his creator has confessed, William became a forceful person in his own right and didn't need any models. The series (totalling thirty-six titles up to the end of 1966) has been translated into many languages and sells particularly well in Scandinavia, Iceland, Italy and Germany (where the William books are used in schools, complete with footnotes). The William books have so far sold more than eight million copies, with the first title, *Just William*, being reprinted no less than forty-three times. The full list of titles, following on from 1924, is: *Still William* (1925), *William the Conqueror* (1926), *William the Outlaw* (1927), *William in Trouble* (1927), *William the Good* (1928), *William* (1929), *William the Bad* (1930), *William's Happy Days* (1930), *William's Crowded Hours* (1931), *William the Pirate* (1932), *William the Rebel* (1933), *William the Gangster* (1934), *William the Detective* (1935), *Sweet William* (1936), *William the Showman* (1937), *William the Dictator* (1938), *William and A.R.P.* (1939) (in post-war years this title was changed to *William's Bad Resolution*), *William and the Evacuees* (1940) (this was similarly changed to *William the Film Star*), *William Does His Bit* (1941), *William Carries On* (1942), *William and the Brains Trust* (1945), *Just William's Luck* (1948), *William the Bold* (1950), *William and the Tramp* (1952), *William and the Moon Rocket* (1954), *William and the Space Animal* (1956), *William's Television Show* (1958), *William the Explorer* (1960), *William's Treasure Trove* (1962), *William and the Witch* (1964), *William and the Pop Singers* (1965) and *William and the Masked Ranger* (1966). William's adventures have also been produced for the cinema, television and radio, and have been running in picture-strip form for many years in a leading women's magazine. In 1939 the script of the first William feature film, *Just William*, was published, together with the six short stories which made up the action of the production. All the William books are collections of short stories, with the exception of *Just William's Luck*, which was a single long story based on the script for a 1948 feature film. In 1949 Richmal Crompton created a new character in *Jimmy* – a rather younger character than William (only seven years old to William's eleven). A sequel, *Jimmy Again*, followed a year later, but this particular hero lacked William's appeal and failed to 'catch on' with the youthful reading public. Miss Crompton has also written nearly thirty adult novels, mainly of a light nature and often telling the story of a family. Typical titles include *Quartet, Frost at Morning, Linden Rise, The Ridleys* and *Matty and the Dearingroydes*. Unmarried, Richmal Crompton lives in Orpington, Kent.

Cross, John Keir

Born in Carluke, Scotland, on 19th August 1914, and educated at Perth Academy. Began his working life as an insurance clerk but, not finding the work to his taste, gave up the job and took to the road as a tramp and travelling busker-ventriloquist. Went to live in Chelsea, London, in 1936 and, as a result of writing the words and music for a musical comedy, joined the staff of the BBC in 1937. He worked as a writer-producer in the Drama, Variety, Features and Children's Hour Departments of the BBC, writing and producing numerous radio plays and features and also writing the occasional song or piece of music. He left the BBC in 1946 to turn freelance but continued to work for radio regularly. He proved particularly skilful at adapting stories and books for broadcasting; examples of his fine work in this field include versions of Masefield's *The Midnight Folk* and *The Box of Delights*, Dickens' *Little Dorrit* and Hardy's *The Trumpet-Major*. Published his first children's book, *'Studio J' Investigates*, in 1944, following it with *Detectives in Greasepaint* and *Mr Bosanko* (1944, 1945), all dealing with the adventures of a group of children who called themselves 'The J's'. Also in this period came *The White Magic*, an account of an expedition to the Arctic. In 1945 came a near-classic in the juvenile science-fiction field, *The Angry Planet*, which told of a journey made by two adults and three children to the planet Mars. *The Owl and the Pussycat* (1946) was a remarkable fantasy, written with great imaginative power, and *The Man in Moonlight* (1947) was an adventure set in the days of the Jacobite Rising and its aftermath. *Blackadder* (1950) was based by Cross on his own very popular radio play about the adventures of two boys in the days of Nelson. *The Flying Fortunes* (1952) dealt with the adventures of a family of trapeze artists. In 1954 came a sequel to *The Angry Planet* titled *S.O.S. from Mars*. *The Sixpenny Year* (1957) was a country farming adventure. Cross also wrote several adult novels, including two rousing historical romances, *Glory* (1950) and *Juniper Green* (1952), and also *The Other Passenger* (1944), a book of strange stories. He has sometimes used the name 'STEPHEN MACFARLANE' as a partial pseudonym, some of his books (e.g. *The Angry Planet, S.O.S. From Mars, Blackadder*) being 'based on notes and manuscripts by Stephen MacFarlane'; *'Studio J' Investigates* appeared under the name of 'MacFarlane' with no mention at all of John Keir Cross. From 1962 Cross was co-writer of the BBC's popular daily radio serial 'The Archers', set in a country village. He knew a good deal about the background for this programme, which deals largely with English farmers and their families, since he maintained a farm at Diptford, near Totnes, in Devon for some years before his sudden death on 22nd January 1967.

Crouch, Marcus

Born 1913 at Tottenham, London, and educated at Tottenham Grammar School and the University of London. He is a Fellow of the Library Association and since 1948 has been Deputy County Librarian of Kent. In 1957 he edited for the Library Association a history of the Carnegie Medal and the children's books which had won it, under the title *Chosen for Children* (a revised edition appeared in 1967). In 1960 came a biographical and bibliographical study, *Beatrix Potter*, which was followed, in 1962, by a survey of children's books in Britain 1900–1960, *Treasure Seekers and Borrowers*. This was a comprehensive and important study and an invaluable reference work for students of the subject; it was also highly enjoyable reading. In a different field, *Kent* (1966) was a delightful and informative book about that county. Marcus Crouch lives in Maidstone, Kent.

Cummins, Maria Susanna

Born on 9th April 1827, in Salem, Massachusetts, USA, the daughter of a judge, and educated at Lenox. Her first book, published anonymously, was the best-selling *The Lamplighter* (1854). It told, with pathos, sentiment and religious overtones, the story of its virtuous heroine, Gerty, and sold in hundreds of thousands for over sixty years on both sides of the Atlantic. It is still in print today. Her other novels, similar in style, included *Mabel Vaughan* (1857), *El Fureidis* (1860) and *Haunted Hearts* (1864). She died on 1st October 1866.

Dasent, Sir George Webbe

Born 1817 in the island of St Vincent, of which his father was Attorney-General, and educated at Westminster School, King's College, London, and Oxford University. He entered the diplomatic service and accepted a post at the British Embassy in Stockholm. It was here that he developed an interest in Scandinavian mythology and also met Jacob Grimm, who encouraged him to make a thorough study of the language of Scandinavia and especially Icelandic. He did this and his first publication was *The Prose or Younger Edda*, a translation, in 1842, followed by his *Grammar Of the Icelandic or Old Norse Tongue* the same year and eventually by his *Icelandic-English Dictionary*. In 1845, on returning to England, he was appointed assistant editor of *The Times*. He was subsequently called to the Bar, appointed Professor of English Literature and Modern History at King's College, London, and knighted (in 1876). In 1859 he translated a collection of Asbjörnsen's and Moe's Norwegian folk tales and fairy stories, under the title *Popular Tales from the Norse*. This was followed, three years later, by Dasent's *Selections* from the latter work, intended for younger readers. In 1874 came his further translated selection from Asbjörnsen and Moe, *Tales from the Fjeld*. Among Dasent's original *Popular Tales from the Norse* was one called *East of the Sun and West of the Moon* which has been used as the title for many subsequent translated collections of Norwegian tales. Dasent's translations of the tales of Asbjörnsen and Moe became so universally popular that his name is, to this day, closely linked with those two masterly scholars. His translations were the main source for all subsequent English editions. Dasent also translated some of the Icelandic sagas, notably *The Story of Bunnt Njal* in 1861, and wrote four novels. He died in 1896.

d'Aulnoy, Countess

Born in 1649 in France, her maiden name being Marie Catherine de Berneville and her father connected with some of the first families in Normandy. She married Francis de la Mothe, Comte d'Aulnoy, and had four daughters by him. She was a woman of outstanding beauty and gifted with many social accomplishments, being especially known for her sparkling conversation and ready wit. She was perhaps the first writer to use the title 'Fairy Tales', as her first collection of magical short stories was entitled *Contes des Fées* (Tales of Fairies), being published in three volumes in 1698, in France. They made their first appearance in English as one of the volumes of her *Diverting Works*, in 1707. They were reprinted many times in subsequent years, some of the most popular appearing in numerous collections; various of the tales appeared in some of Andrew Lang's colour *Fairy Books*, for example. Her stories were usually concerned with handsome princes and beautiful princesses, often being turned into animals or birds, in search of each other or of great wealth and/or happiness, and always full of complicated and engrossing magic. Among her best-known tales are: *The White Cat, The Blue Bird, The Yellow Dwarf, The Fairy With Golden Hair, The Beneficent Frog* and *The Hind in the Wood*. Countess d'Aulnoy wrote more than twenty of these fairy tales and also published several other books, including *Ingenious and Diverting Letters of a Lady's Travels into Spain* (which had reached its eighth edition by 1717 and was reprinted yet again nearly 100 years later) and *Hipolite*. She died in Paris in January 1705. (NOTE: Other English versions, all used at one time or another, of 'd'Aulnoy' are d'Alnois, d'Anois and d'Aulnois.)

Dawson, A. J.

Born in England in 1872. Went to sea as a boy-apprentice but, after two voyages, decided against a seaman's career and left his ship in Australia. He remained there, first working as a farmer, later joining the staff of a Melbourne newspaper. He began writing novels during this period, did a lot of travelling and finally returned to England. He took up dog-breeding, especially bloodhounds and wolfhounds. In 1908 he published his most famous book, *Finn the Wolfhound*, the story of a dog, set in England and Australia and, in many people's view, perhaps the best dog story ever written. It was followed in 1917 by a sequel, *Jan, Son of Finn*. Dawson served in the First World War, took part in several overseas government missions during the post-war period, and was awarded the M.B.E. He wrote over thirty books in all, mainly novels. He died in 1951.

Day, Thomas

Born London, 22nd June 1748, and educated at the Charter-house and at Corpus Christi College, Oxford. He was admitted to the Middle Temple in 1765 but not called to the Bar until 1779; he never practised law, since he had inherited a good income from his father while still a child. He travelled in Europe during his early twenties and also became a fervent disciple of Rousseau, particularly believing that a child should have a joyous upbringing, living energetically and usefully out of doors and learning from his own experiences – and reading nothing but the Bible and Defoe's *Robinson Crusoe*. Day preached the advantages of this way of life for a child to all and sundry and also practised what he preached. He even attempted to bring up two young orphan girls on Rousseau's lines, with a view to providing himself with one of them as a (theoretically) perfect wife. The experiment was not a success, however, and Day eventually married an heiress. Day and his wife settled at Anningsley, near Chertsey, in Surrey, where he continued with his schemes of social reform by cultivating an experimental farm, giving work to local inhabitants and gaining great popularity. He also spoke on reform and other topics from time to time and in various places. In 1773 he wrote, in conjunction with a barrister friend, J. L. Bicknell, a long poem called *The Dying Negro*, which was published in a magazine. Its object was to arouse public sympathy for the negro slaves in the West Indies. This was followed by several more poems and tracts. Then, in 1783, came the first part of the work on which his fame today rests – *The History of Sandford and Merton*. Though originally written for inclusion in R. L. Edgeworth's *Practical Education* in 1880, this first part eventually appeared as a separate publication published by Stockdale's. Its form was actually that of a long-short story. It was such a big success that a second part appeared in 1786, and a third part in 1789. The story was the greatest and most famous of what have become known as the 'didactic' children's books of the eighteenth and early nineteenth centuries. Its main object was to teach, and it was really a long series of episodes and tales illustrating desirable moral attributes for the young reader, a whole string of moral object lessons stressing what was good and what was bad in life. The puppets used in the tales were Tommy Merton, the spoilt, ignorant son of a rich gentleman, and Harry Sandford, the sturdy, hard-working sensible son of an honest farmer. As the result of an incident in which Harry saves Tommy from a poisonous snake, Tommy is placed under the control and guidance of the local clergyman, Mr Barlow, who is also responsible for teaching Harry. Barlow trains both boys and in practically every story Harry is held up as the perfect example of goodness, while poor Tommy is shown up in all his ignorance and stupidity. Eventually, of course, through Barlow's patient tuition, Tommy becomes as fine a lad as Harry. . . . *Sandford and Merton* was the first classic cautionary tale for children, and it succeeded in what it set out to do: for the youthful readers of the period it provided instruction and entertainment. It became a best-selling children's book over the next 100 years and was translated into several languages. A corrected and revised edition, edited by Cecil Hartley, appeared in 1874 with profuse illustrations and this also went into many editions. Day also wrote *The History of Little Jack* for Stockdale's *Children's Miscellany* in 1787; the following year it appeared as a small separate publication. 'Little Jack' is a young wild boy, suckled by a goat in the wilds and raised by a pious old man. When the old man dies Jack makes his way to civilisation, joins the marines and, after many adventures in India and elsewhere, goes to England and makes his fortune in business. Not surprisingly, this tale too is well seasoned with moral lessons. Thomas Day unfortunately never lived to see the remarkable success of his complete *Sandford and Merton* since he was thrown and kicked to death by a horse he had himself raised from a foal on 28th September 1789. He was buried in the family vault at Wargrave, Berkshire.

Defoe, Daniel

Born around 1660 in Cripplegate, London, the son of James Foe, a butcher (Daniel changed his name about 1703), and educated at a Dissenting College at Newington. He was originally intended for a church career, but he decided against this after a time and went into business. He did well, married, and became a friend and confidant of King William III. By this time he had behind him some experience as a merchant-adventurer to Spain and Portugal, and now he decided to take up writing. He wrote many pamphlets on various political, religious and social topics and was soon employed by the British Government as a writer. One of his pamphlets led him into troubles and he was fined, imprisoned and put in the pillory. After more troubles and misunderstandings Defoe decided to retire to the country and begin writing a novel. His first novel was *The Life and Strange Surprising Adventures of Robinson Crusoe of York, Mariner* in 1719, followed in the same year by *Further Adventures of Robinson Crusoe*. He based his story loosely on an actual occurrence of around 1709, when a man named Alexander Selkirk had lived alone on the island of Juan Fernandez, in the Pacific, for five years and was eventually rescued. Though *Robinson Crusoe* was not written for children originally, they soon took it to their hearts via crude chap-book versions, and in time it became regarded as a 'children's classic'. It also inspired a large number of similar stories of castaways on romantic and isolated desert islands – 'robinsonnades' as the French called them. Defoe followed *Robinson Crusoe* with such swashbuckling novels as *Captain Singleton* (1720), *Moll Flanders* (1722), *Colonel Jack* (1722) and *Memoirs of a Cavalier* (1724).

He also wrote *A Journal of the Plague Year* (1722), various other books, and edited a paper, *The Review*, from 1704–13. Including his many pamphlets, he wrote around 250 works. He died on 26th April 1731.

de la Mare, Walter John

Born on 25th April 1873, at Charlton, Kent (now London), and educated at St Paul's Cathedral Choir School. While at school he founded and edited a magazine called *The Choristers' Journal*. On leaving school at the age of fourteen he became a clerk in the offices of the Anglo-American Oil Company, remaining there for eighteen years. In his spare time he wrote many poems and short stories, having some published in such magazines as *Pall Mall Gazette*, *Cornhill* and *The Sketch*. He was so modest about his work that this early material appeared under the pseudonym 'WALTER RAMAL' (a re-arrangement of the letters of his name). His first book, *Songs of Childhood*, appeared in 1902 and comprised a collection of poems. His first adult novel, *Henry Brocken*, was published in 1904 and *Poems* in 1906. In 1908 he left the oil company and became a full-time writer, his second novel, *The Return*, appearing in 1910. That same year his children's book *The Three Mulla-Mulgars* was published (the title was changed to *The Three Royal Monkeys* in 1935); this was a memorable poetical fantasy about the adventures of three royal monkeys during a long journey. More poems followed in *A Child's Day* (1912) and in *Peacock Pie* (1913), a collection of rhymes and verses which really established him as a front-rank writer for and about children. In 1921 came a beautiful fairy play for children titled *Crossings*, with music by Armstrong Gibbs. Over the next thirty-five years de la Mare wrote many more enchanting stories and poems for children (in addition to all his adult work) and some of his titles include: *Down-Adown-Derry* (1922), *Broomsticks and Other Tales* (1925), *Stories from the Bible* (1929), *Poems for Children* (1930), *The Lord Fish and Other Tales* (1933), *This Year, Next Year* (1937), *Animal Stories* (1939), *Bells and Grass* (1941), *The Magic Jacket and Other Stories* (1944), *The Dutch Cheese and Other Stories* (1946), *Collected Rhymes and Verses* (1944) and *Collected Stories for Children* (1947). In general, de la Mare wrote most of his poems and rhymes in the period

1902–27, and most of his stories between 1925–46. In 1923 he published a superlative anthology of general poetry by various writers, supplying copious and fascinating notes on each item; this was *Come Hither* and is one of the classic anthologies of our time. Another collection from other poets, which he edited, was *Tom Tiddler's Ground* (1931). In 1948 Walter de la Mare was made a Companion of Honour and in 1953 awarded the Order of Merit. He held honorary degrees from several universities too. He died on 22nd June 1956.

Delderfield, Ronald Frederick

Born in Greenwich, London, 12th February 1912, and educated at West Buckland School. On leaving school became junior reporter on local newspaper in a small country town, later becoming sub-editor and editor. Served in the RAF, 1940–45, acting as a public relations officer in Europe. His stage play, W*orm's Eye View*, a comedy about life in the RAF, set up a new record as the longest-running play in London during the late 1940s. He subequently wrote many more successful full-length and one-act plays, for stage, TV and radio; also several novels, including *The Dreaming Suburb*, *The Avenue Goes to War*, *A Horseman Riding* and *The Green Gauntlet*. In 1956 he published a superlative 'pre-sequel' to Stevenson's *Treasure Island* called *The Adventures of Ben Gunn* in which he told (in Gunn's own words) of the events leading up to Gunn's marooning on the island, including his service with Flint, Silver, Pew and the rest on 'The Walrus' pirate ship. In this curiously underrated book Delderfield caught the true spirit of Stevenson's original story and made his new supplementary work a minor classic of modern-day children's literature. Still writing busily, Delderfield today lives in Devon.

de Selincourt, Aubrey

Born 1894 in London and educated at Rugby and University College, Oxford. On obtaining his M.A. degree he became a schoolmaster, later being appointed vice-master of Clayesmore School, Hampshire (later Dorset) in 1929, and headmaster two years later. He resigned this post in 1935 and became headmaster of another school. After contributing to various newspapers and magazines he published a book of essays, *Streams of Ocean*. In 1940 he published his first children's book, *Family Afloat*, about the adventures of a family of children on a sailing holiday and replete with plenty of technical details about the hobby (de Selincourt's own chief relaxation was sailing so he knew what he was writing about). Other similar books followed, about the same family and all with a sailing background: *Three Green Bottles* (1941), *One Good Turn* (1943), *One More Summer* (1944) and *Calicut Lends a Hand* (1946). Another children's story was *Micky* (1947) and in 1948 came *The Young Schoolmaster*, a 'career novel' giving a realistic picture of a schoolmaster's life. In 1950 he 'retold' the story of *Odysseus the Wanderer* and later translated *Herodotus* (for Penguin Books). His later titles include: *Six Great Englishmen*, *Six Great Poets*, *Six Great Thinkers* and *Nansen*.

Dickens, Charles

Born on 7th February 1812, at Landport, near Portsmouth, where his father was a clerk in the Navy Pay Office. His miserable childhood is too well known to repeat here and his great career as a novelist even better known. His fame is based, of course, on his series of colourful novels. He wrote very little for children (though they can read with enjoyment many passages from his adult books, especially the early chapters of *David Copperfield, Great Expectations, Oliver Twist, Nicholas Nickleby* and the perennial favourite *A Christmas Carol*). His chief work written expressly for young readers was *Holiday Romance*, which appeared in the American magazine *Our Young Folks*, January–May 1868, and also in *All the Year Round*, January–March the same year. It was published in book form in 1874 (included with *Edwin Drood* and other stories). *Holiday Romance* comprises four parts, each supposed to be told by a different child, aged from six to nine. The four stories are: *The Trial of William Tinkling* (which really sets the scene for the subsequent tales), *The Magic Fishbone, Captain Boldheart* and *Miss Orange and Mrs Alicumpaine*. The middle two stories in particular have been reprinted, either separately or in collections, many times. *Holiday Romance* was perhaps the earliest example of the 'make-believe' type of story which was to become so popular in the years following its publication. Its style and atmosphere have been compared on more than one occasion to those of E. Nesbit or Kenneth Grahame. Dickens also wrote *A Child's History of England* (1852–54), which had originally appeared in *Household Words*, and a *Life of our Lord*, which he wrote for his own children with no thought of it ever appearing in print but which was published in 1935. Charles Dickens died on 9th June 1870.

Dickinson, William Croft

Born Leicester, 1897, and educated at Mill Hill and the Universities of St Andrews and London. Was Librarian at the London School of Economics, 1933–44, and, from 1944, Fraser Professor of Scottish History at Edinburgh University. Editor of the *Scottish History Review* from 1946. Published many books on Scottish history, including several volumes for the Scottish History Society. In 1944 wrote a fine children's book called *Borrobil*, which was a magical fantasy in which two children are transported back to a legendary past by a good magician named Borrobil and encounter the Black King of Winter, the White King of Summer, Morac, Princess Finella and a poison-breathing dragon. Two sequels followed, featuring the same children on similar fantastic visits to the past: *The Eildon Tree* (1947) and *The Flag from the Isles* (1951). Professor Dickinson combined his deep knowledge of history and legend with a fine dramatic style of storytelling in these tales. He was, incidentally, M.A., D.Lit. and LL.D. Died in 1964.

Dimmock, Frederick Hayden

Born in 1895. Probably the most prolific writer on boy scouting ever (not excepting the great 'B-P' either). Joined the staff of the official magazine of the Scout movement, *The Scout*, as an office-boy in 1913. It was to become his life's work. He saw active service in the First World War and was seriously wounded, but recovered and was appointed editor of *The Scout* in 1918. Apart from a brief period in 1919 when he moved over to *Pearsons' Weekly* as assistant editor, Dimmock held the post of *Scout* editor until 1954, when he retired – only to die the following year (26th April 1955) at his home in Welwyn Garden City, Hertfordshire. As well as editing *The Scout*, Dimmock also wrote numerous stories and serials for the paper, one of the most popular being *Lone Scouts of Crusoe Island*. He also wrote many books for boys, usually with a scouting background, and was fond of introducing a dog as a leading character too. He was the originator of the Scouts' famous 'Soap-Box Derbies' and also of the 'Bob-a-Job Weeks'.

Disney, Walt

Born Chicago, USA, 5th December 1901, spending part of his early childhood on his parents' farm in Marceline, Missouri. Later his family moved to Kansas City and young Walter received most of his education there, also doing a daily newspaper-round with his brother Roy. He completed his education in Chicago, when his family returned there, also working part-time in a jelly factory. He studied at the Chicago Academy of Fine Arts, concentrating on drawing and especially cartooning. After service as a Red Cross Ambulance driver during the latter part of the First World War, he submitted hundreds of cartoons to leading U.S. magazines – and collected an equal number of rejection slips. After working for an advertising company in Kansas City, he joined the Kansas City Film Advertising Company and began making his first animated cartoon films. He sold animated advertisements to local cinemas, then formed his own corporation to make cartoon films. After various ups-and-downs he made a series of films which mixed animation with live action called *Alice in Cartoonland*. He made the series in Hollywood in 1923–26, going on to make cartoons about Oswald the Rabbit (1926–28) and finally, in 1928, he created the world-famous Mickey Mouse. The first Mickey Mouse cartoon films were silent, but in late 1928 came the first one with sound, *Steamboat Willie* – the first of hundreds. In 1929 came the first in the successful series of *Silly Symphonies* and in 1932 he made his first colour cartoon, *Flowers and Trees* (though he did not go over entirely to colour until 1934). Donald Duck made his first appearance in 1934 in *The Wise Little Hen* but only in a tiny part; he really made his first

77

impact in *Orphans' Benefit* that same year and went on to 'star' in his own cartoons in the same way as Pluto and Goofy, who were also introduced around this period. In 1936 Disney began production of the world's first full-length feature cartoon film, *Snow-White and the Seven Dwarfs*; it had its première in Hollywood in December 1937 and over the next few years winged its way all over the world, achieving sensational success everywhere it was shown. Disney's subsequent feature cartoons included: *Pinocchio* (1940), *Fantasia* (1940), *Dumbo* (1941), *Bambi* (1942), *Make Mine Music* (1946), *The Adventures of Ichabod and Mr Toad* (1949), *Cinderella* (1950), *Alice in Wonderland* (1951), *Peter Pan* (1953), *Lady and the Tramp* (1955), *The Sleeping Beauty* (1958), *The Hundred-and-One Dalmatians* (1961) and *The Sword in the Stone* (1963). He also produced many live action feature films, primarily aimed at young audiences and including: *Treasure Island* (1950), *Robin Hood* (1952), *The Sword and the Rose* (1953), *Rob Roy* (1954), *20,000 Leagues Under the Sea* (1954), *Davy Crockett* (1955), *Johnny Tremaine* (1957), *Zorro* (1958), *Kidnapped* (1960), *Swiss Family Robinson* (1961), *Babes in Toyland* (1962) and *In Search of the Castaways* (1963). The widely-praised *Mary Poppins* (1964) combined cartoon and live action sequences. In 1949 came the first of Disney's excellent real-life animal and bird colour full-length documentaries, *Seal Island*; it was followed by several more, including *Beaver Valley* (1950), *Water Birds* (1952), *The Living Desert* (1953) and *The Vanishing Prairie* (1954). Although essentially a film-maker, Walt Disney finds a place here because, as a result of his films, a whole new book industry came into being, beginning chiefly in the 1930s, consisting of books based on his productions and his characters. Apart from picture books based on his cartoons and special illustrated editions of his versions of classic stories there are regular publications such as *Mickey Mouse Annual*, *Donald Duck Annual* and so on, as well as drawing and painting books, cut-out books, etc. But though the Disney cartoons may be pleasing enough on the moving cinema screen, when frozen in the pages of a book their characters lose most of their charm and add little to the art of children's book illustration. Printed versions apart, however, the art of Walt Disney has probably brought more delight and genuine pleasure into the lives of children in modern times than that of anyone involved in supplying their entertainment needs. Disney died on 15th December 1966.

Dodge, Mary Mapes

Born New York, 26th January 1831. Her father, a scientist, undertook to build up a run-down old farm in New Jersey, carrying out valuable experiments that were to benefit farmers throughout the USA and elsewhere. Mary was the youngest of his three daughters and helped her father with his work from her teens, keeping the books, studying crop rotation, soils, drainage and so on. When she was sixteen she helped her father run a magazine called *The Working Farmer* and also wrote articles for it. In 1851, when she was still only twenty, she married a lawyer named William Dodge. She had two sons and then, after seven years of married life, her husband died and Mary returned to live with her sons and her parents at the farm. She began writing down some of the stories she told her small sons and, in 1864, her first book, *Irvington Stories*, appeared. Most of the eight stories in the book were taken from American colonial history. Mary was asked by her publisher to write a full-length story, using the Civil War as a background. But she had a different idea in mind. She had always been interested in Holland, especially since she had read and re-read Motley's *Rise of the Dutch Republic*, so she began work on a book about Dutch children and their adventures culminating in a breathlessly exciting race for a pair of prized silver skates; it was *Hans Brinker; or The Silver Skates* and it was published in the USA in 1865 (the same year, incidentally, that *Alice in Wonderland* appeared in Britain). It was an immediate and sensational success, going through more than 100 editions in thirty years and appearing in six different languages. Within four years it had won the coveted Montyon Prize of the French Academy. It has never been out of print over the last hundred years – proof of its enduring popularity with young readers. After her father's death in 1866, Mary Mapes Dodge continued to write stories, articles and poems. Then, in 1870, she became editor of the home-making department of the magazine *Hearth and Home* (on which Harriet Beecher Stowe also worked). Three years later, in 1873, she was appointed founder-editor of the new American children's magazine *St Nicholas*, which was to run for nearly seventy years as probably the best general children's magazine in the world. Under Mary's direction and editorship *St Nicholas* exerted a tremendous influence on children's literature and all to the good. She gathered together a brilliant and distinguished list of contributors, also writing the occasional story herself. Her other books for children include: *A Few Friends and How They Amused Themselves* (1869), *Rhymes and Jingles* (1874), *Along the Way* (1879), *Theophilus and Others* (1876), *Donald and Dorothy* (1883), *The Land of Pluck* (1894) and *The Golden Gate* (1903). Mary Mapes Dodge remained editor of *St Nicholas* for thirty-two years, until her death in 1905, though for the last seventeen years of her life she withdrew more and more from the active management of the magazine and lived mainly in the Catskill Mountains. She died on 31st August 1905. Few people did more to raise the level of children's writing.

Dodgson, Charles Lutwidge

See: Carroll, Lewis

Doyle, Sir Arthur Conan

Born on 22nd May 1859, in Edinburgh, Scotland, and educated at Stonyhurst Academy and Edinburgh University, where he studied medicine and (in 1881) qualified as a doctor. His first regular practice was at Southsea but, lacking both patients and funds, he began to write short stories. Many stories appeared in such magazines as *The Cornhill*, *Blackwood's*, *London Society* and even *Boy's Own Paper*. He also wrote his first novel, *The Firm of Girdlestone*, but it failed to find a publisher. His only boys' serial, *Uncle Jeremy's Household*, ran in the *Boy's Own Paper* in 1887. In *Beeton's Christmas Annual* for 1887 appeared his novel *A Study in Scarlet*, which introduced a character who was soon to become fiction's most famous detective: Sherlock Holmes. A further Holmes novel, *The Sign of Four*, appeared in 1890. But it was the long series of Sherlock Holmes (not forgetting his friend and assistant, Dr Watson) short stories which ran in the *Strand Magazine* from 1891 which really established Doyle's success. The fifty-odd Holmes stories were published in five volumes over the years and were: *The Adventures of Sherlock Holmes* (1892), *The Memoirs of Sherlock Holmes* (1894), *The Return of Sherlock Holmes* (1905), *His Last Bow* (1917) and *The Case-Book of Sherlock Holmes* (1927). Full-length Holmes novels were *The Hound of the Baskervilles* (1902) and *The Valley of Fear* (1915). Sherlock Holmes was inspired primarily by Dr Joseph Bell, under whom Doyle had studied medicine; Bell had had the habit of deducing all kinds of things about a person merely by observing him, his clothes, habits, and so on. Holmes had the same gift – added to *penchants* for pipe-smoking, violin-playing, occasional drug-taking and deerstalker hats. Dr Watson, who chronicled the cases, was good-hearted, sentimental and loyal, though constantly amazed at Holmes' deductive powers. Doyle regarded his detective stories as relatively minor work compared with his 'serious' historical novels such as *Micah Clarke* (1889), *The White Company* (1891) and *Sir Nigel* (1906). He once 'killed off' Holmes in a short story – but was persuaded by public opinion to bring him to life again in a subsequent series. Doyle's *The Lost World* (1912) was also a huge popular success and told graphically of a small band of explorers – headed by the eccentric, bad-tempered Professor Challenger – who became trapped in a land still inhabited by prehistoric monsters. Challenger appeared again in *The Poison Belt* (1913), an exciting 'science-fiction' novel, and *The Land of Mist* (1926). Doyle's most popular short stories, apart from those featuring Sherlock Holmes, are those contained in *The Exploits of Brigadier Gerard* (1896) and *The Adventures of Gerard* (1903). They are stylishly told exploits of a Napoleonic soldier-adventurer and have many humorous touches. Doyle's other titles include: *Rodney Stone* (1896), *Uncle Bernac* (1897), *The Tragedy of the Korosko* (1898) and *The Maracot Deep*, plus several volumes of short stories. He served in the South African War as a doctor and subsequently wrote *The Great Boer War* (1900). He was knighted in 1902. In his later years he became deeply interested in spiritualism. He died on 7th July 1930.

du Bois, William Pène

Born on 9th May 1916, in Nutley, New Jersey, USA, and

educated at Barstow's School, New York, Lycée Hoche, Versailles, Lycée de Nice, and Morristown School, New Jersey. Lived in France with his family between the ages of eight and fourteen. Grew to love the circus during this period and once said he averaged thirty visits every year. His father was an artist, and on leaving school William decided to follow in his footsteps, having a marked talent for drawing. He wrote and illustrated his first book, *Elizabeth, the Cow Ghost*, in 1936, following it with several others, including *Giant Otto* (1936), *Otto at Sea* (1936), *Three Policemen* (1938), *The Great Geppy* (1940) and *The Flying Locomotive* (1941). In 1941 he entered the U.S. Army and was on active service overseas for four and a half years. *The Twenty-One Balloons* (1947 in USA, 1949 in Britain) is his best-known book and won the Newbery Medal in America as the best children's book of its year. Written and illustrated by du Bois in truly striking style, the story tells of a Professor who, after forty years of teaching, sets off on a balloon trip and eventually becomes involved in the great explosion of Krakatoa, finally being discovered in mid-Atlantic amidst the wreckage of twenty-one balloons. Du Bois' subsequent books include *Peter Graves* (1950), *Bear Party* (1951), *Lion* (1956), *Otto in Texas* (1959) and *Otto in Africa* (1961). He has also illustrated books for other authors, including Rumer Godden's *The Mousewife* (1951).

Dumas, Alexandre (the elder)

Usually called 'the elder' to distinguish him from his son of the same name who was also a popular writer. Born in Villers-Cotterets, near Paris, on 24th July 1802, the son of a general in Napoleon's army. The general died when Alexandre was only four and it was a great struggle for his wife to bring the young boy up as she had been left with practically no money. Alexandre received little formal education and began his working life as a lawyer's messenger in Paris, later becoming the lawyer's clerk. He also worked as a secretary on the staff of the Duke of Orleans for a time. He had always been interested in the theatre and soon he tried his hand at writing plays himself. In 1828 the Théâtre Français accepted one of his plays, *Henri III*. The production was an immediate success and from then on Alexandre turned out many action-packed historical melodramas, which made him one of the most popular writers in Paris. Around ten years later he switched from writing successful plays to writing even more successful novels. He wrote so many (in one year alone he was said to have published some forty volumes) that he employed a staff of writers, secretaries and transcribers to assist him, though he was the dominating spirit and plot-developer. The chief of his helpers was Auguste Maquet, a lecturer and writer specialising in history. He supplied the historical research for many stories, with Alexandre Dumas expanding them into full-length, action-filled adventures. In 1844 came one of his two most famous books, *The Three Musketeers*, a romantic adventure recounting the exploits of a young man named d'Artagnan who goes to Paris in 1625 to join the musketeers of King Louis XIII and who teams up with three of the most courageous of them – Athos, Porthos and Aramis. It was followed by several sequels, including *Twenty Years After* (1845), *The Vicomte de Bragelonne* (1848–50) and *The Man in the Iron Mask* (1850). In 1844–45 came his other classic novel, *The Count of Monte Cristo*, dealing with a man's implacable and merciless revenge for false imprisonment. Other well-known novels are *The Corsican Brothers* (1845) and *The Black Tulip* (1850). Alexandre Dumas, the elder, also wrote several children's stories, which have been published in various collections; his most famous fairy tale is probably *The Adventures of a Nutcracker*, based on Hoffmann's original tale (Dumas's version was published in 1845). Although he made much money from his books and plays, Alexandre Dumas didn't keep it for long. He was a great spender and on one occasion built himself a vast house called 'Monte Cristo', just outside Paris. He invited 600 friends to dinner on his first night there. But the creditors were never far away, and, despite his spectacular success as a popular and fashionable writer, he died near to poverty, at Puys, on 5th December 1870.

Eager, Edward

Born in Toledo, Ohio, USA, and attended Harvard University. He worked primarily as a playwright and lyricist. In the world of the New York theatre he wrote the lyrics for *Dream with Music* and *Sing Out Sweet Land*, adapted Pirandello's play *The Pleasure of Respectability* under the title *Call It Virtue* (1963) and worked on adaptations of Goldoni's *The Liar* and Ugo Betti's *The Gambler* with actor-singer-writer Alfred Drake. He also wrote the lyrics for the American TV spectacular *Marco Polo* (1956) and adapted Mozart's *The Marriage of Figaro*, also for television. In addition to his theatre and TV writing Eager also wrote several excellent children's books, beginning in 1951 with *Red Head* and following it with *Mouse Manor* the following year. In 1954 came the first of his fine series of magical and semi-magical stories, *Half Magic*; the others were *Knight's Castle* (1956), *Magic By the Lake* (1957), *The Time Garden* (1958), *Magic or Not?* (1959), *The Well-Wishers* (1961) and *Seven-Day Magic* (1963). It was no coincidence that Eager's books bore a strong family resemblance to those of E. Nesbit, since he considered her the best children's writer of all time and freely acknowledged his debt to her. He first discovered her books as an adult, when he read them to his small son, Fritz. In his own childhood his favourites were the Oz books. Eager's own stories were usually about a family of ordinary children who became caught up in fantastic happenings – or what were almost fantastic. . . . His children were realistic and his situations entertaining, many of them being based on his own experiences as a child, especially during summers spent at Indiana during school holidays. In his later years he lived in Connecticut by a small river. He loved the country life and his hobbies were bird-watching and gardening. In 1964 he worked again with Alfred Drake on the English lyrics to *Ruggantino*, the Italian musical show which was produced on Broadway. He died in the autumn of 1964.

Edgeworth, Maria

Born on 1st January 1767, at Black Bouston, Oxfordshire, daughter of Richard Lovell Edgeworth, a well-to-do Irish landowner and M.P. The latter was a colourful character, opinionated, had definite views on education, was a writer and four times married, and father to around twenty children, of whom Maria was the second. She was left motherless at six and from then on experienced a lengthy succession of step-mothers, half-brothers and half-sisters. Edgeworth was keenly interested in education, being especially influenced by the teachings of Rousseau. A close friend of his was Thomas Day (author of *Sandford and Merton*), also an educationalist, and together the two men did their best to bring Maria up in the best principles of their educational theories. At fifteen, Maria, and the rest of the family, went to live in the family estate their father had inherited at Edgeworthstown in Ireland. Maria herself was now helping in the education of her younger brothers and sisters, and one of her favourite pastimes was telling them stories. The stories would be criticised by the younger Edgeworths and often altered to conform with their preferences. The tales were, in the nature of Maria's stringent upbringing, moral ones and each had an express moral point to make at the end. She wrote several of them down, and after her father had approved them (making a few additions and changes himself) he sent them to a publisher under the title *The Parent's Friend*. In 1796 the publisher (Joseph Johnson) brought the book out under the title *The Parent's Assistant* (much to Maria's disappointment, as she hated the title). This first volume contained ten stories and an Introduction; that same year a second edition appeared, with additional stories, and in 1800 came a third edition in six volumes containing more than twenty stories. A new collection of tales, *Early Lessons*, was published in 1801, containing stories mainly about such child characters as Rosamund, Frank, Harry and Lucy. Each story, as before, pointed a moral and the young reader was persuaded to identify himself with the central character and sigh, at the conclusion: 'I'll be wiser and more sensible next time', or 'What a lesson this has taught me'. Though didactic and, to modern eyes, more than a little dull, Maria's moral tales for children were the first of their kind to have real plots, suspense, surprises and even excitement. They were a step in progress after Day's extremely moral and humourless *Sandford and Merton*, and a step in the right direction: towards *entertaining* young readers as well as instructing them. Some of Maria Edgeworth's best-remembered tales are *The Purple Jar* (featuring a very realistic little girl named Rosamund), *Lazy Lawrence*, *Simple Susan*, *The Birthday Present*, *Forgive and Forget* and *The*

False Key. In 1801 she published *Moral Tales* and in 1804 *Popular Tales*, both intended for rather older children and much more didactic in their tone. Two sequels to earlier stories were *Frank* (1822) and *Harry and Lucy* (1825). As well as her writings for children she produced a series of adult novels, starting with *Castle Rackrent* in 1800 and ending with *Helen* in 1834. Most of these were about the Irish people, whom she had come to know well as a result of living and working (as his agent) on her father's country estate in County Longford. During the Irish potato famine in 1847 she worked passionately to relieve the sufferings of the Irish workers and their families. She died suddenly on 22nd May 1849.

Edwards, Monica

Born in 1912, at Belper, Derbyshire, and educated at Wakefield High School and St Brandon's Clergy Daughters' School, Bristol. Her first book, *Wish for a Pony* (1947), was written to please her daughter, who was one of the two heroines in the story, the other being her daughter's school friend. The book has a Romney Marsh setting (which Miss Edwards knows well from her own childhood holiday visits) and tells of two girls who dream of owning a pony. Their dream comes true, of course, but this is no routine pony book, as the characters are deftly and sympathetically drawn and the Romney Marsh atmosphere comes over well. Subsequent stories in this Romney Marsh cyle include: *The Summer of the Great Secret* (1948), *The Midnight Horse* (1949), *The White Riders* (1950), *Cargo of Horses* (1951), *Hidden in a Dream* (1952), *No Entry* (1954), *Storm Ahead* (1953), *The Nightbird* (1955), *Stranger to the Marsh* (1957), *Operation Seabird* (1957) and *No Going Back* (1960). Miss Edwards' second cycle of stories, this time about Punchbowl Farm, is again based loosely on her own family (indeed her address today is Punchbowl Farm, Thursley, Surrey) and began in 1947 with *No Mistaking Corker*. This series tells how the Thornton family begin farming right from the beginning, with practically no experience. There are, naturally, plenty of horses and ponies and they all add to the healthy, outdoor charm and vigour of the stories. Others in this series include: *Black Hunting Whip* (1950), *Punchbowl Midnight* (1951), *The*

86

Spirit of Punchbowl Farm (1952), *The Wanderer* (1953), *Punchbowl Harvest* (1954), *Frenchman's Secret* (1956), *The Cownappers* (1958) and *The Wild One* (1967). Miss Edwards has also written career novels, including *Joan Goes Farming* (1954) and *Rennie Goes Riding* (1956). In 1954 she published her autobiography, *The Unsought Farm*, and in 1966 another non-fiction book about the farm, *The Badgers of Punchbowl Farm*. She has also written the script of a Children's Film Foundation production, *The Dawn Killer*, which was shown in serial form. She has contributed to various magazines and also broadcast in BBC Children's Hour. Among her more recent books are *Dolphin Summer*, *The Hoodwinkers* and *The Outsider*.

Eliot, Thomas Stearns

Born at St Louis, Missouri, USA, on 26th September 1888, of a distinguished Boston family. Educated at Smith Academy and Harvard, later going on to the Sorbonne in Paris and to Merton College, Oxford. He was a master at Highgate School, London, for a time and later worked in Lloyd's Bank. He wrote his first important poems in 1915, and in 1922 *The Waste Land* brought him awards and fame. He wrote many more books of poetry and several plays. In 1948 he was awarded the Nobel Prize for Literature and also the Order of Merit. His only book for children (and then not intended exclusively for them) was *Old Possum's Book of Practical Cats* (1939), in which eccentric and hilarious cats were described in amusing verses, inimitably illustrated by Nicolas Bentley. T. S. Eliot, one of the world's great modern poets, died in 1964.

Ellis, Edward Sylvester

Born in Geneva, Ohio, USA, on 11th April 1840. Worked for a time as a schoolteacher, then began writing American 'dime novels' (roughly the USA equivalent of British 'penny dreadfuls') and in 1860 published one called *Seth Jones, or The Captives of the Frontier*. This title sold nearly half a million copies in its first six months and continued to sell steadily for many years. It was described by literary experts as 'the perfect dime novel' and set the seal on Ellis's reputation as a popular boys' adventure story writer. He specialised in exciting tales about Red Indians, bear-hunters, trappers and cowboys, all set in the American West. Was the author of the very popular *Log Cabin, Deerfoot* and *Wyoming* series of books. Turned out close on 100 such stories over a period of some thirty years, typical titles including: *Captured by Indians, Lost in the Rockies, Deerfoot on the Prairies, Pony Express Rider, In Red Indian Trails, Redskin and Scout, Blazing Arrow, The Young Ranchers* and *Two Boys in Wyoming*. He also wrote similar tales under seven different pseudonyms. In later years Ellis wrote a six-volume, illustrated *History of the United States* (1896), which was sold on a gigantic subscription plan all over America. He died on 20th June 1916.

Evens, George Bramwell

Better known as 'Romany'. Born in 1884 in Hull, Yorkshire, his parents both being officers in the Salvation Army. Was of genuine gipsy ancestry. Educated in Liverpool and Epworth College, Rhyl. Studied divinity at Queen's College, Taunton. Was a schoolmaster for a short time in Lytham, Lancashire, before spending a year in church work in Colchester, Essex. Attended the Wesleyan Theological College in Handsworth, Birmingham, 1905–8, being ordained in Cardiff in 1908. Became minister at a church in Dalston, East London, later serving as minister of a Methodist Church in Carlisle, 1914–26. The remainder of his ministry was spent in Huddersfield and Halifax. All this time he was developing a deep love of nature, animal and bird life and country matters in general, often touring the countryside in an old Romany caravan he had bought and accompanied by his wife and dog. He also lectured on wild life in Methodist halls and, in the very early 1930s, broadcast talks in the BBC's schools programmes. He was invited to take part in the BBC's radio Children's Hour in Manchester in 1931 and soon became a regular favourite with listeners of all ages. His programme 'Out With Romany' (as he had decided to call himself) usually took the form of a walk in the country, or through a farm, with two young companions, Muriel and Doris (played by Muriel Levy and Doris Gambell) and his dog, Raq, with Romany himself talking about the various creatures and happenings they encountered on the way. By 1934 the programme was the most popular Children's Hour feature in the North of England. By 1938 it was broadcast in all regions throughout the British Isles, and was again one of listeners' top favourites. In 1932 the first in the popular series of 'Romany books' was published – *A Romany in the Country*. Others included *A Romany in the Fields*, *A Romany and Raq* and *A Romany on the Trail*. These particular titles were collections of Romany's writings from the Methodist press and were not actually written as books. In 1937 came a series specially written for children, which featured Romany and a boy called Tim and described their adventures among wild life. The titles were: *Out With Romany*, *Out With Romany Again*, *Out With Romany Once More*, *Out With Romany by the Sea*, *Out With Romany by Meadow and Stream* and *Out With Romany by Moor and Dale*. Another book, told from the point of view of Raq, the dog, was *Romany, Muriel and Doris*, written by Evens' son, G. Kinnaird Evens (he subsequently contributed three further titles to the series: *Romany Turns Detective*, *Romany on the Farm* and *Romany's Caravan Returns*). Romany also contributed prolifically to various newspapers, including long-running weekly columns in the *Yorkshire Post*, *Huddersfield Examiner*, *Cumberland News* and *Methodist Recorder*. He was still at the height of his fame and popularity when he died on 20th November 1943.

Everett-Green, Evelyn

Born in 1856, the daughter of artist G. B. Everett-Green, and studied music at the London Academy, subsequently nursing in a London hospital for two years. In 1883 she moved to Somerset and began her long and prolific writing career, eventually publishing over 300 novels for both adults and children. They included family chronicles and historical adventures, the latter being set against such events as the Wars of the Roses, the Gunpowder Plot, the Plague, the Fire of London and the Monmouth Rebellion. She was a popular best-seller in her day and girls particularly liked her books. Her first book was *Lady Temple's Grandchildren* (1883) and subsequent titles included: *His Mother's Book* (1883), *True to the Last* (1885), *Head of the House* (1886), *The Last of the Dacres* (1886), *Miriam's Ambition* (1889), *My Boynie* (1889),

Daring Dot (1890), *Shut In* (1894), *Dominique's Vengeance* (1896), *'Sister'; a Chronicle of Fair Haven* (1898), *A Clerk of Oxford and His Adventures in the Barons' War* (1898), *Esther's Charge* (1899), *The Heir of Hascombe Hall* (1900), *After Worcester* (1901), *A Hero of the Highlands* (1902), *Dicky and Dolly* (1906), *The Family Next Door* (1906), *General John: a Story for Boy Scouts* (1910), *Dicky and Dolly at School* (1911), *Miss Mallory of Mote* (1912) and *The Imprudence of Carol Carew* (1933). She also wrote forty-one books under the pseudonym 'CECIL ADAIR', including *Cantacute Towers* (1911) and *Quadrille Court* (1913), and at least two as 'EVELYN WARD' – *Patricia Pendragon* (1911) and *The Story of Joan of Arc* (1914). She died in 1932.

Ewing, Juliana Horatia

Born on 3rd August 1841, at Ecclesfield, Yorkshire, where her father was Vicar. She was the eldest daughter of the Rev. Alfred Gatty and Mrs Margaret Gatty, famous as a children's author herself and editor of *Aunt Judy's Magazine*. Juliana had several brothers and sisters and soon became the family story-teller, being nicknamed 'Aunt Judy' because all the other children used to group themselves around her as she told her stories, and also because she was the prime organiser of the nursery and the chief solver of problems. Her first three stories appeared in Charlotte Yonge's magazine *The Monthly Packet* in 1861 and were *A Bit of Green*, *The Blackbird's Nest* and *Melchior's Dream*. With the addition of two more stories and with illustrations by a sister they were published in book form in 1862 under the title *Melchior's Dream and Other Stories*; the book appeared under her maiden name, of course, i.e. Juliana Horatia Gatty. That same year she contributed three short tales to a book of her mother's – *Aunt Judy's Letters*. During this period, too, Juliana and her brothers and sisters ran their own manuscript magazine at home and she wrote many pieces for this. In 1866 Mrs Gatty started her own children's magazine, *Aunt Judy's Magazine*, and Juliana wrote a serial, beginning in the opening number, called *Mrs Overtheway's Remembrances* (later published in book form, 1869). In subsequent years practically all her work first appeared in *Aunt Judy's* before being published in book form. An early exception was one of her most famous tales, *The Brownies*, which appeared in *The Monthly Packet* with illustrations by Cruikshank, in 1865. Many years later Sir Robert Baden-Powell, before he became a Peer, took the name and idea from this story to found the junior section of the Girl Guide movement. *The Brownies and Other Tales* appeared in book form in 1870, also including *The Land of Lost Toys*. In 1867 Juliana Gatty became Mrs Ewing when she married Major Alexander Ewing of the Army Pay Corps, who was also noted as a writer of hymns. The Ewings lived in Canada (where Major Ewing was posted) for the first two years of their married life and Juliana continued to write stories and send them home. From 1869 until 1877 Major Ewing was stationed at Aldershot and they lived in a small military bungalow there. It was here that Juliana became interested in the life of the ordinary soldier and this is why he figures in several of her stories. Her stories tend to fall into two groups – the fairy tales and the Victorian domestic stories. The latter are rather sentimental and over-religious for modern tastes generally, but there are some delightful individual stories which still read well today. She published over 100 stories for children and the best-known include: *A Flat-Iron for a Farthing* (1872), *Lob-lie-by-the-Fire* (1874), *Six to Sixteen* (1875), *Jan of the Windmill* (1876), *Old Fashioned Fairy Tales* (1882), *Jackanapes* (1883), *Daddy Darwin's Dovecote* (1884), *The Story of a Short Life* (1885) and *Dandelion Clocks* (1887). (Dates refer to the first book publication.) Her *Verses for Children* appeared in three volumes in 1888, and her collected works, in eighteen volumes, 1894–96. Several of her later titles were published posthumously. In the last few years of her life she suffered from ill-health and in 1883, when Major Ewing returned from a posting in Ceylon and Malta, he took Juliana to live in Devon, and later to Bath. She failed to improve, however, and died in Bath on 13th May 1885.

Falkner, John Meade

Born on 8th May 1858, at Manningford Bruce, Wiltshire, the son of a clergyman, and educated at Marlborough College, and Hertford College, Oxford. On leaving university he became tutor to the sons of Sir Andrew Noble, then vice-chairman of the Armstrong-Whitworth Company, the great armaments firm. He so impressed his employer that he was offered a post with the firm in 1885. He subsequently became secretary to the Board, a director (in 1901) and finally, in 1915, chairman of this huge company. He was chairman during the momentous years 1915–20, and remained a director until 1926. His energy and intellect were so enormous that he found sufficient time for scholarship, research and book-collecting, as well as carrying out his company duties. He travelled widely in Europe and in South America for his firm, and besides negotiating with foreign governments he studied manuscripts and old documents wherever he could find a library. He was decorated by the Italian, Turkish and Japanese governments as a man of business, and received a gold medal from the Pope for important researches carried out in the Vatican Library. His other interests included palaeography, archaeology, folklore, mediaeval history, architecture and church music. His holidays were often spent in walking and cycling through Oxfordshire and Berkshire and his first publications were *A History of Oxfordshire* and handbooks to this county and also Berkshire. His first novel was *The Lost Stradivarius*, published in 1895; it was primarily a ghost story set in Oxford University and Italy. His most famous novel, and the book by which he is best remembered, is the near-classic *Moonfleet* (1898), a boys' adventure story in the tradition of *Treasure Island* and set in eighteenth-century Dorset. The story is told in the first person by fifteen-year-old John Trenchard, who falls in with local smugglers and has exciting adventures which take him away to Holland with a price on his head before eventually returning to Moonfleet village. The characters are well drawn and the narrator and his inn-keeper friend, Elzevir Block, are especially memorable. The story was once described as an affectionate 'pastiche' of the boys' adventure yarn, but it came to be enjoyed and loved as one of the *genre*'s finest examples. His third novel was *The Nebuly Coat* (1903) and was a scholarly mystery story with a timid architect as its hero. Falkner did write a fourth novel, but he lost it in a railway carriage and never saw the manuscript again. He also wrote a few historical short stories and mediaevalist verse. Towards the end of his life he was made an Honorary Fellow of Hertford College, Oxford, Honorary

J. M. Barrie's *Peter Pan* pictured by various illustrators

40 Edward Ardizzone (1962)

41 Mabel Lucie Attwell (1931)   42 Nora S. Unwin (1951)

43 F. D. Bedford (1911)

44 Betty Bronson as Peter Pan in
Paramount's 1924 silent screen
version. Walt Disney's full-length
colour cartoon appeared in 1953

45 Gwynedd M. Hudson (c 1920s) 46 Arthur Rackham (1906)

Reader in Palaeography to Durham University, and Honorary Librarian to the Chapter Library of Durham Cathedral, which had become, through his untiring efforts, one of the best cathedral libraries in Europe. He died in Durham on 22nd July 1932, and is buried in the churchyard of the small Cotswold town of Burford, a place which he knew and loved well.

Farjeon, Eleanor

Born in 1882 in London, the daughter of Benjamin Farjeon, a popular novelist, and grand-daughter of Joseph Jefferson, the famous American actor, who was renowned for his stage portrayal of Rip Van Winkle. She never went to school, but learned privately at home. She had three talented brothers: Harold, who became a gifted composer and a teacher at the Royal Academy of Music; Joseph, who became a popular light novelist and thriller-writer; and Herbert, who made a distinguished career in the theatre, as author, producer, critic and manager. She was brought up among famous people – who were always in the house visiting her popular father – and also among books: her father had thousands of them and one endearing custom in the household was that after every Sunday lunch each child was given a book, to keep and read as their own. As well as reading, Eleanor also wrote – stories, poems, playlets, rhymes – she turned them out prolifically from an early age and always gave them first to her father for his opinion. When she was seven she could type, correct proofs and read copy! When her father died in 1903 it took Eleanor a long time to recover from the blow. She sought refuge again in her writing and had stories, articles and poems published in various publications. In 1914 her *Nursery Rhymes of London Town* were appearing anonymously in *Punch* and were published in book form two years later. *Singing Games for Children* came in 1919, and in 1921 came the book which won her wide praise, *Martin Pippin in the Apple Orchard*. When it was first published it was intended for adults and was reviewed as such. Older children, especially girls, came to love the stories in the book, however, and it is now issued as a 'juvenile'. Her first real children's book, a miscellany called *Nuts and May*, was published in 1925. Subsequent collections of children's stories were: *The Tale of*

Tom Tiddler (1929), *Kaleidoscope* (1929), *The Old Nurse's Stocking-Basket* (1931), *Perkin the Pedlar* (1932), *Italian Peepshow* (1934), *Jim at the Corner* (1934), *Martin Pippin in the Daisy Field* (1937) and *One Foot in Fairyland* (1938). Other early titles were: *Ameliaranne's Prize Packet* (1933), *Ameliaranne's Washing-Day* (1934), *The Perfect Zoo* (1929), and two books of amusing verses, written in collaboration with her brother Herbert, *Kings and Queens* (1932) and *Heroes and Heroines* (1933). Eleanor Farjeon's own selection of what she considered the best of her children's verse (published in various volumes over the years) was published in three books: *Silver-sand and Snow* (1951), *Children's Bells* (1957) and *Then There Were Three* (1958). Among the collections of her plays written for children to perform themselves, the best is usually considered to be *Grannie Gray* (1939). In 1944 Eleanor and Herbert Farjeon wrote a fairy play, *The Glass Slipper* (based on the story of Cinderella), which was produced on the London stage by the late Robert Donat that year and the one following. *The Silver Curlew* was another children's play, written by Eleanor, and produced in 1948. Both plays were later written as prose stories and published in book form (1955 and 1953). In 1955 Eleanor Farjeon was awarded both the Carnegie Medal and the Hans Andersen Medal for *The Little Bookroom* as the Best Children's Book of the Year; it comprised a collection of her stories written over the years and chosen by herself. *Eleanor Farjeon's Book* (1960) was a Puffin collection, edited by Eleanor Graham, of some of Eleanor Farjeon's best stories and verses. In 1964 she collaborated with William Mayne in producing *The Hamish Hamilton Book of Kings*, and in 1965 *The Hamish Hamilton Book of Queens*. Her last story, *Mr Garden*, appeared in picture-book format in 1966 and the same year saw the publication of *The Eleanor Farjeon Book*, a commemorative anthology of new stories and poems by leading writers for children, in special tribute to Miss Farjeon, a few months after her death. As well as her children's books (which amount to over seventy) Eleanor Farjeon wrote several adult novels, stories and poems. Her own story of her childhood years, *A Nursery in the 'Nineties*, appeared in 1935. In the field of journalism, she contributed regular poems, under the pseudonym 'TOM FOOL', to the *Daily Herald* from 1917–30, and also a weekly topical verse to *Time and Tide*

94

under the name 'CHIMAERA' for several years from 1920. She wrote book reviews too. It might also be mentioned that one of her short stories is considered by many critics to be one of the most perfect children's tales ever written, especially for reading aloud; its title: *Elsie Piddock Skips in Her Sleep*. Eleanor Farjeon died on 5th June 1965.

Farquharson, Martha

See: Finley, Martha

Farrar, Frederic William

Born on 7th August 1831, in Bombay, where his father was a missionary. At the age of three he was sent with his brother to live at Aylesbury, in Buckinghamshire, England, with two maiden aunts, and attended the Latin School there until his parents returned from India in 1839. He was then educated at King William's College, Isle of Man, where he was a boarder and eventually became head of the school. He studied at London University, obtaining his B.A. in 1852. Then he went to Trinity College, Cambridge, where he secured another B.A. in 1854, his M.A. in 1857, and D.D. in 1874. He became a master at Marlborough College in 1854 and was ordained as deacon the same year and as priest in 1857. From 1855 to 1870 Farrar was a master at Harrow, in 1869 also becoming chaplain to Queen Victoria. In 1871 he became Headmaster of Marlborough College and, in 1875, Canon of Westminster. He was made Archdeacon of Westminster in 1883 and Dean of Canterbury in 1895. This highly distinguished and scholarly career, however, does not prevent him from going down in literary history as the man who wrote that famous school story *Eric, or Little by Little*. Published in 1858 (the year after *Tom Brown's Schooldays* appeared) the book was a huge popular success, achieving thirty-six editions in its first forty-five years. The story told of a boy's experiences at 'Roslyn School', which Farrar based on his old school, King William's College, in the Isle of Man. His main preoccupations in telling this tale were with the many varieties of evil that await a young boy away in his first big school and the temptations he should resist. To modern eyes it appears sentimental, over-religious, morbid and cloying and, indeed, was regarded as something of a joke as long ago as the early part of the century (Kipling even pokes fun at it in his *Stalky and Co* [1899]). But the story has many well written scenes and the book as a whole has a powerful narrative style which can often carry young readers through the lachrymose sequences. He followed this remarkable debut with *Julian Home* (1859), a story of life at Cambridge University and again based loosely on his own experiences. In 1862 came *St Winifred's, or The World of School*, a further essay in the pitfalls and evils of public school life and almost as successful with the reading public as *Eric*. *The Three Homes: a Tale for Fathers and Sons* (1873) appeared under the pseudonym 'F. T. L. HOPE' (which, Farrar later explained, stood for 'Faintly Trust the Larger Hope') and told of three schoolboys, Ralph, Martin and Lord Glenullin, their different backgrounds and personalities, and their adventures. Even this lesser-known work (which appeared under the pseudonym until 1896) ran into twenty editions up until 1911. It included the usual sins, temptations and death-bed scene, as before. Farrar's only other books for young readers were *Darkness and Dawn* (1891), set in Nero's time, and *Gathering Clouds* (1895). He also wrote several theological works for adults, the most famous of which is *The Life of Christ* (1874), which was translated into many languages. He was a fine orator and preacher and, in 1885, toured America and Canada lecturing on, among other topics, Robert Browning, and starting a vogue for that poet's works there. Dean Farrar (as he was widely known) had five sons and five daughters by his wife Lucy Cardew. One of his grandsons is Field Marshal Viscount Montgomery. He died on 22nd March 1903.

Farrow, George Edward

Born in 1866. Became one of the most popular children's authors of the day with the publication in 1895 of *The Wallypug of Why* (illustrated by Harry Furniss). This was very much a 'pastiche' of Carroll's *Alice*, with some excellent imaginative touches and truly Carrollian flashes of logical nonsense. The 'Wallypug' was a meek little man, dressed in ill-fitting robes and crown, who was 'a kind of King', but governed by the people, instead of governing them, and having to address his own subjects as 'Your Majesty'. The little girl heroine, who found herself in the land of 'Why' and had many adventures with the Wallypug and all sorts of strange animals, was called Girlie. This first book was followed by several sequels about the Wallypug, including: *The Wallypug in London* (1898), *Adventures in Wallypug Land* (1898), *In Search of the Wallypug* (1903), *The Wallypug in Fogland* (1904) and *The Wallypug in the Moon* (1905). Another success was *The Little Panjandrum's Dodo* (1899), with its sequels *The New Panjandrum* (1902) and *The Adventures of a Dodo* (1908). Farrow wrote many other nonsense tales, most of which were illustrated by Alan Wright, who also supplied coloured plates for *The Wallypug Birthday Book* (1904). Little is known about Farrow's life and he is something of a 'mystery man' to bibliographical researchers. His last book, *The Mysterious Shin Shira*, was published in 1914 and his entry disappeared from the official *Who's Who* after 1919, so it is assumed that he died around 1920, but this is not certain. It *has* been recorded that he had two favourite armchairs, one named Pendennis and the other 'The Toad', in which he used to do much of his writing; that he had a faithful dog named Dick; and that his friends called him 'Gef'.

Fenn, George Manville

Born on 3rd January 1831, in Pimlico, London. His early years were spent in comfort and happiness and he lacked for nothing, but before his eleventh birthday his entire circumstances changed, due to death in the family and other cumulative misfortunes, and he found himself more or less 'thrown on the world' to earn his own living. He spent five unhappy years and later refused to talk about them, maintaining that he only wanted to forget them. He had no regular education, but used to borrow educational works from the second-hand booksellers' barrows, teaching himself French, German and Italian (not to mention English) in this haphazard way. He became apprenticed to a printer, but on completing his apprenticeship he decided he would like to try teaching as a career – if he could teach himself so well, why not others?

97

He studied at the Battersea Training College for Teachers from 1851–54, then became a master at a small elementary school in a remote part of Lincolnshire. He later became a private tutor before returning to London to take up printing again. In 1864 he became part-owner of the *Hertfordshire and Essex Observer*, but the enterprise failed. He had been writing stories, sketches and poems for some time, without getting any published, but his luck turned when he sent a story to Charles Dickens. Dickens accepted the story for his *All the Year Round* and this started a steady stream of commissions for Fenn. His work appeared in *Once a Week*, *Chambers' Journal* and, of course, in *All the Year Round*. His first book, a collection of sketches called *Readings By Starlight*, appeared in 1866. The following year he was appointed editor of *Cassell's Magazine*, later becoming editor and proprietor of *Once a Week* and dramatic critic (for twelve years) of the London *Morning Echo*. He wrote well over 150 books, including many excellent adventure novels for boys. His first boys' story was *Hollowdell Grange* (1867) and subsequent titles included: *In Honour's Cause* (1896), *Fix Bay'nets* (1899), *Dick o' the Fens* (1905) and *Glyn Severn's Schooldays* (1904). Also: *The Dingo Boys*, *The Rajah of Dah*, *Nic Revel*, *Diamond Dyke*, *Charge!*, *Draw Swords!*, *The Kopje Garrison*, *Walsh the Wonder Worker* and – perhaps his most beloved story – *Nat the Naturalist* (1899). Many of his stories ran as serials in such boys' papers as *Young Folks*, *Boys' Champion*, *Boys' Herald* and *Boy's Own Paper*. He had married at twenty-four and his wife bore him six daughters and two sons, one of whom – Clive R. Fenn – also became a popular boys' writer and editor. George Manville Fenn died at his home at Syon House, Isleworth, Middlesex, on 26th August 1909. His final work was the definitive biography of his distinguished friend and writing colleague, G. A. Henty, published in 1907.

Finley, Martha

Born Chillicothe, Ohio, on 26th April 1828, and was a school-teacher by profession, as well as a writer. Her books also appeared under the name 'MARTHA FARQUHARSON'. She is best known for her long series (twenty-eight volumes) of books about *Elsie Dinsmore*, which began in 1867 with the book of that title. This saga began with Elsie as a child and carried the heroine on through childhood, girlhood, wifehood, motherhood and widowhood, finishing with a volume titled *Grandmother Elsie*. There were even more in the series featuring various relatives and descendants of Elsie. The heroine herself would today be regarded as an insufferable little prig: she burst into floods of tears and/or fainted at every conceivable opportunity. But the books were sensationally successful for many years on both sides of the Atlantic and countless small girls (and their elder sisters) collected the whole series as they came out. Each book in the series (which ended in 1905) was bound in either blue or red and had a pansy embossed on the cover. Another series, about *Mildred*, lasted for seven volumes, published between 1878 and 1894; they were just as moralising as *Elsie* but did not catch on as successfully. Martha Finley (or Farquharson) also wrote novels for adults, but it is as the creator of Elsie Dinsmore that she will be remembered. She died on 30th January 1909.

Fisher, Margery

Born 1913 in Camberwell, London, and educated at Amberley House, Christchurch, New Zealand, and Somerville College, Oxford. She was English teacher at Oundle School from 1939–45, having previously taught for three years in a girls' school. In 1961 she published her critical appraisal of modern fiction for children, *Intent Upon Reading*, which immediately became a classic of modern literary criticism. Surveying the entire field of contemporary children's stories, from around 1930 to the present day, with thoroughness, enlightenment and wit, Mrs Fisher produced an important reference work that was also a delight to read and browse over. A second, revised edition was brought out in 1964, with two additional chapters. In May 1962 Mrs Fisher began to publish and edit a regular review of children's literature, *Growing Point*, which is still running successfully today. A short biographical and bibliographical study of John Masefield was published in 1963. In 1965 she edited *Open the Door*, an excellent anthology of children's reading. In collaboration with her husband, author-naturalist-publisher James Fisher, she wrote a biography of

99

Shackleton, in 1958. Today regarded as one of Britain's leading authorities on children's literature, Mrs Fisher is eminently qualified for the work; apart from being a mother of six children she is an experienced teacher (holding both M.A. and B.Litt.) at both school and university levels, critic, lecturer and broadcaster. She also organises courses on reading and writing for pleasure for the National Federation of Women's Institutes. In 1966 she became the first recipient of the Children's Book Circle's 'Eleanor Farjeon Award' for her outstanding work in connection with children's reading. She lives with her family in Ashton, Northampton, where she takes an active interest in local affairs and history.

Fitzpatrick, Sir James Percy

Born in 1862 in South Africa, the son of a noted Cape Colony judge. Became a well-known South Africa politician in the periods which preceded and followed the Boer War. He also became President of the Witwatersrand Chamber of Mines and was connected with the development of the South African railway system. He accompanied Lord Randolph Churchill (father of the late Sir Winston) on his famous expedition through Mashonaland in 1891 and was later sent to prison for a time because of his work as honorary secretary to the Reform Committee in South Africa. He achieved literary fame in 1907 when he published *Jock of the Bushveld*, which became one of the classic best-selling dog stories of all time. Founded on fact, the story tells of a dog and his master trekking across the wild veld in South Africa during the early days of the gold rush there. Adventures of man and dog are vividly presented and there is, too, a valuable general picture of what life was like in those pioneering days on the veld. In 1918 he wrote a short sequel, *The Creed of Jock*, which was published only in the United States. Sir Percy Fitzpatrick, as he is usually known, died in 1931.

Forester, Cecil Scott

Born on 27th August 1899, in Cairo, the son of a government official, and educated at Alleyn's School and Dulwich

College, London. He studied medicine at Guy's Hospital, then left to devote his time to writing and to professional bridge-playing. His first book was a crime novel, *Payment Deferred* (1923), which enjoyed great success. Later he voyaged in a dinghy, with his first wife, through the rivers of England, France and Germany, his 'ship's log' being published in 1929 as *The Voyage of the 'Annie Marble'*; the following year came *The 'Annie Marble' in Germany*. Also in 1929 he wrote *Brown on Resolution*, followed by several further novels. From 1932 until 1939 he spent part of each year scriptwriting for various films in Hollywood. On the outbreak of war in 1939 he entered the Ministry of Information and later sailed with the Royal Navy to collect material for his book *The Ship* (1943). While making a similar research voyage to the Bering Sea for a book on the American Navy he was stricken with arteriosclerosis, a disease which left him crippled. He continued with his writing, however, to the pleasure and gratitude of millions throughout the world. It was in 1937, in his novel *The Happy Return*, that Forester created Captain Horatio Hornblower, R.N., today one of the most popular fictional characters of all time and with readers of all ages. The idea of creating such a character came to Forester when he bought a dusty set of three bound volumes of the *Naval Chronicle*, a monthly journal for naval officers published from about 1790 to 1820, from a second-hand bookshop in Harwich. They cost him about £2 – and supplied the first inspiration from which the great Hornblower saga has grown. The stories are set in the late eighteenth and early nineteenth centuries and tell chiefly of Hornblower's adventures during the Napoleonic wars and his rise from midshipman to Admiral Lord Hornblower. Hornblower is a likeable, unheroic hero, liable to make mistakes and face up to the consequences. He is essentially a believable and human character. *The Happy Return* was followed by *Flying Colours* (1938) and *A Ship of the Line* (1939), which won the James Tait Black Memorial Prize. Other titles in the Hornblower saga are: *The Commodore* (1944), *Lord Hornblower* (1946), *Mr Midshipman Hornblower* (1950), *Lieutenant Hornblower* (1952), *Hornblower and the 'Atropos'* (1953), *Hornblower in the West Indies* (1958) and *Hornblower and the 'Hotspur'* (1962). For the interest of those who would like to read the books through in their correct sequence, here is the chronological order: *Midshipman, Lieutenant, 'Atropos', 'Hotspur', Happy Return, Ship of the Line, Flying Colours, The Commodore, Lord* and *West Indies*. *The Hornblower Companion* – the story of how the Hornblower saga came into being, with thirty maps illuminating all of the major naval exploits of this legendary figure – was published in 1964. In 1963 Penguin Books published in their Peacock series *Hornblower Goes to Sea*, selected adventures taken from *Midshipman* and *Lieutenant*, and in 1964 there appeared *The Young Hornblower*, an omnibus volume containing the first three chronogical books; a further omnibus containing the next four novels, *Admiral Hornblower*, appeared in 1966. In 1954 specially edited and illustrated versions of seven of the Hornblower books were published in 'Cadet' editions. Forester wrote only one book especially for children: *Poo-Poo and the Dragons* (1942), the story of how an ordinary family copes with two large, affectionate dragons, graphically illustrated by Robert Lawson. Latterly, C. S. Forester lived in California with his family, but made occasional visits to London. He died on 2nd April, 1966. An autobiographical volume, *Long Before Forty*, was published posthumously in 1967.

Fouqué, Baron Friedrich de la Motte

Born on 12th February 1777, in Brandenburg, and was descended from a French Huguenot family. Served as a Prussian cavalryman in the two campaigns against Napoleon in 1792 and 1813. Began his career as an author by translating one of Cervantes' works into German. He developed an intense interest in the old Norse sagas and German legends and he wrote a series of enchanting fantastic romances, with fairy and magical elements predominating. The most popular of his shorter tales was *Undine* (1811, published in English in 1818), the story of a water-nymph who married a mortal man and so gained a soul. In 1814 came *Sintram and His Companions* (published in English in 1820), for which he took as his inspiration Dürer's engraving 'The Knight, Death and the Devil' (also sometimes known as 'The Knight and His Companions'), and which told stories of a heroic young knight fighting with the forces of good and evil. Other works included *Peter Schlemihl, Aslauga's Knight* and *The Two Captains*. His stories became very popular in England during the 1840s and 1850s. Today he is chiefly remembered for his water-nymph and for his knights in shining armour. De la Motte Fouqué died in Berlin on 23rd January 1843.

Froissart, Sir John (or Jean)

Born in 1338 in Valenciennes, France, the son of a painter of armorial bearings. Visited England in his early youth and was presented to, and entertained by, King Edward III, and by his Queen, Phillipa of Hainault. On his second visit to England, in 1361, he became Clerk of the Chamber to Queen Phillipa. After her death he became a parish priest in Lestines, France, was subsequently attached to the Court of Winceslaus de Luxembourg, Duke of Brabant, and later was secretary to King John of France. He is famous for his great *Chronicles of England, France, Spain and the Adjoining Countries*, which he began writing at the age of twenty and which was eventually published in four large volumes in his native France. The *Chronicles* tell graphically of historic events in the fourteenth century, with particular attention being paid to battles such as Crecy, Poitiers, etc. He also paid special regard to the gallant knights of the period. Before he described the French wars he painstakingly interviewed those survivors who had actually fought in them, visited the battlefields, talked with local inhabitants and read every report he could trace. To his descriptions he brought vivid colour and sweep and almost persuaded the reader that he had been at the occasion in question himself. Froissart also probably did nearly as much as Malory in perpetuating the romantic picture of the shining knight errant on immaculate horseback. Froissart's *Chronicles* have been published in many different children's editions, under such titles as *The Children's Froissart, The Boys' Froissart*, etc. The work was first translated into English in 1523 by Lord Berners and at the request of King Henry VIII. Froissart died around 1410, reputedly in poverty.

Fuller, Roy

Born in 1912, in Failsworth, Lancashire, and educated at private schools in the area. He was articled to a solicitor at sixteen and qualified as a solicitor himself at twenty-one.

He was appointed Assistant Solicitor to the Woolwich Equitable Building Society in 1938. Shortly before the start of the Second World War he published his first collection of poems; he had already contributed verse to *New Writing* and other magazines, his main influences being W. H. Auden and Stephen Spender. It was while serving with the Royal Navy in Africa that his second book of poems, *The Middle of a War*, came out and this received excellent press reviews from critics who hailed him as the most promising new poet of the Second World War. He has since published several collections of poems and is today considered one of Britain's finest modern poets. In 1946 he published his first novel, which was a children's story, written for his own son and called *Savage Gold*. It told of the adventures of two very human and likeable boys who become involved in a clash between rival mining interests in Kenya. *With My Little Eye* (1948) was a boys' detective novel and won more praise from critics, who especially complimented Fuller on being able to show how an adolescent boy's mind can 'grow up' during the course of a few eventful days. Roy Fuller has since published several adult novels and thrillers, as well as his poetry, but his only children's book in recent years has been *Catspaw* (1966), a parable about the 'cold war between cat and dog'. Since 1958 he has been Solicitor to the Woolwich Equitable Building Society.

Fyleman, Rose

Born in 1877, in Nottingham, and educated there privately and at University College, Nottingham. After working as a schoolteacher for some years she studied singing in Germany, Paris, and at the Royal College of Music in London, of which she became an Associate. She had written odd pieces for children from an early age, using them mainly in her teaching work, and had never submitted anything to a magazine until 1917, when she was in her fortieth year. The first poem she submitted to *Punch* was accepted and appeared on 23rd May 1917 – it was the classic *There Are Fairies at the Bottom of Our Garden*. From then on Rose Fyleman could be said to have 'cornered the market' in fairies. Numerous fairy verses appeared in *Punch* (whose readers welcomed them as a change from reading about the First World War) and other magazines. In 1918 her first collection of fairy poems was published: *Fairies and Chimneys*. Later came *The Fairy Green* (1919), *The Fairy Flute* (1921), *The Rainbow Cat* (1922), *Fairies and Friends* (1925), *Gay Go Up* (1929), *Fifty New Nursery Rhymes* (1931), *The Little Christmas Book*, *The Princess Comes to Our Town*, *Runabout Rhymes* (1941) and *Nursery Stories* (1949). In 1934 she published a sort of International Mother Goose, comprising a collection of nursery rhymes translated from many different languages from all over the world, titled *Widdy-Widdy-Wurkey*; it also became known under its sub-title *Nursery Rhymes from Many Lands* (and was published in the USA as *Picture Rhymes from Foreign Lands*). She translated many more verses and stories from the French, German and Italian, including the *Père Castor* books from the French. She wrote chiefly about gossamer-winged, be-crowned fairies, who carried magic wands and danced around fairy rings in the moonlight and projected the strictly glamorous notion of what fairies are supposed to be like. Younger children love her fairy stories and verses and her teaching experience certainly helped her to appreciate what smaller readers like. Some of her favourite poems include: 'Fairies', 'Differences', 'Yesterday in Oxford Street', 'The Fairy Tailor', 'Dunsley Glen', 'Mrs Brown', 'The Dentist' and 'Mary Middling'. The last three are not about fairies, as Miss Fyleman occasionally wrote about other topics too. In 1930 she edited a fine anthology of stories and verses for children, *Round the Mulberry Bush*. She also wrote children's plays and, in 1933, a children's opera. Her songs for young people were popular too. In 1923 she founded and became the first editor of the children's monthly magazine *Merry-Go-Round*. It was in this magazine that some of A. A. Milne's children's verses first appeared. Some of her other books are: *Forty Goodnight Tales*, *The Dolls' House*, *The Princess Dances*, *Jeremy Quince*, *About Bears*, *Nine Little Plays*, *Adventures with Benghazi* and *Hob and Bob*. Miss Fyleman's favourite recreation was travelling and she toured widely throughout Europe, the United States and Canada. She died on 1st August 1957.

Garfield, Leon

Born 1921, in Brighton, Sussex. His art studies were interrupted by the Second World War, when he joined the army and served for five years in England, Belgium and Germany. He subsequently became a hospital biochemist and began to write in his spare time, as he still does today. In 1964 his first novel for young readers was published: *Jack Holborn*. This powerful and exciting story of a young eighteenth-century boy who becomes caught up with pirates made an outstanding debut and was hailed by critics as one of the best children's stories of the year. His second book, *Devil-in-the-Fog* (1966), also set in the eighteenth century and telling of a boy who grows up with a family of travelling actors, was even more widely praised and won the first *Guardian* Award for children's fiction. Then came *Smith* (1967), again dealing with Garfield's favourite period, the eighteenth century, and drawing a graphic, breathtaking picture of England – and particularly London – with a handful of memorable, larger-than-life characters. It told of a boy who witnessed a murder and was consequently pursued by the murderers. Garfield's excellent, forceful writing and his ability to create striking characters has brought comparisons with Stevenson and Dickens, among others. But he has a style of his own and, more to the point, an imagination of his own, and is certainly one of the most distinguished children's writers of the 1960s. A word of praise is due to Antony Maitland, who illustrated Garfield's books so memorably. Leon Garfield, married, with one daughter, lives in North London.

Garner, Alan

Born in Cheshire. Educated at Alderley Edge Primary School, near Wilmslow, Cheshire, at Manchester Grammar School, and at Magdalen College, Oxford. An outstanding athlete, he won several championships for his county, Cheshire, at sprinting. He served as a 2nd Lieutenant in the Royal Artillery and began writing towards the end of his service. His first children's book, *The Weirdstone of Brisingamen*, was published in 1960 and hailed as an outstanding debut. The story linked two modern children with the powerful forces of ancient magic and entangled them in the age-old fight between good and evil. Garner's next two books – *The Moon of Gomrath* (1963) and *Elidor* (1965) – continued the theme magnificently and he was established as a children's fantasy/allegory-writer of note. Garner's later books are *Holly for the Bongs* (1966), a nativity play (with music by William Maupe), and an account of how it was put on by a group of children in a Cheshire village one Christmas; *The Old Man of Mow* (1967), a story with photographs set amidst the crags of Mow Cop in Garner's beloved Cheshire; and *The Owl Service* (1967), a striking novel for older children, telling how an old Welsh legend comes to influence the present. It won the Carnegie Medal as the Best Children's Book of the Year, and also the *Guardian* award for children's fiction. Today, Garner lives with his wife and three children at Blackden-cum-Goostrey, Cheshire, in a house called 'Toad Hall'. His three great hobbies are archaeology and the history and folklore of Cheshire.

Garnett, Eve

Born in Worcestershire, the youngest daughter of an English Lieutenant-Colonel and an Irish mother, and educated at The Convent, Bideford, Devon; West Bank School, Devon; and The Alice Ottley School. Studied art at Chelsea Polytechnic and the Royal Academy School of Art, where she won the Creswick Prize and Silver Medal. While still a student she used to wander through the East End slums in London and was aghast at the conditions there. She was particularly angered at the pathetic sight of half-clothed, ill-fed children running the streets, but at the same time she was impressed by their cheerfulness in spite of everything. As she walked the back streets Eve Garnett sketched what she saw and one day took some of her work to a publisher. The result was a commission to illustrate Evelyn Sharp's *The London Child*. She managed to obtain special leave of absence from the Royal Academy Schools for this task and toured around schools, playgrounds, children's courts, homes, and so on, until her drawings were finished. Haunted by the conditions she had seen, she resolved to do something to bring to people's notice the prevailing situation of the working-class family. She wrote and illustrated *The Family from One End Street*, starting it in a train and completing it during the upheavals of a house-moving. It was rejected by six consecutive publishers, all of whom condemned it as unsuitable for children. A seventh firm accepted it, but then went into liquidation. After two further rejections it was finally taken by Frederick Muller and published in 1937. It was awarded the Carnegie Medal for that year as the Best Children's Book, subsequently being reprinted about twenty times and translated into several languages, even Japanese. In this heart-warming and very realistic story – which was unique at the time of its appearance – Mr Ruggles is a dustman and Mrs Ruggles takes in washing. They have several cheerful children and each chapter tells of a particular incident involving one of them. The working-class background – and often foreground – of the book was authentically described and completely different from the other family stories then being published for children, which were almost exclusively middle-class. Miss Garnett later described the book as 'a shot in the battle against slums'. But it is no social tract; it is very readable, funny, human and entertaining. In the late 1930s it made children realise that not all their contemporaries owned ponies, had nurseries or attended boarding-schools . . . In 1938 Miss Garnett published a book of pictures of children in Britain, continuing her plea for social reform, titled *Is It Well With the Child?*; the book had a foreword by Walter de la Mare and a preface by Marjorie Bowen. Her subsequent books include: *In and Out and Roundabout: Stories of a Little Town* (1948), *A Book of the Seasons* (1952) (this was an anthology of poems by English writers, illustrating the seasons and decorated with delightful drawings and paintings by Miss Garnett), *Further Adventures of the Family from One End Street* (1956), and *Holiday at the Dew Drop Inn* (1962) which featured Kate Ruggles (from One End Street) and her recovery from measles in a country village. In a foreword to *Further Adventures . . .* Miss Garnett explained that the original MS had been badly burnt in 1941 in a fire and been stored away in a box for years. She rediscovered it and began to decipher the charred pages in the late 1940s and some chapters were published in *Collins' Magazine* in 1950. The work then had to be put aside for various reasons, finally appearing in book form in 1956. This sequel was generally agreed to be just as good as the original book. In 1948 Eleanor Graham commissioned Miss Garnett to do the illustrations for a special Puffin Books edition of Stevenson's *A Child's Garden of Verses*, which was a notable success. Eve

Garnett has also written stories and supplied illustrations for various anthologies, including James Reeves' *A Golden Land*. Her most recent books are *Mr Crundell's Cow* (1967), a story for younger children, and *To Greenland's Icy Mountains* (1968), the story of the eighteenth century Norwegian explorer and missionary Hans Egede. She lives in Lewes, Sussex, the setting of some of her stories. Her greatest interest is painting and has had several exhibitions of her work in London; she also painted forty feet of mural decorations at the Children's House, Bow, London.

Gatty, Margaret

Born on 3rd June 1809, at Burnham Vicarage, Essex, the daughter of Dr Alexander Scott, chaplain to Nelson on board HMS *Victory* at the Battle of Trafalgar and in whose arms Nelson died. Margaret's mother died when her little girl was only two, and for some years Margaret, and her elder sister, Horatia, spent summer with their father in the country in Essex, and winter with their grandparents in the precincts of the Charterhouse in London. In 1817 Dr Scott became Vicar at Catterick, Yorkshire, and his two daughters took up permanent residence with him there. They were educated privately by a governess and Margaret excelled particularly at the study of German and Italian, becoming so proficient as to translate poems in these languages into English. In 1829 and 1830 a few of these translations appeared in the *Bijou*, a literary annual. Around this period the two Miss Scotts, Horatia and Margaret, enjoyed a gay and lively round of engagements and, as well as doing the social whirl, formed literary societies, amateur magazines and interests in such subjects as astrology and demonology. In 1839 Margaret married a penniless young curate, Alfred Gatty, after a period of objection (largely due to Gatty's slender means) by her father. While they were still on their honeymoon, however, Margaret's uncle offered Gatty the living of Ecclesfield, in Yorkshire, and it was at Ecclesfield Vicarage that Margaret was to bear her ten children and live for the rest of her life. (Three of the children were named, in various ways, after Lord Nelson, to mark her father's close association with him.) Money was short after marriage and Margaret began writing, largely to earn a little extra housekeeping money. Her first book was *The Fairy Godmother* (1851), a collection of modern fairy tales with morals. The first part of her most famous work, *Parables from Nature*, appeared in 1855, four further parts being published, the last in 1871. The *Parables* were little stories or fables illustrating the truths and morals to be found in life, but telling the tales with the help of animals, birds, insects, snowflakes, fishes and so on, and explaining at the same time a great deal of information about such creatures and the ways of nature generally. These little moral stories, many of them entertainingly dramatic or humorous, found tremendous favour during the nineteenth century and were still in print until fairly recently. They were originally illustrated by such distinguished artists as Tenniel, Millais, Holman Hunt and Burne-Jones. Subsequent children's books included: *Worlds Not Realised* (1856), *Proverbs Illustrated* (1857), *Legendary Tales* (1858) and *Aunt Judy's Tales* (1859). 'Aunt Judy' was the nickname given to Margaret's second child, Juliana Horatia, because of her prowess as nursery story-teller and organiser-in-chief of her younger brothers and sisters. (Juliana was later to win fame as the popular children's writer, Mrs Ewing.) Margaret Gatty used her own children as characters in many of her stories and often used to refer to them as numbers. *Aunt Judy's Letters* followed in 1862, and in 1866 her publishers invited her to edit a new children's monthly magazine, which was called (naturally enough) *Aunt Judy's Magazine*. It was probably the best general children's magazine to appear in the nineteenth century and included stories, articles and poems by many famous writers, including Lewis Carroll (who contributed *Bruno's Revenge*), Hans Andersen, Mrs Molesworth and F. Anstey. One of the most prolific contributors to *Aunt Judy's Magazine* was Margaret's daughter, Juliana Ewing, many of whose most famous stories made their first appearance there. Margaret Gatty edited the magazine until her death in 1873, when it was taken over by her third daughter, Horatia, with help from Juliana. It finally ceased publication in 1885, a few months after the death of Juliana. *Aunt Judy's Magazine*, incidentally, was the first periodical to endow special beds at Great Ormond Street Children's Hospital in London. It was also one of the first to feature regular reviews of children's books; one of the new titles reviewed during the magazine's first year was *Alice's Adventures in Wonderland,* which received a warm welcome. Though she suffered from increasing ill-health in her last years, Margaret Gatty published three final books in the year before her death: *The Mother's Poetry Book* (1872), *The Book of Emblems* (1872) and *The Book of Sundials* (1872). It should also be noted that in 1863 she had published *The History of British Seaweeds,* in two volumes – a work which remained the standard reference on the subject for many years. Seaweeds were a particular interest of hers and she spent hours on the sea-shore studying and collecting specimens. She died on 4th October 1873, at Ecclesfield Vicarage.

Gilson, Barbara

See: Gilson, Charles

Gilson, Charles

Born 1878, in Dedham, Essex, and educated at Dulwich College, where he was a contemporary of P. G. Wodehouse. He distinguished himself at cricket at Dulwich, once playing for the Young Amateurs of Surrey against the Professionals at the Oval – and taking eight wickets for twenty runs – while still a schoolboy. He also excelled at rugby football, playing for his school and, later, for Croydon and the Eastern Counties. At twenty he entered the army and gained a commission. His first station was Malta and soon afterwards he saw active service in the Boer War in South Africa. During a period of convalescence after being wounded, he began to write. Later he served in China, Japan, the South Sea Islands, Australia, Canada, East Africa and the East Indies. Then, in Singapore, he fell very ill and was sent home to England to be invalided out of the army with the rank of Captain (all his earlier books bear the name 'Captain Charles Gilson'). He began writing stories for boys when he was aged about thirty and his first full-length serial appeared in the magazine *The Captain* in 1907–8, with stirring illustrations by R. Caton Woodville: it was *The Lost Island,* one of his most popular stories and later published in book form in 1910. It dealt with rousing adventures in the Far East – a region Gilson had come to know well during his army service. His first published book for boys was *The Lost Column* (1908), which dealt with the Boxer Rebellion. Other titles of this early period include *The Lost Empire* (1909), *The Spy* (1910), *The Sword of Freedom* (1911), *The Pirate Aeroplane* (1912), *The Race Round the World* (1913) and *The Sword of Deliverance* (1913). During the First World War he joined the Naval Division and served in Antwerp, being 'Mentioned in Dispatches' for his fine record. He subsequently took up important duties as Commandant of more than one army detention barracks. His books published during the war include *A Motor-Scout in Flanders* (1915), *Across the Cameroons* (1916), *Submarine U-93* (1916), *In Arms for Russia* (1917), *In the Power of the Pygmies* (1918) and *The Pirate Yacht* (1918). After the war he left the service, this time with the rank of Major (which is why his later books bear the credit 'Major Charles Gilson'). He returned to his busy writing career and promptly established an all-time record for the famous *Boy's Own Paper*, opening no less than five consecutive annual volumes (Nos. 42–46, 1919–23) with serials, all later appearing in book form: (*The Lost City* [1923], *The Realm of the Wizard King* [1922], *The Treasure of Kings* [1922], *Jack Without-a-Roof* [1923] and *In the Land of Shame* [1924]). He also contributed several serials to such magazines as *Chums* and more to *The Captain*. Further titles of his books include: *The Mystery of Ah Jim* (1919), *Held by Chinese Brigands* (1920), *The Scarlet Hand* (1920), *The Society of the Tortoise Mask* (1921), *Mystery Island* (1928), *The Wizard of the Woods* (1931), *The City of the Sorcerer* (1934), *The Bronze Casket* (1938), *Out of the Nazi Clutch* (1940), *Sons of the Sword* (1941) and *The Secret Agent* (1948). Under the pseudonym 'BARBARA GILSON' he wrote girls' adventure tales such as *Through the Dragon Door* (1934) and *Queen of the Andes* (1935). He also wrote non-fiction titles about *Waterloo* (1941) and *The Battle of the Nile* (1943), as well as three adult novels. Gilson's boys' yarns were always exciting and full of colourful action; he was paricularly at home in writing about the Orient, for which he had an especial fascination. He died on 18th May 1943.

Godden, Rumer

Born in Sussex, 1907, she was taken by her parents to India

when she was nine months old and spent much of her early life there. She began to write when she was seven and produced, with her elder sisters, many stories and poems, which they illustrated and bound themselves. She returned to England around 1920 and completed her education at Moira House School, Eastbourne. Her first adult novel, *Chinese Puzzle*, appeared in the early 1930s, but it was her second, *Black Narcissus*, which established her as a leading novelist. Her later adult novels include *The River, A Candle to St Jude, Kingfishers Catch Fire, An Episode of Sparrows* and *The Greengage Summer*. Her first children's book, *The Dolls' House*, was published in 1947 and set the pattern for her subsequent series of dolls' house stories, which have been hailed as the best of their kind. This first story of everyday life in a dolls' house, with its humours, incidents and fears, had an enthusiastic welcome from critics and public alike; some of the former pointed out that it could be enjoyed both by children (as a straightforward story) and by adults (as a parable on life in the larger world outside the dolls' house). In 1951 came *The Mousewife*, a tender and enchanting story about a mouse and a caged dove and their strange friendship and based on an anecdote in Dorothy Wordsworth's *Journal*. This again can be enjoyed as a tale or as a parable about the oppressed. Another story about dolls, *Impunity Jane*, came in 1955 and told of Jane, a small doll, and her adventures when she was taken as a mascot by a gang of boys. In the same year she wrote an engaging 'story biography' of Hans Christian Andersen. Other tales of dolls and dolls' houses include: *The Fairy Doll* (1956), *Mouse House* (1957), *The Story of Holly and Ivy* (1958), *Candy Floss* (1960), *Miss Happiness and Miss Flower* (1961), *Little Plum* (1962) and *Home is the Sailor* (1964). *St Jerome and the Lion* (1961) is a long narrative poem. A recent children's book, *The Kitchen Madonna* (1967), is one of her finest and tells how two children make an icon; *Two Under the Indian Sun* (1966) (written with her sister Jon) is a fragment of early autobiography which describes the year the two little girls spent in their father's house at Bengal. Her work has been translated into no less than thirteen languages. Today she lives in her native Sussex, in the lovely house at Northiam formerly owned by Sheila Kaye-Smith, the novelist (who also wrote children's stories), and here she keeps her own private collection of dolls' houses.

'Golden Gorse'

The mysterious author who, under this pseudonym, introduced the 'pony story' in 1929 with the publication of *Moorland Mousie*, the life and adventures of an Exmoor pony and of the children who owned him, told in the first person. A sequel, *Older Mousie*, followed soon afterwards. Both stories were illustrated by Lionel Edwards. *Mousie* gave rise to that whole new brand of children's literature, read almost entirely by girls, consisting of books about ponies and their youthful owners and riders.

Goodrich, Samuel Griswold

The original 'PETER PARLEY'. Born on 10th August 1793, in Ridgefield, Connecticut, the son of a Congregational minister. As a child he was horrified to read such fairy tales as *Little Red Riding Hood, Jack the Giant Killer* and *Bluebeard* and thought the idea of adults giving them to children to read was disgusting. He thought such tales too frightening and, what was almost as bad, *untrue*! He resolved at this early age to try to give children true stories to read – and non-frightening ones at that. In 1818 he became a partner in a publishing firm in Connecticut and wrote a few 'toy-books' around this period. In 1826 he moved to Boston and formed his own publishing firm. The following year he produced the first of the many famous and much-imitated 'PETER PARLEY' books, a name which he also used as his pseudonym. It was *Tales of Peter Parley about America* and was followed in 1828 by *Tales of Peter Parley about Europe* and by a long succession of similar tales. He also wrote numerous books about geography, history, science, travel and famous men and women – all for children and all packed with information and moral value. He might well be described as one of the first of America's didactic writers for children. In 1833 he published and edited *Parley's Magazine*, a fine children's periodical which ran until 1844 and numbered some distinguished names among its contributors. In 1828 he had started a magazine called *The Token*, which introduced Nathaniel Hawthorne to the reading public and published some of his popular *Twice Told Tales* for the first time. In Britain, there were several imitators of 'Peter Parley', all using the same pen-name and copying Goodrich's style, etc. (for brief details see under 'Parley, Peter'). The general popularity of the genuine *Peter Parleys* can be appreciated when it is realised that over a period of thirty years (1827–57) no less than seven million copies were sold, of about 120 different titles. Thus, Goodrich had a big and important influence on children's books and their readers during the early and mid-nineteenth century, when countless young people grew up with 'Peter Parley'. He also wrote books of poems and an autobiography. He died on 9th May 1860.

Goodyear, Robert Arthur Hanson

Born 1877, in Barnsley, Yorkshire, and educated at Archbishop Holgate's Grammar School, Barnsley. Made his debut as a professional writer at the age of seventeen, having a serial, *The Football Rivals*, accepted by *The Boys' Friend* in 1895. Soon afterwards he received encouragement from Alfred Barratt (humorist 'R. Andom'), then editor of Henderson's *Nuggets* magazine, and had several stories published in this periodical. After years of writing for the popular weekly magazines and sporting papers he turned his attention to writing hard-cover public school stories for boys. He soon became one of the most popular authors of this type of story, especially during the 1920s and 1930s. Among his typical titles were *The White House Boys*, *Jack O'Langsett*, *Forge of Foxenby*, *With Wat at Wintergleam*, *The Captain and the Kings*, *Three Joskins at St Jude's*, *Blake of the Modern Fifth*, *The Broom and Heather Boys*, *Rival Schools at Schooner Bay*, *The Boys of Ringing Rock*, *Too Big for the Fifth*, *Tringle of Harlech*, *Young Rockwood at School* and *The New Boy at Baxtergate*. In private life one of his favourite pastimes was producing village plays, some of which he also wrote. He lived for the latter years of his life in Wheatcroft, Scarborough, Yorkshire – in a house named 'Wintergleam', one of the many public schools he wrote about. He died there in November 1948.

Goudge, Elizabeth

Born in Wells, Somerset, where her father was Principal of the

Theological College. Her mother came from Guernsey, C.I., and the young Elizabeth spent her childhood holidays there. She was educated at Grassendale School, Southbourne, Hampshire, and at Reading University School of Art, where she studied to be a handicraft teacher. From Reading, she returned to her father's rooms in Christ Church, Oxford University, where he was now Regius Professor of Divinity. Elizabeth had always wanted to write stories but her parents had insisted on her qualifying as a handicraft teacher first, so that she would have something to fall back on if her writing was unsuccessful. So in the evenings, after instilling the arts of weaving, basket-work and leather-tooling to her pupils in Oxford, she would sit down and write. She loved the theatre and so made her first big project a play based on the life of the Brontës, whose books she adored. It was accepted by a London manager for a Sunday night 'try-out' but was never produced commercially. She wrote two more plays, about Jane Austen and Fanny Burney, but they were turned down, so she decided to write a novel. It was *Island Magic* and it was accepted for publication. The story told of a family growing up on the Channel Island of Guernsey and was a small success in both Britain and America. Primarily an adult novel, it could be enjoyed by young readers too. Many more novels followed, some based on settings she knew well from her own experience: *A City of Bells* is set in Wells and *Towers in the Mist* in Christ Church, Oxford. *Green Dolphin Country* was a best-selling novel which won an award of £30,000 given by M-G-M in Hollywood. Her first children's book was *Smoky House* (1940) and was followed by *Sister of the Angels*, *Henrietta's House* and *The Little White Horse* (1946), which won the Carnegie Medal as Best Children's Book of the Year. Set in Victorian times, the story told of little Maria Merry-weather's introduction to the mysterious house called 'Moon-acre' in Devon, and of the strange people she met there, not the least strange being the little white unicorn, and of how she brought back peace and harmony to 'Moonacre' and the village of Silverdew. The characters were vividly brought to life and the countryside beautifully evoked, with the whole story having a marvellous magical quality which defies analysis. Miss Goudge's other children's books are *The Valley of Song* and *Linnets and Valerians* (1964). She has also written a life of Christ for young people called *God So Loved the World* (1951) and a biography of *St Francis of Assisi*. *A Christmas Book* (1967) is an anthology of Miss Goudge's writings about that festive season and can be enjoyed by most ages. She is a Fellow of the Royal Society of Literature and today lives at Henley-on-Thames.

Graham, Eleanor

Born in 1896, in Walthamstow, London, the daughter of P. Anderson Graham, who was editor of *Country Life* magazine for the first quarter of this century. Educated at the North London Collegiate School for Girls. Published her first children's book in 1920; it was *Six in a Family*, a pleasant if not outstanding story of family life. In 1927 she joined Bumpus's famous bookshop, then in Oxford Street, London, to become head of its children's department. She made a big success in this job, leaving in 1930 to join a publishing house for a spell and following this by a nine-month stay in a children's library. She was by now reviewing children's books regularly in *The Bookman* and the *Sunday Times*. She also published two books in America, *Happy Holidays* (1933) and *Welcome Christmas!* (1932), and another book in Britain called *Head o' Mey*, which was the semi-autobiographical story of a Scottish grandmother. In 1934 she became Selector and Secretary of the Junior Book Club, holding this post until 1938. Her most memorable children's story, *The Children Who Lived in a Barn*, appeared in 1938 and told how a family of children lived in a barn on their own resources after their parents had disappeared. She was now contributing reviews and articles to *Junior Bookshelf* too. When Penguin Books started their series of Puffin Story Books in 1941, Eleanor Graham was appointed editor and for more than twenty years (until 1962, in fact) she built up an excellent list of fine children's books in paperback form (Number One Puffin, by the way, was Barbara Euphan Todd's *Worzel Gummidge*). She was succeeded as Puffin editor, in 1962, by Kaye Webb. During her stay she commissioned many original Puffin books, also editing *The Puffin Book of Verse* (1953) and the *Quartet of Poets* (1958), as well as writing her own original *The Story of Jesus* (1959) (reprinted in hard covers the following year). In 1943 she became editor of Methuen's

117

children's books, resigning in 1957. During this period she wrote *The Story of Charles Dickens* (1952) for Methuen's series of 'story biographies' for young readers. In 1962 she re-told and 'presented' Barrie's *Peter Pan*, in a sumptuous edition illustrated by Edward Ardizzone. A short study of Kenneth Grahame and his works appeared as a 'Bodley Head Monograph' in 1963. Now retired from active publishing, Eleanor Graham still reviews children's books regularly for various publications, including *The Times Literary Supplement*, and is regarded as a foremost authority on the subject.

Graham, Harry Jocelyn Clive

Born on 23rd December 1874, in London, and educated at Eton College and Sandhurst. Served as an officer with the Coldstream Guards during the Boer War in South Africa at the turn of the century. As a result of his experiences he published in 1902 a book of *Ballads of the Boer War*. Earlier, in 1899, he established his reputation with the publication of *Ruthless Rhymes for Heartless Homes*, a collection of somewhat savage verses which were the precursors of today's so-called 'sick humour'. They were mainly concerned with the mis-adventures of children, their Mammas and Papas, Aunts and Uncles, etc. Though intended more for their parents, the verses were enjoyed by many children too, rather in the way in which the *Struwwelpeter* pieces had been in earlier years. *Ruthless Rhymes* started a new trend in 'cruel humorous verse' and begat many imitators. *More Ruthless Rhymes* appeared in 1930. Graham also wrote many other volumes of humorous verse and short stories, one of his most popular characters in the latter being 'Reginald Biffin'. In 1930 came an engaging children's book, *Happy Families*. He also wrote lyrics for several musicals, including *Maid of the Mountains*, *White Horse Inn* and *Land of Smiles*, as well as straight plays such as *By Candlelight*. He was a Trustee of the British Museum and worked for a time as private secretary to Lord Rosebery. He died on 30th October 1936.

Grahame, Kenneth

Born on 8th March 1859, in Edinburgh, the son of an advocate who soon afterwards became Sheriff-substitute for Argyll, and descended from an old Scottish family which went back to Robert the Bruce. He spent his early childhood in Scotland but, after his mother's premature death in 1864, went to live with his grandmother and his two brothers and sister at 'The Mount', Cookham Dene, Berkshire. The house was large and rambling, with plenty of grounds and with the River Thames running through part of them. Kenneth loved the place and spent many happy hours roaming through the countryside and along the river banks. Two years later, grandmother and charges moved to Cranbourne, which was less idyllic. He was educated at St Edward's School, Oxford, where he became head of the school and distinguished himself at rugby football and cricket, as well as in the classroom. On leaving school, his dreams of going to Oxford University were shattered by his grandmother's decision to obtain a clerkship for him in the Bank of England. Whilst waiting for this post he worked for his uncle, a Parliamentary political agent in Westminster, for two years. He joined the staff of the Bank of England in 1878 and rose over the years to become Secretary in 1898, a post he held until 1907, when he was forced to retire through ill-health. During his early years at the Bank he wrote essays and verses, getting most of them politely rejected by the various papers and magazines he sent them to. The odd one was published here and there, however, and he persevered. His first traceable published work was an essay on the Berkshire Downs which appeared in the *St James's Gazette* in December 1888. Two years later he was contributing essays, sketches and poems to W. E. Henley's *National Observer*. A collection of the essays and sketches was published in 1893 under the title *Pagan Papers* (also included in this volume were half a dozen stories about a family of children – stories which later made up part of *The Golden Age*). In 1895 he published *The Golden Age*, followed by its sequel *Dream Days* in 1898. Both books contain delightful studies of children and their thoughts and adventures, but are intended chiefly for adults. They have been published in illustrated children's editions but few children actually enjoy them. They are primarily tales about children for adult readers. The two books met with widespread critical approval, with many writers singling out the fairy story *The Reluctant Dragon* (contained in *Dream Days*) for special praise. Kenneth Grahame had married in 1899 and his wife bore him a son, Alistair, the following year. On Alistair's (or 'Mouse's', to give him his family nickname) fourth birthday, in May 1904, his father began to tell him a bedtime story – a story about a mole and a rat (there was a giraffe too, but that soon disappeared) – a story which expanded over the next three years, to include other characters such as a badger and a toad, among others . . . When 'Mouse' went away on a lengthy seaside holiday at the age of seven, the story had to be continued in the form of letters. Kenneth never had any thought of writing the story down in book form until persuaded by a friend who was also a representative of an American magazine. He eventually wrote the story down and called it *The Wind in the Willows*. But the American magazine who had expressed interest turned it down! So did his English and American publishers. At length, Methuen's accepted it in Britain and Scribner's (Grahame's American publishers) changed their mind and decided to publish it. It appeared in Britain on 8th October 1908, with a frontispiece by Graham Robertson – and met with mixed reviews. Critics were puzzled by this sudden change in style and subject matter and seemed disappointed that a sequel to *The Golden Age* and *Dream Days* was not forthcoming. But some reviewers liked it and the public bought it in ever-increasing numbers until, eventually, it became a steady best-seller throughout the world. By 1951 – in a matter of forty-three years – 100 editions had been printed. A stage-play version was written by A. A. Milne in 1929 under the title *Toad of Toad Hall*. And *The Wind in the Willows*, with its endearing adventures of Mole, Rat, Badger and the conceited Mr Toad, which are climaxed in the epic battle against the stoats and weasels, is today one of the true and immortal children's classics of all time. It was Grahame's last book, though mention should be made of a little story called *Bertie's Escapade*, which he had written as a sort of family joke for a family magazine which 'Mouse' and his friends were 'publishing'. The hero was the Grahame's own pet black pig. The story was never intended for publication but was discovered after his death and included in a biography and later in a book by Mrs Grahame. It finally appeared as a separate book, with illustrations by E. H. Shepard (who had so brilliantly illustrated Grahame's previous books) in 1949. Grahame also edited *The Cambridge Book of Poetry for Young People* (1916). He died on 6th July 1932, at Pangbourne, where he was buried, his body later being transferred to Holywell Church-yard, Oxford. His cousin, popular novelist Anthony Hope, wrote the moving epitaph for his gravestone: 'To the beautiful memory of Kenneth Grahame, husband of Elspeth and father of Alistair, who passed the River on the 6th of July, 1932, leaving childhood and literature through him the more blest for all time.'

Green, Roger Lancelyn

Born in 1918 at Norwich, Norfolk, and educated at Dane Court, Pyrford, Surrey; Liverpool College; and Merton College, Oxford. As a schoolboy of ten he devoured the books of Rider Haggard (among those of many other authors), and one in particular, *The World's Desire*, which Haggard wrote in collaboration with Andrew Lang, became his favourite. It was natural that he should seek out the works of Lang and it was this author's poetry, critical essays and other writings which formed the foundation of the young Green's knowledge of English literature. When he went up to Oxford University he found that his own college, Merton, had been Lang's too, and Green chose Lang as the subject of the thesis he wrote for his B.Litt. He also obtained his M.A. degree. While at Oxford he acquired a deep interest in imaginative and romantic literature, especially in the Arthurian legends and the history of the myth in literature. On leaving Oxford he had short spells as a schoolmaster, antiquarian bookseller and professional actor. In the latter profession, he appeared as the pirate 'Noodler' in the 1942–43 London production and provincial tour of Barrie's *Peter Pan* (the stars that season being Ann Todd and Alastair Sim). This engagement fostered an interest in both the play and J. M. Barrie, which later resulted in books about both. He returned to Merton College, Oxford, in 1945 to become Deputy Librarian, a post he held for five years. In January 1946 he published *Tellers of Tales*, a fascinating and unique work about children's books and their authors over the past 150 years or so. Two further revised editions of this brilliant book appeared in 1953 and 1956, with a completely re-written and enlarged edition coming in 1965. A classic of its kind, it is probably the most absorbing work dealing with children's literature that has yet appeared. In October 1946 came his definitive study *Andrew Lang*, and in 1949 *The Story of Lewis Carroll*, a biography intended mainly for younger readers. He was granted a William Noble Research Fellowship at Liverpool University between 1950 and 1952 and during this period published his biography of *A. E. W. Mason* (1952) and prepared *The Diaries of Lewis Carroll*, which were published in two volumes in 1953 under his editorship. *Fifty Years of Peter Pan* appeared in 1954 and gave full details of every production of the play up to that time. He produced five of the useful 'Bodley Head Monographs' on children's authors: *Lewis Carroll* (1960), *J. M. Barrie* (1960), *Mrs Molesworth* (1961), *C. S. Lewis* (1963) and *Andrew Lang* (1962). In 1962 he published the *Lewis Carroll Handbook* (originally by Williams and Madan) in a revised, augmented edition, brought completely up to date to 1960. *Authors and Places* (1963) was an entertaining book about well-known children's authors and the places where they had lived, and *Kipling and the Children* (1965) was a study of Kipling's stories for children. Apart from all these contributions to the study of literary figures (mainly of children's writers), he has been a prolific author in other fields of books for young readers. His children's novels include: *The Wonderful Stranger* (1950), *The Luck of the Lynns* (1952), *The Secret of Rusticoker* (1953), *The Theft of the Golden Cat* (1954), *Mystery at Mycenae* (1957) (in which he told the story of Helen of Troy as a modern detective story), *The Land of the High Tiger* (1958) and *The Luck of Troy* (1961). His collections and re-tellings include: *King Arthur and His Knights of the Round Table* (1953), *Old Greek Fairy Tales, Modern Fairy Stories* (1955), *Fairy Stories* (1957), *The Adventures of Robin Hood* (1956), *Land Beyond the North* (1958), *Tales of the Greek Heroes* (1958), *The Tale of Troy* (1958) – these last two original Puffin titles being combined in *The Heroes of Greece and Troy* (1960) – *The Saga of Asgard* (1960), *Myths of the Norsemen* (1960), *Once Long Ago* (in which he collected and re-told seventy stories from fifty countries) (1962), *Thunder of the Gods* (Norse legends), *A Book of Myths* (1964), *Tales from Shakespeare* (1964), *Tales the*

Muses Told (shorter Greek Myths) (1965), *Ten Tales of Detection* (ed.) (1967), *Tales of Ancient Egypt* (1967), *Sir Lancelot of the Lake* (1967), *Folk Tales of the World* (1967), and *Jason and the Golden Fleece* (1968). He has also edited *A Book of Verse for Children* (1961), *A Century of Humorous Verse* (Everyman), and *The Book of Nonsense* (1956). *Into Other Worlds* (1957) was a history of space-flight in fiction, 'from Lucien to C. S. Lewis'. And, as a change, he has also published a book of poetry, *The Singing Rose, and other poems*. He lives at Poulton-Lancelyn, Bebington, Wirral, Cheshire, in the manor which his ancestors have held for 900 years (two of his children's stories, *The Luck of the Lynns* and *The Theft of the Golden Cat*, are set in his manor, disguised as 'Mereford Hall', its ancient Saxon name). Roger Lancelyn Green is married and has two sons and one daughter.

Greene, Graham

Born on 2nd October 1904, at Berkhamsted, Hertfordshire, where his father was a headmaster, and educated there and at Balliol College, Oxford. From 1926–30 he worked as a sub-editor on *The Times*. His first novel was *The Man Within* in 1929 and he subsequently published many other famous novels, thrillers, travel books and plays. He finds a place here because of his four charming books for children: *The Little Train* (1946), *The Little Fire-Engine* (1950), *The Little Horse-Bus* (1952) and *The Little Steam-Roller* (1953). All illustrated vividly by Dorothy Craigie, they tell simple and entertaining stories of vehicles becoming mixed up in thrilling adventures with criminals, etc. A fact not generally known, perhaps, is that Greene is a cousin, twice-removed, of Robert Louis Stevenson.

'Grey Owl'

Real name: Archie Belaney. Born in 1885 in Hastings, England, and brought up by two aunts there. At fifteen he went to seek his fortune in Canada, where he eventually lived with a tribe of Indians and adopted their way of life, dressing and existing just as they did. The tribe gave him the name 'Wa-Sha-Quon-Asin' ('He Who Walks by Night') and he called himself 'Grey Owl'. He served in the Canadian Army during the First

World War, was wounded in 1917, returning to Canada after being invalided out, and lived with the Ojibways tribe of Indians. In all, he lived with the Indians for thirty-seven years, spoke their tongue, lived their life and married an Indian girl, who later bore him a daughter, 'Little Dawn'. He began writing in the late 1920s, and in 1930 *Country Life* ran a series of his articles, publishing them as a book in 1931 under the title *Men of the Last Frontier*. In 1935 a specially written book, about the life and ways of the Indian in Canada, was published in Britain; titled *Pilgrims of the Wild* it became an immediate best-seller. Grey Owl's account of his life and of his untiring work in saving the beaver from extinction was told in his own unorthodox style and was fresh and unusual. In the same year *The Adventures of Sajo and Her Beaver People* appeared; it was a children's book telling of a little Indian girl and her brother who lived in the Canadian woods and of the two beaver kittens they adopted. In 1936 Grey Owl visited Britain and undertook an extensive lecture tour, which was enormously successful. It was followed by a later, second tour, of which the climax was a Royal Command to lecture at Buckingham Palace before the late King George VI, Queen Elizabeth, and the two little Princesses, Elizabeth and Margaret. Also in 1936 came Grey Owl's final book, *Tales of an Empty Cabin*, stories of Indian and wild life in Canda. He died suddenly, in April 1937. In 1939 Lovat Dickson produced *Half-Breed*, which told the fascinating story of this romantic and unusual character. There was also *The Book of Grey Owl*, which consisted of selections from his writings.

Grimm, Jacob Ludwig Karl, and Wilhelm Karl

Known universally as the Brothers Grimm. Jacob was born in 1785 and Wilhelm in 1786, both in Hanau, Hesse, Germany, the sons of a lawyer. Their father died when they were children and their mother had a hard struggle in bringing up the whole family of six by herself. With the financial aid of an aunt, Jacob and Wilhelm attended the University of Marburg and qualified successfully as lawyers. Jacob became assistant to one of his Professors at Marburg, Friedrich Savigny, who fostered in him a deep interest in early German literature and philology.

THE BOYS' OWN PAPER

No. 536.—Vol. XI   SATURDAY, APRIL 20, 1889.   Price One Penny.
[ALL RIGHTS RESERVED.]

SIR LUDAR:
A 'PRENTICE STORY OF THE DAYS OF THE GREAT QUEEN BESS.
BY TALBOT BAINES REED,
Author of "The Master of the Shell," "A Dog with a Bad Name," "The Fifth Form at St. Dominic's," etc., etc.

47 The most famous, longest-running and – in its time – influential British boys' paper of them all: the '*B.O.P.*' Many distinguished authors and artists contributed to its pages over the paper's 88-year career. It ran from 1879 until 1967 and its title is perpetuated in an Annual

No. 17.—Vol. I.]   JANUARY 4, 1893.

CONTENTS.

THE HAUNTED HOUSE AT HOE. (*New Serial Story.*) By E. EVERETT GREEN. *See pages* 266–267

"THE PRUSSIAN FLUNG HIS ARMS UP WITH A CONVULSIVE MOVEMENT . . . THEN FELL HEADLONG." (*See page* 259.)

48 and 49 Typical covers of *Chums*, an extremely entertaining boys' paper
which specialised in stories of adventure, school and sport. It boasted many

PRICE ONE PENNY.] A CHAT ABOUT DR. W. G. GRACE.

No. 46.—Vol. I.] JULY 26, 1893. [ALL RIGHTS RESERVED.

CONTENTS.

"HE KICKED OFF HIS SHOES, AND PLUNGED IN ALL DRESSED AS HE WAS." (*See page* 722.)

well-known contributors and was noted for its colourful and exciting illustrations. *Chums* ran from 1892 until 1934, continuing as an Annual until 1941

50 *The Captain* was aimed primarily at public and grammar schoolboys and, although it featured stories of most types, concentrated upon the school story of quality. P. G. Wodehouse wrote his earliest fiction for it and John Buchan contributed a serial in 1910. The cover of the magazine's half-yearly bound volume is reproduced above. *The Captain* ran from 1899 until 1924

Wilhelm was also fascinated by the subjects and he and his brother eventually obtained private positions, chiefly as University librarians, which enabled them to pursue their own studies. Jacob created the world-famous 'Grimm's Law', which deals with the development of words from one language to another. Both brothers carried out deep researches into the traditional folk-lore and legendary tales of Germany, talking with old peasants in various parts of the countryside and gathering together different variations of similar tales which had been handed down by word of mouth throughout successive generations. They wrote down each story substantially as they heard it, adding no embellishments, but just polishing up an odd phrase here and there. The first volume of their collection of stories, *Kinder-und-Hausmärchen* (*Nursery and Household Tales*) appeared in 1812, during the winter of Napoleon's epic retreat from Moscow; the second volume was published in 1815 (year of the Battle of Waterloo), with a third volume of historical commentary and notes appearing in 1822. Critical reception was cold and unenthusiastic, with the work even being banned in Vienna as 'superstitious'. Nevertheless, the work was an immediate success with the public and the more discerning literary figures of the day and sold well. It was soon being translated into many languages, with the first English translation by Edgar Taylor appearing in two volumes in 1823 and 1826, under the title *German Popular Tales*. This first English edition was vividly illustrated by George Cruikshank and contained a selection of fifty-five stories from the complete collection of over 200 in the original German version. The stories soon won world-wide fame and popularity, despite the violence and ferocity of many. They dealt mainly with giants, dwarfs, elves, princes and princesses, witches, enchantments and spells and were earthier and crueller than Hans Andersen's and Perrault's. Some of the best-known include: *Snow-White*, *Rumpelstiltskin*, *Tom Thumb*, *Hans in Luck*, *The Golden Goose*, *The Valiant Little Tailor*, *The Frog-King*, *Hansel and Gretel*, *Puss in Boots* and *Rapunzel*. As well as their famous collection of folk and fairy tales the Brothers Grimm also published a *History of the German Language*, a *German Grammar* and a vast *Dictionary* so lengthy and complex that it was still uncompleted at their deaths. They also produced learned works on

German mythology and philology. In general, Jacob could be described as the great scholar of the partnership and Wilhelm the fine writer and storyteller. The brothers were inseparable throughout their lifetime; even when Wilhelm was married 'Uncle Jacob' lived with the family quite happily, with the brothers sharing the same study and books. Both brothers were still writing and researching busily when they died, Jacob in 1863 and Wilhelm in 1859.

Guillot, René

Born 1900 in France and studied at the Faculté de Bordeaux. In 1923 he went to French West Africa as a schoolteacher, specialising in mathematics, and taught at St Louis and Dakar. He remained in this territory for twenty-five years (with the exception of the war years), gaining an unrivalled knowledge and experience of the native and jungle life there. He would often go hunting in the deepest regions of the jungle with a handful of black hunters. At other times he would listen to villagers telling the old jungle legends and traditional tales. He would also trek into the jungle, or up the River Niger in a small boat, watching and learning the ways of the animals, fishes and birds. He studied, too, the primitive beliefs and customs of the African tribes and grew to be accepted by them as a friend. During the Second World War Guillot served in France and Germany, became a Chevalier de la Légion d'Honneur and was awarded the Croix de Guerre and other decorations. After the war he returned to teaching in French West Africa for a time, then, in 1948, returned to Paris and continued his teaching at a school there. Around this time he published his first story – a detective tale which won an award. A distinguished publisher, who happened to be one of the judges on this occasion, talked with Guillot, became fascinated by his stories of life in the jungle and persuaded him to begin writing for children. His first book for young readers was *The White Shadow* (France 1948, Britain 1959), a haunting story of a French girl in Africa who makes friends with an African child. *Companions of Fortune* (France 1950, Britain 1952) was an outstanding story of adventure on the high seas with buccaneers. Soon came a quartet of memorable animal stories:

Sama (1950, 1952), about a baby elephant; *Sirga* (1951, 1953), the adventures of an African child and a lion-cub; *Oworo* (1951, 1954), a chimpanzee; and *Kpo the Leopard* (1955, 1955). Among his many other titles are: *Wind of Chance* (France 1951, Britain 1955), *The 397th White Elephant* (1952, 1954), *Beyond the Bambassu* (1952, 1961), *The Fantastic Brother* (1953, 1961), *Riders of the Wind* (1953, 1960), *The King's Corsair* (1953, 1954), *The Animal Kingdom* (1955, 1957), *A Boy and Five Huskies* (1955, 1957), *The Elephants of Sargabal* (1956, 1956), *Elephant Road* (1957, 1959), *King of the Cats* (1959, 1962), *Grishka and Brother Bear* (1960, 1965), *The Stranger from the Sea* (Britain 1967), *King of Reindeer* (1967) and *Little Dog Lost* (1968). The majority of Guillot's books are set in the country he knows so well – Africa – and his work has been compared several times to that of Kipling and the famous *Jungle Books*; both writers have that rare genius for being able to bring alive the animal and human inhabitants of the jungle on the printed page and to re-create the scents and atmosphere of the forest in a few brilliantly chosen words. Ever-present in his stories is the theme of friendship – between white and coloured men, and between men and animals. His books have won many awards including, in 1950, the Prix Jeunesse (for *Sama*); in 1953, the Belgian Prix M. Proumen (for *The Wind of Chance*); in 1956, the German Children's Book Prize (for *Sirga*); in 1958, the Prix Enfance du Monde (for *Grishka and the Bear*); and, in 1964, the Hans Christian Andersen Prize for his complete works. Guillot retired from teaching in 1962, but still writes prolifically (he has averaged around two books a year over the past sixteen years). Both his wife and son are writers too. Today he lives in Vincennes, near Paris, and in the Saintonge.

Guthrie, Thomas Anstey

See: Anstey, F.

Habberton, John

Born on 24th February 1842, in Brooklyn, New York. Originally worked as a salesman, telegraph operator and printer, before serving with the Union army during the American Civil War. When he left the army around 1866 he entered journalism and worked for various newspapers. From 1876–93 he was literary and dramatic critic of the *New York Herald*. In 1876 he published his first book and the one by which he is almost solely remembered – *Helen's Babies*. It was the humorous story of how a young bachelor uncle looked after his two high-spirited, incredibly mischievous nephews (aged five and three) during the children's parents' holiday. The episodes were based on Habberton's own experiences with his two small sons on one occasion when his wife was away. The boys (in the book) were called Budge and Toddie. The book was a huge popular success with the public, young and old, and has been in print ever since. Habberton tried to repeat his initial success and wrote two sequels – *Other People's Children* (1877) and *Budge and Toddie* (1908) – but nothing else he published ever approached the success of *Helen's Babies*. His other books included: *The Worst Boy in Town* (1880), *Some Boys' Doing* (1901), *The Chautauquans* (1891) and *Caleb Wright* (1901). He also wrote a successful stage play, *Deacon Crankett* (1880). He died, on his birthday, 24th February 1921.

Hadath, Gunby

Born *c*. 1880 in Owersby, Lincolnshire, and educated at St Edmund's School, Canterbury, Kent, and Peterhouse College, Cambridge. Later famous for his excellent public school stories, Hadath himself was something of a real-life school story hero. He was Captain of his school and brilliant at practically every sport. At Cambridge he won a Classical Tripos M.A. degree and his college colours for rugby, soccer and cricket. On leaving Cambridge he taught at a private school in Devon and later became Senior Classical Master at Guildford Grammar School, in Surrey. His first story, *Foozle's Brilliant Idea*, appeared in *The Captain* in 1909 and he soon became a regular and prolific contributor to this boys' magazine, as well as to others such as *Chums* and *Boy's Own Paper*. His articulate and highly intelligent (as well as often very funny) school stories often spotlighted real-life social problems. In one of his *Captain* serials, *Conquering Claybury* (later reprinted in book form as

Schoolboy Grit), for example, the plot concerned the difficulties of a lone council schoolboy pitchforked into public school life – anticipating Warren Chetham Strode's controversial stage play (and later film) *The Guinea Pig* by thirty-five years. Perhaps Hadath's most popular stories were about his creation 'Sparrow' – a wry, thoughtful and scheming schoolboy who invariably got the upper hand of his various adversaries. Three books featuring the character were *Sparrow in Search of Expulsion*, *Sparrow in Search of Fame* and *Sparrow Gets Going*. Hadath's first book, in fact, was a formidable work on ancient philosophy! Some of his more typical titles were: *Grim Work at Bodlands*, *The Secret of the Code*, *Go-Bang-Garry*, *Against the Clock*, *Carey of Cobhouse*, *Brent of Gatehouse*, *The Fattest Head in the Fifth*, *Living Up To It*, *According to Brown Minor* (originally *The Feats of Foozle*), *Major and Minor*, *What's in a Name?*, *Fight It Out*, *No Robbery*, *Honours Easy*, *Pillar to Post*, *The Atom*, *The Swinger*, *The March of Time*, *The New House at Oldborough*, *Revolt at Fallas* and *The New School at Shropp*. He also wrote under the pseudonyms 'JOHN MOWBRAY', 'FELIX O'GRADY' and 'JAMES DUNCAN'. Many of his books were translated into French and Scandinavian and even Braille, and were also published in the United States. He additionally wrote several hundred popular songs, including the successful *Down the Vale* and *In My Garden*. He saw active service in the First World War. He subsequently became a member of the Inner Temple, in London, and on leaving schoolteaching coached pupils for the Bar. He also kept up with his cricket and played for the Gentlemen of Surrey. His wife (whose twin sister was Matron at Dulwich College for many years) alone could read his handwriting, and typed all his stories before sending them to the publishers. Hadath lived in Cricklewood, north London, for many years, but usually spent the winter at St Gervais-Les-Bains, in the French Alps (and was made a Citoyen d'Honneur of the town). He died in January 1954, having more than sixty books to his credit.

Haggard, Sir Henry Rider

Born on 22nd June 1856, at Bradenham, Norfolk, one of a family of ten children and son of the local Lord of the Manor and barrister. Educated at Garsington, near Oxford, and Ipswich Grammar School. In 1875 he went to South Africa as private secretary to Sir Henry Bulwer, Governor of Natal, and from 1877–79 he held the post of Registrar and Master of the High Court in the Transvaal. During his stay in South Africa he became fascinated by its people and its history, making friends with several leading Zulus. He returned to England in 1879 and married. After a brief return to South Africa he began to study for the Bar in London (he was called to the Bar in 1884). His first book was *Cetewayo and His White Neighbours* (1882), which dealt with recent South African history. Two long novels, *Dawn* (1883) and *The Witch's Head* (1884) were received only moderately and Haggard was feeling somewhat disillusioned with literary endeavours when, during a chance conversation with his brother, an argument arose about Stevenson's *Treasure Island*, at the time a sensational best-seller. Haggard bet his brother a shilling that he could write an adventure story just as good. The bet was accepted – and for the next six weeks Haggard spent his evenings (his days were taken up with his legal career) working on a book he had decided to call *King Solomon's Mines*. Several publishers turned it down, until Cassell's finally agreed to accept it on Andrew Lang's strong recommendation (though Lang had not, as yet, even met Haggard). *King Solomon's Mines* was published in the autumn of 1885 and its reception was tremendous, from both public and critics alike. Some even said it was better than *Treasure Island*. Haggard had won his shilling bet . . . From this time onward, Haggard published numerous 'romances' of adventure, legend and history, especially liking the backgrounds of Africa, the Zulus of South Africa, Mexico and Egypt. Among the titles were: *Allan Quatermain* (a sequel to *King Solomon's Mines*) (1887), *She* (1887), *Cleopatra* (1889), *The World's Desire* (in collaboration with Andrew Lang) (1890), *Eric Brighteyes* (1891), *Nada the Lily* (1892), *Montezuma's Daughter* (1893), *The People of the Mist* (1894), *Ayesha: the Return of She* (1905), *Queen Sheba's Ring* (1910), *The Ivory Child* (1916) and *She and Allan* (1921). On his first writing success Haggard had given up his law practice and retired to Norfolk to become a full-time author. He made rural economy his hobby and his relaxation, and published several books on farming and allied subjects in between his more eagerly awaited 'romances'. He loved his home at Ditchingham, Norfolk, where most of his books after 1889 were written. In later life he won a fine reputation as an acknowledged expert in both agricultural matters and international affairs and problems, in which he took a great interest, and also became a local magistrate. In 1911 he was knighted for his public services and in 1919 was made a Knight Commander of the British Empire. But it is for his best-selling novels that the general public best remember H. Rider Haggard. He died in a London nursing home on 14th May 1925.

Hale, Kathleen

Born in Scotland and educated at Manchester High School for Girls, Manchester School of Art and Reading University College of Art. After doing a certain amount of illustration work she wrote and illustrated her first book about the now-famous 'Orlando' in 1938; titled *Orlando the Marmalade Cat: A Camping Holiday*, it introduced Orlando, the sophisticated cat with a coat striped exactly like marmalade and two glowing green eyes, together with his tabby wife, Grace, and their kittens. The book was big in format, vividly presented in excellent colour lithography, and told a warmly amusing story of humanised, talking cats. Kathleen Hale's pictures were on the grand scale and beautifully detailed. She is said to have based her characterisations and illustrations upon her own cats. Orlando caught children's imaginations at once and the book sold many thousands of copies in that immediately pre-war period and during the early part of the war, when the popular marmalade cat brought a touch of colour into children's otherwise austere and worrying days. The next Orlando book appeared in 1941 and was *Orlando's Evening Out*. A whole series followed and included: *Orlando's Home Life* (1942), *Orlando Buys a Farm* (1942), *Orlando's Silver Wedding* (1944), *Orlando Becomes a Doctor* (1944), *Orlando's Invisible Pyjamas* (1947), *Orlando's Trip Abroad* (1949), *Orlando Keeps a Dog* (1949), *Orlando the Judge* (1950), *Orlando's Seaside Holiday* (1952), *Orlando's Zoo* (1954), *Orlando's Magic Carpet* (1958), *The Frisky Housewife* (1959), *Orlando Buys a Cottage* (1963) and *Orlando and the Three Graces* (1965). Kathleen Hale also published several

Peep-Show Books, Puss in Boots, Henrietta the Faithful Hen (1943) and *Manda* (1952) – the latter being about a Jersey cow who went on a visit to Ireland.

Hale, Lucretia Peabody

Born on 2nd September 1820, in Boston, USA, and was the elder sister of Edward Everett Hale, the clergyman and short story writer. She led an uneventful life and wrote two or three minor novels. When she was in her fifties she used to tell her friends' children stories about an imaginary family called the Peterkins. The tales grew so popular and aroused so much laughter and amusement – among adults as well as the children – that she was eventually persuaded to publish them. *The Peterkin Papers* appeared originally in episodic form in numbers of *Young Folks* and subsequently continued in *St Nicholas Magazine* in the late 1870s. They made their first appearance in book form in 1880 and a second edition was published in 1886, including an additional story called *The Peterkins at the Farm*. The Peterkin family, who lived in Boston, consisted of Mr and Mrs Peterkin, Solomon John, Agamemnon, Elizabeth Eliza and the three little boys (who were never named but who loved wearing their india-rubber boots). The book comprised twenty-odd episodes in which they never took the obvious solution to any problem, but went the most roundabout way possible of overcoming their difficulty. Their problems were usually solved by the sensible 'Lady from Philadelphia', who appeared in most of the tales for just that purpose. The stories are very funny and their humour springs from the very absurdity of the situations. The book has been beloved, chiefly by American children, for several generations of readers and has never been out of print in the USA. In 1886 Miss Hale wrote a sequel, *The Last of the Peterkins*. She died on 12th June 1900.

Hamilton, Charles Harold St John

The first eighteen years of this astonishing writer – probably the most prolific of all time – remain relatively shrouded in doubt, mainly because he wished this to be. As a result of tireless researches by various members of the Old Boys' Book

Club, however, the following brief details of Hamilton's early life have been uncovered (though only time and further enquiries will tell whether or not they are fully accurate).

Charles Hamilton was born on 8th August 1876, in Oak Street, Ealing, Middlesex (now London). He was sixth in a family of five brothers and three sisters. He was probably educated at a private school.

He wrote his first story in 1894 at the age of seventeen and, realising he had some sort of gift for writing entertaining boys' stories quickly and easily, he was soon turning out stories by the hundred, mainly for the firm of Trapps, Holmes and Co., who published a variety of boys' and juvenile papers and comics. Using over twenty pen-names, he contributed every type of story – school, adventure, travel, crime, humour and even light romance. In the autumn of 1906 he created the public school St Jim's in the pages of *Pluck*, while in the spring of 1907 *The Gem* was launched as a weekly boys' paper and soon characters such as Tom Merry and Arthur Augustus D'Arcy were popular with millions all over the world. *The Gem* ran until the end of 1939, when it ceased publication owing to the Second World War. In February 1908 came No. 1 of another new paper called *The Magnet* and before long Billy Bunter (the 'Fat Owl' of Greyfriars School), Harry Wharton and Co (comprising Wharton, Bob Cherry, Frank Nugent, Hurree Jamset Ram Singh and Johnny Bull), Herbert Vernon-Smith, Lord Mauleverer, Horace Coker, Loder, Wingate, Skinner, Snoop and Stott, and Messrs Locke, Quelch, Prout and Hacker, together with the rest of the inhabitants of the magical world of Greyfriars, had been introduced to a vast public which read about them unceasingly until the paper finished in 1940 (another war casualty). Hamilton wrote about Greyfriars under the name 'FRANK RICHARDS' and of St Jim's as 'MARTIN CLIFFORD'. Early in 1915 he began his stories of Rookwood, in the *Boys' Friend*, under the name 'OWEN CONQUEST'. For the same paper he wrote about the Rio Kid, under the name 'RALPH REDWAY'; and in *Modern Boy*, under his own name this time, about the adventures of Ken King of the Islands. He also started off the stories about Bessie Bunter (Billy's sister) and the girls of Cliff House in *Schoolfriend* as 'HILDA RICHARDS' (these tales were subsequently taken over by other writers). He also wrote the bulk of the yearly *Holiday Annuals*, and many of his original school stories were reprinted in the monthly *Schoolboys' Own Library*. He wrote under a large number of pseudonyms, many of which are still undiscovered. He created nearly fifty fictional public schools. After the Second World War (when Hamilton was seventy) came the brand-new series of 'Bunter books' – thirty-eight of them. There came too the *Billy Bunter's Own* annuals, the *Tom Merry Annuals*, the Tom Merry and Rookwood series and the Greyfriars Armada and Merlin paperback titles. And so it went on until, over the years, a 'cult' grew up around Charles Hamilton's writings, the Old Boys' Book Clubs were formed, with Hamilton's works taking a lion's share of the proceedings; nostalgic devotees of Greyfriars, St Jim's and Rookwood built up collections of the old papers – and dealers sold them at inflated prices. Hamilton – a kindly, scholarly and quietly humorous man, who took to wearing a skull cap in later years – certainly started something when he created Billy Bunter and Tom Merry. Then, on Christmas Eve, 1961, he died in his sleep – and millions mourned. The man is dead – but his characters carry on and still appear in various forms today. Especially Billy Bunter – who is one character who will never die.

Hardy, Thomas

Born on 2nd June 1840, in Upper Bockhampton, Dorset, the son of a builder and stonemason, and a descendant of Nelson's famous flag-captain of Trafalgar fame. A weak and delicate child, he was first taught by his mother at home, then at four different schools, the final one being Dorchester Grammar School, founded by one of his own ancestors and of which he later became a governor himself. On leaving school in 1856 he was apprenticed to an ecclesiastical architect in Dorchester and later studied Gothic architecture under Sir Arthur Blomfield in London, subsequently becoming a practising architect for six years. All this time he was busily writing poetry, none of which he could get published. His first published work was a humorous sketch called *How I Built Myself a House*, which appeared in *Chambers' Journal* in 1865. In 1871 he published (at his own expense) his first novel, *Desperate*

Remedies. It created no stir among reviewers or readers, but two further novels followed, *Under the Greenwood Tree* (1872) and *A Pair of Blue Eyes* (1873). In 1874 came his first major success, *Far From the Madding Crowd*, followed by several further novels, including such titles as *The Return of the Native* (1878), *The Trumpet-Major* (1880), *The Mayor of Casterbridge* (1886), *The Woodlanders* (1887) and his most famous book, *Tess of the D'Urbervilles* (1891). Most of his stories were set in or around his native county of Dorset, which he always called by its ancient name of Wessex. Many of his books aroused strong resentment and controversy among the eminently respectable and strait-laced Victorians, who took exception to reading about married women falling in love with other men, unmarried men and women living together, illegitimate children and so on, despite the masterly way in which Hardy portrayed his troubled characters. *Tess* upset so many people that Hardy was, in turn, upset by readers' reactions to his novels. This may have been one reason why, soon after the appearance of *Tess*, he turned aside from his adult books to write his one and only story for children. Titled *Our Exploits at West Poley*, it ran in the American magazine *Household* from November 1892 to April 1893; it did not appear in book form until 1952 in Britain. The story tells of two teenage boys in a Somerset village who change the course of an underground stream, with unexpected and hilarious results. The hot atmosphere of the setting and the characters of the boys and their neighbours are beautifully evoked and, on laying the story down, the reader wonders that Hardy did not write other children's tales. In his later career he concentrated upon poetry and his reputation in this category stands very high. He received the Order of Merit in 1910 and held several other distinctions, including honorary degrees of Oxford, Cambridge, St Andrews, Bristol and Aberdeen. He died on 11th January 1928, his ashes being buried in the Poets' Corner at Westminster Abbey.

Harnett, Cynthia Mary

Born in 1893 in Kensington and educated at private schools. Studied at the Chelsea School of Art and then under her artist-writer cousin, the late Vernon Stokes. Collaborated with

Stokes during the 1930s on several books for children, chiefly picture books about country life; one example was *David's New World* (1937), about a boy and the animals he encounters in the country. Cynthia Harnett and Vernon Stokes produced several further animal stories/picture books, typical titles being: *Mudlarks*, *Bobtail Pup*, *Getting to Know Dogs*, etc. In 1949 Miss Harnett wrote her first historical novel for children, *The Great House*, which told of an architect's life around 1700. In 1951 came *The Wool-Pack*, for which she was awarded the Carnegie Medal for that year; it was the story of the son of a Cotswold wool-merchant towards the end of the fifteenth century. Other books include: *Ring Out Bow Bells!* (1953), set in London when Dick Whittington was Mayor and culminating in Henry the Fifth's triumphant return there after the Battle of Agincourt; *The Load of Unicorn* (1959), about one of Caxton's apprentices and giving some fascinating details about the early days of printing; and *Stars of Fortune*. Miss Harnett ensures that every tiny detail in her stories is historically accurate and that the settings and atmosphere are completely authentic. She illustrates her own books too, featuring not so much the story-line or action scenes as informative sketches of what the people wore in those days, what they ate, what they rode in, how they lived, and so on. In 1963 she published *Monasteries and Monks*, which was a history of many of the most famous English monasteries and of the monks associated with them.

Harris, Joel Chandler

Born on 9th December 1848, near Eatonton, Georgia, USA, the son of an Irish labourer. Educated locally, he began work, at the age of thirteen, as a 'printer's devil' on *The Countryman*, a weekly newspaper, and received much of his education from the paper's owner, Joseph Addison Turner. He grew up in the districts of the cotton plantations and came to know and love the Negroes who worked on them. He would listen for hours to their dialect, humour and unusual phraseology – and to the many stories they told one another. He soon began contributing the odd sketch or story to his paper, then, after two years on *The Countryman* (which was published at the Turnwold Plantation), Harris worked on newspapers in Macon, New Orleans and Savannah and finally, in 1876, joined the *Constitution* in Atlanta, where he stayed for twenty-four years. Among his early articles for this paper were a series of humorous sketches featuring the Negro and for them Harris drew on his own knowledge and experiences of the plantations. He had an uncanny ear for dialects and reproduced the Negro way of speaking entirely successfully. He created, as his chief character in those early sketches, an old Negro called Uncle Remus. On 20th July 1879 the first of his famous Uncle Remus animal tales appeared in the Atlanta *Constitution* – it was called *The Story of Mr Rabbit and Mr Fox, as told by Uncle Remus*. The stories soon gained tremendous popularity with all ages and, in 1880, a collection of thirty-four of them was published under the title *Uncle Remus: His Songs and Sayings*. The stories were supposed to be told by Uncle Remus, an aging plantation Negro, to amuse a small white boy, and were about such characters as Brer Rabbit, Brer Fox, Brer Wolf, etc., illustrating in a broadly humorous way how the smaller can outwit the bigger creature by various means; it was usually Brer Rabbit who triumphed, through his own mischief and cleverness, over the other animals. The tales are told in authentic Southern Negro dialect and are difficult to understand at once. As soon as the dialect has been mastered, the stories are outrageously enjoyable. There have been many modern 're-tellings' of the stories, however, for those who do not wish to tackle the dialect original versions. Several further 'Uncle Remus' books appeared, including: *Nights With Uncle Remus* (1883), *Uncle Remus and His Friends* (1892), *The Tar Baby, and Other Rhymes of Uncle Remus* (1904), *Told By Uncle Remus* (1905), *Uncle Remus and Brer Rabbit* (1906), *Uncle Remus and the Little Boy* (1910) and *Uncle Remus Returns* (1918) (the last two posthumously). Harris also wrote a series of stories especially for children, including: *Little Mr Thimblefinger* (1894), *Mr Rabbit at Home* (1895), *The Story of Aaron* (1895), *Aaron in the Wildwoods* (1897) and *Plantation Pageants* (1899). In 1892 he published an autobiographical novel called *On the Plantation: A Story of a Georgia Boy's Adventures During the War* (the American Civil War, of course). He also wrote many other collections of short stories for adult readers, as well as numerous sketches, articles and several novels, all primarily on life in the Southern States. In

1907 Harris and his son Julian started *Uncle Remus's Magazine*, with another well-known writer, Don Marquis, as associate editor. He continued to write new Uncle Remus stories for the magazine until his death, on 3rd July 1908.

Hatch, Richard W.

Born 1898, in Framingham, Massachusetts, USA, and educated at Pennsylvania University and Columbia University. A schoolmaster by profession (with M.A. and B.Sc. degrees) he wrote several adult novels and also a few children's books, the most notable of which were the two 'Lobster' stories – *The Curious Lobster* (1937) and *The Curious Lobster's Island* (1940). These two books were about the adventures of a kindly but very curious old lobster who wanted to find out all about things. With this in mind he travelled to dry land and made the acquaintance of a badger and a bear and the three became firm friends. Their adventures and humorous escapades are enjoyable and were popular around the late 'thirties and the 'forties, and were reprinted in 1951. Hatch served in the U.S. Navy in both World Wars.

Hauff, Wilhelm

Born on 27th November 1802, in Stuttgart, Germany, and educated at Tübingen University. In 1824 he became tutor to the children of General Baron Ernest Eugen von Heigel, the war minister. His first book appeared in 1825 and was a satire. The following year he wrote a historical novel, *Lichtenstein*, which became very popular. To amuse and interest his pupils Hauff wrote and told a number of stories, dealing mainly with Eastern subjects or fairies. He possessed a sound knowledge of both subjects, derived chiefly from the many hours he had spent, as child and youth, in browsing through his grandfather's large library. He collected his stories and published them in 1826, in Stuttgart, under the title *The Story Book for the Year 1826*; they were introduced to Britain in the 1840s and have since appeared in numerous anthologies and collections. The best-known are *The Caliph Stork* (sometimes titled *The Sultan Stork*), *Long-Nose the Dwarf*, *The Tale of Little Muck* and *The*

Cold Heart. Hauff published other adult books and some short poems, becoming editor of the *Stuttgart Morgenblatt* in 1827. He died on 18th November 1827, at the early age of twenty-four.

Hawkins, Sir Anthony Hope

See: Hope, Anthony

Hawthorne, Nathaniel

Born on 4th July 1804, in Salem, Massachusetts, USA, the son of a sea captain. His real name was Hathorne, but he inserted the 'w' when he began writing. His ancestry was Puritan and his forebears included one of the judges at the infamous Salem witch trials in the seventh century. At the age of seven Hawthorne suffered a bad injury to a foot during a game and until the affliction healed a few years later he could play no further sport and took to reading instead. In his early teens he spent a year or so living with his family by a remote lake in Maine, an area which made a deep impression upon him. He graduated from Bowdoin College in 1825, one of his class-mates being Henry Wadsworth Longfellow and another close friend (in the class before him) being Franklin Pierce, who was later elected fourteenth President of the U.S. (in 1852). He then returned to Salem and began writing numerous short stories and sketches, many of which appeared in S. G. Goodrich's magazine *The Token*. He also published (in 1928) an immature first novel, *Fanshawe*. He remained in Salem, almost in seclusion, for eleven years, emerging in 1836 to become editor of Goodrich's monthly *American Magazine of Useful and Entertaining Knowledge*. The following year he compiled the widely read *Peter Parley's Universal History*. Also in 1837 came a collection of his stories and sketches from various papers, magazines and annuals, *Twice Told Tales*, with a revised and enlarged edition following in 1842. From 1839–41 he worked in the Boston Custom House. In 1841 he published *Grandfather's Chair, or True Stories from New England History, 1620–1803*, in three volumes, and, in 1842, *Biographical Stories for Children*. After his marriage to Sophia Peabody in 1842 he went to live in a famous residence, The Old Manse, in Concord, continuing to write stories. In

1846 he returned once more to Salem to become Customs Surveyor, being dismissed three years later for political reasons. He celebrated this apparent setback by writing his greatest novel, *The Scarlet Letter* (1850). This established him as a major writer and soon afterwards he moved to Lenox, Massachusetts, and published another famous novel, *The House of the Seven Gables* (1851). It was at Lenox that Hawthorne wrote the first of his two most famous books for children – *A Wonder Book* (1852). It consisted of imaginative re-tellings of six classical myths – *The Gorgon's Head, The Golden Touch, The Paradise of Children, The Three Golden Apples, The Miraculous Pitcher* and *The Chimaera*. His versions were light-hearted and conversational (told as stories to a group of young children at a country house called Tanglewood), modernised and simplified. In some, the heroines are described as little girls instead of adult women, and much of the grandeur and tragedy of the Greek gods disappears. But Hawthorne's adaptations are enchanting re-creations in their own right and have delighted generations of children down the years. More important, they have led young readers to the original myths and legends, to discover the full stories for themselves . . . Six further re-tellings – *The Minotaur, The Pygmies, The Dragon's Teeth, Circe's Palace, The Pomegranate Seeds* and *The Golden Fleece* – followed in *Tanglewood Tales* (1853). In 1852 he bought Bronson Alcott's (father of Louisa May Alcott) house in Concord and wrote a campaign biography for his friend, Franklin Pierce. When Pierce was elected President of the United States that year, he appointed Hawthorne U.S. Consul at Liverpool, England, where the author stayed between 1853 and 1857. The Liverpool weather apparently did not agree with him, however, and he went to Italy in 1857 for two years, to regain his lost health. The last of his books to be published during his lifetime was *Our Old Home* (1863), an account of his life in England and on living with the English. He died in America on 19th May 1864.

Hemyng, Bracebridge

Born in 1841 and became a barrister of the Middle Temple but, it was said, never held a brief. Famous as the creator of the incredibly successful series of boys' stories about a tough, rakish, adventure-prone young man named Jack Harkaway. The first serial, *Jack Harkaway's Schooldays*, appeared in the magazine *Boys of England* in 1871. Many sequels followed with such titles as *Jack Harkaway at Oxford, Jack Harkaway's Adventures Round the World, Jack Harkaway Among the Pirates* and so on, through every imaginable permutation. The stories were also published in the USA and when Hemyng visited New York he received a tremendous reception from his American admirers. He also wrote countless other stories for both British and American publications. He died in 1901.

Henty, George Alfred

Born on 8th December 1832, at Trumpington, near Cambridge, the eldest son of a stockbroker, and educated at Westminster School and Caius College, Cambridge. He left Cambridge without gaining his degree when he volunteered for service on the outbreak of the Crimean War. He originally went to the Crimea in the Hospital Commissariat in 1855, later moving over to the Purveyor's Department. His first essay into the literary world came when the London *Morning Advertiser* accepted a group of articles based on the siege of Sebastopol. Soon afterwards he was promoted to the post of Purveyor to the Forces. He subsequently resigned his commission, having grown weary of his work. He tried his hand at mining, both in Wales and abroad, but did not find this to his liking either. In 1865 he joined the staff of *The Standard* in London and wrote leaders and reviews and became a journalist-of-all-work. Growing restless again he volunteered to go as a Special Correspondent to cover the Austro-Italian war. He next went to Abyssinia with Napier, accompanied Garibaldi in his Tyrolese campaign, reported the Franco-German war, starved in Paris during the Commune and then turned south to Spain, to rough it in the Pyrenees throughout the Carlist Insurrection. He also toured Asiatic Russia, America, and accompanied the Prince of Wales (later King Edward VII) on his tour of India in 1875. He also covered the Turkish war with Servia in 1876. After all these travels, campaigning experiences, many adventures and journalistic work, he was well equipped for his main writing activities, which were still to come. He had written two or three inconspicuous adult novels in the late 1860s/early 1870s, as well as descriptions of two of the campaigns he had observed: *The March to Magdala* (1868) and *The March to Coomassie* (1874). But his fame and his reputation rest upon his eighty-odd adventure stories for boys, most of which were founded on well-known historical events, wars and battles. Henty based many of his books upon his own experiences as a war correspondent, and if he set a story in a campaign or period with which he was unfamiliar he would carry out weeks of painstaking research to ensure that he was correct in every historical and geographical aspect. His stories were full of action and excitement so that the young reader could enjoy them as 'rattling good yarns' while painlessly, almost unconsciously, absorbing the real-life history in them. As Henty's fellow boys' writer and biographer, George Manville Fenn, wrote: Henty 'taught more lasting history to boys than all the schoolmasters of his generation'. His first book for boys was *Out on the Pampas* in 1868 and typical subsequent titles from his prolific output included: *The Young Franc-Tireurs* (1872), *The Young Buglers* (1880), *In Times of Peril* (1881), *Under Drake's Flag* (1883), *Facing Death* (1883), *With Clive in India* (1884), *The Young Colonists* (1884), *The Lion of the North* (1885), *St George for England* (1885), *In Freedom's Cause* (1885), *The Young Carthaginian* (1886), *With Wolfe in Canada* (1887), *Bonnie Prince Charlie* (1887), *The Cat of Bubastes* (1889), *Captain Bayley's Heir* (1888), *Redskin and Cowboy* (1892), *Beric the Briton* (1893), *The Tiger of Mysore* (1895), *Through Russian Snows* (1896), *With Buller in Natal* (1901), *With Roberts to Pretoria* (1902), *With Kitchener in the Sudan* (1903) and *With the Allies to Pekin* (1904). For around thirty years he averaged three books a year, often lengthy ones comprising 100,000–150,000 words each. His favourite method was to lie at his ease on a sofa in his beloved, trophy-hung, dog-haunted study, at his house in Lavender Hill, London, smoking a well-worn pipe and dictating his current story to a secretary. For many years his titles regularly sold 150,000 copies a year in Britain and 50,000 in America. Several of his stories were serialised in the famous *Boy's Own Paper*. In 1880 Henty succeeded W. H. G. Kingston as editor of Sampson Low's short-lived boys' magazine *Union Jack*. Previously he had been editor for a time of Beeton's *Boys'*

Own Magazine. George Henty – a huge, burly man with massive full beard and immense energy and resourcefulness – was one of the most popular, prolific and best-selling boys' writers of all time. His books still sell well today and there are currently over thirty of his titles in print in Britain alone. He was married twice and had two sons and two daughters. His favourite recreation was yachting and it was on his yacht in Weymouth Harbour, Dorset, that he died on 16th November 1902. His obituary in the London *Sketch* read: 'By the death of George Henty, the boys of England lose one of the best friends they ever had . . .'

Higson, Kit

Born in Blackburn, Lancashire. Wrote regularly for several newspapers and magazines in the 1930s, including the *Clarion* and *Red Magazine*, and also contributed to BBC programmes. She was a prolific writer and turned out many novels, plays, sketches, short stories, articles and children's books. Her two outstanding achievements in this last field were two children's novels – *Hundreds and Thousands* (1937) and *Cop Shooter* (1942). The first was about a lively, good-humoured family and their neighbours, with lacings of broad humour and sentiment, and the second, a touching story of an orphan boy and his faithful dog. Both stories are still in print today and have retained their popularity over the years.

Hildick, E. W.

Born 1925 in Bradford, Yorkshire, and educated at Wheelwright Grammar School, Dewsbury, and Leeds Training College. Worked as a library assistant and then a laboratory assistant before serving in the RAF for two years. He then trained to become a teacher and for four years taught in a boys' secondary modern school in Dewsbury. While teaching he began writing short stories and articles for various publications and, in 1957, won the Tom Gallon Award for Short Story Writing. He had long toyed with the idea of writing a series of stories aimed especially at secondary modern schoolboys, particularly those in the industrial areas of Britain, and in 1958 he published *Jim Starling*. The hero was an ordinary, working-class pupil at the Cement Street Secondary Modern School for Boys in an industrial town called Smogbury – a decided change from the popular public school story heroes of past eras! Hildick's realistic and fast-moving style at once caught on, particularly with the kind of readers he was aiming at, and a whole series of 'Jim Starling' books followed: *Jim Starling and the Agency* (1958), *Jim Starling's Holiday* (1960), *Jim Starling and the Colonel* (1960), *Jim Starling Takes Over* (1964) and *Jim Starling and the Spotted Dog* (1964). Other boys' stories, written in similar vein, include: *The Boy at the Window* (1960), *Mapper Munday's Treasure Hunt* (1963), *Meet Lemon Kelly* (1963), *Birdy Jones* (1963), *Lemon Kelly and the Home-Made Boy* (1967), *Calling Questors Four* (1967), *Birdy and the Group* (1968), *Louie's Lot* (1968) and *Louie's S.O.S.* (1968). *Lucky Les* (1967) was an entertaining story about a cat. E. W. Hildick has also written adult novels.

Hoffmann, Ernst Theodor Amadeus

Born in Königsberg, Germany, on 24th January 1776. After practising as a lawyer, he took up a musical career, both composing and writing musical criticism. His opera 'Undine' was very popular during the early 1800s. In 1814 he began to write the series of romantic and fantastic stories for which he is best remembered today. His most famous single fairy story is 'The Nutcracker and the Mouse King' (1816), which was adapted by Alexandre Dumas the Elder in 1845 as 'Les Aventures d'un Casse-Noisette'; it was from this version that Tchaikovsky was inspired to compose his popular 'Casse-Noisette [or Nutcracker] Suite' which was also the music to the ballet, first produced in 1892. Another of Hoffmann's stories inspired the ballet 'Coppelia', by Delibes, and a further three formed the basis of Offenbach's famous opera 'The Tales of Hoffmann', first staged in 1881. Hoffmann's tales were translated into English in the mid-nineteenth century and have since appeared in many editions and in many forms. He died on 24th July 1822.

Hoffmann, Heinrich

Author and illustrator of the famous – some might say infamous

– picture-book *Struwwelpeter* (1845). Hoffmann was born in 1809 and became a practising doctor in Frankfurt, Germany. He soon found that there were no books suitable for diverting his more youthful patients while they were awaiting their turn for examination and so would often draw humorous pictures for them in a notebook or on a sheet of paper. He added verses to some of his drawings and presented a collection of them to his own children one Christmas. The album chanced to catch the eyes of a pair of publishers, Loening and Rutten, and they offered to publish it. Hoffmann readily agreed and, being something of a perfectionist, insisted on checking proofs of the coloured lithographs of his drawings at every stage – chiefly to ensure that his self-confessed 'amateurish style' was not improved upon in any way. The collection of drawings and verses made its first appearance, anonymously, in 1845, under the title *Lustige Geschichten und drollige Bilder* (Jolly Tales and Funny Pictures) and ran to twenty-three pages. The book was bound only in boards, on the shrewd Dr Hoffmann's own advice, so that copies would not last for too long and parents would have to replace them. The first edition was quickly sold out and was constantly reprinted. In the third edition the pictures and verses were rearranged and the title changed to *Der Struwwelpeter* (Shock-headed Peter), and in the fifth edition an extra story was added, making a total of twenty-four pages. In 1848 came the English translation: *The English Struwwelpeter; or Pretty Stories and Funny Pictures for Little Children*. It sold well but became a 'best-seller' of the day in 1868 when the illustrations were re-drawn, printed from wood-blocks and coloured by stencils; it is these pictures which became so familiar to generations of children in many countries. The verse-stories are short and to the point and tell of such characters as *Shock-headed Peter* (who never cut his hair or his fingernails), *Cruel Frederick* (who was unkind to animals), *Little Suck-a-Thumb*, *Fidgety Philip*, *Little Johnny-Head-in-Air* and so on (and not forgetting *The Dreadful Story of Harriet and the Matches*). The stories were highly moral and the naughty boy or girl received his or her just desserts at the end of each one. Many of the pictures are, to today's eyes, frankly ugly and even terrifying, with boys having their thumbs brutally cut off with long scissors, girls going up in flames, and so on. Luckily, most children accept the pictures as huge jokes and have, over the years, laughed the characters into becoming nursery classics. The book is still in print today – and still in boards. . . . Hoffmann produced a few other picture-books, but none caught on in the same way as *Struwwelpeter*. The most notable of the others was *König Nusskracker und der arme Reinhold* (1851), which was translated by Planché in 1853 as *King Nutcracker; or, The Dream of Poor Reinhold*. Shock-headed Peter and some of the other characters made a brief appearance in this book too. Heinrich Hoffmann died in 1894.

Hogg, Garry

Born 1902 in Harrow, Middlesex, and educated at St George's School, Harpenden, and Wadham College, Oxford, where he obtained his M.A. degree in English Literature. He became a schoolmaster, teaching in both English and French schools, and subsequently worked as a University Extension Lecturer. He began writing in the early 1930s and his first children's book, *Explorers Awheel* (1938), described a cycling tour undertaken by two boys, two girls and their uncle, in south-west England. It was written from first-hand experience of the author's own boyhood cycling tours and met with an enthusiastic reception from critics and young readers, most of whom were cycle-riders themselves. The next in the series of 'Explorers' books was *Explorers on the Wall* (1939) and (again based on personal experience) dealt with explorations and adventures along the Roman Wall in Northumberland. Before starting on *Explorers Afloat* (1940), Garry Hogg charted a cabin-cruiser and took a group of young people on a Thames and canal trip, and again the book benefited from authentic first-hand knowledge and descriptions. In 1941 came a departure from the 'Explorers' – a straightforward and exciting mystery-adventure called *The Secret of the Shuttered Lodge,* and in 1943 another river adventure, *Houseboat Holiday. Sealed Orders* (1948) told of an incident-packed initiative test. In more recent years Garry Hogg has written a wide variety of books, fiction and non-fiction, for both adults and younger readers, but with the emphasis on non-fiction, especially real-life adventure and travel. One recent boys' story was *Climbers' Glory* (1961), set against a background of rock-climbing in North Wales. He also contributes to many magazines and newspapers, as well as to various BBC radio programmes.

Hope, Anthony

Real name: Sir Anthony Hope Hawkins. Born on 9th February 1863, in Clapton, London, where his father, the Rev. Edward Hawkins, was Headmaster of St John's Foundation School for the Sons of Poor Clergy. His mother was Jane Grahame, aunt of Kenneth Grahame (author of *The Wind in the Willows*, etc.), making Anthony that writer's cousin. He was educated at Clapton and then Marlborough College, going on to Balliol College, Oxford, in 1881. He was a brilliant student, gaining a First Class degree in Classics, becoming president of the Union, and excelling at football and athletics. Deciding to take law as his career, he was called to the Bar by the Middle Temple in 1887. He began writing short stories for various magazines in the 1880s and his first book, *A Man of Mark*, was published (at his own expense) in 1890. Several further unimportant novels and a book of short stories appeared over the next three or four years, and in 1893 a series of sketches called *The Dolly Dialogues* ran in the *Westminster Gazette* (appearing in book form the following year). These light social sketches proved popular and 'Anthony Hope' (as he now called his writing self) began to prosper in his second career. He was also becoming increasingly successful as a barrister. But his most famous book was still to come. It is said that in November 1893, while walking home from Westminster County Court after winning a case and pondering on what story he should write next, he happened to pass two men who looked remarkably alike; at the same time the name 'Ruritania' came into his head – and stayed there. By the end of that evening he had the rough outline of *The Prisoner of Zenda* thought out and by the next evening had completed the first chapter. A month later the first draft was ready. The book was published in April 1894, and achieved instant success, as well as enthusiastic commendations from such eminent contemporary writers as Robert Louis Stevenson, Andrew Lang and A. E. W. Mason. The story was an exciting, action-filled one about a young Englishman, whose resemblance to the King of 'Ruritania' (the word Hope introduced to the English language) led him into a series of perilous adventures in that country, particularly in the forest and castle of Zenda, in the Kingdom of the Elphbergs. The hero, Rudolf Rassendyll, the heroine, Flavia (of the red hair) and the villain, Black Michael, soon became classic fictional characters and the book one of the most popular in the English language. A sequel, *Rupert of Hentzau*, continuing the story, appeared in 1898 (after running as a serial in the *Pall Mall Magazine*) and was almost as big a success as its forerunner. Although Hope wrote many more novels, and also plays, it is for *The Prisoner of Zenda* and *Rupert of Hentzau* that he is most remembered. Some of his other titles are: *The Heart of Princess Osra* (1896), *Phroso* (1897), *Sophy of Kravonia* (1906) and *The King's Mirror* (1899) – this last being his own favourite. He had given up his law career in 1894 to concentrate upon his literary work. During the First World War he worked for the Ministry of Information and received a knighthood for his services. He married an American girl, Elizabeth Sheldon, in 1903, and in later years settled at Tadworth, Surrey, where he was the local 'squire'. He died on 8th July 1933.

Hope, Laura Lee

Author of the widely popular American series of young children's books about the adventures of *The Bobbsey Twins*. They were first introduced in the book of that title in the early 1900s and subsequently ran to around fifty sequels. The Twins were Nan and Bert Bobbsey, a pair of lively and adventurous ten-year-olds, and generations of American readers have grown up with them. The series has been published in Britain too.

Household, Geoffrey

Born 1900 in Bristol and educated at Clifton College and Magdalen College, Oxford. On leaving Oxford in 1922 he worked as a banker in Roumania for four years. Deciding then that a banker's life was not for him he went to the USA, where he wrote articles for an encyclopaedia and children's plays for radio. Later he became a foreign salesman, spending three years travelling all over Europe and South America for his company. His first short stories appeared in America in the *Atlantic Monthly* in the mid-1930s and his first novel, *The Third Hour*, in 1937. This was followed by a collection of short stories and, in 1939, by his famous thriller, *Rogue Male*. He served with the Intelligence Corps in the Middle East during the Second World War. His post-war novels include *A Rough Shoot*, *A Time to Kill*, *Fellow Passenger* and *Watch in the Shadows*. All are excellent and intelligent thrillers, spiced with humour and spine-tingling realism, and all are enjoyed by teenage boys as well as by their fathers. Household has written only two novels for children. *The Terror of Villadonga* was published in 1936 and re-issued in 1960 as *The Spanish Cave*. It was an incident-packed adventure story set on the Asturian Coast. *Prisoner of the Indies* (1968) was a historical adventure. In 1961 he wrote *Xenophon's Adventure*, a modern re-telling of the story of the war between Persia and Greece in 401 B.C.

Howard, Edward G. G.

Little is known about this maritime writer's early life, except that he served as a Lieutenant in the Royal Navy and was a shipmate and friend of Captain Marryat's. After leaving the navy in 1832 he became sub-editor of Marryat's *Metropolitan Magazine*. In 1836 he wrote a rousing, realistic (and probably autobiographical) sea story called *Rattlin the Reefer*, which was published as 'edited by the author of *Peter Simple*', largely to ensure a satisfactory sale. It is likely that Marryat, the experienced and successful novelist, actually helped Howard with the book in places too. *Rattlin the Reefer* was attributed to Marryat on more than one occasion because of these circumstances. Howard later wrote several other sea yarns, including *The Old Commerce* (1837), *Outward Bound* (1838), *Jack Ashore* (1840) and (published posthumously) *Sir Henry Morgan the Buccaneer* (1842). He also later worked for Tom Hood on the staff of the *New Monthly Magazine*. Howard died a comparatively young man, on 30th December 1841.

Hughes, Richard

Born on 19th April 1900, at Weybridge, Surrey, of Welsh

descent, and educated at Charterhouse and Oriel College, Oxford. He published a one-act play, *The Sister's Tragedy*, and a book of poems, *Gipsy Night* (1922), while still at Oxford. After travelling throughout the United States, Canada and the West Indies, he published his first novel, *A High Wind in Jamaica*, in 1929. It told the story of a group of children kidnapped (accidentally) by a crew of bloodthirsty pirates and taken to sea. His first book for children was published in 1931 and was *The Spider's Palace, and Other Stories*, a collection of twenty humorous, fantastic and magical short stories, some of which have since appeared in anthologies, etc. Another collection, *Don't Blame Me*, came in 1940. A recent children's story was *Gertrude's Child* (1967). During the Second World War he was employed in the Admiralty and subsequently awarded the O.B.E.

Hughes, Thomas

Born on 20th October 1822, at Uffington, Berkshire, where his grandfather had once been the local Vicar, and educated at Twyford, near Winchester, and at Rugby School, where he was a pupil from 1833-42, under the headmastership of Dr Thomas Arnold. He went on to Oriel College, Oxford, subsequently studying law and being called to the Bar in 1848. In the summer of 1856, Hughes – now married with two children – was living in a house called 'The Firs' in Ridgeway, Wimbledon, London. He was considering what he wanted to say to his son, Maurice, eight, who was soon to go to school; he took to writing a story as the easiest way of bringing out what he wanted. The story was *Tom Brown's Schooldays* and was based loosely on Hughes' own schooldays at Rugby. It was published, under the pseudonym 'An Old Boy', in 1857 and was an immediate success with both reviewers and public alike. It was hailed as the first *real* public school story – which it was, became a best-seller and has been selling ever since. The adventures of young Tom Brown as a new boy at Rugby, his friendship with East, his bullying by Flashman, his feeling for the delicate Arthur, his awe and respect for the great Dr Arnold – all these are described with deep understanding and skill. The humour is there too – and the schoolboy characters are surely the first real and believable schoolboys in Victorian literature. The book had far-reaching and influential effects, both on public school methods and fictional literature. The 'school story' came into being and became one of youth's favourite types of story. A host of other school tales were rushed into print – but *Tom Brown* remained supreme and is still the most famous school story ever written. Its sequel, *Tom Brown at Oxford* (1861) was a comparative failure; it seemed to lack the warmth and intensity of the first book. His only other novel, *The Scouring of the White Horse*, was published in 1859, and was set in his own county of Berkshire. He wrote other books too, including biographies of Alfred the Great, Bishop Fraser, and Daniel Macmillan, the publisher. Hughes became a Q.C. in 1869, was a Liberal Member of Parliament from 1865–74, and was appointed a County Court Judge in 1882. He died in Brighton on 22nd March 1896. There is a statue of him at Rugby School, which he helped to make so famous.

Hunter, Norman

Born 1899, in London, and educated at Beckenham County School, Kent. He entered an advertising agency on leaving school and has been in this profession ever since, mainly as a copywriter. He is chiefly remembered for a superlative and very funny children's book called *The Incredible Adventures of Professor Branestawm* (1933). It was memorably illustrated by W. Heath Robinson and dealt with the escapades of an absent-minded but extremely inventive professor who was for ever creating new gadgets and devices to make life easier or more interesting – anything, in fact, from burglar-alarms to time-machines. He had a high forehead and a habit of wearing five different pairs of spectacles – often all at once. A sequel, very nearly as good, was *Professor Branestawm's Treasure Hunt* (1937). They comprise a pair of the few really funny children's books. Hunter wrote several other books, but none approached the success of the Professor Branestawm stories which, incidentally, made their original appearance in BBC 'Children's Hour' in the form of radio stories told by 'Ajax' (to whom the book was dedicated). His other titles included *Jingle Tales*, *The Bad Barons of Crashbania* and *Simple Conjuring*. Conjuring was one of his specialities and he gave over 200 performances at Maskelyne and Devant's in London shortly before the famous magic theatre was destroyed by German bombing in the Second World War. He also wrote *Advertising Through the Press* and contributed many stories and articles to newspapers and magazines in Britain, America, Australia and New Zealand. He once confessed (not too seriously, it is hoped) that his popular character, Professor Branestawm, was based on himself . . .

Ingelow, Jean

Born on 17th March 1820, in Boston, Lincolnshire, the daughter of a banker and his Scottish wife. The house in which she was brought up in Boston overlooked the River Witham and her early-bred affection for the water and ships later manifested itself many times in her writings. She was educated at home by governesses and tutors and by her mother. She loved writing from an early age and it is said that she once wrote a poem about Catherine of Aragon and Henry VIII on the white shutters of her bedroom because she had no writing paper. When she was fourteen she moved with her family to Ipswich, Suffolk. Her first book of poems, *A Rhyming Chronicle of Incidents and Feelings*, was published in 1850 and brought a compliment from Tennyson. Several more books of poetry followed and by the 1860s she was being hailed as one of the foremost poets of her period. Among her best-known poems and ballads are *Divided*, *Story of Doom* and *High Tide on the Coast of Lincolnshire*. In 1863 she moved to London, living at 6, Holland Villas Road, Kensington, and enjoyed literary success and the friendship of such notables as Tennyson, Browning, Ruskin and Christina Rossetti. In the late 'fifties she began contributing children's stories to the *Youth's Magazine* under the pseudonym 'Orris'. They were collected together and published as *Tales of Orris* in 1860, being reprinted in different form in 1865 as *Stories Told to a Child*. *Studies for Stories* appeared in 1864 and *A Sister's Bye-Hours* in 1868. Her most famous and only full-length story for children, *Mopsa the Fairy*, was published in 1869 – four years after *Alice's Adventures in Wonderland*, to which it owed no little inspiration. A small boy, Jack, climbs into a hollow tree, discovers fairies and is taken off to fairyland on the back of an albatross. His adventures on a river, in the land of enchanted parrots, and over the mountains, with Mopsa, his 'slave-fairy', to a magical palace and finally home again, make engrossing reading and the whole tale has an indefinable and memorable atmosphere which has endeared it to generations of young readers – and is one of the reasons it is still in print today. Inexplicably, Jean Inglelow never wrote another full-length story for children, though collections of tales such as *The Little Wonder Horn* (1872) and *Very Young and Quite Another Story* (1890) were published. Her first adult novel, *Off the Skelligs*, appeared in 1872 and was followed by several others, all of which were very popular during her lifetime. Her poetry was widely acclaimed too and when Tennyson died in 1892 many eminent figures suggested she be made Poet Laureate – an honour which eventually went to Alfred Austin. She died on 20th July 1897, in Kensington, London.

Irving, Washington

Born on 3rd April 1783, in New York City, the son of a Scottish merchant who had emigrated to America. He had little formal education, but read practically every book in his father's excellent library. In 1799 he entered a law firm and read for the Bar. Ill-health forced him to take a European rest-cure between 1804 and 1806. When he returned to America in 1806 he resumed his law studies and was called to the Bar. He did not actually become a practising lawyer but joined his elder brothers in their business as a partner. He had long wanted to write and particularly admired English essaysists of the eighteenth century. He wrote several pieces for New York newspapers under the pseudonym 'JONATHAN OLDSTYLE, Gent.'. In 1807 came *Salmagundi*, a series of amusing and satirical essays, written in collaboration with one of his brothers and a friend. Then, in 1809, he published *A History of New York*, using the now-famous pseudonym 'DIEDRICH KNICKERBOCKER', and it won him immediate fame. The book was mainly intended as a kindly burlesque of the Dutch, who were the first settlers in New York, but was also generally correct in its historical facts. Many descendants of the Dutch settlers were offended, but the work lived on to become a classic of its kind. In 1815, Irving, distressed by the death of his fiancée, left for England, where he remained for the next few years. He began to write a series of sketches and stories, which he sent back to New York, where they were published in periodicals and subsequently in book form (1819–20), making their appearance in Britain in 1820. The title of this collection was *The Sketch Book* and it appeared under yet another pseudonym, 'GEOFFREY CRAYON, Gent.'. It consisted of various sketches made as an American visitor to Britain, touching on such topics as 'Christmas Dinner', 'Stratford-upon-Avon', 'The Stage-Coach', 'John Bull' and so on, together with other pieces and half a dozen American items, including two of Irving's most famous, German-influenced folk tales set in the New York countryside – *Rip Van Winkle* (who slept for twenty years) and *The Legend of Sleepy Hollow* (about Ichabod Crane, a schoolmaster who encounters a ghostly and terrifying 'headless horseman'). The book was an enormous international success, selling thousands of copies on both sides of the Atlantic and on the Continent. Irving was really one of the first American writers to win popular international fame and respect. In 1822 he published *Bracebridge Hall* (which contained a marvellously evocative description of a typical upper-class English Christmas at a country mansion) and in 1824 came *Tales of a Traveller*. In 1826 he was invited to go to Madrid to work on translations of works about Christopher Columbus. He accepted and was so fascinated by the subject that he wrote several original books about Spain and the Spanish, including *The History of the Life and Voyages of Columbus* (1828) and another book popular with young readers, *The Alhambra* (1832). This was a 'Spanish sketch-book' inspired by the picturesque ruins of the great palace, the Alhambra, built by the Moorish Princes at Granada in 1354, and comprising several stories and re-tellings of old legends centred around the Moors and the Spaniards – fairy-tales of a very special and unique kind. Typical titles include *The Legend of the Rose of the Alhambra, The Legend of the Arabian Astrologer* and *The Legend of the Enchanted Soldier*. The collection was revised by Irving in 1848 and has since appeared in numerous translations and editions throughout the world. Appropriately enough, it is extremely popular in Spain. In 1842 Irving was appointed American Minister to Spain, a post he held for four years. In 1846 came his *Life of Goldsmith* and between 1855 and 1859 were published the five volumes of his marathon *Life of Washington* – a particularly appropriate undertaking since Irving had been named after that great statesman. He spent his last few years at 'Sunnyside', an old Dutch house in Tarrytown, in the countryside of New York. He died there on 28th November 1859.

Jacobs, Joseph

Born on 29th August 1854, in Sydney, Australia, and educated at grammar school and university there, subsequently attending London University and King's College, Cambridge, where he obtained his B.A. degree. Was of Jewish origin and became one of the great Jewish historians and researchers of his period. He wrote and edited many Jewish reference books and was editor of the first issues (1896–99) of the *Jewish Year Book*. In 1900 he went to America to become revising editor of *The Jewish Encyclopaedia*, write many articles for the *Encyclopaedia Britannica*, serve as Registrar and Professor of English at the Jewish Theological Seminary in New York City and edit the *American Hebrew* magazine. He was an untiring researcher into folk-lore and was editor of the British journal *Folk-Lore* for a period. In 1890 he published *English Fairy Tales*, a collection of traditional tales he obtained from many sources and re-told in a conversational style, removing any more objectionable scenes of violence. His ambition, as he pointed out in his Introduction, was 'to write as a good old nurse will speak when she tells fairy tales'. In 1894 came a further collection, *More English Fairy Tales*. The two volumes comprised over eighty stories, complete with copious notes, and included such well-known tales as *Jack and the Beanstalk*, *Dick Whittington and His Cat*, *Jack the Giant-Killer*, *Childe Rowland*, *Henny-Penny*, *The Three Little Pigs* and *The Wise Men of Gotham*. It is largely through Jacobs that such traditional English stories have been preserved in the form by which most children know them. In 1892 he edited a collection of *Celtic Fairy Tales*, with a second volume following in 1894. *Indian Fairy Tales* appeared in 1892. In 1889, Jacobs had edited a two-volume edition of *Aesop's Fables*, based directly on those originally published by Caxton in 1484. His other children's books include: *The Book of Wonder Voyages* (1896), *The Story of Geographical Discovery* (1898) and *Europa's Fairy Book* (1915). In 1942 a one-volume selection of over sixty stories from his two-volume *English Fairy Tales* was published. Jacobs was a prolific writer and published numerous works of sociological, historical, literary, philosophical and anthropological interest, in addition to his vast editorial undertakings. He died on 30th January 1916, in New York, where he had made his home for the last sixteen years of his life.

Jansson, Tove

Born 1914, in Helsingfors, Finland, and educated at art schools in Helsingfors, Stockholm and Paris. Published her first children's book in her native Finland in 1946; it was *Comet in Moominland* and introduced, both in her own drawings and story, the endearing Moomintrolls – strange little creatures, reminiscent of small upright hippopotamuses – who live with their friends in a peaceful valley amid the forests of Finland. Moomins are rather shy and fat, love the sunshine and sleep through the winter months, emerging at springtime ready for more adventures. Chief characters in the story (and those that followed) include Moominpapa, Moomimamma, Moomintroll, Snuffkin, Snork, Sniff, the Hemulen, Muskrat, Thingumy and Bob, the Snork Maiden and the mysterious Hattifatteners, who can neither speak nor hear. They all have their peculiar characteristics and habits and small adventures (and sometimes big ones). The stories are full of magical humour and everyday fun – and sometimes tinged with sadness too. The incidents range from the down-to-earth and sensible to the fantastic and nonsensical. Miss Jansson has been compared on more than one occasion to Carroll and Lear, but has really created her own unique fantasy-mythology, and once read about, the Moomins are never forgotten. The first book in the series to be published in Britain was *Finn Family Moomintroll* in 1950 (Finnish publication 1949) and subsequent titles include: *Comet in Moominland* (1951), *The Exploits of Moominpapa* (1952), *Moominsummer Madness* (1955), *Moomin, Mymble*

52 Jacob and Wilhelm Grimm

51 Aesop: *painting by Velasquez*

53 Hans Andersen

54 Captain Frederick Marryat

56 R. M. Ballantyne

55 Frances Hodgson Burnett

57 Mrs Craik

58 James Fenimore Cooper

59 George Alfred Henty

60 Lewis Carroll

61 Robert Louis Stevenson

62 Edward Lear

63 Juliana H. Ewing

64 Kate Greenaway

65 Andrew Lang

66 Louisa May Alcott

67 Beatrix Potter

68 E. Nesbit

69 L. Leslie Brooke

70 Arthur Ransome

71 Rosemary Sutcliff

and Little My (1953), *Moominland Midwinter* (1958) *Who Will Comfort Toffle?* (1961), *Tales from Moominvalley* (1963) and *Moominpapa at Sea* (1966). The stories were originally written in Swedish and have also appeared in newspaper comic-strip form. Today, she still lives in her birthplace of Helsingfors, Finland.

Jefferies, Richard

Born on 6th November 1848, on his father's farm, 'Coate Farm', near Swindon, in North Wiltshire. He received little formal education but roamed the countryside studying wild life, doing odd work on the farm and reading everything he could lay his hands on. When he was fifteen he ran away to France with a boy cousin, intending to walk to Moscow, but the venture ended in failure and Jefferies returned to the farm. In 1866 he joined the staff of the *North Wilts Herald* in Swindon, reporting and reviewing. He also wrote short stories for the paper. Later he wrote for the *Pall Mall Gazette* a series of articles about country life; in 1878 the series was published in book form as *The Gamekeeper at Home*. Several more books about the countryside and wild life appeared over the next few years, as well as half a dozen novels. In 1881 he wrote *Wood Magic*, a strange story about a small boy, 'Sir Bevis', and his conversations and adventures with animals, birds, trees and the winds. The following year came Jefferies' most famous book, *Bevis*, which was an idealised version of his own childhood. The story tells in fascinating detail of the adventures and undertakings of two boys, Bevis and his friend Mark, in the countryside around a farm in Wiltshire. They build their own boat, sail it on a reservoir, camp on an island which they call 'New Formosa' and invent circumstances and settings which anticipate the stories of Arthur Ransome to some extent. Throughout the whole book is a deep feeling for nature in all its aspects and the atmosphere of a hot summer's day permeates the story in an invigorating and memorable way. Jefferies died on 14th August 1887, at Goring, near Worthing, Sussex, after a long and painful illness and at the early age of thirty-eight.

Johns, Captain William Earl

Born in 1893, at Hertford, and educated at Hertford Grammar School. He had early ambitions to join the army and find adventure abroad but his parents had other ideas and articled him to a local surveyor at sixteen. He had barely completed his studies when the First World War broke out and he found himself enlisted with the Norfolk Yeomanry as Trooper Johns, serving first in the Middle East. After a period with the Machine Gun Cavalry Squadron in Salonica, he was commissioned, again in the Norfolk Yeomanry. Later, in 1916, he was seconded to the Royal Flying Corps, learning to fly an aeroplane at the age of twenty-three. He served with 55 Squadron, of the Independent Force, going first to France as a fighter-pilot and subsequently going out on two-seater bomber raids over Germany. It was during one of these, in September 1918, that he was shot down over Mannheim by the famous German air ace Ernst Udet. Wounded, he was taken prisoner and sentenced to death, but managed to escape. He was recaptured and sent to a punishment camp in Bavaria, where he remained until the end of the war. Johns enjoyed life in the RFC (subsequently, of course, the RAF) and decided to stay in. He served as a regular officer until 1930, when he was transferred to the Reserve, retaining his old RFC rank of Captain (he was – and is – very proud of his RFC 'Captain' rank and that is why he has used it to this day). In 1930 he became Air Correspondent to several British and overseas newspapers and magazines. His first book appeared in 1932 and was titled *Fighting 'Planes and Aces*. It was also in 1932 that he became Founder-Editor of the monthly magazine *Popular Flying*; it was in the pages of this that the famous 'Biggles' made his bow in a series of short stories. Johns had been searching for stories featuring a British pilot's adventures during the 1914–18 war, but had only been able to find American yarns. Realising he had the necessary 'know-how' and experience himself, he sat down and created Captain James Bigglesworth, of Squadron No. 266, RFC – and the best pilot of a Sopwith Camel in the Service. That first story was called *The White Fokker* and was succeeded by many more short flying tales featuring 'Biggles'. The first collection of them, *The Camels are Coming*, was published in 1932, and was followed by several more. Then the full-length

Biggles books started to flow from Johns' prolific and expert pen, one of the earliest being *Biggles Learns To Fly* (1935), a retrospective story showing the hero at the start of his illustrious career. Since then Johns has published over seventy Biggles books, with all but a few still in print today. Typical titles include: *Biggles, Secret Agent* (1940), *Biggles Sees It Through* (1941), *Biggles Sweeps the Desert* (1942), *Biggles Breaks the Silence* (1949), *Biggles Takes Charge* (1956), *Biggles Goes Home* (1960) and *Biggles in the Terai* (1966). *Biggles Goes to School* (1951) was another retrospective look at Biggles' early life. Biggles was given a new lease of life after the Second World War when he was seconded to the powerful 'Interpol' as an Air Detective. Biggles is a true, straight hero of the 'old school' – good, brave, loyal to both his country and his friends, a non-drinker, no time for girl-friends – and even practically non-violent (he has only struck a man once in all his adventures and that was in a matter of life and death). And the character is as popular with today's boys as with their fathers before them. Captain Johns' Biggles books alone sell several million copies a year in seventeen different countries and are especially popular in (apart from Britain, of course) France and Germany. During the Second World War, Johns toured all over Britain lecturing for the RAF. It was said that he did more for service recruiting than a million posters. During this period two more well-known fictional characters were created by Johns: 'Worrals of the WAAF' and 'Gimlet', the Commando. He introduced them at the suggestion of the Air Ministry and the War Office respectively, who each wanted to speed up recruiting, and wrote a series of books about them. He has written around 200 books altogether, including several non-fiction titles such as *The Air V.C's* (1934) and *Milestones of Aviation* (1935). Johns has also published a series of science-fiction books for boys. He is, in fact, probably the most successful and biggest-selling author of children's books in Britain – always excepting Enid Blyton, who is in a category by herself – and Biggles is one of the most popular characters in juvenile fiction. W. E. Johns lived in an elegant Queen Anne house at Hampton Court Palace, Middlesex; he also had an estate in Scotland and a villa in the South of France. He usually wrote his stories – in long-hand – during the early part of the morning. He died on 21st June, 1968.

Juster, Norton

Born in Brooklyn, New York. Studied architecture at the University of Pennsylvania and then went to England on a Full-bright Scholarship to study city planning at Liverpool University. Spent three years as legal officer, personnel officer and education officer in the U.S. Navy and was stationed in Morocco and Newfoundland. Today he is a practising architect in the United States. In 1961 (1962 in Britain) he published his first book for children, *The Phantom Tolbooth*, which was a gay, amusing and adventurous fantasy – a modern-day version of *Pilgrim's Progress*, in a sense. It told of a boy, Milo, and his magical visit to the land of Dictionopolis, ruled by King Azaz the Unabridged, to rescue the Princesses Rhyme and Reason. An up-to-date morality tale, scattered with word-jokes and clever (perhaps a little too clever) references and witticisms, it did not lack incident or freshness and was hailed by many leading literary critics as one of the most important children's stories to be published for some years. It was startlingly illustrated by Jules Feiffer. His later books are *The Dot and the Line* (1964), a witty fable about a sensible straight line who fell in love with a frivolous dot, and *Alberic the Wise* (1966), three superlative stories in the old 'fairy-tale' tradition.

Kästner, Erich

Born 1899 in Dresden, Germany, and educated at schools in Dresden, Rostock, Leipzig and Berlin. His first two books were collections of poems. Then, in 1929, he published *Emil and the Detectives* (translated and published in Britain in 1931). This story of a ten-year-old boy whose money is stolen on a train journey to Berlin and the subsequent hilarious adventures of Emil and the gang of Berlin boys who help him catch the thief was an immediate success and has been selling steadily throughout the world for nearly forty years. It was a real and believable story about eminently real small boys at large in a big city, and its way of describing breathlessly exciting incidents in an informal and almost conversational manner was something of a milestone in children's literature. It began the wave (still going on) of stories in which gangs or groups of children outwit criminals (and police), emerging triumphant (and a trifle smug) at the end. But *Emil* was an original – and the hundreds of imitations which have followed have never approached its achievement. It also began the trend – commonplace in modern times – for issuing English translations of important foreign children's books in Britain and America. Kästner's subsequent children's novels included: *Annaluise and Anton* (1932), *The 35th of May* (1933), *The Flying Classroom* (1934), *Emil and the Three Twins* (1935) and *Lottie and Lisa* (1950). *The Animals' Conference* (1949 Switzerland, 1955 Britain) was too full of propaganda to be really enjoyed by children and its nearest equivalent in Britain, probably, is Orwell's *Animal Farm*. *Eleven Merry Pranks of Till the Jester* was a collection of folk tales about the legendary Till Eulenspiegel. In 1963, *Let's Face It*, the first selection in English of Kästner's poems, appeared in Britain; his poetry books have sold over a quarter of a million copies in Germany. He has also written adult novels. In 1959 came *When I Was a Little Boy*, an autobiographical account of Kästner's Emil-ish upbringing (his mother was a ladies' hairdresser too!) in pre-1914 Dresden. *The Little Man* (1966) was a story about a 'Tom Thumb' type hero.

Kingsley, Charles

Born on 12th June 1819, at Holne Vicarage, Dartmoor, Devonshire, the son of a clergyman, and lived there until he was five, when his family moved to Barnack, near Stamford, in the Fen country. In 1830, when Charles was eleven, the family moved to Clovelly, Devon, where Charles Kingsley Snr was appointed Vicar. Young Charles was at first sent away to a small preparatory boarding school at Clifton, near Bristol, but soon returned to attend the grammar school at Helston, in Cornwall. In 1836 the family moved once again, this time to Chelsea, London, and Charles attended King's College, London, and then Magdalene College, Cambridge. He was originally intended for the law, but soon decided to follow in his father's footsteps and become a clergyman. He was ordained in 1842 and became Curate, and two years later, Rector, of Eversley, Hampshire, where he remained for eighteen years. In 1848 he published his first work, a poetical drama about St Elizabeth of Hungary called *The*

Saint's Tragedy. His first novel, *Alton Locke*, appeared in 1850. His first book for children, *Glaucus, or The Wonders of the Deep* (1855), was an instructive work about items to be found on the sea-shore and one of the first of its kind. *Westward Ho!* (1855) was a rousing (if overlong) Elizabethan adventure story not written for children but enthusiastically annexed by them. Its hero was a sea-captain, Amyas Leigh, and the yarn culminated in the defeat of the Spanish Armada. *The Heroes* (1856) was written for his three eldest children, Rose, Maurice and Mary. It comprised the superb re-tellings of three classic Greek myths – Perseus, Theseus, and Jason and the Argonauts. Charles Kingsley's most famous book for children, *The Water Babies* (1863), was written especially for his youngest son, Grenville Arthur. The story goes that one spring morning in 1862, as the family was seated at breakfast, Mrs Kingsley gently chided her husband: 'Rose, Maurice and Mary have their book (*The Heroes*) and baby must have his.' Charles went straight into his study, locked the door and emerged a short while later with the complete first chapter of *The Water Babies*. He completed the story at a more leisurely rate and allowed far too much sermonising to creep in, but it still reads well even today. Many good modern editions tactfully cut the moralising and stick to the main story. It is all about little Tom, a badly treated chimney-sweep, who becomes a tiny water-baby and has many adventures under sea and river, encountering the memorable Mrs Doasyouwouldbedoneby and Mrs Bedonebyasyoudid on his way. *Hereward the Wake*, a fine historical adventure story, was originally serialised in *Good Words* in 1865, being published in book form in 1866. Another book for younger children was *Madame How and Lady Why, or First Lessons in Earth Lore for Children*, serialised in *Good Words* in 1868 and published in hard covers in 1870. He wrote many other adult novels, sermons, tracts, poems, etc. and was an ardent advocate of Christian socialism. His academic and theological careers prospered along with his writing work. In 1848 he was appointed Professor of English Literature at Queen's College, London, but resigned through ill-health within a year. In 1859 he was made Chaplain to Queen Victoria and in 1860 became Professor of Modern History at Cambridge University, remaining there until 1869, when he was appointed Canon of Chester. He became Canon of

162

Westminster in 1873, visiting America and Canada the same year. He died at his beloved Eversley on 23rd January 1875. His brothers, George and Henry, were also writers.

Kingston, William Henry Giles

Born on 28th February 1814, in Harley Street, London, the eldest son of L. H. Kingston, a successful merchant, and grandson of Sir Giles Rooke, who was a judge. Many of his early years were spent in Oporto, Portugal, base of his father's business activities. He was educated at various schools and by private tutors and, from an early age, developed a great love for the sea and ships. He went on many voyages in his youth and came to know several seafaring men, since his father was an ex-sailor himself and had wide contacts in the naval and shipping worlds. Kingston's ambition was to enter the navy, but on the death of his father he inherited the family business and this took up most of his time. He eventually returned to England in 1844 and resumed a business career in London, still maintaining his contacts with Portugal. He edited *The Colonial Magazine* and wrote several pamphlets on emigration, one of his particular interests. He also wrote a series of articles on Portugal which, when they were translated into Portuguese, were instrumental in bringing about an important commercial treaty between England and Portugal. As a sign of appreciation, Kingston received a Portuguese knighthood. His first adult novel, *The Circassian Chief*, was published in 1844, and was followed the next year by *The Prime Minister* and by a collection of travel sketches. His first boys' book was *Peter the Whaler* in 1851 – a vigorous, adventure-filled story of life at sea and ashore which met with great success. There followed a constant stream of exciting, outdoor adventure stories for boys (and for young men – especially sailors), numbering over 130 altogether. He averaged three or four titles a year for the rest of his life and, together with his contemporaries Henty and Ballantyne, supplied the bulk of fictional adventure read – and gratefully received as presents and school prizes – by the boyhood of England in the latter half of the nineteenth century. Typical Kingston titles included: *Mark Seaworth* (1852), *Manco, the Peruvian Chief* (1853), *Salt Water* (1857), *Old Jack* (1859), *Round the World* (1859), *Digby Heathcote* (1860), *Will Weatherhelm* (1860), *Washed Ashore* (1866), *The Perils and Adventures of Harry Skipworth* (1868), *The Wanderers* (1876), *Snow-Shoes and Canoes* (1876), *The Rival Crusoes* (1878), *The Frontier Fort* (1879) and *Arctic Adventures* (1882). He naturally retained his love for the sea and was constantly voyaging around the world in his own yacht, or in merchant vessels or naval craft. He wrote many travel books and an account of Captain Cook and his voyages. He won fame as a translator, too, and it was his version of *Swiss Family Robinson* which originally became widely known in Britain; first published in 1879 it was still being reprinted sixty years later. He also translated many of Jules Verne's novels from the French and introduced these also to an enthusiastic British public. Probably his most popular books (apart from the famous *Peter the Whaler*) were *The Three Midshipmen* (1862), *The Three Lieutenants* (1874), *The Three Commanders* (1875) and *The Three Admirals* (1877) – a quartet of boys' yarns which recounted the adventures of three high-spirited friends from their early days as raw young midshipmen to their mature, but still extremely active, years as high-ranking naval officers. In 1859 he edited *Kingston's Magazine for Boys*, which ran for only three years. Later he became the first editor of Sampson Low's boys' magazine *Union Jack*, in January 1880, only to die after seven months (to be succeeded by Henty). Kingston also edited *The Colonist* and *The East India Review*. He originated a Society devoted to the welfare of seamen. In 1879 he had the distinction of contributing the very first serial story to the famous *Boy's Own Paper*, titled *From Powder Monkey to Admiral*, and later wrote many more stories for the magazine. He was at work on a new serial for *B.O.P.* when he became ill and, realising that it would almost certainly prove fatal, penned a moving farewell letter to his youthful readers, which duly appeared in the magazine shortly after Kingston's death, at Willesden, London, on 5th August 1880.

Kipling, Joseph Rudyard

Born on 30th December 1865, in Bombay, the son of John Lockwood Kipling, a Methodist minister who was also an accomplished artist, and Alice MacDonald, sister-in-law of Sir

Edward Burne-Jones. His father had gone to Bombay to take up a post as Principal at a new school of art there. Rudyard was named after Rudyard Lake, Staffordshire, where his parents had first met. In 1871 little Rudyard and his even smaller sister, Trix, were left in the charge of a Mrs Holloway in Southsea, while their parents were in India. They remained there for six years – and Kipling recalled them as the most unhappy of his life. Their guardian was strict, hateful and over-religious; she also had a bullying son a few years older than Rudyard. Mrs Kipling returned from India in the spring of 1877 and 'rescued' her children. In the autumn of 1877, Rudyard began his first term at the United Services College, Westward Ho!, near Bideford, Devon, his schooldays there later being immortalised in *Stalky and Co* (1899), where he thinly disguised himself as 'Beetle' and his two friends as Stalky and M'Turk (in real life L. C. Dunsterville and G. C. Beresford). In 1882 he returned to India and became a journalist, joining the *Civil and Military Gazette* in Lahore, where his father was still living. He began to write short stories and verse, his first published book being *Departmental Ditties* in 1886. Several books of short stories (set in the India Kipling had come to know so well) followed, including *Plain Tales from the Hills* (1888). By 1894, when he had returned to London, Kipling had published more books and had achieved literary success. In 1894 he wrote *The Jungle Book* and followed it, in 1895, with *The Second Jungle Book*. These collections of stories (most of which first appeared in magazines) are best remembered for the tales about Mowgli, the boy who was adopted and raised by a family of wolves in the Indian jungle and grew up with the wild animals without quite becoming one himself. The Mowgli stories, a remarkable blending of fable, fact and adventure, are unique creations, illustrating the age-old Law of the Jungle and the truth that 'the Jungle is big and the cub is small'. They draw parallels between animals' behaviour and that of humans, at the same time showing how basically different an animal is – and has to be – from a human being. Memorable characters include Akela, the lone wolf, Shere Khan, the tiger, and Kaa, the old python. Other famous 'non-Mowgli' stories contained in *The Jungle Books* are Rikki-Tikki-Tavi, the mongoose, Toomai of the Elephants, and the White Seal. *Captains Courageous* (1897) was a sea story set among the cod fisheries of the Grand Banks of Newfoundland, inspired by the memories of a doctor who used to chat with Kipling about his young days on the Banks. After *Stalky and Co* (1899), Kipling's semi-autobiographical school story, came *Kim* (1901), on one level a Secret Service thriller, on another the story of Kimbell O'Hara, a thirteen-year-old boy at large in India, and on yet another, the most fascinating and illuminating collection of Indian character studies ever written. It is something of a brilliant hotch-potch, a sort of Indian stew; but Kim's journeyings through the roads of the Punjab are strangely memorable and some critics point to *Kim* as Kipling's finest book. *The Just So Stories* (1902) was a delightful and amusing collection of 'nonsense' tales such as 'How the Elephant Got His Trunk', 'The Cat That Walked By Himself', 'The Butterfly That Stamped' and 'The Camel's Hump'. *Puck of Pook's Hill* (1906) and its sequel *Rewards and Fairies* (1910) spotlight different periods and people in English history as Puck befriends two small children, Dan and Una, and takes them through time. These few titles comprise Kipling's books read and enjoyed by young readers. Among his many well-known poems is *If*, which is especially liked by young people. He naturally wrote many further books for adults and gained many distinctions, including the Nobel Prize for Literature in 1907. He declined the offers of the Poet Laureateship and the Order of Merit. From 1902 he settled down in a house at Burwash, Sussex. He died on 18th January 1936, and is buried in the Poet's Corner in Westminster Abbey.

Knatchbull-Hugessen, Edward Hugessen (later Lord Brabourne)

Born 1829. Was for some years a Member of Parliament. He formed the custom of telling bedtime stories to his children and was eventually persuaded to publish a collection of them, *Stories for My Children*, in 1869. The book was an immediate success with public and critics alike and in 1871 came *Crackers for Christmas* and *Moonshine*. Further collections of fairy stories were: *Tales at Tea-Time* (1872), *Queer Folk* (1874), *River Legends* (1875), *Whispers from Fairyland* (1875), *Higgedly-Piggedly* (1877), *Uncle Joe's Stories* (1879), *Other Stories* (1880), *The Mountain Sprite's Kingdom* (1881), *Ferdinand's Adventure, and Other Stories*

(1882), *Friends and Foes from Fairyland* (1886) and *The Magic Oak Tree, and Prince Filderkin* (1894). The author admitted that he modelled many of his stories upon those of Hans Christian Andersen (whom he admired enormously) – but they also had some of the qualities of the Brothers Grimm, inasmuch as his fearsome descriptions of ogres, dwarfs, giants, etc could well have given the sensitive child nightmares! He once replied to a reviewer's criticism of this trait by pointing out that ogres did not live on strawberries and cream and that to paint them as pleasant, agreeable creatures would be contrary to all precedent. Today, his stories are almost forgotten – undeservedly, for they read quite well and have many flashes of humour and irony and no little excitement. Some of his typical story titles are: 'The Ogre's Cave', 'The River King', 'The Battle of the Stoats and Rats', 'The History of a Rabbit', 'The Robber-Band' and 'The Witch of Brooke Hollow'. He died in 1893.

Knight, Eric

Born on 10th April 1897, in Yorkshire. Emigrated to America at the age of fifteen and remained there for most of his life. Served with the Canadian Army in the First World War and with the American Army in the Second. Worked for various U.S. newspapers and magazines, both as writer and cartoonist. Most of his best-known stories and novels were set in his native Yorkshire, including *The Flying Yorkshireman* (1936) and *Sam Small Flies Again*, a book of short stories (1942). Another popular novel was *This Above All* (1941). His most famous book was enjoyed mainly by children and was *Lassie Come Home* (1940 USA, 1942 Britain). This was the moving story of a faithful collie dog who, when sold to a Duke and taken to Scotland, escaped and trekked 400 miles back home to her small boy master in Yorkshire. Sad and memorable, the story had a happy ending – much to every reader's relief. It made a remarkably successful motion picture. Knight died on 15th January 1943.

Knight, Captain Frank

Born in 1905 in London and educated at Whitgift Middle School, Croydon, Surrey. At fifteen he became an apprentice in

167

the Merchant Navy and for ten years served all over the world, eventually obtaining his Extra Master Mariner's Certificate at the age of twenty-four. Throughout the Second World War he taught navigation in the RAF to pupil-navigators of Bomber and Coastal Commands, flying regularly with them, both in Britain and in South Africa. After the war he sold yachts for some time, finally deciding to settle down to writing books for a living. His well-known and popular 'Clipper' series for young readers has won wide approval from critics and public alike and comprises a number of excellent and authentic sea stories set amidst the great sailing boat days of the eighteenth and nineteenth centuries. The 'Clipper' series includes, to date: *The Golden Monkey* (1953), *Voyage to Bengal* (1954), *Clipper to China* (1955), *The Bluenose Pirate* (1957), *He Sailed with Bluebeard* (1958) and *Slave's Apprentice* (1961). Another popular series is set in and around a sailing club at Chichester Harbour in Sussex and about a group of young people who frequent it. Titles include: *Mudlarks and Mysteries* (1955), *Family on the Tide* (1956), *Please Keep off the Mud* (1957) and *Shadows on the Mud* (1960). Other sea stories and historical adventures include: *The Partick Steamboat* (1958), *The Last of Lallows* (1961), *Clemency Draper* (1963), *Up, Sea Beggars!* (1964) and *Remember Vera Cruz!* (1965). Non-fiction titles include: *Captain Anson and the Treasure of Spain* (1959), *Young Drake* (1962), *Young Columbus* (1963), *Stories of Famous Sea Fights* (1963), *Stories of Famous Ships* (1963), *Captain Cook* (1964), *Stories of Famous Explorers by Sea* (1964), *They Told Mr Hakluyt* (1964), *Stories of Famous Explorers by Land* (1965) and *Prince of Cavaliers* (1967) a biography of Rupert of the Rhine. He has also written such maritime works for older readers as: *The Sea Story*, *The Beginner's Guide to the Sea* and *A Guide to Ocean Navigation*, as well as several adult adventure novels.

Kyle, Elizabeth

Born in Ayr, Scotland. Began writing children's stories for various annuals while still in her teens and has been busily writing ever since. Has been active in journalism (mainly Scottish newspapers and magazines) for most of her working life and is a regular contributor to *The Guardian* and the *Glasgow Herald*.

Her first children's novels were published in the early 1940s and include *The Vanishing Island, Visitors from England, The Seven Sapphires* and *Holly Hotel*. Later stories include: *The House of the Pelican* (1954), *Caroline House* (1955), *Run to Earth* (1957), *The Money-Cat* (1958), *Reiver's Road* (1953), *Girl With an Easel* (1962) and *Eagles' Nest* (1964). Her tales invariably have a remarkably felt and evoked distinctive setting, such as Edinburgh, Glasgow, the outer Scottish islands, London or Paris, and are authentically and lovingly described. The youthful characters are caught almost as well as the settings and the stories are usually exciting but believable mysteries and family adventures. Miss Kyle has also written a series of excellent biographies of famous people for young readers, including: *Maiden of Orleans* (Joan of Arc), *Queen of Scots* (Mary Stuart), *Victoria* and *Girl With a Song* (Jenny Lind). Many of her books have been broadcast in the BBC's Scottish Children's Hour. She has also published adult novels and travel books. She lives in Ayr.

La Fontaine, Jean de

Born in 1621 in Château-Thierry, Champagne, France, and educated there. Also attended the seminary of St Magloire when he originally had thoughts of entering the church. He later decided to study law, but abandoned this too and eventually entered the French Civil Service as Master of Waters and Forests – a position held by his father and grandfather before him. The job left him plenty of time in which to write, which he had enjoyed doing since his childhood. He married in 1647, but left his wife and son in 1659 and settled in Paris to devote himself seriously to writing, which he did under the generosity of several patrons. He published little of importance, however, until the first series of his *Stories* in 1664; these were strictly for adults and derived from such other writers as Boccaccio. The first six books of his famous *Fables in Verse* appeared in 1668; books seven and eight appeared in 1678, books nine to eleven in 1679 and book twelve, the last, in 1694. La Fontaine derived most of his *Fables* from Aesop, the Indian collection of Bidpai, and other sources. Like Aesop, the great majority of La Fontaine's fables were centred on animals, birds, insects and so on. Typical titles include: *The Grasshopper and the Ant, The Two*

Pigeons, The Town Mouse and the Country Mouse, The Fox and the Stork, Cat into Lady and *The Wolves and the Sheep*. All the 239 fables have morals. The first of La Fontaine's fables first appeared in English in 1692 in l'Estrange's *The Fables of Aesop and Others*. It was once said that his fables could be read and enjoyed by children, by students and by grown people of the world. Young readers can enjoy the stories and bits of animal lore, while adults can appreciate the writer's touches of sophisticated humour and characterisations. It is generally agreed that the fables should be read in their original French to savour their full quality, but there are several excellent translations available. La Fontaine wrote other poetry, stories and translations during his career, but it is almost entirely for his *Fables* that he is remembered today. He became a French Academician in 1684 and died in 1695.

Lagerlof, Selma

Born in 1858 in Varmland, Sweden, and educated at the Royal Women's Superior Training College, Stockholm, training to become a schoolteacher. She taught at Landskrona from 1885–95. She had dreamed of becoming a writer from early childhood, however, and in 1890 some of her stories appeared in a Swedish magazine. In 1891 her first and most famous novel, *Gosta Berling's Saga*, was published with great success. She wrote many more novels, travel books, religious works, etc. In the early 1900s she was commissioned by the Swedish National Teachers' Association to write a geographical school reader on Sweden and spent three years carrying out detailed researches into the various districts of Sweden, the national folk-lore, natural history and traditions before writing it. The book finally appeared in 1906–7 under the title *The Wonderful Adventures of Nils* and told how a small Swedish boy was changed into a tiny elf and rode all over Sweden on the back of a wild goose, having exciting adventures on the way. From his varied experiences with birds, animals and other creatures and people, Nils – and the young reader – learns much about the countryside of Sweden, its traditions, folk-lore, etc. The story is a long, imaginative fantasy which vividly paints the picture of a country and tells an excellent tale at the same time. The book was translated into English by Velma Swanston Howard – a close, Swedish-born friend of Miss Lagerlof's – and published in America in 1907, subsequently appearing in Britain. In English editions it has usually been issued in two parts, because of its length – *The Wonderful Adventures of Nils* and *The Further Adventures of Nils*. Selma Lagerlof received a Doctor of Literature degree from Upsala University in 1907 and, in 1909, became the first Swedish author to be awarded the Nobel Prize for Literature. She bought back her childhood home – her father's country estate called Marbacka – and returned there to live. She wrote a book about it, *Marbacka*, published in 1924. And she lived – and wrote – there for the rest of her life, apart from various trips abroad. She died in 1940.

Lamb, Charles and Mary

Charles Lamb was born on 10th February 1775, in the Temple, London, and educated at William Bird's day-school off Fleet Street, London, and Christ's Hospital. He became a clerk at the South Sea House in 1789, transferring to the East India Company House in 1792 and remaining there until his retirement in 1825. Mary Ann Lamb, Charles' elder sister, was born in 1764 and also educated at Bird's day-school in London. The family – father, mother, Charles and Mary (John, an elder brother, had left home) – lived in near-poverty, with Mary supplementing income by taking in needlework. In 1796 Mary, in a fit of insanity, wounded her father and killed her mother with a kitchen-knife. She was held in an asylum for a time but was released after about a year to remain in the care of Charles, whose life-long companion she became. Charles began his literary career by publishing poetry and plays. In 1807 he was asked by publisher William Godwin to write a children's book and came up with *The King and Queen of Hearts*, a short story told in rhyme. Also in 1807, Mary Godwin commissioned Mary Lamb to adapt a selection of Shakespeare's plays into short prose stories suitable for children. Mary wrote fourteen and Charles supplied stories for six tragedies, with the twenty tales being published in two volumes that same year under the title *Tales from Shakespeare*. The *Tales* were well received, making, to this day, good introductions to Shakespeare's plays, and have never really been superseded. They certainly brought the plots of Shakespeare to a completely new and untapped audience – adults unfamiliar with them bought the *Tales*, as well as their children – and helped to clarify the stories to many to whom Shakespeare had hitherto been something of a mystery. It may be of interest to note that Charles and Mary jointly received the sum of sixty guineas for the work. Next, Charles wrote *The Adventures of Ulysses* (1808), based on Chapman's translation of the *Odyssey*, re-telling the great stories anew for young readers in a fine, vigorous style. In 1809 Charles and Mary joined forces again to produce *Mrs Leicester's School*, in which new pupils at a girls' school gathered together and each told the story of their own life. There were ten stories, with seven by Mary and three ('Maria Howe', 'Susan Yates' and 'Arabella Hardy') by Charles. The tales, quiet and reflective, are partly based on childhood experiences of Charles and Mary. Also in 1809 came Charles and Mary Lamb's *Poetry for Children*, their last joint work. The poems were not well received and few have survived, though several were written with tenderness, charm and humour. In 1811 Charles wrote a verse version of an old French fairy tale, *Prince Dorus*. Later came Charles Lamb's important writings for adults, his famous *Essays of Elia* (1823) (many of which are enjoyed by children), his literary and dramatic criticisms and further poetry. Charles died at Edmonton, London, on 27th December 1834. Mary survived him by over twelve years and died at St John's Wood, London, on 20th May 1847.

Lamburn, Richmal Crompton

See: Crompton, Richmal

Lancaster, W. J. C.

See: Collingwood, Harry

Lang, Andrew

Born on 31st March 1844, at Selkirk, Scotland, eldest son of the county sheriff-clerk, and educated at Selkirk Grammar School,

Edinburgh Academy, St Andrew's and Glasgow Universities and Balliol College, Oxford, which he entered in 1864. He had a distinguished academic career, becoming a Fellow of Merton College in 1868. Seven years later he resigned his Fellowship, married and moved to London, where No. 1, Marloes Road, Kensington, was to become his home for the remainder of his life. Here, he began earning his living by writing; his first book had been a collection of verses published in 1872. Now he turned out an astonishing amount of articles for newspapers, magazines and the ninth edition of the *Encyclopaedia Britannica*. He also wrote poetry, literary reviews and essays. As a child he had always been fascinated by Scottish ballads and folk tales and had devloped a strong interest in the subjects of mythology, folk-lore, fairy origins, etc., and now he published the first of his several books on them. Many other topics brought forth books and articles from his prolific pen, but in 1884 came his first story for children, *The Princess Nobody*, based on a set of illustrations by Richard Doyle and on traditional fairly lore. In 1888 came his sixteenth-century fairy romance set in Scotland and called *The Gold of Fairnilee*. It was followed in 1889 by *Prince Prigio*, a humorous fairy court story in the tradition of Thackeray's *The Rose and the Ring*. Also in 1889 came the first book of traditional fairy stories collected and edited by Lang (though most were actually 're-told' by his wife, Leonora), *The Blue Fairy Book*. It was an immediate success and led to a whole series of similar books being edited by Lang – twenty-five in all, though only half were fairy-tale collections. Each title had a colour to describe it and the entire series, individually and collectively, was a remarkable success. Here, for the record, are the titles in the series: *The Blue Fairy Book* (1889), *The Red Fairy Book* (1890), *The Blue Poetry Book* (1891), *The Green Fairy Book* (1892), *The True Story Book* (1893), *The Yellow Fairy Book* (1894), *The Red True Story Book* (1895), *The Animal Story Book* (1896), *The Pink Fairy Book* (1897), *The Arabian Nights Entertainments* (1898), *The Red Book of Animal Stories* (1899), *The Grey Fairy Book* (1900), *The Violet Fairy Book* (1901), *The Book of Romance* (1902), *The Crimson Fairy Book* (1903), *The Brown Fairy Book* (1904), *The Red Romance Book* (1905), *The Orange Fairy Book* (1906), *The Olive Fairy Book* (1907), *The Book of Princes and Princesses* (1908), *The Red Book of Heroes* (1909), *The Lilac Fairy Book*

(1910), *The All Sorts of Stories Book* (1911), *The Book of Saints and Heroes* (1912) and *The Strange Story Book* (1913). *My Own Fairy Book* (1895) collected Lang's own fairy stories in one volume. A modern addition to the series was *The Rose Fairy Book* (1951), comprising selected tales from various titles in the old fairy book series. Despite the vast bulk of the rest of his work, it is for this children's series that Lang is best remembered and loved today. In 1893 he published a sequel to *Prince Prigio* titled *Prince Ricardo* (the adventures of Prigio's son). Later, in 1906, came a collection of further stories about Prigio and the fairy court of Pantouflia, *Tales of a Fairy Court*. The Ricardo and Prigio stories were also later reprinted in *Chronicles of Pantouflia* (1932). His superb *Tales of Troy and Greece* (1907) were evocative re-tellings of Greek myths. Among Lang's other re-tellings were: *Johnny Nut and the Golden Goose* (1887), *The Story of the Golden Fleece* (1903) and *The Story of Joan of Arc* (1906). An exciting 'romance' written by Lang in collaboration with his great friend H. Rider Haggard was *The World's Desire* (1890), which told of the last adventures of Odysseus and Helen of Troy. Lang also produced several novels, short stories, translations, poems, literary and critical works, etc. His *History of Scotland* appeared in 1900. He received Doctorates of St Andrew's University in 1888 and of Oxford University in 1904. Andrew Lang, who had no children, died on 20th July 1912, at Banchory, near Aberdeen, and was buried at St Andrews.

Leaf, Munro

Born on 4th December 1905, in Baltimore, Maryland, USA. He first worked as an English schoolteacher for some years before writing his first book, *Lo, the Poor Indian*, in 1934, under the pseudonym 'MUN'. That same year, a chance, overheard conversation between two small boys (who were free with the use of the word 'ain't') led him to write a light-hearted book for children called *Grammar Can Be Fun* (1934), which he illustrated himself with a 'match-stick figure' style that quickly became associated with him. The work became a best-seller and a whole series of a similar humorous, but genuinely informative, books followed, including: *Manners Can Be Fun* (1936), *Safety Can Be Fun* (1938), *Arithmetic Can Be Fun* (1949), *History Can Be Fun*

(1950), *Geography Can Be Fun* (1951) and *Science Can Be Fun* (1958). In 1936 he wrote his most famous book, *The Story of Ferdinand the Bull*, which was graphically illustrated by Robert Lawson and later made into a successful colour cartoon by Walt Disney. It became a tremendous best-seller in many countries, as well as America, and was bought and appreciated as much by adults as by children. The story told of a gentle bull whose favourite pastime was smelling flowers. One day he sat on a bee and his subsequent antics convinced people he was the fiercest bull in all Spain. He was taken off to the packed bull-ring, where an expectant audience awaited the greatest bull-fight of the year. They were disappointed – Ferdinand just sat down and sniffed a flower . . . He was returned to his meadow and to the quiet life he loved so much. Many symbolic meanings were read into the simple tale – quite unnecessarily. Leaf told a lovely, simple story and Lawson supplied beautiful illustrations. Children loved it for its humour and excitement, adults for its wit and observation – and both loved the pictures. *Ferdinand* was one of the most popular and best-loved characters of the late 1930s and is still loved to this day. It was recently reprinted in a Latin translation titled *Ferdinandus Taurus*. Leaf's other children's books include: *The Watchbirds* (1936), *Robert Francis Weatherbee* (1936), *Noodle* (1937), *Wee Gillis* (1938), *Fair Play* (1939) and *John Henry Davis* (1940). In 1957 he wrote *Three Promises to You* for the United Nations. He was a director of Frederick A. Stokes Publishing Company from 1932–39.

Lear, Edward

Born on 12th May 1812, in Highgate Village, London, one of the twenty-one children of a stockbroker of Danish descent and his English wife. Edward's Danish grandfather had been a naturalised Englishman who had changed his name from Lor to Lear. Edward's father went bankrupt in 1825 and the family was forced to split up and live in humble circumstances. Ann, the eldest daughter, took charge of Edward and they lived together in London, with frequent visits to another elder sister, Sarah, who was married and living in Arundel, Sussex. He had no formal education, as he was an extremely delicate child and, indeed, suffered chronically all his life from asthma, bronchitis and epilepsy; his sister taught him basic subjects and he had a natural gift for writing poetry and drawing. By the time he was fifteen he was practically earning his own living by undertaking artistic commissions from hospitals and medical researchers and doctors, colouring prints, painting on screens and fans – and, his favourite speciality, drawing and painting pictures of birds. At eighteen he was even taking in pupils. In 1831, through the influence of a friend, Edward was commissioned by the Zoological Society to make coloured drawings of the parrots in the London Zoo. The work took a year and, in 1832, Lear's *Illustrations of the Family of Psittacidae* was published in a large folio volume – the first luxury coloured bird book to appear in England in this format. The work received wide praise and Lear's reputation as a brilliant natural history artist was made. During the next three years or so he illustrated Dr Gray's *Tortoises, Terrapins and Turtles* (not published until 1872), Professor Bell's *British Mammalia*, John Gould's *Indian Pheasants* and *Birds of Europe and Toucans* and several volumes in Sir William Jardine's *Naturalist's Library*. Then the thirteenth Earl of Derby invited Lear to illustrate a book he was preparing on his private zoo at his country residence, Knowsley Hall, near Liverpool. Lear spent four happy years with Lord Derby and his family at Knowsley Hall and was a particular favourite of the Earl's grandchildren. Lear – like Lewis Carroll – got on especially well with children and they, in their turn, loved his humour and the wonderful nonsense verses he made up on the spot for them. They were usually in the form which came to be known as the 'limerick' and it is thought that Lear got the idea of the form from a work called *Anecdotes and Adventures of Fifteen Gentlemen* (1822) which contained several such verses, including one which he always remembered and which began 'There was an old man of Tobago'. Edward Lear did *not* invent the limerick – but he did popularise it and, one might say, made the form his own. In 1846 he published (anonymously) a collection of his verses titled *A Book of Nonsense*, illustrated by himself. The first verse in the book, and one which set the tone and pattern for the whole book was:

'There was an Old Man with a beard,
Who said, "It is just as I feared! –

> Two Owls and a Hen, four Larks and a Wren,
> Have all built their nests in my beard!" '

The book was an immediate success and when it was reprinted in 1861 Lear added further verses and pictures and also put his name on the title-page for the first time. Many people believed the book had been written by Lord Derby (since Lear had dedicated it to the Earl's grandchildren, etc.) but Lear soon became accepted as the author. Since 1837 Lear had been regularly spending most winters abroad and visited many countries all over the world, painting and making notes as he went. In 1841 he had published *Views in Rome and Its Environs*, and in 1846, *Illustrated Excursions in Italy*. He was also making for himself a rapid reputation as a fine landscape painter. In 1846, too, came the results of his four years with Lord Derby's zoo – *Gleanings from the Menagerie at Knowsley Hall*. Again in 1846 (an eventful year for Lear) he was summoned by Queen Victoria to give her a series of twelve drawing lessons; he taught her at Osborne, then later at Buckingham Palace, and the two got on together very well. Lear's subsequent nonsense books were: *Nonsense Songs, Stories, Botany and Alphabets* (1871), *More Nonsense* (1872), *Laughable Lyrics* (1877), *Queery Leary Nonsense* (1911), a book of more recently discovered verses, *Teapots and Quails* (1953) and a still more recently found MS, *ABC, Penned and Illustrated by Edward Lear* (1965). Famous characters from his nonsense songs and verses include 'The Jumblies', 'The Owl and the Pussy Cat', 'The Pobble', 'The Dong with the Luminous Nose', the 'Quangle Wangle', the 'Pelican Chorus' and 'Mr and Mrs Discobbolus'. There was also a memorable nonsense story, *The Story of the Four Little Children Who Went Round the World*. He illustrated all his books himself. He wrote and illustrated several more books about his travels and, for about the last twenty years of his life, lived at San Remo, Italy, due to failing health. His constant companions were his cat, Foss (who lived to the age of seventeen) and a faithful servant. Lear never lived to complete his greatest ambition, which was to illustrate the complete works of Tennyson. He died at San Remo on 29th January 1888.

Lewis, Cecil Day

Born on 27th April 1904, at Ballintogher, Ireland, the son of a clergyman. Educated at Sherborne and Wadham College, Oxford, where he edited *Oxford Poetry*, an anthology, in 1927. He worked as a schoolmaster in Oxford, Helensburgh and Cheltenham until 1935, when he decided to turn to full-time writing. He went on to make a reputation for himself as one of Britain's most distinguished younger poets, with much of his best work appearing during the 'thirties and 'forties. He also translated Virgil's *Georgics* and *Aeneid* into verse, and wrote several critical works and novels. Under the pseudonym 'NICHOLAS BLAKE' he wrote several excellent detective stories, including *A Question of Proof* (1935) and *Malice in Wonderland* (1940). In 1933 he wrote a fine boys' adventure story set in Elizabethan days and titled *Dick Willoughby*. In 1944 came a young readers' handbook to poetry, *Poetry for You*, followed by *Enjoying Poetry* in 1952. His most famous children's book was *The Otterbury Incident* (1948), which was partly based on the French film *Nous les Gosses* but with the action transplanted to England. The story told of two gangs of boys who come up against crooks, eventually helping to catch them. This was no routine boys' thriller, though, and was beautifully written and characterised. It is generally regarded by leading critics and librarians as one of the post-war classics of children's literature. He held the Chair of Poetry at Oxford University, 1951–55, and was appointed Poet Laureate on 1st January 1968.

Lewis, Clive Staples

Born on 29th November 1898, in Belfast, Ireland, the son of a solicitor, and educated at Malvern College and then privately. He entered University College, Oxford, in 1917, only to be called up for active service with the Somerset Light Infantry a few months later. He was wounded and invalided out in 1918, returning to Oxford at the beginning of 1919. He had an exceptionally brilliant scholastic career and after obtaining a double First was in 1925 elected Fellow and Tutor in English Literature at Magdalen College, Oxford. He held this position until 1954 when he became Professor of Medieval and Renaissance Literature at Cambridge University. His first two books were of poetry and published, in 1919 and 1926, under the pseudonym 'CLIVE HAMILTON'. He subsequently published many books, chiefly dealing with theological and literary matters – two of the best known are *The Screwtape Letters* (1942) and *Mere Christianity* (1952). *Out of the Silent Planet* (1938), *Perelandra* (1943) and *That Hideous Strength* (1945) comprised his popular trilogy of science-fiction stories (with allegorical overtones). The first concerned a trip to Mars, the second a voyage to Venus (this was the title given, in fact, to a paperback re-issue in 1953) and the third was a kind of 'spiritual thriller'. The same chief characters appeared in each book. To children's literature, C. S. Lewis gave the lasting gift of the seven-volume saga of Narnia, which began in 1950 with *The Lion, the Witch, and the Wardrobe*. Narnia is a strange kingdom dominated by the fight between good (represented by the great lion Aslan) and evil (usually controlled by a witch and her followers). Various children can, at certain times, enter Narnia and become caught up with many adventures there – the first family of children in this first book enter the kingdom through the back of the wardrobe in the spare room. These imaginative, haunting stories can be read on two levels – as straightforward tales of high fantastic adventure, or as great allegorical and moral stories. No brief description can do justice to this major cycle in the field of children's fantasy – the books have to be read for themselves. The subsequent volumes in the Narnia series, in publication order, are: *Prince Caspian* (1951), *The Voyage of the 'Dawn Treader'* (1952), *The Silver Chair* (1953), *The Horse and His Boy* (1954), *The Magician's Nephew* (1955), *The Last Battle* (1956). In strict *chronological* sequence, *The Magician's Nephew* comes first, followed by *The Lion, the Witch and the Wardrobe*, *The Horse and His Boy*, *Prince Caspian*, *The Voyage of the 'Dawn Treader'*, *The Silver Chair* and *The Last Battle*. The Carnegie Medal for the Best Children's Book of 1956 was awarded to Lewis for *The Last Battle*, but the award was obviously an honour for the whole Narnia series, completed in that year. The entire series was admirably illustrated, incidentally, by Pauline Baynes. It has been translated into several languages and has received critical acclaim wherever it has appeared. Lewis received many honours during his career, including Hon. Doctor of Divinity at St Andrew's University – a rare distinction for a man not in Holy Orders. He died in 1963.

Leyland, Eric

Born 1911, in Ilford, Essex, the son of a clergyman, and educated at Brentwood School and University College, London. He studied librarianship with a view to making it his career and, in 1938, became Chief Librarian of Chingford, in East London. He held this post until 1946, when he was appointed Chief Librarian and Curator of Walthamstow, in the same area of London. In 1949 he resigned to become joint Principal, with his wife, of Normanhurst School, Chingford. Since 1939 he has written and/or edited more than 200 books for boys, including adventure, mystery and school stories, collections of short stories and non-fiction titles. Among his books are the David Flame series, the Steven Gale series, the Abbey School series, the Max and Scrap series, the Hunter Hawk series (in collaboration with T. E. Scott Chard), the Men of Action series, and the Boys' Book of . . . series. He has also written histories of the Victoria Cross and the submarine. He has written TV scripts, contributed to such magazines as *Boy's Own Paper* and *Eagle*, lectured all over Britain on books and the English language, worked as literary adviser to publishing firms, edited series of books and reviewed books regularly for various publications. He is a Fellow of the Library Association. He is undoubtedly one of the most popular purveyors of light boys' fiction in Britain. He has two grown-up children and lives at Woodford Green, Essex.

Lindsay, Norman

Born 1879 in Creswick, Victoria, New South Wales, Australia, the son of a country doctor, and educated locally (where he edited and illustrated the school magazine). At seventeen he joined his brother, Lionel, on the staff of an illustrated magazine in Melbourne. When the publication ceased he did varied freelance art work, including illustrations for a police gazette, jam labels and Sunday School texts. His illustrations to an edition of *The Decameron* helped him to obtain a post on the weekly *Bulletin* in Sydney, where he remained for many years. His first adult novel, *A Curate in Bohemia*, written when he was twenty-one, was published in 1913. In 1918 he published a superlatively funny and vigorously original children's nonsense story called

The Magic Pudding (published in Britain in 1931 and later re-issued) which deserves wider recognition than it appears to have received. The hilarious Australian story is about Bunyip Blue-gum (a Koala bear), Bill Barnacle the sailor, Sam Sawnoff the penguin – and Albert, a magic pudding which replenishes itself automatically as it is eaten and is prone to irascibility if people don't feel hungry. Albert is dogged by two pudding-thieves (a Possum and a Wombat) who are finally thwarted by his friends after a series of wildly inventive adventures. Lindsay's only other children's book was *The Flyaway Highway* (1936), another engaging fantasy. He also wrote a trio of stories dealing with boyhood and adolescence in Australia, one of which, *Saturdee* (1933), has been described as 'an Australian Tom Sawyer'. The other two titles were *Redheap* (1930) and *Halfway to Anywhere* (1947). Lindsay has also written several further adult novels, the most famous being the best-selling *The Cautious Amorist* (1934).

Linklater, Eric

Born 1899 at Dounby in the Orkney Islands, Scotland, and educated at Aberdeen Grammar School and Aberdeen University, where he began by studying medicine but later switched to English. He served with the Black Watch regiment during the First World War and was badly wounded at Passchendaele. After the war he became assistant editor of *The Times of India* at Bombay, in 1927 was an assistant Professor of English Literature at Aberdeen University, and between 1928 and 1930 he travelled to America on a Commonwealth Fellowship. During this period he published his first novel, *Poet's Pub*, followed, in 1931, by *Juan in America*. He subsequently wrote many more novels, plays, biographies, historical works and volumes of poetry. During the Second World War he again served in the army. In 1944 he published the first of his two books for children, *The Wind on the Moon*, which won the Carnegie Medal as Best Children's Book of the Year. It is a delightful fantasy-farce about two small girls, Dinah and Dorinda, who turn into kangaroos and join a zoo. There they meet characters such as Mr Parker, the giraffe who is also a detective, and Bendigo, a bear who reads *The Times*. Adventures follow fast and furious, with the girls reverting to their human shape and rescuing their father from a dictator's prison in Europe. Linklater recalls that the early part of the story originated during a rainy walk in Scotland with his two small daughters; he improvised the tale desperately trying to stop their crying. Later, in the comfort of home, he began to write it all down ... In 1949 came his second children's novel, *The Pirates in the Deep Blue Sea*, which is a mad fantasy involving two boys, Timothy and Hew, with their grown-up friend, Sam Sturgeon, in a hunt for treasure, during which they encounter bloodthirsty pirates, mermaids and a talking octopus – another exhilarating romp, written with great wit, dash and exuberance. From 1945–48 he was Lord Rector of Aberdeen University and in 1954 was awarded the C.B.E. He has travelled extensively in most parts of the world, but makes his home in Ross-shire, Scotland.

Lofting, Hugh

Born on 14th January 1886, at Maidenhead, Berkshire, and educated at a Jesuit boarding-school in Derbyshire. His ancestry was part-English and part-Irish. It has been said that, as a child, he kept a minature zoo and wild life 'museum' in his mother's linen cupboard – until it was discovered! He also enjoyed making up and telling stories to his brothers and sisters. In 1904 he went to the USA to study at the Massachusetts Institute of Technology. Later he completed his studies at the London Polytechnic and worked for a short time as an architect. He subsequently became a civil engineer, working in Canada, Africa and the West Indies, and in 1912 he settled in New York, where he also married. In 1916 he joined the British Army and served during the First World War in Flanders. While writing letters home to his children he tried to think of stories he could tell them (as he could scarcely describe his life in the trenches). He had become particularly moved by the sad plight of the army horses, who served as loyally as the men did but, when injured, did not have the benefit of medical surgery and were usually shot. He thought the ideal answer to the problem might be a special animal doctor – and if he could converse with the animals as well, it would be even better ... Out of these imaginings the unique character of 'Dr Dolittle' was born. Lofting first told stories of the Doctor in illustrated letters sent to his children in America from the Front. After the war Mrs Lofting persuaded her husband to send some of the stories to a publisher. They were immediately accepted and *The Story of Dr Dolittle*, illustrated by the author, was published in New York in 1920; it made its appearance in England in 1922. Dr John Dolittle, M.D., was originally a real human beings' doctor, but he kept so many animals in his house and garden that, in time, he lost all his human patients (with the exception of the cats'-meat-man) and decided to become an animals' doctor and adviser. With the help of Polynesia the parrot he learns how to talk to animals and, along with some of his animal-friends – Jip the dog, Gub-Gub the baby pig, Dab-Dab the duck and Too-Too the owl – he goes off on the first of his many adventures (in this first book, to Africa to cure the monkeys of a terrible sickness). In later books the Doctor acquires a secretary, Thomas Stubbins, who tells several of the stories in the first person. The subsequent books in the series (with English publication dates – original appearance in most cases was a year earlier in America) were: *The Voyages of Dr Dolittle* (1923) – which won the Newbery Medal in the USA as the Best Children's Book of the Year, *Dr Dolittle's Post-Office* (1924), *Dr Dolittle's Circus* (1925), *Dr Dolittle's Zoo* (1926), *Dr Dolittle's Caravan* (1927), *Dr Dolittle's Garden* (1928), *Dr Dolittle in the Moon* (1929), *Dr Dolittle's Return* (1933), *Dr Dolittle and the Secret Lake* (1949), *Dr Dolittle and the Green Canary* (1951) and *Dr Doolittle's Puddleby Adventures* (1953) (posthumously published stories collected and edited by Lofting's wife). Several newly-illustrated Dr Dolittle books, mostly in picture-book format, were issued in 1968 to coincide with the interest stimulated by the successful motion picture version titled *Dr Dolittle*. Also in 1968 appeared *Dr Dolittle: a Treasury*, a selection of choice episodes from the entire series, with many previously unpublished Lofting drawings. Other children's books include: *The Story of Mrs Tubbs* (1923), *Porridge Poetry* (1924), *Noisy Nora* (1929), *Gub-Gub's Book* (1933), *The Twilight of Magic* (1931) and *Tommy, Tilly and Mrs Tubbs* (1936). Hugh Lofting's books have been translated into more than a dozen languages and the Dr Dolittle books, in particular, are popular with children all over the world. He lived in California during his later years and died there on 26th September 1947.

Lorenzini, Carlo

See: Collodi, Carlo

Lucas, Edward Verrall

Born on 12th June 1868, at Eltham, Kent (now London), one of a Quaker family. Moved to Brighton, Sussex, in early childhood and spent over twenty years there, attending various schools, being apprenticed to a bookseller and finally, from 1889–92, working as a reporter on the *Sussex Daily News*. Studied at University College, London, also contributing verses and articles to the *Globe*, which he later joined permanently, remaining on the staff for several years. He subsequently contributed to many newspapers and magazines and wrote a wide variety of books, including novels, collections of essays, criticism and travel books. He was assistant editor of *Punch* in the early years of the century and later became its film reviewer. He compiled several popular anthologies, including the best-selling *The Open Road* (1899). In 1897 he edited *A Book of Verses for Children*, which included useful and copious notes. *The Flamp, and other Stories for Children* appeared also in 1897 and included the amusing *The Schoolboy's Apprentice*. *Another Book of Verses for Children* followed in 1907, then *Anne's Terrible Good Nature, and Other Stories* (1908), *The Slow-coach* (1910), a children's caravanning holiday story, and *Playtime and Company* (1925). Lucas also edited several volumes of old children's stories and verses, including: *Old Fashioned Tales, Forgotten Tales of Long Ago, Runaways and Castaways, The Original Poems and Others* (by Jane and Ann Taylor and Adelaide O'Keefe), etc. He was Chairman of Methuen's, the publishers, for some years. He was also an authority on Charles and Mary Lamb and edited both their Works and their Letters. He died on 26th June 1938.

Lunn, Sir Arnold

Born 1888 in Madras, India, and educated at Harrow School and Oxford University. In 1913 he published a novel called *The Harrovians*, a realistic picture of public school life at Harrow as seen through the eyes of a schoolboy. The book was exceptionally well received by both press and public and still reads well as a detailed day-by-day account of Harrow life in the early 1900s. Sir Arnold later went on to enjoy a distinguished career as a leading British mountaineer and winter sports expert. He is the former president of the Ski Club of Great Britain, the former editor of the *British Ski Year Book*, and the author of many books on these subjects, such as: *Mountain Jubilee*, *The Englishman and the Alps*, *The Complete Ski-Runner*, *The Story of Ski-ing*, *A Century of Mountaineering*, as well as several travel books on Switzerland, Italy, etc. He lives in London.

Lynch, Patricia Nora

Born 1898 in Cork, Eire, and educated at convent schools in Ireland, England and Belgium. She has been absorbed in Irish history, legends and folk-lore since she was a small child and first heard the old stories from her mother and from an old traditional Irish storyteller who was a neighbour. By the time she was a schoolgirl she had acquired the art of storytelling and recalls that her classmates always used to press her for a tale at every opportunity. Her first book, *The Cobbler's Apprentice*, was published in 1932 and was followed by *The Turf-Cutter's Donkey* (1934), *King of the Tinkers* (1938), *The Grey Goose of Kilnevin* (1939), *Fiddler's Quest* (1941) and *Long Ears* (1943). Her stories are usually set in the enchanting Irish countryside and deal with tinkers, fairs, leprechauns and magic of a special kind – though, particularly in some of her later books, she writes of real-life and very contemporary Irish characters, including some eminently believable children. She has written well over forty books for children, which have been translated into eight languages, broadcast as radio plays all over the world and won several literary awards, including the Silver Medal at the Tailteann Festival, Ireland (for *The Cobbler's Apprentice*), the Certificate of Service to Literature in America and the Irish Women Writers' Award. In 1953 she began the series of popular 'Brogeen' books with *Brogeen and the Green Shoes*. She has since written a dozen books about this appealing little Irish leprechaun shoe-mender. Other, non-Brogeen books include: *Strangers at the Fair* (short stories) (1946), *The Dark Sailor of Youghal* (1953), *The Turf-Cutter's Donkey Goes Visiting* (1936), *The Turf-Cutter's Donkey Kicks Up his Heels* (1949), *The Mad O'Haras*,

185

Delia Daly of Galloping Green (1953), *Tinker Boy* (1953), *Fiona Leaps the Bonfire* (1957), *Jinny the Changeling* (1959), *Ryan's Fort* (1961), *The House by Lough Neagh* (1963), *Holiday at Rosquin* (1964), *Mona of the Isle* (1965) and *The Kerry Caravan* (1967). Different types of books have been *Knights of God: Stories of Irish Saints* (1948) and *Tales of Irish Enchantment*, a book of Irish legends. Today, Patricia Lynch – probably Ireland's most distinguished living writer of children's books – lives on the heights just outside Dublin, where she writes prolifically, usually producing at least two new books every year.

McCulloch, Derek

Born on 18th November 1897, in Plymouth, Devon, and educated at Croydon and Plymouth. Enlisted, at the age of seventeen, in the Public Schools Battalion, was later commissioned and saw much active service during the First World War. He was seriously injured, losing an eye, a leg and a lung, before being invalided out of the army. He joined the BBC in 1926 as a London announcer and in 1933 became Organiser of Children's Hour, being appointed the programme's Director in 1938, a position he held until 1950. As the friendly, soft-spoken 'Uncle Mac' of BBC Children's Hour he won countless admirers among both children and adults. He produced and introduced thousands of broadcasts and was especially associated with the popular 'Toytown' series, in which he played the role of Larry the Lamb as well as narrating. His first books were humorous ones with such titles as *Nonsericks* and *Gardening Guyed*. He also published several children's books including: *Cornish Adventure, Cornish Mystery, Television for Children, Every Child's Pilgrim's Progress, Every Child's Birthday Book, Travellers Three* and *The Son of the Ruler*. He also edited many editions of the BBC Children's Hour Annual. From 1950–53 he was children's editor of the *News Chronicle*. He was awarded the O.B.E. in 1939. He lived in Banstead, Surrey, for many years, and died on 1st June 1967.

MacDonald, George

Born on 10th December 1824, at Huntly, Aberdeenshire, Scotland, one of the six sons of a weaver, and educated at the local school and at Aberdeen University. On leaving university in 1845 he became private tutor to a family of children in London for three years. Then he decided to enter the Church and studied for the Congregational ministry at Highbury Theological College. In 1850 he was appointed minister of the Trinity Congregational Church at Arundel, Sussex, but resigned after three years, having displeased his congregation with his somewhat broad and unconventional religious views. Now married, MacDonald moved to Manchester, where he lectured and preached, at times being near to poverty. The publication of his first book, *Within and Without*, a poetic drama, in 1855, created no literary stir, but brought him the friendship and help of Lady Byron, widow of the poet. She sent him for a much-needed holiday to Algiers (he suffered nearly all his life with a tubercular illness) and, on his return to England, helped him to settle at Hastings. He now resolved to concentrate upon a literary career and published his *Poems* in 1857, followed the next year by his first prose work, *Phantastes: a Faerie Romance* (but intended for adult readers). It was a great success and in 1859 he and his increasing family moved to London, where he was able to meet many prominent literary figures. His success was consolidated with his series of popular novels about Scottish country life, including *David Elginbrod* (1862). It was around this period that MacDonald became Professor of Literature at Bedford College, London. He was now living with his wife and their eleven children in a lovely old house near the Thames at Hammersmith called 'The Retreat' (later William Morris, the poet, lived there and re-named it Kelmscott House). It was here that Lewis Carroll's yet unpublished *Alice's Adventures Underground* was read aloud to the family by Mrs MacDonald (Carroll being a close family friend). It was the MacDonald children's enthusiasm for the story that finally decided Carroll to publish it. In 1867 came MacDonald's *Dealings with the Fairies*, which contained several fairy tales, including 'The Light Princess', 'The Giant's Heart', 'The Shadows', 'The Golden Key' and 'Cross Purposes'; his other three short fairy stories – 'The Carosyn', 'Little Daylight' and 'The Day Boy and the Night Girl' – were also included in a later edition published after Mac-Donald's death. In 1868 he was invited to contribute a full-length children's serial story to the magazine *Good Words for the*

Young. He wrote *At the Back of the North Wind* and it ran regularly in the magazine for almost two years, eventually being published in book form in 1871, with fine illustrations by Arthur Hughes (who illustrated most of MacDonald's children's stories). This haunting and memorable story of Diamond, the cab-horse, and young Diamond, the little boy who was swept off to the land at the back of the north wind and had many adventures both there and as a young horse-cab driver in the streets of London, is MacDonald's best-known and most-loved children's book. MacDonald became editor of *Good Words for the Young* in 1869 and ran a further serial of his own during 1870 called *Ranald Bannerman's Boyhood*, a semi-autobiographical story, also published in book form in 1871. *The Princess and the Goblin* ran in the magazine from late 1870 to mid-1871, appearing as a book the following year. This was a fairy adventure story about Curdie, the miner's son who braves many strange challenges, among horrifying goblins inhabiting the inside of a mountain, to save Princess Irene. *The Princess and Curdie* was serialised in 1877 (published in book form in 1883) and was a sequel. Both stories symbolised the fight between good and evil in an exciting and colourful way and once read are never forgotten. Mac-Donald gave up the editorship of *Good Words for the Young* in 1872, after his story *Gutta Percha Willie* had finished serialisation. The latter appeared as a book in 1873 but was comparatively unsuccessful. He continued to contribute, however, and in 1875 another story, *A Double Story*, was serialised, published in book form as *The Wise Woman* later the same year and subsequently re-issued in 1895 as *The Lost Princess*. His only other children's book was *A Rough Shaking* (1890), which again was something of a failure. Another 'faerie romance' for adults was *Lilith* (1895). He spent much of the later period of his life at Bordighera, Italy, where he found the climate so much more suited to his constitution than that of England. George MacDonald died in Ashtead, Surrey, on 18th September 1905, after a long illness, and his remains were taken to be buried with his wife's at Bordighera.

MacFarlane, Stephen

See: Cross, John Keir

72 Charles Hamilton
('Frank Richards', etc.)

73 C. S. Lewis

74 William Mayne

75 Kenneth Grahame

76 Eleanor Farjeon

77 A. A. Milne

78 Philippa Pearce

79 Richmal Crompton

80 Anthony Buckeridge

81 Enid Blyton

82 Noel Streatfeild

83 Malcolm Saville

84 W. E. Johns

Mackenzie, Sir Compton

Born on 17th January 1883, in West Hartlepool, his real name being Edward Montague Compton. Educated at St Paul's and Magdalen College, Oxford. He originally studied law but later decided to concentrate on writing. His first successful novel, *The Passionate Elopement*, was published in 1911 and was followed by such best-sellers as *Carnival* (1912), *Sinister Street* (1913), *Poor Relations* (1919), *The Four Winds of Love* (1937) and *Whisky Galore* (1947). He has written a wide variety of other books and during the 1920s he wrote stories for the celebrated *Joy Street* series of yearly children's annuals. In 1924 he published a brilliant magical fantasy for children called *Santa Claus in Summer* which included all the favourite nursery rhyme characters. It was re-issued in 1960. He was Rector of Glasgow University from 1931–34 and was founder, and editor for many years, of *The Gramophone*, from 1922. He is currently engaged in writing and publishing his autobiography in eight volumes (or 'octaves', as he calls them) under the general title *My Life and Times*. He was awarded the O.B.E. in 1919 and knighted in 1952.

Marchant, Bessie

Born in 1862, in Petham, Kent, and educated privately. A girl's adventure story writer who was called, on more than one occasion, 'the girls' Henty' – and with good reason. Most of her vigorous, action-packed books were set in foreign countries and swept along at a swift, exciting pace; they blew like an invigorating breath of fresh air through the rest of the girls' fiction available in the 'nineties and early twentieth century and created for Miss Marchant a huge and enthusiastic readership. A brief selection from her many titles (with the story's setting in brackets) will give an indication of her range: *Joyce Harrington's Trust* (Argentina), *A Mysterious Inheritance* (British Columbia), *Heroine of the Ranch* (Tierra del Fuego), *The Countess from Canada* (Canadian backwoods), *Daughters of the Dominion* (Canadian frontier), *Girl and a Caravan* (Persia), *A Courageous Girl* (Uruguay), *The Girl Captives* (Indian frontier), *Three Girls on a Ranch* (New Mexico), *Cynthia Wins* (Canadian Rocky Mountains), *A Dangerous Mission* (Russian Revolution) and, at home in

England in 1916, *A Girl Munition Worker*. Bessie Marchant also wrote books for younger children and many stories for various magazines, annuals, etc. She published well over 150 full-length books during her forty-year career. She was married to the Rev. J. A. Comfort and lived for some years in Charlbury, Oxfordshire. She died in 1941.

Marryat, Frederick

Born on 10th July 1792, in Westminster, London, the son of Joseph Marryat, M.P. for Sandwich and Chairman of the Lloyds committee. He was educated at Ponders End, Middlesex, but he was unhappy at school and attempted to run away to sea several times before he was fourteen. When he *was* fourteen, his father relented and Marryat entered the Royal Navy as a midshipman under Lord Cochrane in the frigate 'Impérieuse'. He saw service in many parts of the world, loved the sea life and was a Commander at the age of twenty-three. He enjoyed a distinguished and adventurous naval career, often performing acts of heroism, and saved people's lives on various occasions. In 1818 he was awarded the Royal Humane Society's Gold Medal for his courage. He was elected a Fellow of the Royal Society in 1819 for inventing a mercantile flag-signalling code. In 1826 he became a C.B. He published his first novel, *Frank Mildmay; the Adventures of a Naval Officer*, in 1829, and its quick success, combined with other factors (including a growing family, for he had married in 1819) caused him to resign his naval command at the end of 1830. He decided to concentrate upon full-time professional writing and his next novel, *The King's Own*, appeared in 1830. From 1832–35 he edited *The Metropolitan Magazine*, serialising five of his own novels in it during that time. He wrote more than thirty books in all, his adult novels (though often enjoyed by young readers) including: *Newton Foster* (1832), *Peter Simple* (1834), *Jacob Faithful* (1834), *Mr Midshipman Easy* (1836), *Japhet in Search of a Father* (1836), *The Pirate and Three Cutters* (1836), *Snarley-Yow; or the Dog Fiend* (1837), *The Phantom Ship* (1839), *Poor Jack* (1840), *Percival Keene* (1842) and *The Privateer's-man, One hundred Years Ago* (1846). Most of these were sea adventure stories, also containing some humour of a broad variety. Marryat's life at sea furnished him with unrivalled background (and often foreground) material and atmosphere, and his vigorous yarns have an almost salty taste to them, so well does the author convey his settings. In 1841 Marryat – encouraged by his children to write a book in the manner of *Swiss Family Robinson* – published his first story intended specifically for children: *Masterman Ready*. It told of the Seagrave family who are shipwrecked on a desert island, together with a wise old sailor, Ready, and a coloured Nanny, Juno. A good, exciting shipwreck story, it is marred at times by its didacticism. Marryat's next children's story, *The Settlers in Canada* (1844), was about another family, the Campbells, who had to cope with marauding Red Indians on Lake Ontario. *The Children of the New Forest* (1847) – probably Marryat's most famous and popular book – was set in the time of the Roundheads and Cavaliers and told of the Beverly children, who had been rescued from the Roundheads and were living with an old retainer in the New Forest – and never far from discovery. Marryat's last story for young readers was *The Little Savage* (1848). He died about two-thirds of the way through the story, which was completed by his son Frank. It was a strange, haunting tale about a boy left alone on an island off Peru and his life with only the wild animals for company and comfort. In between writing his books, Marryat had unsuccessfully stood for Parliament in 1833 and visited America in 1837. He spent his last years as a (not very successful) farmer at Langham Manor, Norfolk. He died there on 8th August 1848 – his death being hastened, it was said, by the loss of his eldest son at sea.

Martin, J. P.

Born *c*. 1880 in Scarborough, Yorkshire. Entered the Methodist ministry in 1902, serving for several years as a missionary in South Africa, and later as a Chaplain in the First World War, mainly in Palestine. He went into semi-retirement soon after the end of the Second World War and settled in the village of Timberscombe, Somerset, continuing to serve the Chapel there until his death. During the early 1930s he invented a character called 'Uncle' for stories he used to tell his grandchildren. In 1964 his book about that same character, titled *Uncle*, was published and instantly and enthusiastically acclaimed for its exuberance and inventiveness. 'Uncle' is an elephant who lives at a lovely country home called Homeward, has a B.A. degree, likes wearing a purple dressing-gown and drives a traction-engine. His companions include Old Monkey and Cat Goodman – and his enemy is Beaver Hateman. *Uncle* was compared by some critics to Kenneth Grahame's 'Toad', and the author, J. P. Martin, to Lear and Carroll. Three more books in the series followed: *Uncle Cleans Up* (1965), *Uncle and His Detective* (1966) and *Uncle and the Treacle Trouble* (1967). Martin died in March 1966.

Martineau, Harriet

Born on 12th June 1802, at Norwich, the daughter of a woollen manufacturer of Huguenot descent. She had little formal education since, from early childhood, she was delicate, prone to illnesses of several kinds and, from the age of twelve, was extremely deaf. Added to this, her family upbringing was strict and religious to a degree; her parents were devout Unitarians and, from her teens, Harriet was too. She began writing theological articles for the Unitarian *Monthly Depository*, and in 1823 came her first book, *Devotional Exercises for Young Persons*. In the late 1820s the family was poverty-stricken (Mr Martineau having died after losing all his money) and Harriet and her sisters took in needlework to live. She had by now developed an intense interest in political economy and had the idea of writing stories to illustrate various principles of the subject. In 1832 the first volume of her lengthy series *Illustrations of Political Economy* appeared. It was a great success and Harriet became a great social and literary success in London, where she became regarded as a leading expert on economic matters. In 1841 she published, in four quarterly numbers, a work for children called *The Playfellow*, consisting of four stories: *The Peasant and the Prince, Feats on the Fjord, The Crofton Boys* and *The Settlers at Home*. All four were subsequently reprinted as separate books, the most popular and best-known being *Feats on the Fjord* (1844) and *The Crofton Boys* (1856). The former was one of the first attempts to set a children's story *about children* in another country – in this instance, Norway. It was rather overloaded with information about the country and its customs, but it also had incident and humour. *The Crofton Boys* was something of a milestone since it was probably the first boys' school story, appearing sixteen years before *Tom Brown's Schooldays*. It told of young Hugh Proctor's schooldays at Crofton School – none too happy ones as he was crippled for life during one early incident there. As usual, Harriet Martineau piled the moral and religious matter on far too generously, but the story has its entertaining moments and was certainly popular with youthful readers for many years. Another children's book was *The Billow and the Rock* (1846). Harriet Martineau wrote numerous other books, chiefly on political economy, religion, sociology and history, as well as a few novels. Her younger brother was James Martineau, the great theological philosopher and author. She died on 27th June 1876.

Masefield, John

Born on 1st June 1878, in Ledbury, Herefordshire, the son of a solicitor, and educated at King's School, Warwick. At thirteen he joined the 'Conway', the Merchant Navy training ship then situated in the Mersey. At fifteen he went to sea as an apprentice and sailed around Cape Horn. After a year or so as a seaman he suddenly became ill while in Chile and left the sea to work at various jobs in New York for about three years. He returned to London in 1897 and began to write for newspapers and magazines. His first book of poems, *Salt Water Ballads*, was published in 1902. Though practically all Masefield's work can be read and enjoyed by young readers, it is his books written specifically for children that are noted here. *A Book of Discoveries* (1910) tells of two young brothers and their discoveries of the joys of the countryside as they explore, chart rivers, dig for flints and generally do their best to out-Bevis Bevis – a very special kind of book, superlatively illustrated by Gordon Browne. *Martin Hyde: the Duke's Messenger* and *Jim Davis, or The Captive of the Smugglers* appeared respectively in 1910 and 1911 and are both excellent boys' adventure stories. *The Midnight Folk* (1927) and its sequel *The Box of Delights* (1935) are both wonderful and imaginative fantasy-adventures featuring a small boy named Kay Harker – two of the most magical and evocative stories ever written for children. *Dead Ned* (1938) ends with its hero being hanged for a murder he never committed (period: late eighteenth century) and its sequel, *Live and Kicking Ned* (1939) begins with him being rescued and nursed back to life by friends – both superb high adventure stories, etched out with some fine character studies. Masefield's sea stories are also enjoyed by young people; they include *A Mainsail Haul* (1905), *A Tarpaulin Muster* (1907), *The Bird of Dawning* (1933), *Victorious Troy* (1935) and *Captain Margaret* (1908). His poems need no praise here–superb and stimulating, the best-known are probably *Reynard the Fox* and *Sea Fever*. He became Poet Laureate in 1930, was awarded the Order of Merit in 1935, and was made a Companion of Literature by the Royal Society of Literature in 1961. He also received a doctorate from Oxford University in 1922. He died on 12th May 1967.

Mayne, William

Born 1928 in Yorkshire, the eldest of five children of a doctor, and educated at the Choir School in Canterbury, Kent (about which he later wrote several children's novels). He always had ambitions to become a writer and had written his first full-length book by the age of sixteen. In 1953 his first novel for children, *Follow the Footprints*, was published, and his second, *The World Upside Down*, the following year. *A Swarm in May* (1955) was the book which first really established him as one of the leading children's authors of the day. Set in the Choir School in Canterbury, it gave a warm and evocative picture of everyday life in that unique establishment and won wide praise. A sequel, *Choristers' Cake*, appeared in 1956. He has since produced more than twenty children's books, some intended for younger readers. His titles include: *The Member for the Marsh* (1956), *The Blue Boat* (1957), *A Grass Rope* (1957) (for which he won the Carnegie Medal for the Best Children's Book of the Year), *Underground Alley* (1958), *The Thumbstick* (1959), *The Rolling Season* (1960), *Cathedral Wednesday* (1960) (another Choir School story), *Summer Visitors* (1961), *The Changeling* (1961), *The Twelve Dancers* (1962), *Words and Music* (1963) (Choir School story), *A Parcel of Trees* (1963), *Plot Night* (1963), *Sand* (1964), *Whistling Rufus* (1964), *No More School* (1965), *Pig in the Middle* (1965), *Rooftops* (1966), *Earthfasts* (1966) and *The Battlefield*

(1967). Most of his books are for older children, especially young readers with imagination, who revel in Mayne's superb evocation of place and atmosphere, to say nothing of brilliant characterisation. Several of his stories are set in the Yorkshire Dales, where he spent his own childhood, and where he has worked as a successful schoolteacher. He has also edited, with Eleanor Farjeon, *The Hamish Hamilton Book of Kings* (1964) and *The Hamish Hamilton Book of Queens* (1965) and, as sole editor, *The Hamish Hamilton Book of Heroes* (1967). With Margery Gill as illustrator he wrote two picture-books, *A Day Without Wind* (1964) and *The Old Zion* (1966). Today he lives in his beloved Yorkshire in a comfortable stone cottage by the Fells, where he does all his writing, as well as reading a great deal. One of his hobbies is composing music and he is also interested in vintage cars.

Meade, L. T.

Born in 1854. Her full name was Elizabeth Thomasina Meade and she later became Mrs E. T. Smith. She was one of the most – if not *the* most – prolific of girls' writers of the late nineteenth/ early twentieth centuries, publishing around 250 books, ranging from stories for very young children to those for young ladies on the brink of married life. She was one of the first to pioneer the girls' school story and was to her generation what Angela Brazil was to be to hers. Her most popular school story was *A World of Girls* (1886), set in Lavender House School. Other widely read books include: *The Autocrat of the Nursery* (1884), *Polly, a New-Fashioned Girl* (1889), *Bashful Fifteen* (1892), *The Manor School* (1904) and many others with such titles as *The Seven Maids*, *Rebel of the School*, *A Very Naughty Girl*, *The Girls of St Wode's*, *Wild Kitty*, *Betty: a Schoolgirl* and *Queen Rose. Beyond the Blue Mountains* (1893) was part allegory, part fairy tale and also enjoyed great success. Miss Meade also wrote several historical adventure stories for girls. She was one of the first editors of the girls' magazine, *Atalanta*, which ran from 1887–98 and which published stories and serials by many well-known children's authors. After an industrious and extremely successful career, during which she published around half a dozen full-length books a year, L. T. Meade died in 1914.

Mee, Arthur Henry

Born on 21st July 1875, in Stapleford, Nottinghamshire, the son of a railway fireman. He was educated at the local school and at the age of fourteen became a proof-reader's assistant on the *Nottingham Evening Post*. At sixteen he joined the *Nottingham Daily Express* for four years, during which time he taught himself shorthand and thoroughly learnt his craft of reporting. He was editor of the *Nottingham Evening News* at twenty and soon afterwards combined this post with prolific contributions to numerous London magazines, especially *Tit-Bits*. It was only a matter of time before he went to Fleet Street and he became assistant editor of the short-lived London daily newspaper, the *Morning Herald*, as well as continuing his free-lance articles and columns for such magazines as *St James's Gazette*, etc. He subsequently became editor of *Black and White* and, from 1903–5, was literary editor of the *Daily Mail*. His first book, published in 1900, was a biography of Joseph Chamberlain. On 17th March 1908 there appeared the first fortnightly part of his momentous *Children's Encyclopaedia*, under the auspices of Lord Northcliffe; by the time the 50th and final part appeared, on 1st February 1910, the work had become a sensational success and its appearance an important landmark in the history of modern publishing. Nothing quite like it had been attempted before, but after its publication it had numerous imitators. Under Mee's editorship the work aimed at supplying to young readers a complete and wide-ranging compendium of knowledge, in carefully-chosen illustrations and easy-to-read style. It included nursery rhymes for the youngest reader and articles on the construction of dams and world politics for the older children. After the serial publication came the complete set of hard-cover volumes – eight to begin with and later ten volumes. The sets sold in hundreds of thousands and became a standard fixture in most homes which contained children. It was translated into French, Italian, Spanish, Portuguese, Arabic and Chinese, repeated its success in America and still sells steadily, in a revised edition, today. On the ending of the fortnightly *Children's Encyclopaedia*, Mee founded a similar but monthly children's magazine which, after several tentative titles, finally became most famous as *My Magazine*; this was also issued in yearly bound volumes and became a virtual 'sequel' to the 'C.E.' He edited it for twenty-five years and, in 1921, used much of its material for a further set of volumes called *The Children's Treasure-House*. Mee's famous and unique *Children's Newspaper* started publication in 1919 and ended as recently as 1965. Other serial publications (later appearing in volume form) which he edited included: *The Harmsworth Self-Educator* (1905–7), *Harmsworth's History of the World* (1907–9), *The World's Great Books* (1909–10), *Harmsworth's Natural History* (1910–11), *Harmsworth's Popular Science* (1911–13), *I See All: A Pictorial Encyclopaedia* (1928–30) and *Arthur Mee's Thousand Heroes* (1933–34). Other popular children's works included: *The Children's Bible* (1924) (in which the Bible was condensed to 250,000 words and illustrated with well-known paintings), *One Thousand Beautiful Things* (1925), *The Children's Shakespeare* (1926), *The Children's Bunyan* (1929) *Arthur Mee's Story Book* (1930), *One Thousand Famous Things* (1937) and *Arthur Mee's Book of the Flag* (1941). From 1936 until he died he edited his extremely popular series of travel books about Great Britain, *The King's England*, in thirty-seven illustrated volumes. He made his home at Eynsford, Kent, for many years. He died on 27th May 1943.

Meredith, Hal

See: Blyth, Harry

Meynell, Laurence

Born 1899 in Wolverhampton and educated at St Edmund's College, Old Hall, Ware, Dorset. Served in the H.A.C. during the First World War, subsequently becoming an articled pupil in a land agency. In 1924 he won Harrap's Novel Competition with his first novel, *Mockbeggar*, and began his career as a professional writer. He subsequently wrote numerous novels and mystery thrillers, also publishing novels under the pseudonym 'ROBERT ETON'. When he began writing for children he used the pseudonym 'A. STEPHEN TRING' and it was under this name that *The Old Gang* was published in 1947. This robust and amusing story of modern life in a boys' grammar school was an immediate success; the characters were realistic and the dialogue authentic.

In 1949 (still as Tring) he published *Penny Dreadful*, the adventures of a boisterous day-schoolgirl, Penny; her escapades were continued in a series which included such titles as *Penny Triumphant* (1953), *Penny Penitent* (1953), *Penny Puzzled* (1955) and *Penny Dramatic* (1956). *Barry's Exciting Year* came in 1951, about a typical schoolboy and his battles with the 11-plus. His adventures were continued in *Barry's Great Day* (1954) and *Barry Gets His Wish* (1957). These again appeared under the Tring credit. Writing under his own name, Meynell published a biography of Brunel, the tunnel- and bridge-maker, *Builder and Dreamer*, in 1952 (in 1954 he wrote a story, *Bridge Under the Water*, which told of Brunel's Thames tunnel). His other titles include: *Young Master Carver* (1952), *Smoky* (1953), *Under the Hollies* (1954), *Policeman in the Family* (1953), *Animal Doctor* (1956), *Young Architect* (1958) and *The Hunted King* (1959). He has also written a popular series of girls' stories about 'Nurse Ross'. Meynell's particular subject is Dr Samuel Johnson and he is vice-president of the Johnsonian Society. Married to novelist Shirley Darbyshire, he lives at Great Missenden, Buckinghamshire.

Mills, Annette

Born in Chelsea, London, and educated in Norwich. She originally studied for her L.R.A.M., intending to become a pianist and composer. Instead, she switched her attention to dancing and, after much more study and practice, found a partner and toured the music halls of England as an acrobatic dancer. After an accident, she gave up dancing and, returning to her piano, began to write and compose songs and numbers for leading musical revue stars of the London stage. She went on to write many popular songs of the late 'thirties and 1940s, including 'When You're Home Sweet Home Again', 'With a Feather in Her Tyrolean Hat' and the enormously successful 'Boomps-a-Daisy'. As a result of her new success she toured music-halls once more and did many broadcasts for the BBC. She also organised shows for the services in the Second World War, toured army, RAF and naval bases, wrote radio plays and sketches and appeared in revues. Then she spent three years in hospital following a serious car accident. Soon after BBC TV re-opened after the war in 1946, Annette Mills told a story in a children's programme. Then she made further appearances, later suggesting that one or two little puppets might appear with her, walking on her piano-top. Puppet expert Jan Bussell and his wife Ann Hogarth (who 'pulled the strings') produced several possible characters, including a little mule who appeared in an 'act' with a clown named Crumpet. The clown was dropped but the wooden mule was Miss Mills' guest in her next programme – and stayed on to become one of British television's most famous and beloved children's characters: Muffin the Mule. Subsequently she 'co-starred' with several more of Muffin's puppet friends, including Peregrine Penguin, Oswald Ostrich, Louise Lamb and Peter Pup (not forgetting Prudence Kitten, designed by George Fry). She won several TV Awards. A whole industry grew up around Muffin, including special toys, records, nursery furniture, crockery and so on. Annette Mills went on to write a whole series of 'Muffin' books and annuals, illustrated by her artist-daughter Molly Blake, including *My Annette Mills Gift Book*, which featured all the popular characters. Annette was the elder sister of film actor John Mills. She died, much mourned by her many young admirers, on 11th January 1955.

Milne, Alan Alexander

Born on 18th January 1882, in London, and educated at Westminster School and Trinity College, Cambridge, where he was editor of *Granta*. He disappointed his schoolmaster father by obtaining only a third-class degree in mathematics, and finally persuaded him that it was a writing career he had set his heart upon. With a financial start of a little over £300 from his father, Milne became a free-lance journalist in London in 1903, writing 1,000 words a day but earning only £20 in his first year's work. One of the magazines which had published his work, however, was *Punch*, which he took as a good sign. By the end of his second year as a free-lance he was self-supporting and in 1906, at the age of twenty-four, he was appointed Assistant Editor of *Punch*, the magazine he admired so much. He held this post, also contributing to the magazine, until 1914 and the outbreak of the First World War, when he joined the Royal Warwickshire Regiment and served at the Front. During his service he wrote his first children's book (in 1915) and it was published at the end of 1917; it was *Once On a Time* and was a light-hearted, humorous fairy story concerning the rival courts of Euralia and Barodia. It was rather overlooked by critics and public alike at the time, but has since been reprinted at least twice. Milne also began writing plays whilst serving in the army, including *Make-Believe* (first produced in 1918), consisting of three charming one-act plays for children. Soon after the end of the war, Milne achieved stage success with several light comedy plays, including *Mr Pim Passes By* (1919), *The Dover Road* (1923) and *The Truth About Blayds* (1923). He was also contributing to *Punch* and other magazines. Three collections of his essays, from *Punch* and elsewhere, were also published. In 1923 Milne was invited by his old friend and fellow-*Punch* contributor, Rose Fyleman (famous for her children's fairy stories and poems), to write some children's verses for a new magazine she was starting called *Merry-Go-Round*. He at first refused, then changed his mind and sent a set of verses called *The Dormouse and the Doctor*. Miss Fyleman was delighted and urged Milne to write a whole book of similar poems. He liked the idea and wrote more, using as his model his three-year-old son Christopher Robin (he had married Daphne de Selincourt in 1913). Christopher Robin had already appeared in his father's poem 'Vespers' (better-known, perhaps, as 'Christopher Robin is saying his Prayers') which won wide popularity (both as poem and song) and also distinction, being included in Queen Mary's dolls' house library at Windsor Castle. These new verses about Christopher Robin and his toys began to appear regularly in *Punch* starting on 9th January 1924. The complete collection was published later in the same year under the now-famous title, *When We Were Very Young*. It was an immediate, even sensational, success, in both Britain and America. The book was dedicated to 'Billy Moon', which was the name Christopher Robin gave himself as soon as he began to talk. A second collection of similar outstanding children's verses, *Now We Are Six*, followed in 1927. The two books comprise probably the best verses ever written for – and about – young children. In 1926 Milne published *Winnie-the-Pooh*, with a sequel, *The House at Pooh Corner*, following in 1928. In these two enchanting books Milne introduced his son,

Christopher Robin, once again, but this time in prose stories which featured such characters as Pooh, Piglet, Eeyore, Owl, Rabbit, Tigger and Kanga (with Roo in her pouch). They were based loosely on bedtime stories told to Christopher Robin. Readers first met Pooh Bear in the earlier verse collections, when he started by being known simply as 'Edward Bear'. The change of name came when the real Christopher Robin became a great admirer of an American Black Bear who lived on the Mappin Terraces at the London Zoo and whose name was Winnie. When young C. R. decided to give 'Edward Bear' a new name he joined 'Winnie' to 'Pooh' (the name of a swan he had once known) and the final result is now famous the world over. Most of the characters in the stories were based on C. R.'s real-life toy animals; today those original toys – Winnie-the-Pooh, Piglet, Eeyore, Tigger and Kanga – reside in a glass case in the offices of E. P. Dutton and Co in New York – Milne's American publishers. It may be of interest to note that the original 'Pooh' came from Harrod's store in London and was C. R.'s first birthday present. These unique tales of a small boy and his make-believe adventures with his toy-animals-come-to-life in an English wood are among the best ever written for children. In those four short years, from 1924 to 1928, A. A. Milne made a historic, important and highly entertaining contribution to the field of children's literature and one on which his future fame will doubtless rest. In 1929 Milne adapted Kenneth Grahame's *Wind in the Willows* as a stage play, *Toad of Toad Hall*; it has since been produced many times on the stage, and is a regular attraction of the London Christmas season. In 1925 Milne also published *A Gallery of Children*, a book of child studies, with striking coloured illustrations by Dutch artist Le Mair. No small part of the great success of Milne's earlier quartet of children's books, incidentally, were the superb and 'just-right' illustrations of E. H. Shepard. Milne's only further contributions to children's entertainment were a one-act play, *The Ugly Duckling*, in 1943, which is still a favourite school production today, and a book comprising two recently discovered fairy tales, *Prince Rabbit* and *The Princess Who Could Not Laugh* (1966). He wrote several more plays, novels and essays for adults. Alan Alexander Milne died on 31st January 1956.

Mitchison, Naomi

Born on 1st November 1897 in Edinburgh, Scotland, and educated at Dragon School, Oxford. She came of a distinguished family, her father being Professor J. S. Haldane, the physiologist, her uncle Viscount Haldane, the statesman, and her brother Professor J. B. S. Haldane, the noted scientist and biologist (and himself the author of a humorous classic for children, *My Friend, Mr Leakey*, published in 1937). She married G. R. Mitchison, a barrister, in 1916. She originally intended to become a scientist but, developing her interest in history, she began to write stories with historical backgrounds, particularly concentrating upon ancient times. Her first book was *The Conquered* (1923), which was set at the time of the Roman conquest of Gaul and was probably the first 'naturalistic' historical novel for young people (the characters spoke colloquially and behaved naturally in a twentieth-century manner). Next came a quartet of books of tales about Ancient Greece and Rome, ranging from the fifth century B.C. to the fifth century A.D.: *When the Bough Breaks* (1924), *Cloud Cuckoo Land* (1925), *Barbarian Stories* (1927) and *Black Sparta* (1928). In 1930 the best of the stories contained in these four books were collected into a volume titled *The Hostages*, which was reprinted in 1964. A historical fantasy, *The Corn King and the Spring Queen*, appeared in 1931, and the following year came *An Outline for Boys and Girls and Their Parents* which Mrs Mitchison edited. This was a critical survey of modern knowledge, written by a team of distinguished contributors, and it enjoyed a wide success. Later books include: *The Big House* (1950), *Graeme and the Dragon* (1954), *The Land the Ravens Found* (1955), *The Far Harbour* (1957), *Judy and Lakshmi* (1959), *The Rib of the Green Umbrella* (1960), *Karensgaard* (1961) and *The Fairy Who Couldn't Tell a Lie* (1963). She has also written adult novels, a biography, a book of poems, etc., and has contributed to a variety of newspapers and magazines. Since 1937 Mrs Mitchison – who has three sons and two daughters – has lived in Carradale, Argyll, Scotland.

Moe, Jörgen E.

Born in Norway, 1813. Was a lyrical poet and theologian, later becoming Bishop of Christianssand, in Norway. But he will be chiefly remembered for his association with Peter Asbjörnsen: together, the friends, inseparable from childhood, collected innumerable traditional Norwegian folk tales and fairy stories, wrote them down and published them in a permanent form. Moe wrote other books too and in one of them, *Blind Anne*, he recalls the way in which he and Asbjörnsen used to collect the material for their folk-tale books. Moe died in 1882. (For a full account of Moe's work in association with Peter Asbjörnsen, see entry under Asbjörnsen.)

Molesworth, Mrs Mary Louisa

Born on 29th May 1839, in Rotterdam, Holland, her maiden name being Stewart. She left Holland before she was two and was taken by her parents to settle in Manchester, where her father built a very successful career for himself as a merchant and shipper. Both her parents were of Scottish descent. In Manchester, Louisa lived with her three brothers and two sisters (all younger than her except for one brother) in a small house in Rusholme Road, near the city's centre, until she was about fifteen; then, in 1855, the family moved out to the suburb of Whalley Range. During her childhood Louisa used to love visiting her maternal grandmother in Dunfermline, Scotland, where the old lady spent many hours telling her stories. Louisa was educated first by her mother at home, then at a boarding-school in Switzerland and finally at private classes held by the Rev. William Gaskell, husband of the author of *Cranford*. In 1858 Louisa became engaged to Major Richard Molesworth, nephew of Viscount Molesworth, and they married in 1861, living first at various army camps, then at Tabley Hall, Cheshire. She had seven children, but in 1869 a double tragedy occurred when both her thirteen-week-old baby son and her six-year-old daughter died. Louisa Molesworth began writing a long, adult, three-volume novel soon afterwards, possibly to help take her mind off the sad business, and it was published in 1870 under the title *Lover and Husband*. It appeared under the pseudonym 'ENNIS GRAHAM' (after an old childhood friend) since her father considered that writing was not becoming to a lady. After publishing three more adult novels, and moving to

Edinburgh, she wrote her first book of children's tales, *Tell Me a Story*, in 1875, and it appeared with illustrations by Walter Crane. *Carrots: Just a Little Boy* was published the following year and its characters were based upon her own family. It was this book which established Mrs Molesworth as a children's writer of note, and in 1877 came what was to become her most famous book, *The Cuckoo Clock*. It told the story of a little girl who was befriended by a wise, humorous and often bad-tempered cuckoo from a clock and of the exciting adventures she had in such places as Butterfly Land and the other side of the moon. *The Cuckoo Clock* was the last book to appear under the pseudonym of 'Ennis Graham'. In 1878 she went to live at Caen in Northern France with her children and widowed mother (she had now legally separated from her husband, Major Molesworth). She went on to write a total of just over 100 books, some of the most popular being: *The Tapestry Room* (1879), *A Christmas Child* (1880), *The Adventures of Herr Baby* (1881), *Hoodie* (1882), *Christmas Tree Land* (1884), *Us: An Old-Fashioned Story* (1885), *Four Winds Farm* (1887), *The Old Pincushion* (1889), *The Carved Lions* (1895), *The Ruby Ring* (1904) and *Fairies Afield* (1911). Many of her stories originally appeared in such magazines as *Little Folks*, *Aunt Judy's Magazine*, *The Child's Pictorial* and *The Monthly Packet*. Mrs Molesworth has been called 'the Jane Austen of the nursery' and the description is perhaps apt. She was probably at her best in writing about younger children whom she brought to life with remarkable realism. Many of her stories today seem dated but, on the other hand, they can be read and appreciated as period pieces. Her fairy tales and fantasies are as delightful now as when they were first written. In 1883 Mrs Molesworth returned to settle in London, living in Sloane Street for the last twenty years of her life. She died on 20th July 1921.

Mowbray, John

See: Hadath, Gunby

Mulock, Dinah Maria

Better known under her married name of 'MRS CRAIK'. Born 20th April 1836, in Stoke-on-Trent, where her father was a minister, and educated at Brampton House Academy there, and at other schools. Wrote her first verses when she was ten and at fourteen she saw her first published poem appear in the local newspaper (celebrating the birth of the Princess Royal). Her early youth was not a happy one since her father was somewhat uncongenial and his ministries often changing. She spent a short while in London, studying music and drawing, then returned to Stoke-on-Trent to care for her two ailing young brothers and her mother. By the time she was twenty, one brother and her mother were dead. With her remaining brother she moved to London and decided to concentrate upon writing. In 1849, when she was twenty-three, she published her first novel, *The Ogilvies*, which was a great success. With the appearance of her most famous novel *John Halifax, Gentleman* in 1856, she became established as one of the period's most popular authors. Her other adult novels included *Olive* (1850), *The Head of the Family* (1851) and *A Life for a Life* (1859). Her novels are sentimental to a degree and often melodramatic too. But *John Halifax, Gentleman* is still enjoyed today by all ages. She wrote several popular children's stories, some of them appearing in the magazine *Good Words for the Young*. In 1852 came *Alice Learmont*, a Scottish-flavoured fairy story, inspired by the Border legend of Thomas the Rhymer, followed the next year by *A Hero: Phillip's Book*, another story set in Scotland. A collection of re-told fairy stories, *The Fairy Book*, appeared in 1863. In 1872 came *The Adventures of a Brownie*, in which a prankish sprite becomes involved with a family, and in 1874 *The Little Lame Prince*, probably her most popular children's book; it is the touching story of little Prince Dolor, lame and sad, who has adventures by means of a wonderful magic cloak. Curiously enough, it has always been much more successful in America than in Britain. In 1865 Miss Mulock married George Lillie Craik, a partner in the Macmillan publishing firm, and subsequently became known to her reading public as 'Mrs Craik'. Altogether, she published nearly fifty volumes, including novels, essays, children's stories and verse. Around 1870 she and her husband adopted a little girl of two named Dorothy, who was said to have been the inspiration of several of her later children's stories, especially *The Adventures of a Brownie*. Mrs Craik died on 12th October 1887.

Nesbit, Edith

Born on 15th August 1858, in Kennington, London, the youngest of a family of six. Her father, John Collis Nesbit, was a noted agricultural chemist and ran his own agricultural college and farm in Lower Kennington Lane, where the family lived. He died when Edith was only three and she subsequently attended a number of different schools, both in England and – when her mother took her family abroad for the sake of Edith's elder sister – on the Continent. She began her schooling in Brighton, continued it in Stamford, Lincolnshire, and later attended an Ursuline Convent School in France, followed by a school in Germany. On the family's return to England they lived at Halstead Hall, in Kent. Her first published work – a poem called 'The Dawn' – appeared in the *Sunday Magazine* in 1876, when she was seventeen. Other poems appeared in *Argosy* and *Good Words*. In 1880 she married Hubert Bland, destined to become a leading Socialist writer and a pioneer member (with Edith) of the Fabian Society. The marriage got off to a bad start with Bland losing all his money in an ill-fated business venture and becoming seriously ill for a period. With a baby and a convalescent husband to look after and the rent of the small house in Lewisham, which they had taken, to be paid, Edith set out to make some money by her writing. For the next fifteen years she wrote numerous short stories, romantic novels, verses, and a few children's stories and 're-told' versions of Shakespeare and episodes in English history. During 1896–97 she was asked to contribute a series of childhood reminiscences to the *Girl's Own Paper*, which she did – and enjoyed doing so much that it gave her an idea for a possible children's book. . . . Christmas 1897 saw the appearance of a story called *The Treasure Seekers* in the *Illustrated London News* – and it appeared under the pseudonym 'ETHEL MORTIMER'. Further stories in the series appeared over the next few months in the *Pall Mall Magazine* and the *Windsor Magazine*. The complete *The Treasure Seekers* was published in book form at Christmas 1899 – and E. Nesbit (as her name always appeared on the title-page) had finally found her true metier: as a superlative writer of children's books. *The Treasure Seekers* told of the amusing and very real attempts of the six Bastable children – Dora, Oswald, Alice, Dicky, Noel

206

and H. O. – to restore the fallen fortunes of their house. It was received with acclamation by critics and young readers alike. During 1899, too, a series of magical short stories appeared in the *Strand Magazine*, being published in book form in 1900 under the title *The Book of Dragons* and illustrated by H. R. Millar, the brilliant artist who was so successfully to illustrate most of her later works. Also in 1899, E. Nesbit and her husband moved to the beautiful Well Hall, at Eltham, Kent, where they were to live for the next twenty-three years. Another collection of short stories, chiefly from the *Strand*, was published in 1901 as *Nine Unlikely Tales for Children*, with another book about the fortunes – and misfortunes – of the Bastable family, *The Would-be-Goods* appearing in the same year. From now on most of her books appeared first as serials in the pages of the *Strand* (dates given here denote first book publication). In 1902 came the first of her full-length 'magic' books, *Five Children and It*, introducing the bad-tempered Psammead, who granted a family of children (Cyril, Robert, Anthea, Jane and baby brother, the Lamb) one wish a day – usually with surprising consequences. The combination of magic and fantasy with ordinary, everyday proceedings and extremely likeable, realistic children, made an enchanting and memorable story and E. Nesbit's reputation as a leading children's writer was established for all time. The same children were involved with a Phoenix and a magic flying carpet in *The Phoenix and the Carpet* (1904), and embarked upon a quest into past times in search of the other half of a magical amulet in *The Story of the Amulet* (1906). *The New Treasure Seekers*, completing the Bastable trilogy, appeared in 1904 and a further collection of stories, *Oswald Bastable and Others*, in 1905. *The Railway Children*, about a family down on their luck who go to live in the country near a railway line, was published in 1906 and is probably the least well constructed of her books. At the other extreme, her next book, *The Enchanted Castle* (1907), is perhaps her most haunting and memorable book. Impossible to summarise, the story concerns three children (again so very believable and natural) who discover an old castle and a magic ring which makes them invisible, and their subsequent adventures. Two famous highlights are the scene in which a garden of mythological statues comes alive to enjoy a lively banquet, and the eerie incident in which the 'Ugly-Wuglies', grotesque creatures made by the children from brooms, umbrellas, coats, masks and so on, also come alive and pursue their creators. *The House of Arden* (1908) and *Harding's Luck* (1909) were two interlinked historical fantasies; in the first a young brother and sister go into their family past, by the good offices of the magic white Mouldiwarp, and in the second, their cousin Dickie, a lame slum boy, makes periodic visits to the past in which he is of noble birth. *The Magic City* (1910) was about a boy and girl who shrink to the size of the city they have built from household articles and ornaments and have many adventures there. *The Wonderful Garden* (1911) featured three children staying with their greatuncle in the country (and how beautifully the atmosphere of a hot sunny English country afternoon is captured) and their attempts to create their own magic. *The Magic World* (1912) was another collection of stories and *Wet Magic* (1913) recounted the adventures of a group of children who rescue a mermaid and later become caught up in underwater battles; it was E. Nesbit's last full-length book for children. Her husband was going blind, and in 1914 he died. She had money difficulties and found it such a struggle keeping Well Hall going that she was forced to take in paying guests during the First World War. In 1917 she re-married. Her new husband was Thomas Terry Tucker, a marine engineer and and old family friend. In 1921 they left Well Hall and went to live in a tiny cottage at Jesson St Mary's, near Dymchurch, Kent. Tucker persuaded Edith to write a few more children's stories and these were published posthumously in 1925 as *Five of Us – and Madeline*. *Wings and the Child* (1913) was an interesting book in which she gave her views on child upbringing, etc. She died at her home on 4th May 1924, after a long illness. She had three children by her first marriage – Paul, Iris and Fabian.

Newbery, John

Born in 1713, at Waltham St Lawrence, Berkshire, the son of a farmer. After helping his father on the farm he decided to give up this kind of work, and at sixteen took a job as assistant to William Carnan, a printer, merchant, and editor of *The Reading Mercury*. When Carnan died in 1737, Newbery married his widow and took control of the business, which was now printing and publishing books, as well as selling them, in addition to retailing medicines, cutlery and haberdashery. In 1740 he made a tour of Britain to obtain experience and knowledge of the book trade. Four years later he moved to London, eventually settling his business at the sign of 'The Bible and Sun' in St Paul's Churchyard, and rapidly began to expand his book publishing, printing and selling enterprises. He particularly decided to tread new ground in the production of children's books and, in 1744, brought out *A Little Pretty Pocket-Book* in gilt and flower-embossed covers for 6*d*. Newbery was an astute publicist and one of his typical advertisements remarked: 'The books are given away, only the binding is to be paid for.' Many more books for children flowed from the sign of The Bible and Sun and were eagerly bought by parents and (when they could afford it) by children themselves. Stories and books of instruction included *The Circle of the Sciences* (1745–46), *The Land of Cakes* (1746), *The Nutcracker* (1750), *Be Merry and Wise* (1758), *The Renowned History of Giles Gingerbread* (1765) and *Mother Goose's Melody* (*c*. 1765). In 1765, too, came *The History of Little Goody Two-Shoes*, which has sometimes been attributed to Oliver Goldsmith (though published, of course, by Newbery). This has been described by F. J. Harvey Darton as 'almost the first piece of English fiction deliberately written to amuse children only'. Until then nearly every children's book had been very brief, very didactic or very solemn (though Newbery himself had been trying to add a lighter touch to his own publications over the years). *Goody Two-Shoes* actually dared to tell a lengthy story about the adventures of a girl who is turned out of her home, together with her parents (who soon afterwards die) and brother, and her experiences as a teacher, in preventing cruelty to animals and finally marrying the Squire (with brother Tommy turning up at the end after having made his fortune!). It was like a breath of enjoyable fresh air through the musty rut of children's books of the mid-eighteenth century and a definite turning-point. Newbery also published the first children's periodical, *The Lilliputian Magazine* (1751). He was an energetic, likeable character who, as well as publishing, printing, writing and selling books, also commissioned many other authors to write for him, including Dr Johnson, Smollett and Goldsmith. He still continued to sell patent medicines too. Newbery's name was known throughout Britain and America by the end of his life; he is even immortalised in Goldsmith's *The Vicar of Wakefield*, where he is described as 'the philanthropic bookseller in St Paul's Churchyard, who has written so many little books for children: he called himself their friend, but he was the friend of all mankind'. John Newbery is truly 'the father of children's literature' and all subsequent young readers owe an immeasurable debt to him. His name is honoured in the United States by the annual award of the Newbery Medal by the American Library Association for the best children's book of the year. He died in 1767.

Nichols, Beverley

Born on 9th September 1898, in Bristol, and educated at Marlborough College and Oxford University, where he was editor of *Isis*, founder-editor of *The Oxford Outlook* and President of the Union. He also published his first novel, *Prelude*, while he was at Oxford. He subsequently combined writing with travel and wrote a famous autobiography at twenty-five called, aptly enough, *Twenty-Five*. He later wrote the popular *Down the Garden Path* (1932) about his experiences in living in a country cottage, became a popular newspaper and magazine columnist, and wrote plays and revues. His first children's book, *The Tree That Sat Down*, appeared in 1945. This excellently written imaginative fantasy about a little girl, Jill, who runs a tree-shop for the animals in the wood but meets evil opposition from a boy called Sam and a witch, met with wide praise and great success. Two more adventures of Jill appeared – *The Stream That Stood Still* (1948) and *The Mountain of Magic* (1950). The trio represents an outstanding and underrated tour-de-force in the field of children's imaginative writing and it is to be regretted that Mr Nichols has not written further books for young readers.

Norton, Mary

Born in the early 1900s in Leighton Buzzard, Bedfordshire. Her earliest ambition was to become an actress and she was a member of the Old Vic Theatre Company, under Lillian Baylis's direction, for about a year during the 'twenties, also making other stage appearances. She gave up the theatre to marry Robert C. Norton, one of a famous ship-owning family, and went to live with him in Portugal. It was here that her four children – two girls and two boys – were born and also where she first began writing. When the Second World War started, her husband joined the navy. She wanted to return to Britain but had to travel to New York first, with her four children. She was unable to obtain a passage home at once and lived in the States for a while, writing occasional adult stories and articles. When she eventually returned to Britain in 1943 she began writing a children's book, as well as taking up her acting work once again. Her first book was published in 1945 and was broadcast as a radio play in BBC Children's Hour around the same time; titled *The Magic Bed-knob*, it introduced three children and their adventures with an old bed which had a magic knob on it and which took them wherever they wished. The most endearing and memorable character in the story was an elderly village spinster, Miss Price, who was learning industriously to be a witch and only succeeding in fits and starts. This story, and its successor, *Bonfires and Broomsticks* (1947), had plenty of lively humour and imagination and were partially based on stories Mrs Norton told her own children. After a space of five years came the book which immediately established Mary Norton as one of the foremost children's writers of her generation. This was *The Borrowers* and it won the Carnegie Medal as the Best Children's Book of 1952. Now a modern children's classic, it introduced a family of tiny people who live beneath the floorboards of an old house and furnish their minute 'rooms' with odd things they find lying around and 'borrow' for their own use. Thus their seats are cotton-reels, their wall-clocks are wrist-watches, their table a pill-box, their chest of drawers a pile of match-boxes, their pictures postage-stamps, and so on. Their names are Pod, Homily and little Arrietty (even their names are borrowed) and they dread cats and being seen by anyone. They make friends, though, with a little boy staying in the house and he brings them dolls' furniture and other useful luxuries until the housekeeper discovers their home and they have to make their escape ... Mrs Norton has said that the original idea for *The Borrowers* came from her own childhood when she used to play out elaborate games with small highly-painted china dolls on the floor of her home. Three further sequels were published, completing a perfect quartet of imaginative books for children: *The Borrowers Afield* (1955), *The Borrowers Afloat* (1959) and *The Borrowers Aloft* (1961). *The Borrowers Omnibus* (1966) contained all four books. Mary Norton's two earlier books, *The Magic Bed-knob* and *Bonfires and Broomsticks*, were reprinted as one complete story in 1957 under the title *Bed-knob and Broomstick*. She has also written plays for stage and radio.

Paget, Francis Edward

Born on 24th May 1806 and educated at Westminster School and Christ Church College, Oxford, receiving his degree in 1828. He was a firm upholder of the Oxford Movement and became Rector of Elford, near Lichfield, in 1835, a post which he held for the remainder of his life. He wrote several religious books and a work on old and new churches, but is perhaps best remembered as editor of *The Juvenile Englishman's Library* (1844–49), a series of twenty-one amusing, instructive and moral volumes for young readers, one of which was a story called *The Hope of the Katzekopfs*, written by the Rev. Paget himself. This has been described as 'the first real fairy story of its kind, written in English' and is an amusing tale set in a fairy court, and a forerunner of similar stories by Thackeray and Lang. The moral gets the upper hand in the final stages but there is plenty of enchantment and incident before that happens and the story is an important step in the history of the English fairy tale. *The Hope of the Katzekopfs* was published in 1844 under the pseudonym 'WILLIAM CHURNE OF STAFFORDSHIRE'. He died on 4th August 1882.

'Parley, Peter'

The pseudonym originated in America by Samuel Goodrich, who wrote, edited and published over 100 books on geography, history, science, travel, famous people, etc., largely in the form of didactic stories; he also edited *Peter Parley's Magazine*. (For full details see Goodrich, Samuel.) The 'Peter Parley' pseudonym was widely used and the style copied in many books published in England around the mid-nineteenth century and some of the authors and publishers who used it were William Martin (1801–67), George Mogridge (1787–1854), Thomas Tegg (1776–1845), Charles Tilt, Edward Lacey and Samuel Clark. The whole subject and history of 'Peter Parley' and his pirating is complex in the extreme, but a full report may be found in Harvey Darton's excellent *Children's Books in England* (1932).

Parry, David Harold

Born in 1868 and came from a long line of distinguished painters; his father and uncle were both well-known artists of the Manchester School. D. H. Parry himself studied art in London and Paris and painting was his greatest love throughout his life. He began his writing career in the late 1880s, contributing to Cassell's *Saturday Journal* and *Answers*. But it was through his friend, Max Pemberton, that his work was guided into boys' fiction. Pemberton was starting a new weekly boys' paper called *Chums* and he invited Parry to write the first serial for it. Parry accepted and the serial, *For Glory and Renown*, a historical war story, began in the first number of *Chums* in 1892. It began a long association and Parry was still writing for the paper in 1935. From 1892 Parry turned out an incredibly prolific amount of work, including fiction and factual articles, for practically every boys' paper of his period, including *The Captain*, for which he wrote the first serial, *The King's Red Coat*, in 1899. He was perhaps even better known to boys of his generation under his pseudonym 'MORTON PIKE', under which he wrote about highwaymen and Robin Hood. During one seven-year period, he wrote more than two million words about Robin Hood. Some of his most popular stories were *Guy of the Greenwood, Gilbert Nameless, The Red Rapiers* and *The Black Dragoons*. He also wrote under the name 'CAPTAIN WILTON BLAKE'. He came to be regarded as a great authority on the Napoleonic Wars. His *History of the Victoria Cross* became a well-known classic. So did his magnificent *History and Costumes of the Regiments of the British Army*, which he also illustrated. He was an expert in all military matters and it was recognised that his army and historical stories were correct in every detail. He lived and wrote in Norfolk nearly all his life, in a little secluded home known as

'Ben Gunn's Cottage', near Barton Broad. He died there in January 1950, at the age of 82.

Pearce, Ann Philippa

Born in 1920 in King's Mill House, Great Shelford, Cambridge-shire, where her father was a corn-miller. She spent much of her childhood leisure boating, fishing, bathing and skating on the river which ran past the house's large, sunny garden – activities and settings which played such an important part in her first two children's books. She won a scholarship to Girton College, Cambridge University, and subsequently worked as a script-writer and producer in the BBC Schools Department and also in the Education Department of the Oxford University Press. Her first book, *Minnow on the Say* (1955), was hailed everywhere as the best children's novel published for years and it is truly a memorable book. Simply, the story is of two boys, from different backgrounds, who combine in an unusual treasure-hunt from a canoe on the River Say. Character-drawing, the evocation of summer days by the river and superb writing (coupled with sympathetic illustrations by Ardizzone) went to make the book an outstanding one. Her second book, *Tom's Midnight Garden* (1958), equalled, if not surpassed, her first and was awarded the Carnegie Medal as the Best Children's Book of 1958. In this fascinating 'time story' a boy goes to stay with his aunt and uncle in a modern flat in a converted old house. When the grandfather clock strikes thirteen at midnight, he goes downstairs to investigate, enters the garden – and finds him-self back in Victorian days, talking and playing with a little girl who gradually grows older as he makes repeated visits. Again the atmosphere is magically created, the story haunting and the 'twist' ending so ingenious that it makes the reader turn back to the first page and re-read the book so as to appreciate the whole exercise once again. *Minnow on the Say* and *Tom's Midnight Garden* are two of the real and undisputed classics of modern children's literature. Miss Pearce's only other stories to date are *A Dog So Small* (1962), an unusual tale about a small working-class London boy who has an imaginary dog and spends much of his time day-dreaming (he ends up with a mongrel (real-life) dog instead of the chihuahua of his thoughts and learns a few salutary facts along the way), and *The Strange Sunflower* (1966) about a boy who dreams he enters sunflower land. In 1963 she collaborated with Sir Harold Scott on *From Inside Scotland Yard*. She is also general editor of the *People of the Past* series (Oxford University Press, 1966).

Peck, George Wilbur

Born on 28th September 1840, in Henderson, New York, and brought up and educated in Wisconsin. After serving in the Union army he worked on a New York newspaper, then bought a newspaper in LaCrosse, Wisconsin, which he called *The Sun* (*Peck's Sun*, as it later became known). Four years later, in 1878, he moved the paper to Milwaukee and, in 1882, began to write and publish in it the humorous adventures of *Peck's Bad Boy and His Pa*, which became immensely successful and boosted *The Sun* to a big nation-wide circulation. They also boosted Peck's political ambitions – he became so popular that he was voted Mayor of Milwaukee in 1890 and Governor of Wisconsin from 1890–94. The humorous sketches told of the many and often rather brutal tricks played by Hennery the Bad Boy upon his (usually) drunken father or upon the long-suffering Grocery Man. Broad, even coarse, in their humour, they were nevertheless vigorously written and often very funny. They were certainly enjoyed by all ages for many years after their initial appearance in the pages of *The Sun*. They appeared in book form in 1883 under the title *Peck's Bad Boy and His Pa*, followed by *Peck's Bad Boy and His Pa: Part II, The Grocery Man and Peck's Bad Boy* later the same year. Several further titles in the series appeared, culminating with *Peck's Bad Boy with the Cowboys* in 1907. George W. Peck died on 16th April 1916.

Pemberton, Sir Max

Born on 19th June 1863, in Birmingham, and educated at Merchant Taylors' School and Caius College, Cambridge. Became the first editor of the successful boys' magazine *Chums*, from 1892–93, and wrote a first-class adventure serial, *The Iron Pirate*, for the first volume. It was a great success and later published in book form (1893). In 1910 he wrote a sequel, *Captain Black*, also serialised in *Chums* and published as a book in 1911. Another serial, *The Sea Wolves*, ran in Volume 2 of *Chums*, and in 1917 came *The Man of Silver Mount*. He gave up the editorship of *Chums* after a year to concentrate upon his writing, returning to the field to become editor of *Cassell's Magazine* from 1896 to 1906, many of his own stories appearing in that publication also. He wrote many adult novels, short stories, stage plays and revues and a biography of Lord Northcliffe. He founded the London School of Journalism in 1920, became a director of Northcliffe Newspapers and a J.P., and was knighted in 1928. He was a keen sportsman and particularly liked golf, rowing and motoring. He died on 22nd February 1950, at the age of eighty-six.

Perrault, Charles

Born on 12th January 1628, in Paris, the son of a lawyer. He was educated at Beauvais and in 1651 became a member of the Paris Bar and a qualified lawyer and advocate. After a period of success at the Bar he worked for a while as secretary to his brother, Claude, the architect who designed, among other buildings, the Paris Observatory and the east frontage of the Louvre. Then, after becoming acquainted with Louis XIV's great minister, Colbert, the latter had him appointed Controller of the Royal Buildings and later helped him to become a member of the French Academy. Perrault's name first became known for his famous controversy with Boileau over the relative merits of the ancient and the modern writers (Perrault strongly supported the modernists). This led to his writing several poems and books on the subject, chiefly during the late 1680s and early 1690s. In 1697 came his most famous work: *Histoires ou contes du temps passé, avec des moralités – Histories and Tales of Long Ago, with Morals*. It comprised eight delightful (though a trifle fierce in places) fairy tales: 'The Sleeping Beauty', 'Little Red Riding Hood', 'Bluebeard', 'Puss in Boots', 'Diamonds and Toads' (or 'The Fairies'), 'Cinderella' (or 'The Glass Slipper'), 'Riquet with the Tuft' and 'Hop o' My Thumb'. The book's dedication (to 'Mademoiselle' – Elizabeth Charlotte d'Orleans, the King's niece) was signed 'Pierre D'Armancour', who was Perrault's young son (aged eighteen at the time) and the strong implication was that Pierre had written the work. But there are two schools of thought in this matter. Some scholars believe that Pierre did actually write the Tales; others that the dedication was a transparent bluff by Perrault, who actually wrote the collection of stories and wished his son to receive the credit; still other people believe that both father and son prepared the work together. Whoever was responsible, it is generally agreed that the Tales – based for the most part on old traditional folk tales – were set down beautifully and simply and are among the world's most famous and enchanting fairy stories. In the frontispiece of the original edition was shown an old nurse spinning as she told stories to three children; above the illustration ran the inscription *Contes de Ma Mère L'Oye* (Tales of Mother Goose). It is the first appearance of 'Mother Goose' in a children's book. (Controversy has raged for many years on the true origin of 'Mother Goose' – readers are referred to Darton for full details.) Earlier Perrault had published three verse tales – *Donkey-Skin*, *The Ridiculous Wishes* and *Patient Griselda* – which have often been printed in collections of Perrault's fairy tales, usually paraphrased into prose. Charles Perrault died in Paris on 16th May 1703.

Phillpotts, Eden

Born on 4th November 1862, in India, and educated at a private school in Plymouth. On leaving school he went to London to study for the stage, his ambition always having been to become an actor – or a painter. When he realised his talents in these directions were not as promising as he had imagined, he became a clerk in an insurance office for several frustrating years. In the early 1890s he decided to devote himself to writing and went on to become a prolific and distinguished author, particularly famous for his fine Dartmoor cycle of novels, including *Widecombe Fair* (1913). He also wrote such popular and long-running stage plays as *The Farmer's Wife* (1916) and *Yellow Sands* (1926). It is for his superlative school stories that he finds a place here, however. When Jerome K. Jerome and Robert Barr started a humorous magazine, *The Idler*, in the 'nineties, Phillpotts was an early recruit to the staff. Among his stories for this periodical was a series about 'The Human Boy', warmly written, authentically observed and beautifully characterised tales, told from the boy's angle, set in a small private school presided over by the awesome but often kindly Dr Dunston. They were so popular that they were collected together in book form in 1899 as *The Human Boy*. Later titles in the series included *The Human Boy Again*, *The Human Boy and the War*, *The Human Boy's Diary* and *From the Angle of Seventeen*. These school stories are among the funniest and most entertaining ever written and were said to be based loosely on Phillpotts' own schooldays in Plymouth. A shy, retiring man, Phillpotts spent almost his entire life in Devon, living chiefly at Torquay and, later, Exeter. He died in 1960 at the age of ninety-eight.

Pike, Morton

See: Parry, D. H.

Porter, Eleanor Hodgman

Born on 19th December 1868, in Littleton, New Hampshire, USA, the daughter of Francis Hodgman. She left school early, owing to ill-health, living an outdoor life for a time. She later studied at the New England Conservatory of Music and developed a fine singing voice. In 1893 she married John L. Porter. She published her first novel, *Cross Currents*, in 1907 and followed it the next year with a sequel, *The Turn of the Tide*. Both were popular sentimental novels. In 1911 came *Miss Billy*, the lightly told adventures of a young girl, followed by *Miss Billy's Decision* (1912) and *Miss Billy Married* (1914). Her most famous character was created in *Pollyanna* (1913), which became a remarkable international best-seller. The heroine was again a friendly young girl who liked nothing better than to spread her own particular 'glad' philosophy around to everyone she met. The book was dramatised and also filmed at least twice. It was followed in 1915 by *Pollyanna Grows Up*. Later books included *Just David* (1916) and *Dawn* (1919). She died on 21st May 1920. (After her death, at least four subsequent writers wrote more books about the ever-popular 'Pollyanna'. Titles include: *Pollyanna of the Orange Blossoms*, *Pollyanna's Jewels*, *Pollyanna's Debt of Honour* and *Pollyanna's Western Adventure* [1924–29, by

Harriet Lummis Smith]; *Pollyanna in Hollywood, Pollyanna's Castle in Mexico, Pollyanna's Door to Happiness* and *Pollyanna's Golden Horseshoe* [by Elizabeth Borton]; *Pollyanna's Protégé* [by Margaret Piper Chalmers]; and *Pollyanna at Six Star Ranch* [by Virginia May Moffitt]. The 'Pollyanna' series – also known as 'the Glad Books' – have sold over three million copies and been translated into many languages.)

Porter, Gene Stratton

Born Geneva Grace Stratton, on 17th August 1868, in Wabash County, Indiana, the daughter of a farmer. Near her home was the great Limberlost Swamp and there she studied birds, animals, moths and other wild life. In 1886 she married Charles Porter, a chemist, and they continued to live in the Limberlost area, which Mrs Porter loved so much. She wrote magazine articles, illustrated with her own photographs, and her expert knowledge of both natural history and photography brought her regular journalistic appointments. For two years she was photographic editor of *Recreation*, for a further two years she was on the natural history staff of *Outing*, and for another four years she was specialist in natural history photography on the *Photographic Times Annual Almanac*. Her first novel was *The Song of the Cardinal* (1902), but it was *Freckles* (1904) that brought her fame and fortune. It told the story of a boy who lived in the Limberlost Swamp and was full of the zest of the open air and the hum of insects which the author knew so well. It became a best-seller and was followed by *At the Foot of the Rainbow* (1908) and then by another best-seller, *A Girl of the Limberlost* (1909). The latter told of Elnora Comstock, a young girl who lived in the Indiana swampland, bullied by her unloving mother and collecting moths and butterflies to sell in order to raise money for her schooling. It was, like most of Mrs Porter's stories, very sentimental; but, again, its superb natural history background and atmosphere of shimmering heat made it a memorable tale. Subsequent novels include: *Music of the Wild* (1910), *The Harvester* (1911), *Moths of the Limberlost* (1912), *Laddie* (1913) (a fictional treatment of the author's own upbringing in Limberlost country), *Michael O'Halloran* (1915) and *Keeper of the Bees* (1925). Her natural history studies include: *Birds of the Bible*

(1909), *Homing With the Birds* (1919) and *Friends in Feathers* (1922). Gene Stratton Porter's books enjoyed a huge popular success in their time and she must be counted one of the biggest-selling authors of the first half of this century. At the time of her death, in a motor accident in Los Angeles on 6th December 1924, nearly ten million copies of her books had been sold.

Potter, Helen Beatrix

Born on 6th July 1866, at 2, Bolton Gardens, Kensington, London, the only daughter of wealthy parents whose family had made their fortune in the Lancashire cotton trade. Rupert Potter, her father, was a non-practising barrister and a skilled amateur photographer. Though she never wanted for anything, Beatrix's childhood was a lonely one, relieved by the company of her younger brother, Bertram, when home from school, and by eagerly awaited holidays in Scotland and the Lake District. She especially liked it when her father rented Wray Castle, near Lake Windermere, for the summer, for she loved the neighbouring countryside and she had made great friends with Canon Rawnsley, the Vicar of Wray, whom she admired for his tireless work in preserving the Lake District from development and disfiguration (he later, in fact, became a co-founder of the National Trust). Beatrix never attended school but received her education from governesses at home in Bolton Gardens. Her all-consuming interests were animals and drawing and painting. She kept small pets in her nursery, including a family of snails, a pair of mice, a rabbit, bats and a hedgehog (who drank milk from a doll's tea-cup). From a small child she did innumerable and exquisite drawings of plants, flowers and animals and was almost entirely self-taught. As she grew older she became engrossed with fungi and did hundreds of microscopically detailed sketches of various types in the hope of using them in a textbook. This never transpired, however, and she turned to a different form of artistic outlet. Her first published illustrations appeared around 1893 in a book of verses by F. E. Weatherley called *A Happy Pair*, in which she depicted rabbits and other small animals. Though quiet and almost shy with adults, Beatrix loved children and was always at ease with them. She often illustrated her letters to child friends with little animal drawings

85 Drawing by Hans Baumhauer from Selma Lagerlof's *The Wonderful Adventures of Nils*

86 *Struwwelpeter*, by Heinrich Hoffmann

87 Moominpappa, from
Finn Family Moomintroll,
by Tove Jansson

88 Illustration by Hilda van Stockum from *The
Silver Skates* by Mary Mapes Dodge

89 Detail by Charles Folkard
from Collodi's *Pinocchio*

90 Drawing by Vincent O. Cohen from *Heidi*,
by Johanna Spyri

and told them stories and anecdotes about them. One day, in 1893, she wrote to a little sick boy named Noel Moore, son of one of her former governesses, who lived in Wandsworth, London. The letter began with the words: 'I don't know what to write to you, so I shall tell you a story about four little rabbits whose names were Flopsy, Mopsy, Cottontail and Peter', and went on to tell the story of Peter Rabbit and his adventures in Mr McGregor's garden, in both words and delightful little drawings. Eight years later she borrowed the letter (carefully preserved by little Noel), thinking it might make the basis for a children's book. Beatrix enlarged the original story, added more illustrations and submitted it to Frederick Warne and Company, the well-known publishers of children's books. They – and several other firms – turned it down. Undeterred, she had it privately printed and had sold nearly the whole of the first edition of 250 when Warne's (to whom she had sent a copy of the finished book) changed their minds and agreed to publish if she would do coloured illustrations instead of the existing black-and-white ones. This she did, finding no difficulty with the animals, but having to draw and re-draw Mr and Mrs Mc-Gregor; she was never happy in depicting human figures. So it was that the first edition of *The Tale of Peter Rabbit* appeared in 1902, in the now-familiar format – $5\frac{3}{4}$ ins × $4\frac{1}{4}$ ins with facing pages of text and coloured illustration at every turn. The book was a success and Beatrix Potter, at thirty-six, found herself a professional children's author. Her second book (and many think her best), *The Tailor of Gloucester*, was also issued privately by the author since she thought, in her usual shy manner, that Warne's would not be interested in another book from her so soon. They saw it, liked it and, with a few changes, published it in 1903. John Masefield once described *The Tailor of Gloucester* as 'a gem of English prose'. The illustrations are perfect too. This was originally written for Freda Moore, Noel's sister, after she had been ill. Her dealings with her publishers had brought Beatrix into constant touch with Norman Warne, the youngest member of the famous firm, and in 1905 they announced their engagement. The Potters objected to the coming marriage and many quarrels ensued, ending at the close of the year when Norman suddenly and tragically died. Beatrix, who was making good money from her books, decided to move away from

London and she bought Hill Top Farm, Sawrey – a picturesque village she knew well from family holidays, situated on the borders of Lancashire and Westmorland. She made a great success of the farm and before long owned a good deal of land, including much of the village itself. In 1913 she married William Heelis, her lawyer, and they settled at Castle Farm, Sawrey. From this time onwards she wrote few books and concentrated upon her new career as master farmer and sheep-breeder. But ever since *The Tailor of Gloucester* she had regularly been turning out her miniature classics, all in the same format and all loved by successive generations of children: *The Tale of Squirrel Nutkin* (1903), *The Tale of Benjamin Bunny* (1904), *The Tale of Two Bad Mice* (1904), *The Tale of Mrs Tiggy-Winkle* (1905), *The Pie and the Patty-Pan* (1905), *The Tale of Mr Jeremy Fisher* (1906), *The Story of Miss Moppet* (1906), *The Story of a Fierce Bad Rabbit* (1906), *The Tale of Tom Kitten* (1907), *The Tale of Jemima Puddle-Duck* (1908), *The Roly-Poly Pudding* (later *The Tale of Samuel Whiskers*) (1908), *The Tale of the Flopsy Bunnies* (1909), *Ginger and Pickles* (1909), *The Tale of Mrs Tittlemouse* (1910), *The Tale of Timmy Tiptoes* (1911), *The Tale of Mr Tod* (1912), *The Tale of Pigling Bland* (1913), *Appley Dapply's Nursery Rhymes* (1917) and *The Tale of Johnny Town-Mouse* (1918). Many of the tales are set in farms, houses and surroundings she knew well in and around Sawrey. The year 1918 saw the end of her best period. The few books she published after this date are in a different style, format and standard, though they are all well worth reading. They include *The Fairy Caravan* (USA 1929, Britain 1952), about a group of animals who travel around the countryside in a caravan; and *The Tale of Little Pig Robinson* (1930). In addition there are three further titles (two of which have appeared in only limited editions in Britain) published in America: *Sister Anne* (USA 1932), a long novel based on the story of Bluebeard; *Wag-by-Wall* (USA 1944, Britain, limited edition, 1944), a story about an old countrywoman and an owl; and *The Tale of the Faithful Dove* (USA 1956, Britain, limited edition, 1955), the story of a bird and its rescue from a chimney by a mouse. In 1966 – her centenary year – there appeared *The Journal of Beatrix Potter from 1881 to 1897*. This was transcribed from her 'secret' code writings by Leslie Linder, after years of work. It is a fascinating personal diary and social document.

In her later years she discouraged admirers who called at her farmhouse in Sawrey and considered the raising of pedigree Herdwick sheep much more important than the old picture-books she had produced all those years ago. When she died, at the age of seventy-seven, on 22nd December 1943, she left all her land in the Lake District to the National Trust and with it her farmhouse at Hill Top, which is today maintained as a museum to her memory.

Pudney, John

Born 1909, in Langley, Buckinghamshire, and educated at Gresham's School, Holt, Norfolk. Worked as a writer-producer for the BBC, then joined the *News Chronicle* as a columnist. Served in the RAF during the Second World War and among many other poems wrote the famous 'For Johnny', which was first featured in the film *The Way to the Stars*. After the war he returned to the *News Chronicle*, then joined Odhams to work on magazines. Later he became book-reviewer for the *Daily Express*, a director of a well-known publishing house and, apart from all this, has found time to write more than fifty books, including novels, poetry, non-fiction, an autobiography, film scripts, radio programmes – and many children's books. In 1950 he published the first of his popular 'Fred and I' series of boys' adventure novels, *Saturday Adventure*, telling of the exploits of two boys and their Uncle George, a scientist. *Sunday Adventure* followed in 1951 and a further 'Adventure' for each day of the week was published annually until 1956, when *Friday Adventure* completed the series. *Thursday Adventure* (1955) was produced as a film by the Children's Film Foundation as *The Stolen Airliner*. In 1961 came the first in a new series about 'Fred and I', this time divided into seasons, *Spring Adventure*. It was followed by *Summer Adventure* (1962), *Autumn Adventure* (1964) and *Winter Adventure* (1965). For younger children he has written a series about life in a village called Hartwarp: *The Hartwarp Light Railway* (1962), *The Hartwarp Dump* (1962), *The Hartwarp Balloon* (1963), *The Hartwarp Circus* (1963), *The Hartwarp Bakehouse* (1964), *The Hartwarp Explosion* (1965) and *The Hartwarp Jets* (1967). He has also written other younger children's stories and such non-fiction titles as *Six Great Aviators* (1955) and *The Golden*

Age of Steam (1967), and edited an anthology *Flight and Flying* (1968). John Pudney lives with his wife and several pet animals in the heart of the countryside near Uckfield in Sussex.

Pullein-Thompson, Christine, Diana and Josephine

The three daughters of well-known adult novelist Joanna Cannan have all followed in their mother's footsteps. In 1936 Miss Cannan published a children's book called *A Pony for Jean* which was one of the earliest 'pony books' and did much to set the standard and style for those to come in later years. She wrote another book in this category in 1957, *Gaze at the Moon*. In the 1940s and early 1950s, Miss Cannan's daughters began writing pony stories for girls. Diana published *I Wanted a Pony* in 1946, following it with several more, including *Three Ponies and Shannan* and *A Pony for Sale*. In more recent years, she has done well at creating an entirely different kind of world – that of working-class London – in *The Boy and the Donkey* (1958) and *The Secret Dog* (1959). Christine's titles include: *A Day to Go Hunting*, *The Horse Sale*, and *Phantom Horse*. Josephine's books include: *I Had Two Ponies*, *Show Jumping Secret* and *Prince Among Ponies*; she is also an official horse show and show-jumping judge and Visiting Commissioner to the Pony Club of Great Britain.

Pye, Virginia

Born 1901 in London. Wrote a popular series of children's novels about the Price Family (Tom, fourteen; Susan, twelve; Alan, ten; and also usually included in the circle, Johanna Allard, twelve, a close family friend). The stories were realistic and warmly human, with plenty of humour and incorporating adventures and incidents that could quite well happen . . . The first in the series was *Red Letter Holiday* (1940), followed by *The Snow Bird* (1941), *Primrose Polly* (1942), *Half-Term Holiday*, *The Prices Return*, *The Stolen Jewels* and *Johanna and the Prices* (1951). Also wrote many short stories, both for children and adults, contributing to several magazines. Her chief recreation is music.

224

Pyle, Howard

Born on 5th March 1853, in Wilmington, Delaware, the son of Quaker parents, and educated at the Friends' School and at a private secondary school there. He had always had a liking and talent for drawing and writing and, on leaving school, he studied art for three years under a Mr Van der Weilen at a small art school in Philadelphia. He lived at home while he studied and helped his father with his ailing leather business. After his three years at art school had finished he became more and more involved in the family leather business and in Wilmington social life. His artistic ambitions might well have languished but for an accident of good fortune. During the spring of 1876 he happened to visit a picturesque island called Chincoteague off the Virginia coast. He was so impressed with the place that he wrote down his thoughts about it and illustrated his text with sketches. His mother urged him to submit it to *Scribner's Monthly*, which he eventually did. The illustrated article was accepted at once and a further letter invited Pyle to go to New York to take up a promising career as a magazine illustrator. He at once left and settled down in New York, where he obtained plenty of work, though some of the early illustrations were criticised in some quarters as being 'coarse'. In fact, Pyle was bringing a much-needed breath of fresh air into American illustration and it wasn't long before people began to recognise this. He had many little illustrated fables published in the famous *St Nicholas* magazine for young people, and much other work, both written and drawn, in other magazines. He became more and more interested in writing fairy stories, first old, traditional ones, which he re-told, then later, ones which he created himself. In 1883 came his first published book, the incomparable and now classic *The Merry Adventures of Robin Hood*, which he wrote and illustrated. The tales had first appeared in *Harper's Young People* magazine, but for book publication Pyle drew new illustrations. It is, in the opinion of many, his most perfect book, in conception, style, illustration and quality; it is also probably the best modern re-telling of the old Robin Hood legend. Two books of illustrated fairy tales and humorous verses followed – *Pepper and Salt* (1886) and *The Wonder Clock* (1888). Then came two powerful historical novels – *Otto of the Silver Hand* (1888), a story of the robber barons in medieval Germany, and *Men of Iron* (1892), set in fifteenth-century England in the reign of Henry IV. Naturally he illustrated both himself. Pyle had returned to settle at Wilmington by 1880 and worked at all his books from there. And it was from Wilmington in 1903 that he wrote to Scribner's, the publishers, suggesting that he embark on an ambitious re-telling of the adventures of King Arthur and his Knights of the Round Table. He would, of course, illustrate and design the work himself. He was told to go ahead and, over the next seven years, produced four impressive volumes – *The Story of King Arthur and His Knights* (1903), *The Story of the Champions of the Round Table* (1905), *The Story of Sir Launcelot and His Companions* (1907) and *The Story of the Grail and the Passing of Arthur* (1910). The quartet forms one of the loveliest re-tellings of the Arthurian cycle ever written – and the illustrations are superb. The work has become a young people's classic and a part of American literature. Earlier, in 1895, Pyle had published two very different but equally fine children's books: one was *Jack Ballister's Fortunes*, a full-blooded adventure tale of pirates, and the other, *Twilight Land*, another, perhaps more subtle, collection of fairy stories. Among his other titles were: *The Rose of Paradise* (1888), *The Garden Behind the Moon* (1895), *The Ghost of Captain Brand* (1896), *The Price of Blood* (1899) and a superb volume of articles, stories and pictures about pirates and buccaneers (a subject always close to Pyle's heart) titled *Howard Pyle's Book of Pirates* and published posthumously in 1921. He also illustrated many books written by other authors and concerned chiefly with American history and heritage. Other works he illustrated included Baldwin's *Story of Siegfried* (1882), Dowd's *Book of the American Spirit* (1923), Holmes' *Autocrat of the Breakfast Table* (1893), Lodge's *Story of the Revolution* (1898) and Irving's *History of New York* (1886). From 1894–1900 Pyle taught illustration at the Drexel Institute of Arts and Sciences in Philadelphia, subsequently setting up his own art school in his native Wilmington. Many of his devoted students later became famous artists and illustrators in their own right and included such names as Maxfield Parrish, N. C. Wyeth, Frank Schoonover, Jessie Wilcox Smith and Thornton Oakley. Students came from all over America to study with Pyle and he gave his knowledge and his art freely and gladly. Later in life he painted several outstanding murals for various public buildings. In 1910 he decided to go to Italy to see some of the great art collections and buildings he had heard and read so much about. After being there for about a year he became ill and died, in Florence, on 9th November 1911. Howard Pyle is today recognised as the first great American illustrator and his simple yet strong style, with its kindly humour, dramatic power and vigorous exuberance, marked a turning-point in this specialised and important branch of art.

'Quiz, Roland'

Real name: Richard Martin Howard Quittenton. Born in 1833. Popular writer specialising in stories for juvenile publications in the late nineteenth century. Best known for his fantasy tales of giants, fairies, magicians, sorcery, damsels in distress and courageous heroes, which ran as serials in Henderson's *Young Folks* in the 1870s and later. Most famous were *Tim Pippin* and *Giantland*, which were later re-issued in book form, the most recent editions being in 1947. Almost as well-known as the stories were the graphic illustrations by 'Puck' (John Proctor). 'Roland Quiz' died in 1914.

Rae, Gwynedd

Born 1892, in London, and educated at Manor House School, Brondesbury, London, and privately. Wrote and published her first book for children in 1930: *Mostly Mary*, comprising the humorous adventures of a likeable small bear named Mary Plain, who lives in a zoo in Berne and constantly goes off to have escapades, sometimes with two adults whom she calls 'the Owl Man' (because he wears glasses) and 'the Fur-Coat-Lady' (because she wears one). A whole series of Mary Plain books followed over the years and established themselves with younger readers, especially small girls. The original titles were illustrated by Harry Rountree, with different artists taking over later. Titles in the series include: *All Mary* (1931), *Mary Plain in Town* (1935), *Mary Plain on Holiday* (1937), *Mary Plain in Trouble* (1939), *Mary Plain in Wartime* (1942) (subsequently reprinted in 1949 as *Mary Plain Lends a Paw*), *Mary Plain's Big Adventure* (1944), *Mary Plain Home Again* (1948), *Mary Plain to the Rescue*

(1950), *Mary Plain and the Twins* (1952), *Mary Plain Goes Bob-a-Jobbing* (1954), *Mary Plain Goes to America* (1957), *Mary Plain, V.I.P.* (1961) and *Mary Plain's 'Whodunit'* (1965). Miss Rae also published two adult novels: *And Timothy Too* and *Leap Year Born*.

Ransome, Arthur

Born on 18th January 1884, in Leeds, where his father was Professor of History at the University, and educated at a preparatory school in Windermere and at Rugby, where he occupied Lewis Carroll's study. On leaving school he worked in the offices of Grant Richards, the publishing firm in London, writing many articles and stories for various periodicals and newspapers in his spare time. He published a collection of his own pieces in 1904 and another in the following year. He wrote and edited other books before gaining critical recognition with studies of *Edgar Allan Poe* (1910) and *Oscar Wilde* (1912). In 1913 he went to Russia to learn the language and study folk-lore with a view to obtaining enough material for a book of Russian fairy tales. The result was *Old Peter's Russian Tales* (1916), a delightful and widely popular collection of native folk tales, told by an old Russian peasant, Peter, to his two grandchildren. Ransome remained in Russia throughout the Revolution, sending regular reports back to the *Daily News* and *Manchester Guardian*, as well as writing two books on the Russian situation. After he left Russia he travelled widely, often sailing his own boat, in the Baltic, China, Egypt and the Sudan. Later he lived in East Anglia, near the Norfolk Broads, during a long spell of illness, which kept him away from the seas he loved so much. In 1929, whilst living in his cottage on the banks of Lake Windermere – the district in which he had spent so many happy childhood holidays – Arthur Ransome began to write *Swallows and Amazons* and, though he didn't know it at the time, to create a 'new age' in children's literature. *Swallows and Amazons* was published in 1930 – when Ransome was forty-six years old, had a quarter-century of writing behind him and had published more than twenty books. The story introduced the Walker children: John, Susan, Titty and Roger (the 'Swallows') and the Blacketts, Nancy and Peggy ('the Amazons') and their adventures ashore and afloat on Lake Windermere. Another character was the Blackett's Uncle Jim, or 'Captain Flint' as he was called by the children. He is generally regarded as a light-hearted 'self-portrait' of the author himself. This first edition had no illustrations and caused little comment among reviewers; the second edition had illustrations by Clifford Webb and end-paper maps by Steven Spurrier. *Swallowdale* appeared in 1931, again illustrated by Webb – and again being largely by-passed by reviewers. But in 1932 came the turning-point. *Peter Duck* was published and received enthusiastic notices in *The Times* and (by Hugh Walpole) in *The Observer*. Other writers enthused – and caught up with the first two books in the series. By the time *Winter Holiday* (1933) appeared, Ransome had established himself as one of the most highly praised and popular children's authors of the century. The rest of the series includes: *Coot Club* (1934), *Pigeon Post* (1936) – it won the first Carnegie Award as the Best Children's Book of the Year – *We Didn't Mean to Go to Sea* (1937), *Secret Water* (1939), *The Big Six* (1940), *Missee Lee* (1941), *The Picts and the Martyrs* (1943), and finally, *Great Northern?* (1947). Ransome illustrated all the stories from *Peter Duck* onwards, also re-illustrating the first two in the series in 1938. His dozen children's novels are supreme examples – indeed, instigators – of the modern holiday adventure story. His children are true, realistic children and their adventures are of the kind that can be enjoyed by anyone. And what countless things his readers can learn from the stories . . . The arts of sailing, camping, cooking, tying knots, bird-watching and a thousand other things are imparted, excitingly and expertly, all as integral parts of the story. Two books which rather stand apart from the others are the two imaginative 'holiday romances', *Peter Duck* and *Missee Lee*, which feature the children in gripping and colourful, but rather improbable, adventures abroad. They are equally enjoyable – but different in conception. Two earlier books of Ransome's should perhaps be mentioned: '*Racundra*'*s' First Cruise* (1923) and *Rod and Line* (1929), the latter being a book of angling essays (fishing being one of his chief pleasures in life). Arthur Ransome had an Honorary Doctorate of Letters conferred on him at Leeds University in 1952 and was made a C.B.E. in 1953. He lived until his death on 3rd June 1967 on the banks of his beloved Windermere – setting of so

229

many of his famous 'Swallows and Amazons' books (which, incidentally, have been translated into no less than twelve foreign languages).

Redway, Ralph
See: Hamilton, Charles

Reed, Talbot Baines
Born on 3rd April 1852, in Hackney, London, the third son of Sir Charles Reed, Chairman of the London School Board and Member of Parliament successively for Hackney and St Ives, Cornwall. He was educated at Priory House School, Clapton, and the City of London School, where he was a contemporary of Herbert Asquith, later to become Prime Minister. When scarcely seventeen he was awarded the Medal of the Royal Humane Society for saving his cousin from drowning in the sea off Londonderry. In 1868 he began working for his father's type foundry business in the City of London (eventually rising to be, at the time of his death, managing director). He was naturally an expert in type-founding and his first book was *A History of Old English Letter Foundries* (1877), which became a standard book on the subject. When, in the autumn of 1878, he heard about the coming publication of a new boys' magazine called the *Boy's Own Paper*, Reed submitted a sporting story and had it accepted right away. In fact, it was given the 'star' spot on page one of the first number of *BOP* when it appeared in January 1879; it was the first of a series of sketches of sporting life at Parkhurst School and titled 'My First Football Match'. The sketches were credited to 'An Old Boy' and were later collected in book form as *Parkhurst Sketches* (1889). Two weeks after his first Parkhurst piece had appeared came the first of a short series of articles titled 'Boys of English History'. His first real school story appeared in the *BOP* in August 1879, in two chapters, and was called 'The Troubles of a Dawdler'. Then, at *BOP* editor George Hutchison's suggestion, Reed wrote his first full-scale serial, *The Adventures of a Three Guinea Watch* – this time under his own name. It was an immediate success and he subsequently wrote a further ten serials for the paper, mainly

about public school life, though some described City life. They were all later reprinted in book form (with the exception of the shorter, below-standard 'The Heroes of New Swishford') and ran into many editions. Details (*BOP* serial appearance year, followed by publication in hard covers): *The Adventures of a Three Guinea Watch* (1880; 1883), *The Fifth Form at St Dominic's* (1881; 1887), *My Friend Smith* (1882; 1889), *The Willoughby Captains* (1883-84; 1887), *The Heroes of New Swishford* (1884), *Reginald Cruden* (1885; 1894), *A Dog With a Bad Name* (1886-87; 1894), *The Master of the Shell* (1888; 1894), *Sir Ludar* (1888-89; 1889) (set in the days of Queen Elizabeth I), *The Cock House at Fellsgarth* (1890; 1893) and *Tom, Dick and Harry* (1892-93; 1894). Another public school serial, 'The Boys of Templeton', ran in Cassell's *Boys' World* in 1906 and had previously appeared as a book titled *Follow My Leader* (1885). *Roger Ingleton, Minor* (1891) was a mixture of family drama, set among young people of both sexes, and melodramatic incident. Although, ironically, Reed himself attended a day-school, his fine descriptions of public boarding-school life are generally agreed to be extremely accurate. Apart from his stories he reported the Universities Boat Race each year for the *BOP* and also wrote a regular non-political leading article for the *Leeds Mercury* (edited by his cousin, Talbot Baines) for many years. He was married to the daughter of S. M. Greer, an Irish County Court judge and M.P. for Londonderry, and they had three children. He was putting the finishing touches to a long historical novel, *Kilgorman* (1895), a story about the Rebellion in Ireland in 1798, when he died, following a long illness, at his Highgate home, on 28th November 1893. It was undoubtedly Reed who shaped the traditional school story as readers later came to know and love it.

Reeves, James

Born in Harrow, Middlesex, and educated at Stowe School and Jesus College, Cambridge University. He is one of the foremost poets of the post-war period and has published his *Collected Poems* as well as several works about poetry and its understanding and appreciation. Also a noted critic, reviewer and anthologist. Has produced many books for children since the war, including collections of poetry (his own and that of others), anthologies, stories, re-tellings of Bible stories and legends, and adventure novels. Titles include: *The Wandering Moon* (1946), poems for children; *The Blackbird in the Lilac* (1952), more poems for children; *English Fables and Fairy Stories* (1954); *The Merry-Go-Round* (1955), an anthology of over 400 poems for young people; *Pigeons and Princesses* (1956), five fairy stories; *Mulbridge Manor* (1958), a children's adventure story set in a sleepy English country town; *A Golden Land* (1958), a superlative collection of stories, poems, pictures and songs for children, edited and introduced by Reeves; *The Exploits of Don Quixote* (1959), Cervantes' story re-told for young readers, plus Ardizzone's illustrations; *Titus in Trouble* (1959), an exciting, Ardizzone-illustrated picture book; *Ragged Robin* (1961), children's poems; *Fables from Aesop* (1961); *Sailor Rumbelow and Britannia* (1962), stories for children; *A First Bible* (1962); *Three Tall Tales* (1964); *The Strange Light* (1964), a fascinating story about a small girl who strays into a land peopled by children's book characters awaiting their summons into yet-to-be-written books; *The Road to a Kingdom* (1965), Bible stories; *The Story of Jackie Thimble* (1965), the adventures of a boy whose height is only 1 ft 4 in; *Understanding Poetry* (1965), *The Cold Flame* (1967), the re-telling of a story by Grimm, and, again illustrated by Ardizzone, *Rhyming Will* (1967). James Reeves is an outstanding figure in contemporary children's literature and probably the best writer of original young people's poetry now living. His anthology, *A Golden Land*, is generally regarded as one of the finest examples of its kind. Another recent work he edited was *The Cassell Book of English Poetry* (1965). He also contributes to many leading newspapers and magazines.

Reid, Mayne

Born on 4th April 1818, in Ballyroney, County Down, Ireland, the eldest son of a Presbyterian clergyman. He was intended for the ministry but had no real desire to follow his father in the church. On leaving college he was set up as a tutor by his parents, but Reid became restless and wanted travel and adventure. In 1840 he sailed for New Orleans and was soon working as a store clerk in the lawless town of Natchez, Missouri. He later did a variety of jobs including those of trapper, actor, poet and newspaper reporter. He also became tutor to a judge's family and then a schoolteacher. He soon tired of teaching and became a trader, making several journeys up the Platte, Missouri and Red Rivers, where he had dealings with the Red Indians, getting to know them and their ways very well. Later he became a lieutenant in the U.S. Army and fought in the Mexican war of 1847. He had been writing regularly for the *New York Herald* and the *Spirit of the Times* and continued sending despatches from the front. During a brave and dashing war career he was severely injured in Mexico and retired with the rank of captain. During his convalescence he began writing his first adventure story, *The Rifle Rangers*. It was published in 1850, after Reid had arrived in London the previous year (with the original idea of raising volunteers in the Hungarian insurrection, which collapsed before he had a chance of carrying out his plans). *The Rifle Rangers* (sub-titled 'The Adventures of an Officer in Southern Mexico') was based loosely upon his own action-filled army experiences, as was his second book, *The Scalp Hunters* ('Romantic Adventures in Northern Mexico'), which appeared in 1851. Though neither work was intended for boys, the two titles were soon being eagerly read by them and enjoyed for their graphically described encounters with marauding Red Indians and picture of adventuring pioneers in the American West. Reid wrote over seventy further books, chiefly adventure stories, including: *The Boy Hunters of the Missisippi* (1852) (his first written specifically for young readers), *The Forest Exiles* (1854), *The White Chief* (1855), *The Bush Boys* (1856), *Quadroon* (1856), *The War Trail* (1857), *The Plant Hunters* (1857), *The Wild Huntress* (1861), *Maroon* (1862), *The Boy Slaves* (1865), *The Headless Horseman* (1866), *The Giraffe Hunters* (1867), *The Child Wife* (1868) (based on Reid's own marriage, in 1855, to fifteen-year-old Elizabeth Hyde), *Castaways* (1870), *The White Squaw* (1871), *The Death Shot* (1873) and *The Free Lances* (1881). Some of his early books ran as serials in such boys' magazines as *Boys of England* and *Marvel*. In 1867 Reid started and edited a new London evening newspaper, *The Little Times*, much of it being written by himself. But it lasted for only a month. By the autumn of the same year Reid and his wife had settled in Rhode Island, USA, and he later became an American citizen. He started a new American boys' paper,

233

Onward, again writing most of it himself, and this too was a failure, closing after fourteen monthly numbers, leaving him almost penniless and in a poor state of health. An old war wound in his leg was causing trouble and, towards the end, he walked with the aid of crutches. He had originally lived at Stokenchurch, Buckinghamshire, and Gerrards Cross in the same county, during his long stay in England (and had written all his earlier best-sellers there) and had a great affection for the country. The doctors recommended his return and, after a stay in Ireland, he gradually regained much of his health in Derbyshire, later living in Frogmore, Ross-on-Wye, Herefordshire. He began writing again and, in March 1883, returned to live in London. But he soon became ill again and died in London, on 22nd October 1883. His obituary, in the London *Times*, began: 'Every schoolboy, and everyone who has ever been a schoolboy, will learn with sorrow of the death of Captain Mayne Reid . . .'

Richards, Frank

See: Hamilton, Charles

Richards, Hilda

See: Hamilton, Charles

Robinson, Joan G.

Born in 1910, in Gerrards Cross, Buckinghamshire, and educated at Ledge Point School, Westgate-on-Sea, Kent. Began her popular series of books about the adventures of 'Teddy Robinson' in 1953, with *Teddy Robinson*. The character originated when Mrs Robinson's small daughter Deborah was visited by her teacher one day. During her stay she asked Deborah how her beloved teddy bear was, referring to him as 'Teddy Robinson'. Mrs Robinson at once formed the idea of writing some stories about the teddy bear and Deborah. The stories were not told to her daughter and then written down. On the contrary, they were carefully thought out and written before Deborah heard them for the first time. Today, the endearing character is one of the most popular contemporary nursery heroes. The titles of the rest of the series include: *More About Teddy Robinson* (1954), *Teddy Robinson's Book* (1955), *Dear Teddy Robinson* (1956), *Teddy Robinson Himself* (1957), *Another Teddy Robinson* (1960) and *Keeping Up With Teddy Robinson* (1964). A *Teddy Robinson's Omnibus* has also been published, containing the first three titles in the series. Another series by Mrs Robinson is the one about a typical little girl called 'Mary-Mary'. The titles include: *Mary-Mary* (1957), *More Mary-Mary* (1958) and *Madam Mary-Mary* (1960); again all three titles are contained in *The Mary-Mary Stories* (1965). *When Marnie Was There* (1967) is an outstanding, hauntingly beautiful story about a small girl and her playmate, who is not all that she seems. . . . Another title by this author is *Susie at Home*, again about a little girl. Joan G. Robinson – who illustrates all her own books as well as writing them – has also written a series of more than a dozen books on religious subjects for small children, using the pseudonym 'JOAN GALE THOMAS'. Titles include: *My Book About Christmas, A Stands for Angel, If Jesus Came to My House* and *Ten Little Angels.* Joan G. Robinson and her husband, Richard, have also illustrated several books for younger readers by other authors.

'Romany'

See: Evens, G. Bramwell

Ruskin, John

Born in London on 8th February 1819, the son of a wealthy Scottish wine-merchant, and educated privately and at Christ Church, Oxford University. His academic career was cut short by ill-health allied to an unhappy love affair and, after touring Europe, he returned to live with his parents in 1841. One day a twelve-year-old schoolgirl, Euphemia Chalmers Gray, visited the house and, it is said, challenged the melancholy Ruskin to write her a fairy story. In only two sittings he produced *The King of the Golden River*. It was not published until ten years later, in 1851 – and then anonymously. He never wrote another fairy-tale as he was soon taken up with his massive writings on art and architecture, which do not concern us here. But *The King of the Golden River* was enormously successful and still lives on today.

It tells the sombre story of little Gluck and his two cruel brothers, Hans and Schwartz, who are visited in their home in Stiria (near the German Black Forest) by a mysterious stranger. Gluck treats him kindly, but his brothers do not and the stranger vows vengeance. Gluck soon meets the King of the Golden River in a melting golden mug and the King helps the lad win back his rightful inheritance. The story is colourful and exciting, but modern children often find it difficult to read in its original form. It was originally published with memorable illustrations by Richard Doyle and went through three editions in its first year. Ruskin was a great admirer of Kate Greenaway and her work and it was in 1885 that he edited a new edition of the popular old picture-rhyme story-book *Dame Wiggins of Lee and Her Seven Wonderful Cats* (originally published in 1823) with additional verses by himself and extra illustrations by Miss Greenaway. Ruskin was also an enthusiastic reader of the Brothers Grimm and it was largely through his Introduction to a new edition of their Tales in 1868 that many British parents were at last persuaded to allow their children to read the stories. John Ruskin became a distinguished and highly influential writer on art, economics and sociology, as well as being appointed the first Slade Professor of Fine Arts at Oxford University. He died in the Lake District on 20th January 1900.

Russell, William Clark

Born on 24th February 1844, in New York, the son of a composer, and educated at private schools. He joined the Merchant Navy at the age of fourteen as an apprentice and made several arduous voyages, under conditions of hardship, to places such as India and Australia. He retired from the sea in 1866 and, after journalistic experience, devoted himself to writing popular novels, based largely upon his own naval career, from the age of thirty. His first novel, *John Holdsworth, Chief Mate*, was published in 1875, and was followed in 1877 by *The Wreck of the 'Grosvenor'*, which made his reputation. He went on to become the leading sea-story writer of his generation and was enjoyed as much by boys as by adult readers. His other titles (among over fifty) include: *An Ocean Tragedy* (1881), *Round the Galley Fire* (1883), *The Frozen Pirate* (1887), *The Death Ship* (1888) and

The Romance of a Midshipman (1898). He also wrote biographies of *Dampier* (1889), *Nelson* (1890) and *Collingwood* (1891), as well as books of verse. He lived in Bath, Somerset, for many years and, in later life, became an invalid, losing the use of his legs. He died on 8th November 1911.

Salten, Felix

Born 1869, in Budapest, and educated in Vienna. Wrote several adult novels and plays but is best remembered for his classic story tracing the life of a wild deer, *Bambi*, originally translated from the German and published in the USA in 1926. It was first published in Britain in 1928, with an enthusiastic foreword by John Galsworthy, and has since been reprinted many times. *Bambi* (sub-titled 'A Life in the Woods') is set in a mid-European forest and tells the beautifully observed story of a deer from birth to full maturity. The story was originally written mainly for adult readers, but children everywhere quickly came to know and love it, especially after the appearance of the popular Walt Disney full-length colour cartoon made from it in 1942. Salten's subsequent books include: *Bambi's Children, A Forest World, Perri, Florian, Good Comrades, Renni the Rescuer, Fifteen Rabbits* and *Fairy Tales from Near and Far*. He died in Switzerland in 1945.

Saville, Malcolm

Born in 1901 at Hastings, Sussex, and educated at Richmond Hill School, Richmond, Surrey, and other private schools. Was the son of a well-known Hastings bookseller and so grew up in an atmosphere of books and reading, which he loved from an early age. At twenty-one he obtained a post in the Publicity and Sales Promotion Department of the Amalgamated Press, remaining with this firm until 1936, when he joined the Sales Promotion Department of George Newnes' publishing house. He retired from Newnes in 1966, at which time he had been General Books Editor for several years. He was also editor of the magazine *My Garden* for a period in the mid-1940s. In 1942, the father of four children, he decided to write his first children's book, determining to make it a convincing and exciting adventure story featuring believable and likeable youngsters. Dediccated to his own children, *Mystery at Witchend* was published in 1943 and achieved remarkable success, also being broadcast as a popular radio serial in BBC Children's Hour. His second book, *Seven White Gates* (1944), was also broadcast and featured the same characters as the first book, who had formed themselves into 'The Lone Pine Club'. Both stories were set in the highlands of Shropshire, an area which Saville knew and loved well and described graphically. A whole series of 'Lone Pine' books followed and have remained this author's most successful stories. The titles include: *The Gay Dolphin Adventure* (1945), *The Secret of Grey Walls* (1947), *Lone Pine Five* (1949), *The Elusive Grasshopper* (1951), *The Neglected Mountain* (1953), *Saucers over the Moor* (1955), *Wings Over Witchend* (1956), *Lone Pine London* (1957), *The Secret of the Gorge* (1958), *Mystery Mine* (1959), *Sea Witch Comes Home* (1960), *Not Scarlet But Gold* (1962), *Treasure at Amorys* (1964) and *The Man With Three Fingers* (1966). Saville's other very popular series (too numerous to list individually) feature 'The Jillies', 'The Buckinghams', 'Michael and Mary', 'Nettleford' and, for younger readers, 'Susan and Bill'. His latest series comprises loosely-linked Secret Service thrillers which deal with the adventures of a young (around twenty-one) bachelor Secret Service agent and his two friends (and intermittent girl-friends) in such places as Florence, Provence and Rome. The titles so far include: *Three Towers in Tuscany* (1963), *The Purple Valley* (1964), *Dark Danger* (1965), *White Fire* (1966) and *Power of Three* (1968). They are in the nature of an enthusiastic experiment for Saville, who feels that the modern 'in-between' teenage reader needs a well told story, with a touch of romance, a few thrills and a foreign locale, to 'bridge the gap' between children's stories and adult novels. Saville reports that the response to date has been extremely encouraging (especially from girl readers) and he plans several more titles in this series. Apart from his various series and three or four unconnected children's adventure stories, Malcolm Saville has also written: *Country Scrapbook for Boys and Girls* (1944), *Open-Air Scrapbook for Boys and Girls* (1945) and *Seaside Scrapbook for Boys and Girls* (1946); these titles recently formed the basis for *Malcolm Saville's Country Book* and *Malcolm Saville's Seaside Book* (1962). *Jane's Country Year* (1946) was a widely praised 'guide to the English countryside' told month by month through the eyes of a town girl recuperating at a country farm for a year. *King of Kings* (1958) was a fine, plainly re-told life of Christ, *Strange Story* (1967) an unusual re-telling of the story of Jesus, and a title from the late 'forties was *Adventure of the Lifeboat Service*. *Come to London* (1967) was a personal introduction to the sights of the capital. Today, Malcolm Saville has eight grandchildren as well as his own four children and his books have sold a total of nearly one and a half million copies. Two of his titles (*Trouble at Townsend* and *Treasure at the Mill*) have been filmed by the Children's Film Foundation and many have been serialised by the BBC. He is firmly established as one of Britain's most popular and best-selling children's authors. He is particularly noted for his outstanding flair for atmosphere and situation; whether his story is set in Shropshire, Sussex, Dorset, Kent, Westmorland or Yorkshire (not to mention foreign settings) the young reader is always able to visualise exactly where the action is taking place. Many are often led to discover the place for themselves in their holidays. Saville encourages his readers to write to him and receives several thousands of letters every year, from all over the world. He makes a point of answering every one. He lives in Barcombe, near Lewes, in Sussex.

Scott, Sir Walter

Born on 15th August 1771, in Edinburgh, Scotland, the son of a lawyer. He was educated at Edinburgh High School and University, studied law and became an advocate in 1792. In 1799 he was made Sheriff-Depute of Selkirk and in 1806 Clerk of Session in Edinburgh. Was of Border descent and his first book, published in 1802, was a collection of traditional Scottish Border songs and ballads, titled *Minstrelsy of the Scottish Border*. He later wrote many famous poems, essays and stories, beginning his epic series of great historical novels with *Waverley* in 1814. Other famous titles in the series are *Ivanhoe* (1820), *Kenilworth* (1821), *The Fortunes of Nigel* (1822), *Quentin Durward* (1823), *Redgauntlet* (1824) and *The Talisman* (1825). Scott's works are still read and enjoyed by some young readers today, especially those who revel in history. His novels cover many different historical periods, all brought vividly to exciting life

239

and each introducing brilliantly described characters, both real and imaginary. Scott almost certainly created the historical novel or 'romance' as we know it today. The only work he wrote especially for young people (and particularly for his six-year-old grandson, John Lockhart) was *Tales of a Grandfather* (1827–30), which is a history of Scotland from the earliest times up to the 1745 Rebellion; the latter portion tells of the history of France. Scott was created a baronet in 1820 and died on 21st September 1832.

Seton, Ernest Thompson

Born on 14th August 1860, in Wellington Terrace, South Shields, Durham, one of fourteen children. Emigrated to Canada with his family at the age of six, first settling at Lindsay, Ontario, where he lived a largely outdoor life and began to develop his great love of nature and animals. His family later moved to Toronto, where he was educated at the Toronto Collegiate Institute. He also studied at the Ontario Art School, the Royal Academy, London, and an art school in Paris. Back in Canada and the United States, he began to contribute nature drawings and true accounts of animal life to various magazines and papers, the first appearing around 1884. Much of his early work appeared in such magazines as *St Nicholas* and *Scribner's* and during the 1890s he supported himself in New York by this free-lance work. In 1898 Seton (whose real name had been Seton Thompson) collected a group of his animal tales and published them in his first book, *Wild Animals I Have Known*. It was a huge success and his future career as a naturalist writer-illustrator was assured. Seton was a firm believer in the outdoor life for a young boy and it was in 1902 that he organised the Woodcraft Indian Movement; in 1910 he helped form the Boy Scouts of America and was Chief Scout of the United States from 1910 to 1916. He could perhaps be described as 'the American Baden-Powell' in this respect and, like his illustrious English counterpart, wrote the first scouting handbooks – in Seton's case, especially for the Boy Scouts of America. In 1903 he wrote and illustrated *Two Little Savages* ('Being the Adventures of Two Boys Who Lived as Indians and What They Learned'), which was a largely autobiographical story about boys who enjoy a

240

rapturous holiday in Canada, camping in the woods and re-creating the life of the Indians. It was dedicated, not surprisingly, 'To Woodcraft'. Ernest Thompson Seton's many books of animal, nature and woodcraft stories include: *The Trail of the Sandhill Stag* (1899), *The Biography of a Grizzly* (1900), *Lobo, Rag and Vixen* (1900), *Lives of the Hunted* (1901), *Krag and Johnny Bear* (1902), *American Woodcraft for Boys* (1902), *Monarch, the Big Bear of Tallac* (1904), *Animal Heroes* (1905), *Woodmyth and Fable* (1905), *Biography of a Silver Fox* (1909), *Scouting for Boys* (1910), *The Arctic Prairies* (1911), *Rolf in the Woods* (1911), *Woodcraft and Indian Lore* (1912), *Wild Animals at Home* (1913), *Wild Animal Ways* (1916), *The Preacher of Cedar Mountain* (1917), *Woodland Tales* (1921), *Bannertail: the Story of a Grey Squirrel* (1922), *Lives of Game Animals* (1925), *Katug the Snow Child* (1929), *Famous Animal Stories* (1932), *The Gospel of the Redmen* (1936), *Biography of an Arctic Fox* (1937), *Mainly About Wolves* (1937), *Great Historic Animals* (1937) and *Santana, Hero Dog of France* (1945). Seton often drew the analogy between men and animals, stressing that 'man has nothing that the animals have not at least a vestige of, the animals have nothing that man does not in some degree share . . .' His own nature and animal stories were completely authentic, being based on his own experiences with and close observation of the creatures in their natural surroundings. His autobiography was *The Trail of an Artist-Naturalist* (USA 1940, Britain 1951). In his later years Seton was appointed Naturalist to the Government of Manitoba. He died on 23rd October 1946, in New Mexico, where he had devoted his final years to the preservation of American Indian lore.

Seuss, Dr

Real name: Theodor Seuss Geisel. Born on 2nd March 1904, in Springfield, Massachusetts, USA, and educated at Dartmouth College and Oxford University. After a year's travelling in Europe he returned to the United States and worked as a cartoonist and satirical and humorous magazine writer before spending five years in Hollywood as a screen artist. He later won renown as the creator of several nationally famous advertising campaigns in America including the memorable 'Quick, Henry, the Flit!' series for the Standard Oil Company. After a while he became restless with this type of work and decided to try his hand at writing and illustrating a children's picture book. The result was *And To Think I Saw It on Mulberry Street*, eventually published in 1937 after being turned down by several firms. It was a hilarious 'tall tale' told by a small boy who saw a milk cart in a street and added and embroidered so many other details to the original practically empty scene on describing it to his father that, by the end of the story, a double-page spread was needed to picture them all. The brilliant *The 500 Hats of Bartholomew Cubbins* followed in 1938 and consolidated his arrival as a new children's illustrator and story-teller of genius. Subsequent titles, both written and illustrated by Dr Seuss, include: *The King's Stilts* (1939), *Horton Hatches the Egg* (1940), *McElligot's Pool* (1947), *Thidwick, the Big-Hearted Moose* (1948), *Barthlomew and the Oobleck* (1949), *If I Ran the Zoo* (1950), *Scrambled Eggs, Super!* (1953), *Horton Hears a Who* (1954), *On Beyond Zebra* (1955) and *If I Ran the Circus* (1956). In 1957 came the first of his now-celebrated 'Beginner Books' series: *The Cat in the Hat*. This original picture-book used a vocabulary of only 175 different words to tell a highly amusing story and was intended to help children learn to read in a colourful and diverting way. It entertained as it taught and was followed by many successors by both Dr Seuss and by others. The 'Beginner Books' have sold over thirty million in the United States alone and more than a million and a half in Britain. Other titles in this series by Dr Seuss include: *The Cat in the Hat Comes Back* (1958), *One Fish, Two Fish, Red Fish, Blue Fish* (1960), *Green Eggs and Ham* (1960), *Dr Seuss's ABC* (1964), *The Beginner Book Dictionary* (1965) (drawings by P. D. Eastman), *Fox in Socks* (1966) and *The Beginner Book Dictionary in French* (1967). Other contributors to the series include Helen Palmer (Mrs Geisel in private life), P. D. Eastman (art director of the series) and noted humorist Bennett Cerf. The 'Beginner Books' began publication in their British editions in the autumn of 1961 (though *The Cat in the Hat* appeared as a 'single' in 1958). Dr Seuss has also published several other books not in the 'Beginner Books' series, including *Yertle the Turtle* (1958), *Happy Birthday to You* (1959), *The Sneetches and Other Stories* (1961) and the unusual *Dr Seuss's Sleep Book* (1962). The pseudonym 'Dr Seuss' originated during his period as a journalist, when he wanted a name to append to a series of humorous articles supposed to have been written by a wise old man. 'Seuss' came from his mother's maiden name – and the originally fictional 'Dr' was officially consolidated in 1955 when he received an Honorary Doctorate of Humane Letters from his old college at Dartmouth. He has written several screenplays, including the classic animated colour cartoon *Gerald McBoing-Boing*, which won an Academy Award in 1951. A documentary film, *Design for Death*, on which he and his wife collaborated, won another Academy Award earlier, in 1947. Dr Seuss's wife is a keen and constant collaborator on the majority of his children's books, too. He is one of America's top best-selling authors – and one of the highest-paid – also receiving around 50,000 'fan' letters every year. With the invaluable help of his lively, amusing and carefully planned picture-story books he has surely helped countless children (and also 'backward' pupils) to learn to read far sooner than they might otherwise have done. Today, the 'Dr Seusses' live in a converted windmill at La Jolla, near San Diego.

(Note: the publication dates of Dr Seuss's books given here are those of the American editions, unless otherwise stated.)

Sewell, Anna

Born on 30th March 1820, at Great Yarmouth, Norfolk, and educated at home. Her parents were Quakers and her childhood, though economically up-and-down, was a very happy one. Her mother was Mary Sewell, who was to become a writer of popular best-selling ballads and verses, and her father, Isaac Sewell, had a variety of jobs. Running along a carriage road to her home (at Stoke Newington at that time) when she was fourteen, Anna slipped in a downpour of rain and badly twisted her ankle. The injury was treated wrongly and never healed, making Anna virtually a cripple for the rest of her life. In 1835 the family moved to Brighton, where Isaac Sewell had obtained a post as a bank manager. Ten years later they moved to Lancing, Sussex, where Anna was able to drive her father to the station every day in a pony and trap. After more moves and a year's stay in Germany for treatment for her lameness (which never improved, however), Anna settled down with her mother at Old Catton, near Norwich. By 1871 Anna

243

Sewell was a complete invalid and confined to the house, spending much of her time lying on a sofa. She had always loved animals, especially horses and ponies, and when, one day, she happened to read Horace Bushnell's *An Essay on Animals*, which pleaded in particular for better treatment for horses, Anna made up her mind to write the life story of a horse, making the same plea, indirectly, in her book. She began writing it in 1871 and did not complete it until 1877. In her diary around this time she wrote: 'I have . . . been writing . . . a little book . . . its special aim being to induce kindness, sympathy and an understanding treatment of horses.' She was only able to write a little at a time, feeling more and more ill as time went by, and often scribbled a few lines down in pencil leaving it for her devoted mother to make a fair copy of the work. The book – titled, of course, *Black Beauty* – was published in 1877 and was the only book Anna Sewell wrote. This outstanding 'autobiography of a horse', often described as probably the most successful animal story ever written, caught on at once and did incalculable good in persuading people to be kind to horses in particular and animals in general. Campaigners for the prevention of cruelty to animals distributed the book, together with pamphlets and appeals – and the story was the cause of at least one Home of Rest for Horses being built in England. Anna lived long enough to realise what a success her book had been, before dying on 25th April 1878. At her funeral, her mother ordered the bearing-reins to be removed from all the horses in the funeral train, in respect for Anna's wishes.

Sherwood, Mrs Mary Martha

Born on 6th May 1775, in Stanford, Worcestershire, the daughter of George Butt, a clergyman. She was educated at home until the age of fifteen, when she was sent to Reading Abbey, a French School which later moved to London. There she was a classmate of Mary Russell Mitford and Letitia Elizabeth Landon, both later to become well-known writers too. Her father died in 1795 and the family moved to Bridgnorth, Shropshire. There she taught in Sunday School and sought to teach religion to the poor; with this object in mind she wrote her first book, *The Traditions*, in 1794, followed by other religious stories and tracts. In 1803 she married her cousin, Captain Henry Sherwood, of the 53rd Regiment, accompanying him to India in 1805. Here she came under the influence of missionary Henry Martyn, who inspired her to write even more deeply religious works than she already had. They included *The Indian Pilgrim* (1817) and *Little Henry and His Bearer* (1814), the first missionary book for children. Mrs Sherwood also founded the first orphan institution during her stay in India. Before she left India she began what was to be her most famous work – *The History of the Fairchild Family*, which was published in three parts (in 1818, 1842 and 1847), the first section being the most notable. The book was extremely didactic and moral to say the least and was intended as a sort of 'awful warning' to youthful readers who should ever err from the straight and narrow path in any way. Her explicitly stated belief, upheld throughout the book, was that: 'All children are by nature evil, and while they have none but the natural evil principle to guide them, pious and prudent parents must check their naughty passions in any way that they have in their power, and force them into decent and proper behaviour and into what are called good habits.' Even on the title-page the book is described as 'a child's manual, being a collection of stories calculated to show the importance and effects of a religious education'. Mr and Mrs Fairchild believed in bringing up their three children – Lucy, Emily and Henry (all names of Mrs Sherwood's own children) – in the strictest possible way, punishing every act of naughtiness, e.g. quarrelling, lying, disobeying, stealing an apple, and so on, with blood-curdling lectures, threats of eternal hell and damnation and numerous dramatic illustrations – such as the occasion when Mr Fairchild took the entire family to see a gibbeted murderer hanging in rusty chains and pointed out that the man's downward path had no doubt started in a quarrel (a quarrel which may have begun in play, like the children's . . .). Parts of the book, such as this incident, were terrifying to young readers, but the author (and many parents) hoped the graphic prose would drive home the moral and the lesson. *The History of the Fairchild Family* was bought and read in vast numbers, later coming to be ridiculed and condemned. It was still in print more than a hundred years after its first appearance.

On the Sherwoods' return to England in 1816 they settled in Worcester. Mrs Sherwood took in pupils, brought up her growing family and continued to write regularly, producing well over 300 stories, tracts and articles, in addition to a long and detailed diary. Though her books are virtually unreadable today, it is generally agreed that she possessed a masterly prose style and an excellent understanding of the child mind. She died on 22nd September 1851. Mrs Sherwood's sister, Mrs Lucy Cameron (1781–1858), also wrote many religious stories and tracts, chiefly directed at improving the young and the poor.

Sinclair, Catherine

Born on 17th April 1800, in Edinburgh, Scotland, the fourth daughter of Sir John Sinclair, a prominent politician and the first President of the Board of Agriculture. She worked as her father's secretary from the age of fourteen until he died in 1835, when she devoted herself to writing. She published two popular novels, *Modern Accomplishment* (1836) and *Modern Society* (1837) before a chance remark to her by Sir Walter Scott led to her writing her most popular work. Scott said, 'In the rising generation there will be no poets, wits or orators, because all the play of the imagination is now carefully discouraged.' This was, of course, directed against the flood of didactic, moralising stories being fed non-stop by parents to their children. In her Introduction to *Holiday House* (1839), Miss Sinclair emphasised that she had 'endeavoured to paint that species of noisy, frolicsome, mischievous children, now almost extinct, wishing to preserve . . . remembrance of days long past, when young people were like wild horses on the prairies, rather than like well-broken hacks on the road . . .' She succeeded, and *Holiday House* blew through the children's book world of the period like a gust of fresh spring air, blowing away just a few, at any rate, of the dusty didactic cobwebs. F. J. Harvey Darton described the book as 'the best original children's book written up to that time, and one of the jolliest and most hilarious of any period.' It told of the doings of two perfectly natural, lively children, Harry and Laura, their tetchy old governess, Mrs

Crabtree, and their nice, sympathetic Uncle David, who was apt to tell the children wonderfully funny and nonsensical stories from time to time. One of Uncle David's stories was a *Nonsensical Story of Giants and Fairies*, often reprinted separately in later anthologies and described by Roger Lancelyn Green as 'the first example of real laughter and sheer delight in children's literature.' One of the giant-characters in the story was so tall that he 'was obliged to climb up a ladder to comb his own hair.' Miss Sinclair had originally told several of the stories in the book to her own nephew and niece. When she wrote them down in *Holiday House* they were enjoyed by countless young readers everywhere in a book which was to become a milestone in juvenile literature and which was to sell well for 100 years. Catherine Sinclair's other children's stories include *Charlie Seymour* (1838) and *Frank Vansittart, or The Model Schoolboys* (1853). Then, in 1861, she published a series of 'hieroglyphic' picture-letters (with pictures inserted in place of many of the words) which became 'overnight best-sellers', with six of the letters selling over 100,000 within three years. Her picture-letters consolidated the earlier success of *Holiday House* and made her a true nursery favourite. In her later years she performed many social services, such as setting up drinking-fountains and seats in various parts of her native Edinburgh. She also wrote many stories, sketches and articles about Scotland and the Scottish people. She died in Kensington, London, on 16th August 1864.

Sleigh, Barbara

Born in 1906, in Acocks Green, Birmingham, and educated at St Catherine's School, Bramley, Guildford, Surrey, and West Bromwich Art School. Her first children's book was *Carbonel* (1955), a memorable story about a magical witch's cat which has a nice line in dry humour. A sequel, *The Kingdom of Carbonel*, appeared in 1959. Other books include: *The Patchwork Quilt* (1956), *North of Nowhere* (1964) (comprising twenty-six re-told fairy tales from different countries), *Jessamy* (1967) and *Pen, Penny Tuppence* (1968). Miss Sleigh is married to David Davis, head of the BBC's radio children's programmes, and has taught at Holly Lodge High School and Goldsmith's College,

London. She also broadcasts occasional book reviews for the BBC.

Southey, Robert

Born in Bristol on 12th August 1774, and educated at Westminster School and Balliol College, Oxford. Poet Laureate from 1813 until his death. Wrote many poems, biographies, histories, theological works, etc. He appears here because, until fairly recently, he was credited with having originated the tale of *The Three Bears* in his book *The Doctor* (1834–37). This was disproved around 1950 when it was discovered that Eleanor Mure had written the tale down in book form in 1831 and that even at that date the story was 'a celebrated one'. So Southey had merely re-told the story (which featured an old woman, incidentally – little Goldilocks did not appear until later versions) with a few of his own embellishments. Southey, who was Coleridge's brother-in-law, died on 21st March 1843.

Spring, Howard

Born on 10th February 1889, in Cardiff, the son of a jobbing gardener. Left school at the age of eleven to help raise his eight brothers and sisters. He joined the staff of a newspaper (the *South Wales Daily News*) as a messenger boy, later becoming a reporter. He subsequently joined the *Manchester Guardian*, where he stayed until 1931. He was appointed Book Critic of the London *Evening Standard* and wrote the first of his long series of best-selling novels, *Shabby Tiger*, in 1934. Among his other famous novels are *My Son, My Son* (originally titled *O Absalom!*) (1938) and *Fame is the Spur* (1940). He also wrote three superlative children's books – *Darkie and Co.* (1932), *Sampson's Circus* (1936) and *Tumbledown Dick* (1939) – which only go to prove what an outstanding children's writer he might have been had his best-selling adult novels left him sufficient time. *Heaven Lies About Us* (1939) is a short autobiography describing his childhood experiences. He died in Cornwall in 1965.

Spyri, Johanna

Born in 1829, in Hirzel, a village near Zurich, Switzerland, and was one of six children born to a country doctor and his wife. As a little girl, Johanna Heusser (as she was before her marriage) lived a lively open-air life amid the beautiful flower-covered mountain slopes and helped to tend the goats. She took a sympathetic interest in the occasional patients her father brought home for special care. When she grew up she married a young lawyer named Bernhard Spyri, who later became town clerk of Zurich, where the couple went to live. Johanna first began to write to earn money with which to help wounded refugees arriving in Zurich from the Franco-Prussian War. She began to sell short stories for children. Then, in 1880, her first really long story was published; it was *Heidi*, which was an immediate success and ran through thirteen editions in its first ten years. It was translated into English in 1884 and was equally successful in Britain and America. *Heidi* tells the story of a little Swiss girl (rather like Johanna herself) who lives in the Alps with her grandfather, is sent to live in a big town, becomes unhappy and homesick, and eventually returns to her beloved mountain meadows and goats. The whole authentic atmosphere of the sparkling-clean Swiss Alps is there and the character of Heidi is delightful. The story makes a wonderful introduction to Switzerland for the young reader. Several different people have translated and illustrated *Heidi* since its first appearance. (One of the translators, Charles Tritten, also wrote two sequels: *Heidi Grows Up* and *Heidi's Children*, which proved popular.) Over the years, *Heidi* has maintained its place in the affections of young readers (especially girls) and is cited time and time again as a 'favourite book'. Johanna Spyri wrote many other books for children (and, as she often pointed out, 'for those who love children too') and some of these were translated into English as well. But none ever came anywhere near to rivalling the fame and success of *Heidi*. Johanna Spyri died in Zurich in 1901.

Stables, William Gordon

Born on 21st May 1840, in Aberchirder, Marnoch, Banffshire, Scotland, and educated at Aberdeen Grammar School and later at the University, where he studied medicine and qualified as a doctor. As a young man he shipped on board a small whaling brig on a voyage to Arctic regions. In 1863 he entered the Royal Navy as a surgeon and again sailed to the Arctic, and later the Antarctic – experiences which were to serve him in good stead when he came to write his many adventure stories set in those regions. Dr W. G. Stables (C.M., M.D., R.N.) served in the Royal Navy for nine years and for a further two years in the Merchant Service, serving in such places as Africa, India, the South Seas and the Mediterranean. After an eventful naval career he was invalided out on pension around 1874. The following year he settled down at his house, 'The Jungle', Twyford, Berkshire, and began his writing career. His first story was *The Cruise of the 'Snowbird'*, written as a serial for the *Boy's Own Paper* in 1880 (published in book form in 1882), followed by a sequel *Wild Adventures Round the Pole* (serial 1881, book 1883). His first actual book to appear was *Wild Adventures in Wild Places* (1881). Over the next thirty years he published around 150 books – an average of five a year. They were nearly all boys' adventure stories set in various parts of the world. He was a most prolific contributor to the *Boy's Own Paper*, writing nineteen full-scale serials for it, each having well over 60,000 words. Typical titles (and the dates in which they ran in *BOP*) include: *For England, Home and Beauty* (1887), *The Cruise of the Good Ship 'Boreas'* (1895), *Frank Hardinge: Adventures from Torrid Zones to Regions of Perpetual Snow* (1896), *The Cruise of the 'Arctic Fox'* (1900), *The Shell-Hunters* (1902), *The Butterfly Hunters* (1904), *From the Slums to the Quarter Deck* (1907), *The Ivory Hunters* (1907) and *From Fisher Lad to Fleet Surgeon* (1908). His tales often traced the arduous but triumphant climb of an ordinary lad to the top of his profession. Stables also wrote numerous articles for the *BOP* on natural history, domestic pets and other topics, as well as conducting a regular 'Advice' column for boys, who wrote in with their problems and queries (he was particularly fond of recommending cold baths, brisk early-morning walks and bowls of hot oatmeal porridge as 'cures' for most ailments and 'problems'!). He was also regarded as a leading authority on dogs of all breeds and often acted as judge at dog shows. His publications included books on animals in general and on dogs in particular; he also wrote historical novels for adults. A formidable man with a striking personality, Gordon Stables (he usually dropped the 'William') was a well-known figure in Fleet Street in the '80s and '90s wearing, as he often did, his full Highland dress, complete with kilt and sporran. During the last twenty-five years of his life he spent much of his time in a caravan called 'The Wanderer' and toured around the English countryside in it writing as he went (he disliked the word caravan, in fact, and preferred the term 'land-yacht'). His experiences resulted in a book, *The Cruise of the Land Yacht 'Wanderer'* (1886). He died on 10th May 1910, a few days before his 70th birthday, leaving six children.

Stevenson, Robert Louis

Born on 13th November 1850, at 8, Howard Place, Edinburgh, Scotland, the only child of a civil engineer, Thomas Stevenson, and his wife, Margaret Balfour. His family had included several famous engineers, who had built such lighthouses as Skerryvore and Bell Rock. But Robert Louis (he was actually christened 'Lewis' and he later changed the spelling but retained the pronunciation) had, like his mother, weak lungs and was an extremely delicate child. Whilst he had had literary ambitions from childhood, his father insisted that he study law, since he had neither the inclination nor aptitude for engineering. For much of his childhood he was confined to his home and nursery, in the care of his parents and his beloved and dedicated nurse, Alison Cunningham. He later attended a preparatory school and then Edinburgh Academy; finally came Edinburgh University, where he became something of a bohemian. In 1871 he began to read for the Scottish Bar, being called in 1875. He made little effort to practise law, however, and concentrated instead upon writing essays and articles which began to appear in such periodicals as *Cornhill Magazine* and *The Portfolio*. A tour he made with a friend in a canoe through France and Belgium provided the subject of his first book, *An Inland Voyage*, which appeared in 1878. A tour made a few months later resulted in *Travels With a Donkey in the Cevennes* (1879). His entertaining *New Arabian Nights* appeared in magazine form during 1878 and in book form four years later. In 1880 he married Fanny van der Grift Osbourne in San

251

Francisco and they returned, with her young son by a previous marriage, Lloyd, to live in Edinburgh. In 1881, while staying in a cottage at Braemar, Scotland, there came an incident which prompted Stevenson to write his most famous book – and one of the most celebrated boys' adventure stories ever written: *Treasure Island*. Twelve-year-old Lloyd Osbourne was passing a wet afternoon away by drawing a map of an imaginary desert island, when his step-father came in and, after watching with interest for a few minutes, set to with coloured pencils and helped him to complete it, even adding descriptive names for various points of the island – and crosses showing where hidden treasure lay. Lloyd said how wonderful it would be to have a story written about their island. Stevenson liked the idea and had completed the first chapter by next morning. The story was written enthusiastically and quickly, with a chapter finished each day and read to Lloyd. Half-way through the book, a visitor, Dr Japp, was so impressed that he took what Stevenson had so far written to the editor of *Young Folks*, who accepted *The Sea Cook* (as Stevenson had called his story) and re-titled it *Treasure Island*, running it as a serial between October 1881 and January 1882. It caused little comment or interest at this time, but when it was published as a book in late 1883 it became a widely read and nationally hailed best-seller, welcomed by many reviewers as a work which would surely revolutionise the boys' adventure story and give it a much-needed jolt from the over-wordy and generally routine rut into which it had fallen in recent years (with a few honourable exceptions). In *Young Folks*, by the way, the story was credited to 'Captain George North'. The book has never been out of print since and has even, in more recent years, resulted in fictional 'sequels', involving many of the same characters, written by other hands. And in Long John Silver, that one-legged, cunning, villainous sea-cook, Stevenson created one of the most memorable characters in all fiction. In the meantime, Stevenson had been contributing another serial to *Young Folks*: *The Black Arrow*, which ran from June to October 1883, being published in book form in 1888. This was a historical drama set against the background of the Wars of the Roses, featuring Richard, Duke of Gloucester, as a leading character, and telling of a boy's fight to gain his rightful inheritance. It was a

ERIC

OR, LITTLE BY LITTLE

A TALE OF ROSLYN SCHOOL

By FREDERIC W. FARRAR

Tis one thing to be tempted, Escalus,
Another thing to fall.
Measure for Measure, Act ii. Scene 1.

LONDON
A. & C. BLACK, SOHO SQUARE
1903

91 (a) Frontispiece and
(b) title-page from a 1903 edition
of F. W. Farrar's celebrated *Eric
or, Little by Little*

92 Drawing by H. M. Brock
from Desmond Coke's *Youth,
Youth . . . !* (1919)

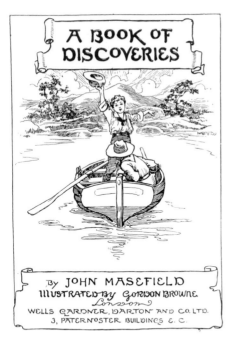

93 and 94 Two fine examples of title-pages by Gordon Browne

95 A trio of typical Kate Greenaway children

96 Beatrix Potter's *Peter Rabbit*

97 Helen Bannerman's *Little Black Sambo*

98 Frontispiece photograph (by Wm. Ransford, Hampstead) of 'The Members of the Exploring Party', from the 1914 edition of Sir Arthur Conan Doyle's *The Lost World*. Doyle – who posed for the picture with friends – is seen 'disguised' as Professor Challenger in the centre of the group

99 Two of H. R. Millar's superlative illustrations to E. Nesbit's stories. The first from *The Magic City* ('A long procession . . .')

100 . . . and the second from *The Enchanted Castle* ('This is an enchanted garden . . .')

good, exciting tale, but not in the same class as Stevenson's other boys' adventure stories. *Kidnapped*, Stevenson's last serial for *Young Folks*, ran from May to July 1886, appearing as a book later the same year. This story of the adventures of a young Scot, David Balfour, in the Highlands of 1751, and of his exploits in company with the colourful, reckless Alan Breck Stewart, was on a par with *Treasure Island* and again achieved enormous success. Its sequel, *Catriona*, appeared in 1893 (following serialisation in a girls' magazine called *Atalanta*) and continued David Balfour's adventures. Stevenson's famous macabre tale *Dr Jekyll and Mr Hyde* was also published in 1886. And, showing a completely different side to his brilliance, *A Child's Garden of Verses* came out in 1885. This collection of poems written especially for children and dedicated to his old nurse, hauntingly brings into focus the private, imaginative world of the child, his thoughts, his play, his likes and his fears. Based on Stevenson's own childhood memories, the verses – including such well-known ones as 'My Shadow', 'The Land of Counterpane' and 'The Lamplighter' – are delightfully true to the child reader and sadly and evocatively nostalgic to the adult. His other famous books include *The Master of Ballantrae* (1889), *The Wrong Box* (with Lloyd Osbourne) (1889), *The Wrecker* (with Lloyd Osbourne) (1892), *Island Night's Entertainments* (1893), the unfinished *Weir of Hermiston* (1896), and *St Ives* (concluded by Arthur Quiller-Couch) (1897). Dogged by bad health all his life, he went to live on the South Sea Island of Samoa, hoping a more congenial climate would improve things. There he lived happily among the natives – who christened him 'Tusitala' (Teller of Tales) – from 1890 until his death on 3rd December 1894. High on a hill in Samoa lies his grave, with the moving Requiem:

> *Here he lies where he longed to be;*
> *Home is the sailor, home from sea,*
> *And the hunter home from the hill.*

Stoker, Bram

Born 1847 in Dublin and was a child-invalid, not starting to walk until his eighth year. Educated privately and at Trinity College, Dublin University, where he was a leading athlete and gifted student. He worked in the Irish Civil Service for several years before becoming Henry Irving's acting manager at the Lyceum Theatre, London. After writing a few undistinguished novels he published *Dracula* in 1897, soon to become one of the classic horror tales of English literature. What is not generally known is that Stoker published a book of children's stories, *Under the Sunset*, in 1881 – long before he made his name with *Dracula*. The stories were strong, moral ones, complete with sombre illustrations, and were not intended for squeamish children, featuring as they did, for example, a plague, the King of Death and a bloody giant. There were, at least, no vampires. Stoker died on 20th April 1912.

Stowe, Harriet Beecher

Born on 14th June 1811, in Litchfield, Connecticut, USA, the daughter of Lyman Beecher, a great Congregational minister, and also the sister of Henry Ward Beecher, the most famous preacher and reformer of his day. Her upbringing was strict and puritanical and she was educated privately, her father often acting as her tutor. At the age of thirteen Harriet attended the girls' school at which her sister, Kate, was a teacher. After being a pupil there for a year Harriet stayed on to teach moral philosophy. In 1832 her family moved to Cincinnati, where Harriet continued to teach, also writing stories and sketches, which were published in various magazines. In 1836 she married an eminent clergyman, Calvin E. Stowe, with whom she went to live in Maine around 1850. It was there that she began to write her famous book *Uncle Tom's Cabin*, based on sights she had seen in Kentucky and Louisiana among the Negro slaves and their white masters. The story originally appeared as a serial in a magazine, *The National Era*, in 1851–52, being published in book form in 1852. It caused a sensation and made Harriet famous almost overnight. It was soon translated into every major language and became a world best-seller (within 100 years it was to sell three million copies in the United States alone). *Uncle Tom's Cabin* is not really a children's book at all, but, over the years, the younger readers tended to 'take it over' (as they have done with many other books written originally for adults) and to this day it is still read widely by children, who shed many a tear over its pathos. The story tells of the sufferings of Uncle Tom, a Negro slave in the American South, who is unceasingly bullied and ill-treated by a Yankee overseer named Simon Legree. Other characters include Little Eva, daughter of Uncle Tom's white owner; Eliza, the mulatto girl; Topsy, the mischievous Negro child (remembered for her much-quoted saying: 'I just growed!'); and Miss Ophelia, a prim spinster. Harriet Beecher Stowe wrote the book to help the abolition of slavery. 'God wrote the book,' she once said, 'I took his dictation.' The book led to deep controversy and was said to have been one of the causes of the start of the American Civil War. President Lincoln, meeting the author, is reported to have greeted her, half-jokingly, half-seriously: 'So this is the little lady who made the big war!' The book certainly played a major part in the emancipation of the slaves and by this one story Harriet Beecher Stowe qualifies as one of the outstanding reformers of the nineteenth century in America. She visited Britain in 1853 and was received with acclaim. She had seven children and also found time to publish many further books, articles, stories, etc. Her collected works run to sixteen volumes – but she is remembered today almost entirely by *Uncle Tom's Cabin*. She died on 1st July 1896.

Strang, Herbert

The large number of popular books for boys written by 'Herbert Strang' during the first thirty years of the century were, in fact, all the work of a two-man partnership. The prolific team consisted of George Herbert Ely (who died in 1958) and James L'Estrange (who died in 1947). (A glance at their names will show how they arrived at their joint pseudonym.) The two men wrote over fifty books, but neither ever wrote a complete one on his own. The plots were worked out together. Then L'Estrange, who had travelled widely, supplied the local colour and Ely did the actual writing. The partnership began in 1903 in Glasgow and was actually more than a literary one, since they both later joined the Oxford University Press, for which they worked for more than thirty years. Typical titles include: *With Drake on the Spanish Main* (1908), *Humphrey Bold* (1909) *King of the Air* (1909), *The Cruise of the Gyro-Car* (1911), *The*

Flying Boat (1912), *Bright Ideas* (1920) and *Martin of Old London* (1925). The stories were of most types (with the exception of school stories, for some reason), with special emphasis on wonderful new flying inventions, or dealing with the lengthy, detailed and action-filled adventures of one young man at a certain period of history. They were extremely popular in their day and were particularly in demand for school prizes. *Herbert Strang's Annual* started in 1908 and appeared regularly for many years; its title was eventually changed to *The Oxford Annual for Boys* (edited by Herbert Strang), which continued until the late 1930s.

Streatfeild, Noel

Born in December 1897, at Amberley, near Arundel, Sussex, the daughter of William Streatfeild, a country vicar (who later became Suffragan Bishop of Lewes, in Sussex). Her great-great grandmother was Elizabeth Fry, the great nineteenth-century prison reformer. While she was still a baby, her father was appointed Vicar of St Leonards-on-Sea, Sussex, and it was at the Vicarage there that Noel spent most of her childhood, growing up with her three sisters and brother. She was something of a 'rebel', constantly chafing at parental and school disciplines and longing to grow up so that she could have more 'say' in what she did. She was educated at St Leonards-on-Sea and later, when her father became Vicar of Eastbourne, at Laleham School, Eastbourne. She showed a marked dramatic talent from childhood and often took part in her father's parish's concerts and plays. She decided she would like to make acting her career and she eventually studied at the Royal Academy of Dramatic Art. When she left the Academy she joined a provincial repertory company and appeared in many plays, especially Shakespearean. She subsequently appeared in revue, pantomime and many plays, also touring in South Africa and Australia. It was during this period of her life that she obtained the first-hand, authentic experience which was to be so useful later on when she came to write stories featuring theatrical families. In 1929 she was travelling home to England after an Australian tour when she heard that her father had died. She decided she needed a 'safer' career than the stage and one which would bring her a reasonably steady income; surprisingly enough she chose writing, but felt confident she could succeed. Years before, she had subscribed to a correspondence course in writing, produced two fairy stories (which her tutors described as 'unsaleable') and promptly sold them to a children's magazine. But she began her writing career with a novel, *The Whicharts* (the title originating in a childhood mispronunciation of 'The Lord's Prayer' beginning: 'Our Father Whichart . . .'). It was published in England and America in 1931 with success and was followed by other adult novels. She was eventually invited to try her hand at a children's story and the result was the widely praised, best-selling *Ballet Shoes*, published in 1936. It tells the story of three children – Petrova, Pauline and Posy Fossil – who train for stage careers, concentrating particularly on the one who has her heart set on becoming a ballet dancer. There are plenty of dramatic productions included too and the diet is by no means all ballet. The story ends with one girl going abroad to complete her ballet training, another going off to Hollywood to become a film star – and the other changing her mind and deciding she wants to fly aeroplanes after all! Next came *Tennis Shoes* (1937), which describes the training of a child to become a championship tennis player. Then, in 1938, came *The Circus is Coming* which won the Carnegie Medal as the Best Children's Book of the Year. Noel Streatfeild spent a period travelling around with a circus before she wrote this story, so as to get every detail correct and the atmosphere just right. It tells of two children, Peter and Santa, who run away from the threat of being sent to an orphanage and stay with their uncle, who turns out to be nothing less than a clown with a touring circus. In 1940 came Noel Streatfeild's only children's 'thriller', *The House in Cornwall*, followed by *The Children of Primrose Lane* (1941), which tells of a group of wartime evacuee children who discover a German spy, *Curtain Up* (1944), another story of children training for the stage, and *Party Frock* (1946), describing how a whole village pageant is organised by a family of children so that one of them, Selina, can wear her wonderful present from America – a party frock . . . *The Painted Garden* (1949) tells how a girl is chosen to star in a Hollywood film version of *The Secret Garden*; *White Boots* (1951) is about two girls who want to

257

become ice-skating champions; and *Wintle's Wonders* (1957) tells the story of two girls who are members of a professional children's dancing group. In 1953 came *The Fearless Treasure: A Story of England From Then to Now*, which unfolds England's history through the adventures of a group of children who go back into the past. In the same year Miss Streatfeild edited a collection of new short stories written specially for her – and for children – by many well-known authors: *By Special Request*. In 1953 *The Bell Family* ran as a very popular serial in the BBC Children's Hour programme; later it was adapted into a television serial, and in 1954 the story was published in book form. In 1960 came another story about the Bell Family – *New Town*. More recent family stories are *Apple Bough* (1962), *The Children of the Top Floor* (1964), *The Growing Summer* (1966) and *Caldicott Place* (1967). Apart from her popular series of children's novels, Noel Streatfeild has written several more adult novels, as well as two fictionalised autobiographies telling of her own experiences as a member of a country vicar's family: *A Vicarage Family* (1963) and *Away from the Vicarage* (1965). Her books for younger children include: *Dennis the Dragon* (1939), *The Grey Family* (1956), *Bertram* (1959), *Look at the Circus* (1960) and *Let's Go Coaching* (1965). Other titles include: *Magic and the Magician* (1958) (a study of E. Nesbit and her children's books), *Lisa Goes to Russia* (1963), *Confirmation and After* (1963) and *Enjoying Opera* (1965). *The Years of Grace* (1950) and *Growing Up Gracefully* (1955) are companionable handbooks for growing girls, and *The Day Before Yesterday* (1956) is a book of articles on aspects of life and characters in the late-nineteenth/early-twentieth centuries. These last three titles were edited by Miss Streatfeild. Noel Streatfeild is one of the most popular and successful of contemporary writers for children and her work is highly regarded by readers and critics alike. She creates likeable and believable children and goes to endless trouble in researching the background material for her stories. She was the sister-in-law of the late Kitty Barne, another Carnegie Medal winner. Today, Noel Streatfeild is still writing busily and lives in the heart of London's Belgravia.

Suddaby, Donald

Born 1900, in Leeds, Yorkshire, and educated at Manchester Cathedral School. His first book, *Lost Men in the Grass*, was published in 1940 under the pseudonym 'ALAN GRIFF' (it was later reprinted under his own name). This is an exciting imaginative fantasy about three men who are reduced to the size of ants and their battles against attacking insects, birds and animals. In 1950 came *The Star Raiders*, the story of a space voyage to the planet Venus and what three explorers discovered there. Subsequent titles include: *Masterless Swords* (1951), *The Death of Metal* (1952), *Village Fanfare* (1954), *New Tales of Robin Hood* (1955), *The Moon of Snowshoes* (1955), *Merry Jack Jugg – Highwayman* (1956), *Prisoners of Saturn* (1957), *Fresh News from Sherwood* (1959), *Crowned With Wild Olive* (1961), *Tower of Babel* (1962), *A Bell in the Forest* (1964) and *Robin Hood's Masterstroke* (1965). Suddaby was at his best in his Wellsian fantasies such as *Lost Men in the Grass*, *The Star Raiders*, *The Death of Metal*, *Village Fanfare* and *Prisoners of Saturn* and brought a poet's sweep and descriptive power to his tales. He died on 17th March, 1964.

Sutcliff, Rosemary

Born in 1920, at West Clandon, Surrey. Until she was ten she accompanied her father (who was a naval officer) and mother to his various stations until he retired, when the family settled down in North Devon. From the age of two Miss Sutcliff has suffered from a polyarthritic complaint which has restricted her physical movement. She was consequently unable to begin proper schooling until she was nine, when she attended a 'Dame school' in Chatham, Kent. Up to then her mother taught her and also read her many stories about the Roman Empire, old legends and fairy tales, and stories by Whyte-Melville, Kenneth Grahame and Kipling. They paved the way for Miss Sutcliff's later Roman stories and her treatments of ancient legends and historical subjects. She was especially influenced by Kipling's writings. On leaving school she trained as a painter at Bideford School of Art and subsequently became an expert professional miniaturist. She was a member of the Royal Society of Miniature Painters and her work has been exhibited at the Royal Academy. In her mid-twenties she virtually gave up painting to concentrate on writing, which she now found more satisfying and enjoyable. She began by re-telling a series of old British legends and submitting the collection to a publisher. The legends were rejected but had impressed the publisher's children's editor so much that Miss Sutcliff was invited to write a similar book, but this time about the legends of Robin Hood. So it was that, in 1950, her first two books appeared: *The Chronicles of Robin Hood* and *The Queen Elizabeth Story*; the latter was a charming story of a little girl who lived in a Devon village and longed to see Queen Elizabeth the First. In 1951 came *The Armourer's House*, about a little girl who goes from her home in Devon to live with her armourer uncle in the London of Henry the Eighth; and in 1952 appeared *Brother Dusty-Feet*, the adventures of a boy who runs away to join a band of strolling theatrical players in Tudor times. Rosemary Sutcliff's career took a decided step forward with *Simon* (1953), which was set in the English Civil War. But her stature as a children's writer of major importance was consolidated with the publication of *The Eagle of the Ninth*, which described graphically the last years of Roman rule in Britain. Its success was underlined by the fact that the BBC's Children's Hour programme broadcast the serial version of the story twice – the second time by public request. Later books include: *Outcast* (1955) (Roman), *The Shield Ring* (1956) (Viking settlers in Britain versus the Normans), *The Silver Branch* (1957) (Roman), *Warrior Scarlet* (1958) (Bronze Age), *The Lantern Bearers* (1959) (another in the magnificent series about the Romans in Britain, and it also won the Carnegie Medal as the Best Children's Book of the Year), *The Bridge Builders* (1959) (a short story of life on the Roman Wall), *Knight's Fee* (1960) (Norman England), and *Dawn Wind* (1961) (Britain defeated by Saxon invaders). *Beowulf* (1961) was a dramatic re-telling of the Anglo-Saxon poem and was re-printed in a Puffin edition in 1966 as *The Dragon Slayer*. A study of *Houses and History* appeared in 1960 and a critical survey of *Rudyard Kipling* in the same year. Novels for older readers are: *Lady in Waiting* (1956), *The Rider of the White Horse* (1959) and *The Sword of Sunset* (1963), the last being a memorable story about the real King Arthur. *The Hound of Ulster* (1963) was a new version of the Irish Cuchulain saga. Miss Sutcliff's more recent books include *The Mark of the Horse Lord* (1965), telling of a Roman gladiator, *Heroes and History* (1965) a collection of pieces about legendary British heroes such as Hereward the Wake, Robin Hood, King Arthur, etc.; *The Chief's Daughter* (1967), a story for younger readers; and *The High Deeds of Finn Mac Cool* (1967), legendary tales about one of Ireland's greatest heroes. Today, Rosemary Sutcliff lives and writes in a country cottage near Arundel in Sussex.

Swift, Jonathan

Born on 30th November 1667, in Dublin, of English parents, and educated at Kilkenny and at Trinity College, Dublin. He subsequently went to England and became secretary to Sir William Temple, the statesman and essayist, at Moor Park. During this period he met Esther Johnson (whom he came to call 'Stella'), later to play a large part in his life and the only person he is said to have really loved. He returned to Ireland in 1694 and became a clergyman at Kilroot, near Belfast. While there, he wrote his two early satires, *The Tale of a Tub* and *The Battle of the Books* (both eventually published in 1704). In 1699, after another spell in England, he returned again to Ireland to become Chaplain to the Lord Deputy, the Earl of Berkeley; he was also appointed Vicar of Laracor. He began to pay frequent visits to London and much of the remainder of his life was devoted to active participation in religious and political issues being debated in England and Ireland. He wrote a vast number of pamphlets, articles and books and was chiefly anti-Whig in his attacks. He was perhaps the most prolific writer of his time. In 1726 came his famous *Gulliver's Travels* (the actual title being *Travels into Several Remote Nations of the World, by Lemuel Gulliver*). Swift intended the work as an adult satire, pin-pointing the foibles and follies of the human race. But the story was gradually adopted by young readers (who had no real books of their own at this time) who read it simply as a rollicking and amusing adventure yarn about a sailor shipwrecked upon the land of tiny people – the Lilliputians – and among other strange peoples. (The other chief voyages were to Brobdingnag, Laputa and the land of the Houyhnhnms.)

The book has usually been published in expurgated form in recent times, since parts of the original are assuredly not suitable for children. It has been translated into every major language and illustrated by a wide variety of distinguished artists. Swift had been appointed Dean of St Patrick's Cathedral, Dublin, in 1713 – but he never achieved the bishopric he wanted so much. In his later years he became more and more bitter and, for the last ten years of his life, suffered from serious illness and insanity. He died in Dublin on 19th October 1745 and is buried in St Patrick's Cathedral there.

Tarkington, Booth

Born on 29th July 1869, in Indianapolis, Indiana, USA, the son of a lawyer, and educated at Purdue and Princeton Universities. His first novel was *The Gentleman from Indiana* (1899), but it was his second book, *Monsieur Beaucaire* (1900), a romantic historical trifle, which became a best-seller and made his name. He went on to write many famous novels, including *The Magnificent Ambersons* (1918) and *Alice Adams* (1921), both of which won Pulitzer Prizes. He won many other distinctions, but he finds a place here because of his delightful *Penrod* (1914), which told of the amusing adventures of a twelve-year-old boy in a U.S. Middle-Western community and was said to have been inspired by Tarkington's nephews. At the peak of its popularity in America it even out-sold *Tom Sawyer*. It was followed by two sequels: *Penrod and Sam* (1916) and *Penrod Jashber* (1929). All three were collected in an omnibus volume, *Penrod: His Complete Story*, in 1931. *Seventeen* (1916) was about an older boy (William Baxter) and his first romance. Booth Tarkington died on 19th May 1946.

Taylor, Ann and Jane

Ann Taylor was born on 30th January 1782, in Islington, London, and her sister, Jane, on 23rd September 1783, in Holborn, London. They were the daughters of Isaac Taylor, the engraver and writer (known as 'the elder' to differentiate him from his writer son of the same name). In 1786 the family moved to Lavenham, Suffolk, and resided there for ten years.

262

Isaac Taylor became a minister at Colchester, Essex, in 1796, again taking his family with him. Both Ann and Jane began to write verse in childhood and by 1799 Ann had seen publication of a rhymed answer to a puzzle in the *Minor's Pocket Book*, with Jane achieving print five years later with a poem 'The Beggar Boy' in the same periodical. The publishers of the *Minor's Pocket Book* (Darton and Harvey) invited the sisters to submit a collection of their verses for publication in book form. So it was that *Original Poems for Infant Minds* by 'Several Young Persons' appeared in 1804. A young writer named Adelaide O'Keefe (said by some to be a friend of the Taylors, though averred by others that she was 'brought in' by the publishers) contributed thirty-four poems. The collection was, on the whole, a delightful one, drawing on the daily lives of ordinary children for most of the verses. A considerable number, however, were also in the form of 'awful warnings' or moral verse-stories, with such titles as 'Never Play With Fire', 'To a Little Girl Who Has Told a Lie', 'Careless Matilda' and 'Negligent Mary'. The best-known verse in the collection is Jane Taylor's 'The Star' which begins with the classic 'Twinkle, twinkle, little star. . . .' Ann was responsible for such titles as 'Meddlesome Matty', 'The Two Gardens' and 'My Mother'. *Original Poems* was an enormous success and went into numerous editions, also being translated in several countries abroad. It was followed by *Rhymes for the Nursery* (1806), *Limed Twigs to Catch Young Birds* (1808), *Hymns for Infant Minds* (1810) and *Original Hymns for Sunday Schools* (1812). The writing partnership broke up after the last title, as a result of Ann's marriage to the Rev. Joseph Gilbert. In 1810 Isaac Taylor Snr took up an appointment as a Nonconformist minister at Ongar, Essex, and, since the whole family were now writing books (father, mother and two sons, in addition to the already successful works of Ann and Jane) they became known as 'The Taylors of Ongar'. Though both Ann and Jane wrote further occasional books separately, they never achieved the early success of their verses for children. Jane died on 13th April 1824. Ann spent her last years at Nottingham and died on 20th December 1866.

Thackeray, William Makepeace

Born on 18th July 1811, in Calcutta, India, where his father was employed by the East India Company. In 1817, soon after his father's death, he was sent back to England to live with an aunt in Chiswick, where he attended his first school. When his mother and step-father returned to England, he was sent to the Charterhouse School in Smithfield. He later spent a year at Trinity College, Cambridge, not achieving much academic success, but enthusiastically following the social rounds and making several influential friends. He began writing verses and drawing caricatures for undergraduate magazines too. Following much European travel, a short spell as a law student at the Middle Temple and a great deal of journalistic work – including prolific contributions to *Fraser's Magazine* and *Punch* – his famous novel *Vanity Fair* was published in 1847–48. It at once established him in the top rank of English novelists and second only to Dickens among living novelists. Other successful novels subsequently appeared, including *Pendennis* (1848), *Henry Esmond* (1852) and *The Virginians* (1857). In 1854, whilst staying in Rome with his two daughters, he drew a set of picture cards as part of the Twelfth Night festivities and wove a story around them to amuse his children and their friends. In 1855 the story – by then elaborated and injected with shafts of satire – was published as *The Rose and the Ring*, described as 'A Fireside Pantomime by Mr. M. A. Titmarsh', and was a great success. It was a humorous 'extravaganza' set in the Royal Fairy Courts of Paflagonia and Crim Tartary and featured such characters as Prince Giglio, Princess Rosalba, Fairy Blackstick and Gruffanuff, the Palace porter. It was also graphically illustrated by Thackeray. It was virtually his only children's book – and even then it was written with an eye on adult readers, who relished its touches of political and social satire. But younger readers accepted it purely as a light-hearted and nonsensical fairy-tale. Thackeray died on 24th December 1863, in London, and is buried at Kensal Green.

Thompson, Ruth Plumly

Born Philadelphia, USA, 1895. Author of many children's books, including no less than nineteen titles about the magical country of Oz, originally created by L. Frank Baum in *The Wonderful Wizard of Oz*. After Baum's death in 1919 other writers continued the Oz saga, the most prolific and popular being Miss Thompson. Among her titles are: *The Princess of Cozytown* (1922), *The Cowardly Lion of Oz* (1923), *The Lost King of Oz* (1925), *Pirates of Oz* (1931) and *King Kojo* (1939). The series was continued until 1951.

Thornton, Edward

See: Brooks, E. S.

Todd, Barbara Euphan

Born in the late 1890s at Arksey Vicarage, Doncaster, Yorkshire, and educated at St Catherine's School, Bramley, Guildford, Surrey. On leaving school at the end of 1914, soon after the beginning of the First World War, she worked on the land and as a V.A.D. until 1918. She had composed her own verses and stories from the age of nine and it was perhaps natural that she should turn to writing as a way of earning her living. She contributed many verses, stories and articles to a variety of magazines and became a regular contributor and later a reviewer to *Punch*. Her verses about children were particularly popular with *Punch* readers and in the late 1920s a collection of them was published under the title *The Seventh Daughter*, when she used the pseudonym 'Euphan'. Another book of verses was *Hither and Thither*. In 1927 she wrote her first children's book (in collaboration with Marjory Royce), a family story titled *The Very Good Walkers*. In the early 1930s came another book, *Mr Blossom's Shop*, which was broadcast in the BBC's Children's Hour programme. In 1936 she introduced her most famous character – and one of the most beloved in modern children's literature – in *Worzel Gummidge*. Worzel was a turnip-headed, bottle-straw-footed scarecrow who lived in a field at Scatterbrook Farm in the heart of the English countryside. He was rather bad-tempered and moody, given to philosophising and impersonating humans, but with a heart of gold and an impeccable sense of logic. The book told of two children, John and Susan, and their hilarious adventures with

Worzel when they stayed at Scatterbrook recovering from whooping-cough. It was broadcast as a serial in BBC Children's Hour shortly after publication, with the role of Worzel being played by the late Hugh E. Wright, and the broadcasts were enormously successful, making the scarecrow a nation-wide favourite with both children and parents. (*Worzel Gummidge*, incidentally, was chosen to be Penguin Books' 'Puffin Story Book No. 1' when the popular series was first launched in December 1941.) Many more titles about Worzel Gummidge succeeded that original one and they include: *Worzel Gummidge Again* (1937), *More About Worzel Gummidge* (1938), *Worzel Gummidge and Saucy Nancy* (1947), *Worzel Gummidge Takes a Holiday* (1949), *Earthy Mangold and Worzel Gummidge* (1954), *Worzel Gummidge and the Railway Scarecrows* (1955), *Worzel Gummidge at the Circus* (1956), *Worzel Gummidge and the Treasure Ship* (1958) and *Detective Worzel Gummidge* (1963). Several of these later stories have also been broadcast. In 1943 Miss Todd wrote (in collaboration with Esther Boumphrey) *The House That Ran Behind*, a family caravanning adventure. Her late husband was Commander J. G. Bower, R.N., D.S.O., who wrote adventure novels, often set in the submarine service in which he served, under the pseudonym 'Klaxon'; in 1950 came *Aloysius Let Loose*, the humorous adventures of a preparatory schoolboy, written by husband and wife under that same pseudonym. *The Shop By the Sea* (1965), *The Clock Shop* (1967) and *The Boy With the Green Thumb* (1968) were stories for younger readers.

Tolkien, John Ronald Reuel

Born on 3rd January 1892, in Bloemfontein, South Africa, and educated at King Edward VI School, Birmingham, and Exeter College, Oxford, where he gained his M.A. – the first of his many academic honours. He joined the Lancashire Fusiliers in 1915 and served during the First World War until 1918. In 1920 he became Reader in English Language at Leeds University, being appointed Professor of English Language in 1924. He was Rawlinson and Bosworth Professor of Anglo-Saxon at Oxford University 1925–45, Fellow of Pembroke College 1926–45, and Merton Professor of English

Language and Literature 1945–59. He is today Fellow of Merton College, Oxford. His first book was *A Middle English Vocabulary*, published in 1922. It was followed in 1925 by *Sir Gawain and the Green Knight*, which he co-edited. Studies of Chaucer and Beowulf were followed in 1937 by *The Hobbit*. A 'hobbit' is a sort of furry gnome created by Professor Tolkien and the hero of the story is Bilbo Baggins, a quiet hobbit who is called upon to set out and destroy a terrifying dragon who is tormenting neighbouring villagers. His courage and humour carry him through the adventure safely and the reader is swept up by the tide of the author's superb, pulsating prose. *The Hobbit* was, though refreshingly unusual, obviously a children's book (it was also, incidentally, illustrated by the author). Its breathtaking, unique successor, the epic heroic romance cycle called *The Lord of the Rings*, was not intended for children, though it can be read by practically any age from around eleven or twelve upwards. The cycle was published in three volumes: *The Fellowship of the Ring* and *The Two Towers* appeared in 1954, and *The Return of the King* in 1955. In *The Lord of the Rings* Professor Tolkien created an entire new mythology, expanding on the one he first imagined in *The Hobbit*. The basic story is that of the quest for a powerful magic ring, by which the owner can rule the world and everyone in it. An evil figure, Sauron, wants the ring; a good wizard, Gandalf, sends a party of hobbits (and various companions) to destroy the ring. On the highest level the story is the ageless one of good versus evil; on a lower plane it is a tremendously exciting adventure yarn. And the writing is colourful and outstanding, varying in style according to the different types of incidents it describes. Distinguished critics have compared the cycle to Spenser, Malory, Aristo and Beowulf, containing elements of Norse, Teutonic, Celtic and fairy-tale myths and legends. The work has gone through a dozen editions in as many years, sold nearly three million copies in nine languages throughout the world, become a fantastic 'cult' in the USA, and remains one of the few true modern classics of our time. Among Professor Tolkien's other works are: *On Fairy Stories* (1938) (reprinted as *Tree and Leaf* in 1964), a critical study; *Farmer Giles of Ham* (1949), set in pre-Arthurian times in Britain and telling of the hero's dealings with a dragon and a giant; *The Adventures of Tom Bombadil* (1962), a tale

267

in verse, supposed to be from 'The Red Book', the imaginary source of hobbit lore mentioned in *The Lord of the Rings*; *Smith of Wootton Major* (1967), a medieval, short story of winter and *The Road Goes Ever On* (1968), in which composer Donald Swann supplies music to songs taken from the author's books. Professor Tolkien lives in Headington, Oxford, where he is currently working on a new saga called *The Silmarillion*, again set in 'Middle Earth' (the setting of his earlier cycle).

Tourtel, Mary

Creator of the famous 'Rupert Bear' picture-stories, which have been delighting children for nearly fifty years. Mary Tourtel had written several children's stories, and illustrated them, when, in 1920, the *Daily Express* newspaper in London ran a few of them. Later that same year, it was suggested that she contribute a regular daily picture-serial about a new character. She chose a boy-bear named 'Rupert' and, on 8th November 1920, the very first story, 'The Adventures of a Little Lost Bear', began in the newspaper. The captions were written by Miss Tourtel's husband, who was a sub-editor on the *Daily Express* at that time. The daily feature became so popular that the Rupert League was founded and many thousands of children from all over Britain (and abroad) joined. The series ran successfully until 1935, when Mary Tourtel's sight failed and she had to give the work up after an unbroken run of fifteen years. After an unsuccessful two-week period in which the story was told in photographs of bears and other animals, A. E. Bestall took over the Rupert stories and pictures and has been doing them ever since. As well as contributing her daily strip-pictures to the *Daily Express*, Mary Tourtel also produced little books of Rupert stories, Rupert Annuals, Rupert painting books, and so on. Her favourite character of Rupert, with his red jersey, checked trousers and muffler, has an indefinable charm, and his adventures an engaging quality of cosy fantasy; the combination is difficult to resist.

Travers, Pamela Lyndon

Born during the early 1900s in Australia, of an Irish father and

Scottish mother. She was a voracious childhood reader and began to write stories while still a child. After a brief period on the stage she began writing literary and dramatic criticisms, as well as poetry which was lauded by the Irish poet and editor 'A.E.' (George Russell), who published much of it in his *The Irish Statesman*. Longing to work in a wider literary scene than could be offered by her native Australia, she came to England in the 'twenties and contributed to various publications. In 1934 came her first and most famous book: *Mary Poppins*. It introduced the most lovable English Nannie in children's literature – the severe, always-correct, prim, kindly and magical Mary Poppins. She was blown into the Banks' household by an east wind, promptly sliding *up* the banisters and proceeding to unpack a seemingly bottomless carpet-bag. Taking charge of Jane and Michael (not to mention the twins) Mary took them on a breathtaking series of magic adventures and escapades. In doing so she carved herself a permanent niche among the immortals of children's stories and over the years has become a world-wide favourite. Her popularity was increased even more by the enormous success of Walt Disney's musical film version, which opened in 1964. Subsequent books in the series are: *Mary Poppins Comes Back* (1935), *Mary Poppins opens the Door* (1944), *Mary Poppins in the Park* (1952) and *Mary Poppins From A to Z* (1963). P. L. Travers' other books for children are: *I Go By Sea, I Go By Land* (1941), a story about child-evacuees to America during the Second World War (and written while the author was working for the Ministry of Information in wartime America) and *The Fox at the Manger* (1963), a Christmas story inspired by an old carol, telling of the part played by the fox at the Nativity. Today, Miss Travers lives in a Regency house in Chelsea, London.

Treadgold, Mary

Born in London and educated at St Paul's Girls' School and Bedford College, London. In the 1930s she entered publishing, initially with Raphael Tuck and later as Heinemann's first Children's Books Editor. She was a Talks Producer with the BBC's Overseas Service from 1941 until 1960. In the autumn of 1940 – whilst sheltering from enemy air-raids in a garden

'Anderson' – she began writing her first children's book, *We Couldn't Leave Dinah*. As a publisher's editor she had had to read hundreds of submitted 'pony stories' – the majority of which were very poor. She decided she could do better. And so the book was published in 1941 – and won the Carnegie Award for that year as Best Children's Book. It is set in an imaginary Channel Island, just invaded by the Germans at the beginning of the Second World War, and tells of the Templeton children on holiday there. They get left behind in the confusion and are, anyway, not keen to leave behind Dinah, Caroline Templeton's beloved pony. They make contact with the 'Resistance', have exciting but credible adventures and finally make their escape. The story was one of the first of the popular 'pony stories' and certainly one of the very best of its kind. *No Ponies* (1946) was set in the South of France, again in wartime. *The Adventure of the 'Polly Harris'* (1949) was a smuggling adventure set on the River Thames, and *The Winter Princess* (1962) was about a group of children who visit an old lady living at Hampton Court. *The Heron Ride* (1962) and *Return to the Heron* (1963) dealt with the adventures of children resident at a riding-school. *Maids Ribbons* (1966) and *Elegant Patty* (1967) were stories for younger children.

Trease, Geoffrey

Born 1909, in Nottingham, and educated at Nottingham High School and Queen's College, Oxford. His first children's book, *Bows Against the Barons*, was published in 1934 and aroused interest because the hero, Robin Hood, was depicted as a revolutionary trying to inflame the peasants to rise up against their enemies. Despite the unusual political approach, the story was a rousing adventure which showed imagination and flair. Also in 1934, Trease contributed a school serial to the *Boy's Own Paper* called *The New House at Hardale*. Subsequently came a whole series of fine historical novels for young people. They include: *Comrades for the Charter* (1934) (The Chartist Movement); *The Call to Arms* (1935) (politics and war in South America); *In the Land of the Mogul* (1938) (East India Company); *Cue for Treason* (1940) (Spying in Tudor times); *The Grey Adventurer* (1942) (The Fire of London and settlers in

Virginia); *Trumpets in the West* (1947) (Monmouth Rebellion); *Silver Guards* (1948) (Cavaliers and Roundheads); *Hills of Varna* (1948) (Renaissance); *A Crown of Violet* (1952) (Athens in Socrates' time); *The Baron's Hostage* (1952) (Barons' Revolt under Simon de Montfort in thirteenth-century England); *Word to Caesar* (1955) (about a 'king' of the Roman Underworld in the second century A.D.); *Thunder of Valmy* (1960) (French Revolution); *Follow My Black Plume* (1963) (Garibaldi Rising in Italy); *A Thousand for Sicily* (1964) (Revolt of the Thousand against the Kingdom of Naples in 1860); *The Dutch are Coming* (1965) (17th-century London); *The Red Towers of Granada* (1966) (medieval England and Spain); *The White Nights of St Petersburg* (1967) (Russian Revolution); and *The Runaway Serf* (1968). In 1949 Trease began his series about a group of modern teenagers growing up in the atmosphere of a contemporary day-school, with *No Boats on Bannermere*; succeeding titles were *Under Black Banner* (1951), *Black Banner Players* (1952), *Black Banner Abroad* (1954), and *The Gates of Bannerdale* (1956). Other stories about modern young people growing up were *The Maythorn Story* (1960) and *Change at Maythorn* (1962). Other, non-fictional, books by Trease include: *Tales Out of School* (1949, rev. ed. 1964), an excellent critical survey of children's story-books; *Fortune My Foe* (1949), a 'story-biography' of Sir Walter Raleigh; *Enjoying Books* (1951); *Seven Queens of England* (1953); *The Young Traveller in England and Wales* (1953); *The Shadow of Spain* (1953), three historical plays for boys and girls; *Seven Kings of England* (1958); *Seven Stages* (1964), biographies of famous historical theatrical figures; *This is Your Century* (1965) and *The Grand Tour* (1967), the evolution of the famous European tour from Elizabethan to Victorian times. In 1952 he translated *Companions of Fortune* into English – the book which introduced the outstanding French children's writer René Guillot to a wider audience. Geoffrey Trease lives in Malvern, Worcestershire.

Treece, Henry

Born in 1911 in Wednesbury, Staffordshire, and educated at Wednesbury Grammar School and Birmingham University, where he was captain of boxing. During the 1930s he worked at a variety of jobs, including those of dance band pianist and artist's model, before settling down to teaching. It was while employed as a schoolmaster at Tynemouth School that he began to have his verses published in various 'little magazines', and in the late 'thirties he became one of the leaders of the poetical 'New Apocalyptic Movement', jointly editing three anthologies of new poetry. During the Second World War he served in the RAFVR as an Intelligence Officer and assisted John Pudney in the editing of *Air Force Poetry*. During the 'forties he published several volumes of verse, turning to fiction in the early 1950s, when he wrote adult novels. In 1954 he published his first children's adventure novel, *Desperate Journey*, to be followed over the next twelve years by nearly thirty further books for young readers, not to mention more adult novels. He specialised – and was at his superb best – in historical fiction, especially that set in ancient times. He had made a close study of the Viking and Roman periods and always brought them vividly to life in his stories. He wrote with a poet's imaginative flair and this, combined with his considerable historical knowledge, made him one of the finest novelists of this type for older children. His Roman stories include: *The Eagles Have Flown* (1954), *Legions of the Eagle* (1954), *War Dog* (1962), *The Bronze Sword* (1965) and *The Queen's Brooch* (1966). Treece's Viking novels include: *Viking's Dawn* (1955), *The Road to Miklagard* (1956), *Viking's Sunset* (1960), *Horned Helmet* (1963), *The Last of the Vikings* (1964), *The Splintered Sword* (1965) and *Vinland the Good* (1967) (his last book). Other historical subjects were: *Hounds of the King* (1955) (King Harold and the Battle of Hastings); *Men of the Hills* (1957) (the Stone and Bronze Ages in Britain); *The Children's Crusade* (1958) (the famous thirteenth-century disaster); *The Bombard* (1959) (The Battle of Crecy and after); *Wickham and the Armada* (1959), *The Golden One* (1961) (adventures in thirteenth-century Constantinople) and *Swords from the North* (1967) (Hardrada in the service of the Byzantine emperor). There is also a series of modern children's 'thrillers' – *Ask for King Billy* (1955), *Hunter Hunted* (1957), *Don't Expect Any Mercy* (1958) and *Bang, You're Dead* (1966). Other titles include: *The Return of Robinson Crusoe* (1958), *The Jet Beads* (1961), *Know About the Crusades* (1963), *The Burning of Njal* (1964) and *The Windswept City*

(1967) (for younger children). Many of his books were also published in the USA and several translated into other languages (*The Children's Crusade* appeared in six different languages, as well as being serialised in a British national magazine, and is probably his most successful children's book). For many years, and up to the time of his death, he was Head of the English Department at Barton-on-Humber Grammar School, in Lincolnshire. He died at his home in Barton-on-Humber on 10th June 1966.

Tucker, Charlotte Maria

Born on 8th May 1821, in Barnet, Hertfordshire, one of ten children (five sons and five daughters) of Henry St George Tucker, an expert in Indian affairs who later became Chairman of the East India Company, and his Scottish-born wife, who was related to James Boswell. When Charlotte was one year old her family moved to London and she received her education at home. She began to write stories, verses and plays as a child and continued throughout her early youth, though just for the entertainment of herself and her family and friends. During this period she also became a devout evangelist, and after her father's death in 1851 she decided to incorporate religious and educational ingredients into her stories and try to have them published in order to benefit young readers. Her first book was accepted and was published under the title *The Claremont Tales* in 1852. This – and all her subsequent writings – appeared under the pseudonym 'A.L.O.E.' (A Lady of England). There followed a prolific stream of titles from her pen, nearly all didactic, austere and pious, many of them almost certainly appearing 'old-fashioned' and dated even when first published. They all had a heavily-underlined moral. But they were well-intentioned, widely-read – and favourite Sunday school prizes. She wrote nearly 150 titles in all (including her later missionary tracts), including: *Wings and Stings* (1855), *The Rambles of a Rat* (1857), *The History of a Needle* (1857), *Old Friends With New Faces* (1858), *The Crown of Success* (1863), *The Silver Casket* (1863), *Fairy Know-a-Bit* (1866), *The Lake of the Woods* (1867), *Cyril Ashley* (1870), *The Hymn My Mother Taught Me* (1871), *The Children's Tabernacle* (1871), *A Wreath of Smoke*

273

(1871), *Edith and Her Ayah* (1872) and *The Giant-Killer; or The Battle We Must All Fight* (1890). As well as her moral and allegorical tales, Miss Tucker also wrote several natural history and animal stories. She donated all the proceeds from her books to charities. When her mother died, in 1869, she decided to take up missionary work and began an intensive study of Hindustani. She went to India in 1875 and spent the rest of her life as a dedicated and busy missionary among the Hindus, chiefly in the Lahore district. Her many missionary tracts and stories were circulated widely in India, being translated into several tongues. She died at Amritsar, India, on 2nd December 1893, after a long illness.

Twain, Mark

Real name: Samuel Langhorne Clemens. Born on 30th November 1835, in Florida, Missouri, USA, one of the three sons of a Justice of the Peace (they had a sister too). When Samuel was five the family moved to Hannibal, Missouri, where he received local schooling. His father died when he was twelve, and he became a printer's apprentice, working for the two local newspapers. He began his writing career, too, on the Hannibal *Journal*, subsequently working as a journeyman printer and travelling throughout various parts of the USA. In 1857 he became an apprentice river pilot on the Mississippi steam-boats, gaining his pilot's licence in 1859. Returning to journalism in Virginia City in 1861 (when the outbreak of the Civil War ended steam-boating), he first used his famous pseudonym 'MARK TWAIN', deriving from the two words called out by river pilots on the Mississippi when taking soundings and signifying two fathoms. In 1865 his story *The Celebrated Jumping Frog of Calaveras County* was published in a prominent newspaper and established Twain's reputation as a top humorist. *The Innocents Abroad* (1869), an account of a tourists' trip to the Mediterranean, gained him further acclaim and, after his marriage, he moved to Hartford, Connecticut, where he was to write many of his most famous stories. In 1876 came *The Adventures of Tom Sawyer*, based largely upon his own experiences as a boy in Hannibal in the 1840s. It is a lively, episodic story of a boy's adventures, big and small, in a little town on the banks of the

Mississippi. It was an immediate success and soon appeared in England and many other parts of the world. Ninety years later it still remains one of the best and most popular boys' stories ever published. *The Adventures of Huckleberry Finn* (1884) spotlights one of the leading characters in *Tom Sawyer* – the resourceful, adventurous 'Huck', the son of the local drunkard. Told in brilliant Southern American first-person dialect, the book tells of the adventures of Huckleberry Finn, running away from his brutal father, and Jim, a runaway Negro slave, as they float down the Mississippi on a raft. The book is generally regarded as Twain's masterpiece and by many as 'the great American novel'. Ernest Hemingway once said that 'all modern American literature stems from this one book'. Like *Tom Sawyer* it has appeared all over the world and has become one of the most widely read novels of all time. Twain later wrote two sequels to his original *Tom Sawyer* book: *Tom Sawyer Abroad* (1894) and *Tom Sawyer: Detective* (1896). Another children's book is *The Prince and the Pauper* (1882), the Prince being Prince Edward (later King Edward the Sixth) of England, and the Pauper a poor London beggar named Tom Canty. The two boys change places, with resulting and entertaining complications. Many of Twain's other humorous books are read and enjoyed by young readers too. He died at Redding, Connecticut, on 21st April 1910.

Upton, Florence K.

Born on 22nd February 1873, in New York, the daughter of English parents, and educated there. In 1889, when she was sixteen, her father died suddenly, leaving Mrs Bertha Upton with four children (the eldest eighteen) to bring up alone. Florence had always shown a marked talent for drawing, and on leaving school on her father's death managed to obtain illustrating work almost immediately, which helped the family finances. In 1893 the family travelled to England and stayed several months at the original family home in Hampstead, London. It was while in Hampstead that Florence Upton illustrated her first book – and created that now-universal nursery favourite 'the Golliwogg'. Thinking to help family finances further, she decided to prepare a children's book and found a group of

275

wooden Dutch dolls to serve as models for her drawings (she could never draw without models). As she was beginning work, her aunt discovered an old, rather tattered 'nigger doll' (as they were then called) which had once been a favourite childhood toy (it had originally been purchased, or won, at an American fair) and Florence at once decided to make him the 'hero' of her book. She hit on the name 'Golliwogg' and the first book, *The Adventures of Two Dutch Dolls*, appeared in 1895, with verses by Bertha Upton and eye-catching colour pictures by Florence. It was an immediate success and youthful readers asked for more. A whole series of 'Golliwogg' books followed: *The Golliwogg's Bicycle Club* (1896); *The Golliwogg at the Sea-side* (1898); *The Golliwogg in War* (1899); *The Golliwogg's Polar Adventures* (1900); *The Golliwogg's Auto-Go-Cart* (1901); *The Golliwogg's Air-Ship* (1902); *The Golliwogg's Circus* (1903); *The Golliwogg in Holland* (1904); *The Golliwogg's Desert Island* (1906); *The Golliwogg's Christmas* (1907); and *The Golliwogg in the African Jungle* (1908). All were in the identical long, flat 11 in × 8½ in format and sold in vast numbers. Two picture-books which did not feature the Golliwogg or the Dutch Dolls were not nearly as successful. They were: *The Vegemen's Revenge* (1897) and *The Adventures of Barbee and the Wisp* (1905). The Golliwogg originally appeared in this unique series of books with rather longer and softer black hair than later generations came to know and love him in toy form. He was dressed in white shirt, red bow-tie, pale blue jacket with yellow buttons and red trousers. The Dutch dolls, for the record, were Sarah Jane, Peg, Meg, Weg and the Midget – the last being a tiny version of the others. Soon after the publication of the first Golliwogg book, manufacturers stepped in and marketed the toy Golliwogg, which every child craved – and usually received. Unfortunately, Florence Upton omitted to patent her creation and so only received royalties on her books instead of the vast fortune she would otherwise have made. For, apart from the toys, there were Golliwogg pottery figures, Golliwogg wallpapers, Golliwogg paperweights, Golliwogg materials and so on. The correct spelling of Golliwogg should be noted, incidentally – all too often the final 'g' is omitted. In 1917, anxious to help the war effort, Florence Upton donated her entire collection of manuscripts, drawings and original

Golliwogg and Dutch dolls to be auctioned at Christie's in London in aid of the Red Cross. They fetched 450 guineas, which was used to buy an ambulance, known affectionately as 'Golliwogg'. The Golliwogg and the Dutch dolls were presented by the purchaser (Miss Faith Moore) to Chequers, the Prime Minister's official country residence in the Chilterns. There, amidst the forbidding Cromwellian relics and paintings, sit Golliwogg and his friends in a glass case in the Long Gallery. Though she enjoyed illustrating the colourful, rather garish, Golliwogg books and derived much satisfaction from seeing the pleasure they gave children, Florence Upton really wanted to make her name as a serious portrait painter. By the early 1900s she had a studio in Paris and travelled widely and studied in Holland under George Hitchcock. She also contributed drawings to *Punch* and several other magazines. Later she had a studio in Great College Street, London, and began to find success with her paintings, some being exhibited at the Royal Academy, the Paris New Salon and the Exposition Internationale in Nantes. Towards the end of her life she developed a great interest in spiritualism. She died in London on 16th October 1922, and is buried in Hampstead cemetery, where her gravestone records the fact that she invented the Golliwogg.

Uttley, Alison

Born 18th December 1884, at Castle Top, Cromford, Derbyshire. Her childhood days spent in this picturesque farm in the heart of rural England have supplied memorable material for several nostalgic books. After attending a local village school she was educated at Lady Manners School, Bakewell, Manchester University, and Cambridge University, gaining a B.Sc. degree. She began writing professionally in the 1920s, contributing to such periodicals as *The Spectator*. In 1929 came the first of her long series of stories about *The Squirrel, The Hare* and *The Little Grey Rabbit*. The stories, published in the format and approximate size of the Beatrix Potter books, were illustrated by Margaret Tempest and today include over thirty titles. Though not strictly intended for children, *The Country Child*, which followed in 1931, is often enjoyed by them. It was the first of Mrs Uttley's evocative recreations of her youthful days on the Derbyshire farm and countryside where she grew up. Similar reminiscences were *Ambush of Young Days* (1937), *The Farm on the Hill* (1941), *Country Hoard* (1943), *Country Things* (1946), *Carts and Candlesticks* (1948) and *Peck of Gold* (1966). *Moonshine and Magic* (1932) and *Candlelight Tales* (1936) were collections of fairy stories with a magic all their own. In 1937 came *The Adventures of No Ordinary Rabbit*, followed in 1939 by *A Traveller in Time*, an outstanding story of a young girl who steps from the present back into Tudor times and becomes caught up in its intrigues. Also in 1939 was born her most popular and famous character – Sam Pig – who made his bow in *Tales of Four Pigs and Brock the Badger*. Sam was the youngest and liveliest of the four piglets featured in the book and in 1941 came the well-deserved *The Adventures of Sam Pig*, followed by many more titles in the series. *The Sam Pig Storybook*, an opulent collection of thirty-five adventures, was published in 1965. Mrs Uttley is also responsible for such other popular series as the *Little Brown Mouse* books, which began in 1950 with *Snug and Serena Pick Cowslips*, and the *Little Red Fox* tales, which started in 1954 with *Little Red Fox and the Wicked Uncle*. Both series are illustrated by Katharine Wigglesworth. *The Washerwoman's Child* (1946) was a three-act play based on the life of Hans Andersen. Other titles include: *Cuckoo Cherry-Tree* (1943), *The Spice-Woman's Basket* (1944), *The Weather-Cock* (1945), *John Barleycorn* (1948), *The Cobbler's Shop* (1950) and *Magic in My Pocket* (1957). *Cuckoo in June* (1964) is a collection of countryside essays. Alison Uttley has lived in Beaconsfield, Buckinghamshire, for many years. At one time she lived at Downs House, Bowdon, Cheshire – once the home of another famous children's writer, Mrs Juliana Ewing.

Verne, Jules

Born on 8th February 1828, at Nantes, France, the son of a lawyer. His father wanted him to follow in his footsteps, but young Jules wanted adventure and even went so far, at the age of eleven, as to 'run away to sea'. He was brought back from the ship's first port of call, however, and returned to his school, promising his tearful mother that henceforth he would travel 'only in the imagination' – a prophetic remark. At sixteen Jules

Verne began to study law and also work in his father's office. When his studies took him to Paris he spent much of his time there writing plays and stories; he also met Alexandre Dumas the Elder, who encouraged his writing and produced one of his plays on the stage. Stimulated with what small success he was achieving in Paris, Verne wrote to his father and told him he was giving up his law studies to concentrate on writing. He obtained a post as secretary to the Théâtre Lyrique and wrote in his spare time. He had a few stories and articles published, but nothing of note. Then he married a young widow with two small daughters, left his theatre job and took a post on the the Paris *Bourse* or Stock Exchange. Still he wrote, but to little material effect. One day he completed a treatise on ballooning and submitted it to a magazine; it was rejected. When it came back for the second time he was so disappointed and angry he threw the manuscript on the fire – luckily his wife was there to quickly rescue it. She persuaded him to take it to publisher and writer Jules Hetzel, who refused it as a treatise, but suggested Verne re-wrote it in fictional form. Overjoyed, Verne went back and wrote his first novel *Five Weeks in a Balloon* – the adventures of three men who travel over Africa in an ingenious hydrogen balloon – which was published in 1863. Hetzel was delighted with his new protégé and explained to him that he was about to launch a new magazine called *Le Magazin d'Éducation et de Récréation*. Would Verne be interested in writing regular serials for it, which would subsequently be published in book form? Verne was, and signed a unique contract with Hetzel under which he would agree to provide two full-length stories a year for twenty years – or forty stories in a lesser period. They would be known collectively as Verne's *Voyages Extraordinaires*. Verne gave up his Stock Exchange job and set about his mammoth task with enjoyment and anticipation. *Five Weeks in a Balloon* had met with immediate success and now all he had to do was maintain that success. He did – over the next forty years. He produced over sixty novels and many shorter works, including: *A Journey to the Centre of the Earth* (1864), *From the Earth to the Moon* (1865), *The Adventures of Captain Hatteras* (sometimes published in two parts as *I, The English at the North Pole* and *II, The Wilderness of Ice*) (1866), *The Children of Captain Grant* (sometimes in three

279

parts as *I, The Mysterious Document, II, On the Track* and *III, Among the Cannibals*) (1868), *Round the Moon* (1870), *Twenty Thousand Leagues Under the Sea* (1870), *A Floating City* (1871), *Around the World In Eighty Days* (1873), *Dr Ox* (1874), *The Mysterious Island* (sometimes in three parts as *I, Dropped From the Clouds, II, Abandoned* and *III, The Secret of the Island*) (1875), *Michael Strogoff* (1876), *Hector Servadac* (1877), *The Steam House* (sometimes in two parts as *I, The Demon of Cawnpore* and *II, Tigers and Traitors*) (1880), *The Giant Raft* (sometimes in two parts as *I, The Giant Raft* and *II, The Cryptogram*) (1881), *The School for Crusoes* (1882), *The Green Ray* (1882), *The Clipper of the Clouds* (1886), *The Purchase of the North Pole* (1889), *Carpathian Castle* (1892), *Propeller Island* (1895), *Second Fatherland* (this was a sequel to Wyss's *Swiss Family Robinson* and is sometimes in two parts as *I, Their Island Home* and *II, The Castaways of the 'Flag'*) (1900), *Master of the World* (1904) and *The Lighthouse at the End of the World* (1905). Verne's stories were usually incident-packed adventures and/or what later became known as 'science-fiction' (though some of it later turned out to be 'science-fact' and it was Verne who prophesied such inventions as the incandescent bulb, the submarine, the electric clock, the airship and radio among many more). He would make a lengthy and serious study of his subject before starting his latest work and was painstaking with his detail. Even celebrated scientists looked forward to reading Verne's latest book, since they knew he was always completely up-to-date with their discoveries and, as often as not, improved on them. Unusual explorations, shipwrecks, inventions, discoveries, space-voyages, secret codes, floating islands, giant ocean liners, airships, balloons and adventures by the thousand – Jules Verne had them all at his finger-tips and enthralled readers of all ages (but especially boys) throughout the world. He was an enthusiastic yachtsman and always liked to call his boats 'St Michel' after his son, Michel. In 1886 came a tragedy which affected the rest of Verne's life. His nephew, Gaston, had a nervous breakdown and fired at Verne with a loaded revolver. He was seriously injured in the leg and, despite several operations, remained crippled till the end of his days. He was forced to give up his beloved sailing since he could no longer keep his balance aboard on the sloping decks. But, in spite of continual discomfort, he continued to write. It was, incidentally, the *Boy's Own Paper* which was largely responsible for introducing Verne's works to the young English reading public. No fewer than sixteen of his books were serialised in the *BOP*, beginning with *Dick Sands, the Boy Captain* in 1879. Boys' adventure story author W. H. G. Kingston translated many of Verne's stories into English. Verne spent his last twenty years at Amiens, where he took an active part in civic affairs. He was honoured by the French Academy and received the Legion of Honour. He died at Amiens on 24th March 1905 – 'father' of science-fiction and master of invention. His statue at Nantes, his birthplace, shows three readers at his feet and includes a train, a ship and a balloon, representing travel by land, sea and air.

Vipont, Charles

See: Vipont, Elfrida

Vipont, Elfrida

Born 1902 in Manchester and educated at Manchester High School for Girls, and The Mount School, York. After reading history at Manchester University she studied music and singing in London, Paris and Leipzig, subsequently becoming a professional singer. Her first book for children, *Blow the Man Down* (1939) was published under the pseudonym 'CHARLES VIPONT'. It was an exciting historical adventure story about a young man 'press-ganged' into Cromwell's navy. In 1948 (and under her own name) came *The Lark in the Morn*, a sensitive story about a schoolgirl, Kit Haverard, a member of a Quaker family, and her emergence as a talented singer. A sequel, *The Lark on the Wing*, was published in 1950 and won the Carnegie Award as the Best Children's Book of that year. It told of Kit's experiences after leaving her Quaker school whilst living in London and of her realisation as a singer. The two 'Lark' books, in fact, take the heroine from schooldays to the beginning of her singing career and imminent marriage. Miss Vipont, a Quaker and ex-professional singer, drew upon her own experiences, in part, for these outstanding stories. *The Spring of the Year* (1957) and *Flowering Spring* (1960) remain in the

Haverard family and tell of Kit's niece, Laura, and her dream of becoming an actress. In 1955 came another story for boys written as 'CHARLES VIPONT': *The Heir of Craigs*, a late-seventeenth-century adventure with Jacobite plots as its background. Other titles include: *The Story of Quakerism, 1652–1952* (1952); *The High Way* (1957), an anthology of religious writings through the ages for young people; *Sparks Among the Stubble* (1959), a group of inspiring life-stories; *The Story of Christianity in Britain* (1960); the 'Dowbiggins' series of family stories; *Search for a Song* (1962), an unusual family story set in the Lake District; and a series of stories for younger children – *Larry Lopkins, Stevie* and *The Offcomers* (1965); *The Secret Passage* and *The China Dog* (1967). *Terror By Night* (1966) was a collection of ghost stories. Elfrida Vipont married in 1926 (she is Mrs R. P. Foulds) and has four daughters, one of whom is an actress, and several grandchildren. She devotes much of her time to serving on various Quaker committees all over the world and to lecturing to young people. She lives in a seventeenth-century house in Yealand Conyers, near Carnforth, in Lancashire.

Walkey, Samuel

Born 1871, in Cornwall. At the age of sixteen he entered a bank as a clerk. Being good at his job, promotion came quickly and regularly; by the turn of the century Walkey had become a bank Inspector and, later still, a Staff Controller. These posts necessitated being away from home frequently and Walkey took up the writing of boys' stories to while away the lonely evenings spent in strange places. A Cornish acquaintance, the distinguished author, Sir Arthur Quiller-Couch, saw Walkey's work, liked it and introduced him to Max Pemberton in 1895. The latter had recently relinquished the editorship of *Chums*, the popular boys' magazine, but still held an important position with Cassell's, the periodical's publishers, and it was largely through him that Walkey's first serial, *In Quest of Sheba's Treasure*, ran in the 1895–96 volume of *Chums*. With his next serial, the following year, Walkey achieved an enormous success. It was a swashbuckling, stirring pirate yarn called *Rogues of the Fiery Cross* and was illustrated by the prolific artist Paul Hardy, who subsequently illustrated nearly all Walkey's

stories. From then onwards, Walkey wrote many adventure
serials for *Chums*, mainly with pirates, sailors, adventurers and
French Revolution heroes as their leading characters. Titles
(dates refer to original publication in *Chums*) include: *King of the
Seas* (1899), *With Redskins on the Warpath* (1901), *Under Nelson's
Flag* (1906), *Yo-Ho! For the Spanish Main* (1909), *Jack-a-Lantern*
(1910), *Hurray! For Merry Sherwood* (1911), *Captain Swing* (1914),
For Drake and Merrie England (1915), *Under the Black Flag* (1916),
Powder-Monkey Jack (1926), *Drake Goes West* (1932) and *The
Treasure of Pirates' Island* (1940) (a long complete story
and, it is believed, his last). Many of his serials were later
published in book form. He invariably called himself 'S.
Walkey' and never used his christian name as an author. He
always wrote in his spare time and retained his bank job for
many years. Walkey was probably the finest writer of pirate
stories that ever lived (always excepting R. L. Stevenson for his
Treasure Island, which is in a class by itself anyway). He eventually retired to his native Cornwall and died there in the 1950s.

Walpole, Sir Hugh

Born on 13th March, 1884, in Auckland, New Zealand, the
son of a clergyman who later became Bishop of Edinburgh.
Educated at King's School, Canterbury, and Emmanuel
College, Cambridge. He was a schoolmaster at Epsom College
for a year after leaving Cambridge, but did not find the job at
all to his liking. All the petty jealousies and rivalries of the
common-room were portrayed vividly in his story of the tragic
feud between two public schoolmasters, *Mr Perrin and Mr Traill*
(1911), his third novel. Between 1919 and 1927 he wrote a fine
trio of semi-autobiographical stories of boyhood: *Jeremy*
(1919), *Jeremy and Hamlet* (1923) and *Jeremy at Crale* (1927).
He wrote many excellent novels, the most famous being the
the long family saga, *The Herries Chronicle* (1930–33). He also
wrote some notable literary studies, including works on Conrad
and Trollope. He was knighted in 1937, never married, and
died in 1941.

Walton, Mrs Octavius Frank

Born around the mid-1800s, and little about her life appears to be traceable. Many of her books were published by the Religious Tract Society between 1872 and 1900 and were chiefly deeply moral and religious tales of suffering, pathos and despair for young people and were much in demand as Sunday School prizes. Despite her stern moralising and pitiful little heroes and heroines, her stories were widely read during the Victorian era, especially her trio of 'best-sellers' comprising *A Peep Behind the Scenes* (1877), about a long-suffering little girl in a travelling fair; *Christie's Old Organ, or Home, Sweet Home* (1882), the story of a waif who inherits a barrel-organ; and *Shadows: Scenes and Incidents in the Life of an Old Armchair* (1884). These three titles were reprinted many times. Mrs Walton's first book was *My Little Corner: a Book for Cottage Homes*, published anonymously in 1872. Other typical stories included: *Angel's Christmas* (1877), *Saved at Sea* (1879), *Little Faith* (1890), *Nobody Loves Me* (1883) and *Poppy's Presents* (1886). *Our Gracious Queen* (1886) was a Jubilee tribute to Queen Victoria. Mrs Walton is believed to have died around the early 1900s.

Ward, Evelyn

See: Everett-Green, Evelyn

Warner, Susan

See: Wetherell, Elizabeth

Watkins-Pitchford, Denys James

Born in Lamport, Northamptonshire, 1905. Educated privately before studying at the Schools of Painting and Engraving of the Royal College of Art, in the former under Sir William Rothenstein. Assistant art master at Rugby School for many years. Under the pen-name 'B.B.' became well known for his descriptive and evocative writings on the English countryside. His first book, appearing in the late 1930s, was *Wild Lone*, the story of a Pytchley fox. There followed *Manka the Sky Gipsy* (the story of a wild goose), *The Countryman's Bedside Book* and *The Sportsman's Bedside Book*. In 1942 came *The Little Grey Men*, a tale of the last gnomes in Britain, who leave the shelter of their

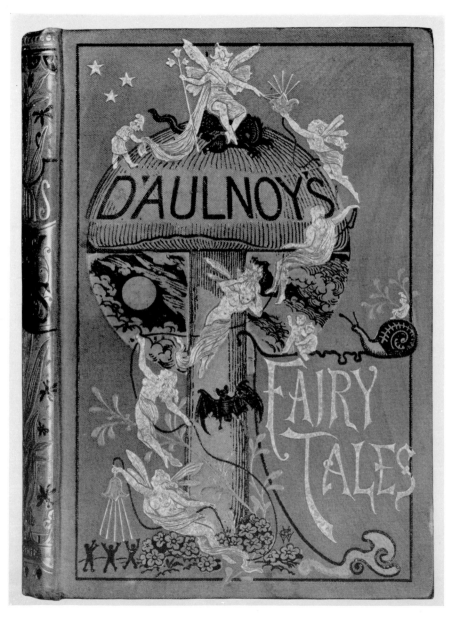

101 A fine example of pictorial binding for a children's book of about 1860

102 Illustration by
E. H. Shepard from
A. A. Milne's *The
House at Pooh Corner*

103 Illustration by
Diana Stanley from
Mary Norton's *The
Borrowers*

104 Illustration by E. H. Shepard from Kenneth Grahame's *The Wind in
the Willows*

oak-tree home to voyage upstream in search of their missing brother, Cloudberry. Their names are Sneezewort, Baldmoney and Dodder. Illustrated by the author with numerous scraper-board drawings, the book was a magnificent achievement and was awarded the Carnegie Medal for 1942. The book was re-issued in a new edition in 1946 with new illustrations (again by the author), this time in the form of coloured oil paintings. A further edition, different again, was published in 1952, with a small selection of the original scraperboard drawings plus a coloured frontispiece. In 1948 came a sequel to *The Little Grey Men* and featuring the same gnomes again—*Down the Bright Stream*. The same year 'B.B.' published a collection of traditional fairy tales, *Meeting Hill*, followed by a companion volume, *The Wind in the Wood*, in 1952. Both were illustrated by the author superbly in full colour. All this author's books are both written and illustrated by him alone, incidentally, but the title-page invariably reads 'by "B.B.", Illustrated by D. J. Watkins-Pitchford'. Another children's book which caught the atmosphere of the open air was *Brendon Chase* in 1944, the story of two truant boys living wild in the woods. Other country books, which can be enjoyed by young and old, include: *Idle Countryman, The Fisherman's Bedside Book, Dark Estuary* and *Letters from Compton Deverell*. His more recent children's books include *The Forest of Boland Light Railway* (1955) and *The Wizard of Boland* (1959) (both set in the enchanted Forest of Boland, inhabited by gnomes, wizards, animals, birds and leprechauns, and full of humour and absurdity); several stories for younger children, including *The Whopper* (1967), *At the Back o' Ben Dee* (1968) and *Ben the Bullfinch* (1968); the first two titles in a series about a bachelor hedgehog – *Monty Woodpig's Caravan* and *Monty Woodpig and his Bubblebuzz Car*; and a series of books featuring 'Bill Badger' aboard his canal-barge: *Wandering Wind* (the first in the series), and others including *Bill Badger's Big Mistake, Bill Badger's Whispering Reeds Adventure, Bill Badger's Winter Cruise, Bill Badger and the Pirates* and *Bill Badger's Finest Hour*.

Webb, Marion St John

Born in the 1890s at West Hampstead, London, later moving

to Neasden with her parents. She moved back to Downshire Hill, Hampstead Heath, while still a little girl and lived there until she was about twenty. During this period she had ambitions to be an artist and studied painting and drawing at private classes. The family moved to Rickmansworth, Hertfordshire, around 1910 and she now developed her singing talents, passing several examinations. She also edited an amateur magazine called *The Spur*, which circulated mainly among fellow tennis club members. For a competition in the magazine, she entered, anonymously, the first of her 'Littlest One' poems. It won and was later published by the *Daily News*. *The Littlest One*, her first book, appeared in 1914 and comprised a collection of verses, told in the first person, by a little boy of about six, complete with lisp and 'cute' spelling. It was enormously popular and sold 50,000 copies during its first seventeen years. *The Littlest One Again* (1923), *The Littlest One's Third Book* (1925) and *The Littlest One – His Book* (1927) met with similar success. Many other children's books, stories and verses followed the success of *The Littlest One*, usually touched with humour and fantasy. The 'Mr Papingay' series of four books were probably the most popular of her stories, appearing originally in the pages of a women's magazine. The titles were *The Little Round House*, *Mr Papingay's Caravan*, *Mr Papingay's Flying Shop* and *Mr Papingay's Ship*. These comprised the magical and surprising adventures encountered by a little boy, Robin, in company with the kindly and eccentric Mr Papingay, his little niece, Penny, and a whole gallery of weird and amusing characters, including Aunt Muffin, the Fat Boy, the Lodger and the Home-Made Fairy. Other titles by Miss Webb included: *The Magic Lamplighter*, *Knock Three Times*, *Eliz'beth*, *Phil and Me*, *The Girls of Chequertrees*, *The Little One in Between*, *The House With the Twisting Passage* and *Twice Ten*. She was married to Sidney Hastings Webb and, despite her wonderful way of getting into the child mind and knowing just what her young readers liked, she never had any children of her own. During the period ranging roughly from 1915 to 1935 her fantasies, fairy tales and verses were among the most popular of their kind in Britain. And it is interesting to note that the *Littlest One* verses appeared a full ten years before Milne's *When We Were Very Young*. Marion St John Webb died in 1930.

Webster, Jean

Born on 24th July 1876, in Fredonia, New York State, USA, and educated at the Lady Jane Grey School, Binghamton, and at Vassar. She was related to Mark Twain's mother, who was her aunt, and her father handled Twain's business affairs as well as being his partner in publishing. Her real name was Alice Jane Chandler Webster. Her first stories appeared in the *Vassar Miscellany* and her first book was *When Patty Went to College* (1903), about a young girl's experiences at school and college (a later sequel, *Just Patty*, appeared in 1911). The book for which she is most famous, *Daddy-Long-Legs*, was published in 1912 and told the wryly humorous story (well-laced with sentiment) of how a young orphan girl found romance. It became an immediate best-seller and has never been out of print since. It was also produced on the stage, as a film (twice), and a musical comedy version called *Love From Judy* was successfully produced in 1953 on the London stage. A sequel, *Dear Enemy*, was published in 1915 but failed to achieve the huge popularity of its predecessor. In 1915 she married, but died shortly after the birth of her daughter, on 11th June 1916.

Welch, Ronald

Real name: Ronald O. Felton. Born in Wales. Became a schoolmaster and taught history at Berkhamsted and Bedford. He is today Headmaster of Okehampton Grammar School, Devon. His first book for young readers was *The Gauntlet*, published in 1951. It was an unusual and dramatic tale of a modern boy who is taken back in time to the fourteenth century to experience his ancestors' adventures in and around a castle at Carreg Cennen in the hill country of the Welsh border. In 1954 came the first of his series of stories about a Welsh military family, the Careys of Llanstephan. It was *Knight Crusader* and it was awarded the Carnegie Medal for the outstanding contribution to children's literature for that year. The book recounted the adventures of a young crusader-knight, Philip d'Aubigny, in the Holy Land in the twelfth century, culminating in its tough warrior-hero's arrival in Wales to claim his inherited estates. Subsequent titles in the Carey saga are: *Captain of Dragoons* (1956) (Charles Carey in the service of Marlborough), *Mohawk Valley* (1958) (Alan Carey taking part in the capture of Quebec with Wolfe), *Captain of Foot* (1959) (Christopher Carey serves under Wellington in the Peninsular War), *Escape from France* (1960) (Richard Carey and the French Revolution), *For the King* (1961) (Neil Carey in the Royalist Army in the Civil War in England), *Nicholas Carey* (1963) (the hero becomes involved in national uprisings in Italy during the 1850s and takes part in the Crimean War) and *The Hawk* (1967) (Harry Carey in the time of Elizabeth I). Mr Welch's deep knowledge of history (and especially military history, great battles and old weapons) combined with his excellently imagined stories make outstanding reading for all ages. *Ferdinand Magellan* (1955) was the story of the first voyage round the world made by that great Portuguese sea-captain. *Bowman of Crecy* (1966) told of a band of outlaws in England and how the tough masters of the long-bow proved themselves in King Edward III's victorious battles against the French. His pen-name comes from the Welch Regiment, in which he served, following in the family tradition set by his grandfather and father.

Westerman, Percy F.

Born 1876, in Portsmouth, and educated at Portsmouth Grammar School. He published his first boys' adventure story, *A Lad of Grit*, in 1908 and went on to write around 150 more over the next fifty or so years, thus averaging an output of three books a year. He specialised in exciting but conventional sea and flying stories, some of which featured his best-known character 'Standish of the Air Police'. Typical titles include: *Under the White Ensign*, *The Junior Cadet*, *Sea Scouts of the 'Petrel'*, *The Pirate Submarine*, *Captain Blundell's Treasure*, *Standish Gets His Man*, *Winning His Wings*, *The Quest of the 'Golden Hope'*, *With Beatty off Jutland*, *The White Arab*, *The Bulldog Breed* and *Captain Starlight*. Westerman was one of the most popular and successful boys' writers in the period between the two World Wars – a fact which is borne out by his being voted 'the most popular boys' author' during a national poll taken in English children's public libraries in the 1930s. His books were translated into

Danish, Dutch, Norwegian, Swedish, Polish and Hungarian. He died on 23rd February 1960, at the age of eighty-four.

Wetherell, Elizabeth

Real name: Susan Warner. Born on 11th July 1819, in New York City. She was a devout Presbyterian. She wrote her first book – *The Wide Wide World* (1850) – to raise money to assist her impecunious lawyer father to pay some of his debts. It was eventually accepted by a publisher after being turned down by many and became one of the great best-sellers of its time. It told the story of an orphan girl, Ellen Montgomery, with a great deal of sentiment, moralising and religious comment. Miss Warner published it under a pseudonym ('Elizabeth Wetherell') which was her great-grandmother's name. Later came several further novels in the same style and which were all enormously successful. They included: *Queechy* (1852), *The Old Helmet* (1863), *Melbourne House* (1864), *Daisy* (1868) and *Diana* (1877). She also collaborated with her younger sister, Anna Warner (pseudonym 'Amy Lothrop') on several titles, including *Mrs Rutherford's Children* (1853–55) and *Wych Hazel* (1876). Anna wrote several novels of a type similar to her sister's. Susan Warner also wrote many hymns, the best-known probably being 'Jesus Loves Me'. She died on 17th March 1885.

White, Elwyn Brooks

Born on 11th July 1899, at Mount Vernon, New York State, and educated at Cornell University. After service in the First World War he worked as a reporter for the *Seattle Times*, worked his passage to Alaska as a ship's steward, became a production assistant in a New York advertising agency, finally joining the staff of the famous *New Yorker* magazine, for which he wrote the 'Talk of the Town' column. He also contributed regularly to *Harper's Magazine*. He collaborated with James Thurber on a humorous book in 1929, subsequently publishing many books of humour and literary criticism. His two children's books have become minor classics of their kind. *Stuart Little* (USA 1945, England 1946) told of the adventures of the hero, who was the second son of Mr and Mrs Little, of New York. The only unusual thing about him was that he was a mouse . . . *Charlotte's Web* (USA 1952, England 1955) was about a rather unprepossessing little pig who was lovingly reared by a little girl, Fern, and eventually saved from the fate of the frying-pan by the genius of his friend, Charlotte, the spider. Both amusing, yet strangely touching, tales are told with simplicity and unforced charm.

White, Terence Hanbury

Born 1906, in Bombay, India, and educated at Cheltenham College and Queen's College, Cambridge. His first adult book, *Loved Helen* (poems), was published in 1929 and followed by several others. *The Sword in the Stone* (1939) told the story of King Arthur's boyhood in light-hearted style and was followed by *The Witch in the Wood* (1940) and *The Ill-Made Knight* (1941). *Mistress Masham's Repose* (USA 1946, England 1947) is an outstanding fantasy about a little orphan, Maria, who lives in a huge estate called Malplaquet in the wilds of Northamptonshire, with her wicked governess (who is aided and abetted in her cruel treatment of Maria by the nasty local vicar). The vast mansion is dilapidated and Maria, the governess and the cook live in two or three rooms which at least still have a roof over them. Maria discovers the existence of a community of Gulliver's tiny Lilliputians on an island in the lake of Malplaquet and the story turns on her efforts to help them and prevent her evil guardians from capitalising on their discovery, one of the modern fantasies that deserves to live on for many more generations. *The Master* (1957) was a powerful story of two children held prisoner on the Atlantic island of Rockall by a strange man who has plans for ruling the world and who can already control men's minds by his mental powers. In 1958 came *The Once and Future King*, which collected four of White's Arthurian subjects together in one revised volume to tell the story of King Arthur from the beginning to the end (the four titles included were *The Sword in the Stone*, *The Queen of Air and Darkness*, *The Ill-Made Knight* and *The Candle in the Wind*). In addition, he published many further books primarily of adult interest. White had a great affection for Ireland and spent much of his time there. He was particularly interested in natural history, bird-life (especially falcons and falconry), sport – and, as evidenced by his Arthurian subjects, mediaeval history and legends. He died in 1964.

Wiggin, Kate Douglas

Born on 28th September 1856, in Philadelphia, USA, and educated at the Abbott Academy, Andover, Massachusetts. Her maiden name was Smith and she acquired the name she later won fame with when she married Samuel Wiggin in 1881. She trained to become a teacher and was a keen and lifelong student of child education (especially kindergarten). She organised and opened the first free kindergarten school in the West of America; it was in San Francisco. She also helped her sister, Nora Archibald Smith, to found a kindergarten teaching training school. She first began writing children's books in order to raise money for her school. The first was *The Story of Patsy* in 1883, followed by the over-sentimental *The Birds' Christmas Carol* (1887) and *Timothy's Quest* (1890). *The Story Hour* (1900) was the first of many collaborations with her sister. Her most famous children's book was *Rebecca of Sunnybrook Farm* (1903), which became a best-seller over many years. It told the story of ten-year-old Rebecca Rowena Randall who left her poor widowed mother and brothers and sisters and went to live on a farm in Riverboro, Maine, with her two spinster aunts. They were unused to children, and waspish Aunt Miranda, in particular, gave Rebecca a bad time ('an ounce of good behaviour is worth a pound of repentance' was a typical maxim). But sunny Rebecca, with her little straw hat and pink sunshade (her dearest possession) and her generous, winning ways, made many new friends and emerged from her experiences triumphant and happy. Rebecca was once described as 'the nicest child in American literature' and the tag is an apt one. The story has a great deal of charm (as does its heroine) and was dramatised and filmed with success (Shirley Temple portrayed Rebecca in the 1937 film production). A sequel, *The New Chronicles of Rebecca*, followed in 1907 (this book has been issued with varying titles, including *More About Rebecca of Sunnybrook Farm*). Another popular book by Mrs

Wiggin was *Mother Carey's Chickens* (1911). Between 1906 and 1911 Mrs Wiggin and her sister, Nora Archibald Smith, compiled and edited *The Library of Fairy Literature* – the five volumes which comprised the work being *Fairy Ring* (1906), *Magic Casements* (1907), *Tales of Laughter* (1908), *Tales of Wonder* (1909) and *Talking Beasts* (1911). The collection of around a hundred fairy and folk tales, and fables, was excellent. She also wrote several light-hearted travel books about a character called 'Penelope', based loosely upon her own tour of the British Isles in the 1890s. The greater part of *Rebecca of Sunnybrook Farm* was written at the home of her friend, Charles Henry Nevill, at Bramhall Hall, Cheshire, during one such tour. With her sister she wrote several works on child education too. Her first husband died in 1889 and six years later she married again. She died on 24th August 1923.

Wilde, Oscar

Born on 16th October 1854, in Dublin, and educated at Porotra Royal School, Enniskillen, Trinity College, Dublin, and Magdalen College, Oxford. At the outset of his writing career (though his *Poems* had appeared in 1881) he wrote two books of beautiful, sad and haunting fairy tales: *The Happy Prince* (1888) and *A House of Pomegranates* (1891). The two collections together contained nine stories: 'The Happy Prince', 'The Selfish Giant', 'The Devoted Friend, 'The Remarkable Rocket', 'The Nightingale and the Rose', 'The Young King', 'The Birthday of the Infanta', 'The Star-Child' and 'The Fisherman and His Soul'. Some, Wilde had originally told to his sons, Vyvyan and Cyril. Written in magnificent prose, the stories are perhaps better appreciated by adults than children, though many young readers do undoubtedly enjoy them. Overtones of religious allegory and 'Biblical' language tend to put some children off, however. Later, of course, Wilde went on to produce his more famous works. Following his last tragic years, he died in Paris on 30th November 1900.

Wilder, Laura Ingalls

Born on 7th February 1867, at Lake Pepin, Wisconsin. The

detailed story of her own childhood and growing-up as a member of a pioneer family in Wisconsin during the 'seventies and 'eighties are the subject of her popular and widely-hailed series of children's books, the first of which was published when she was sixty-five. *The Little House in the Big Woods* (1932) began the saga with five-year-old Laura living with her family in a log hut in the Wisconsin Woods. *Farmer Boy* (1933) introduced Almanzo Wilder and his childhood on a New York State farm (he was later to marry Laura). *Little House on the Prairie* (1935) told how Laura and her family left their Wisconsin Woods home to set off for the West by covered wagon. *On the Banks of Plum Creek* (1937) sets the family down in Minnesota, and *By the Shores of Silver Lake* (1939) finds them in Dakota Territory. In *The Long Winter* (1940), the Ingalls experience a blizzard-swept winter in a small town. *Little Town on the Prairie* (1941) and *These Happy Golden Years* (1943) tell of Laura's venture into teaching and of her marriage to Almanzo Wilder. The stories, though told in the third person, are all true and give the reader a vivid, dramatic and humorous picture of authentic American pioneering. As a piece of social history the saga is invaluable; as a story for young people it is superb. Laura Ingalls Wilder died on 10th January 1957, as she was nearing the age of ninety.

Wilkins, Vaughan

Born 1890 in London and educated at Merchant Taylors' School, London. Entered journalism soon after leaving school. Served in France, Egypt and Palestine during military service, 1914–18. Was Assistant Managing Editor, *Daily Express*, 1929–33, and was later appointed Assistant Editor of the *Sunday Referee*. Won wide recognition and success with such adult novels as *And So – Victoria* and *Being Met Together*. In 1945 came his first book for children: *After Bath*. Sub-titled 'The Remarkable Case of the Flying Hat', it was a fantasy-adventure telling how two children, William and Garland, go off to search for the lost magic of Minchester. Funny, exciting and outrageous in turn, the tale tends to become rather more serious towards the end and develops into a battle between good and evil, a striking contribution to juvenile literature, showing a rare wit and imagination in many passages. Wilkins' *The City of Frozen Fire* (1950) was an exciting adventure story. He died in 1959.

Williams, Ursula Moray

Born 1911 at Petersfield, Hampshire, and educated privately and at a finishing school in Annecy, in the French Alps. She studied art in Winchester, subsequently contributing stories and illustrations to several children's publications. Her first major success was *The Adventures of the Little Wooden Horse* (1938), which she also illustrated. The appealing toy's experiences, sad, exciting, funny and happy, as he went off in search of a fortune for his master and maker, Uncle Peder, made a big impression on young readers (and their parents) and have stood the test of time well, as recent reprints have shown. *Peter and the Wanderlust* (1939) was an original and entertaining story about a boy and a 1902 Viking motor-car, bringing in the famous veteran car run from London to Brighton as one of its highspots. Her varied titles since then include: *Gobbolino, the Witch's Cat* (1942), *The Good Little Christmas Tree* (1943), *Jockin the Jester* (1951), *The Binklebys at Home* (1951), *Hobbie* (1958), *The Moonball* (1958), *The Noble Hawks* (1959), *Beware of This Animal* (1963), *Johnny Tigerskin* (1964), *High Adventure* (1966), *Cruise of the Happy-Go-Gay* (1967), *Goodbody's Puppet Show* (1967) and *A Crown for a Queen* (1968). Her twin sister, Barbara Moray Williams, has also illustrated several books. Ursula Moray Williams, who has four sons, lives near Tewkesbury, Gloucestershire.

Williamson, Henry

Born 1897, in Bedfordshire. At seventeen he enlisted in the army and served in France throughout the First World War. He first won fame with his quartet of adult novels published under the collective title *The Flax of Dream* (comprising *The Beautiful Years*, 1921; *Dandelion Days*, 1922; *Dream of Fair Women*, 1924; and *The Pathway*, 1928). In 1923 he left his home in London to live in a tiny, centuries-old hut in a Devon village. He lived there alone, wandering through the countryside and watching wild life. He had always loved animals, birds and fishes – now he made the most of his opportunity to get to know them better. He reared a baby otter, which used to follow him around like a pet dog. When the otter vanished, after being injured in a rabbit-trap, Williamson resolved to write the detailed story of an otter, told from the animal's own viewpoint. He studied the ways of otters for a considerable time, becoming utterly absorbed in their world. Then, in 1927, he published *Tarka the Otter*, after revising and re-writing it no less than seventeen times, so determined was he to make it absolutely authentic and accurate in every way. It received wide and glowing praise from leading literary figures of the day and won the Hawthornden Prize for that year. It has never been out of print since. Although not strictly intended for children, they have taken it as their own over the years, as they have several of his subsequent nature stories. Other titles include: *The Peregrine's Saga* (1923), *The Old Stag* (1926), *Salar the Salmon* (1935) and *The Phasian Bird* (1948). Since around 1950 he has been absorbed in his huge novel-cycle with the collective title *A Chronicle of Ancient Sunlight*; more than a dozen volumes have been published so far. Today, Henry Williamson still lives in his beloved Devon. Apart from writing, he has also farmed in both Devon and Norfolk.

Wodehouse, Pelham Grenville

Born on 15th October 1881, in Guildford, Surrey, the third son of a judge who was based in Hong Kong. He was educated at preparatory schools in Guernsey and Dover, then at Dulwich College, London. His first job was as a clerk in the Hong Kong and Shanghai Bank in the City of London, where he remained for two years. His earliest writings appeared in a variety of magazines, including *The Public School Magazine*, which serialised his first full-length work *The Pothunters*, a school story, in 1901; it appeared in book form in September 1902. A whole series of further public school stories – all excellent of their kind – followed, including *A Prefect's Uncle* (1903), *Tales of St Austin's* (1903), *The Gold Bat* (1904; first published as a serial in the boys' magazine *The Captain*, 1903–4), *The Head of Kay's* (1905; serialised in *The Captain*, 1904), *The White Feather* (1907; serialised in *The Captain*, 1905–6) and *Mike* (1909; serialised in

The Captain, 1907–8, in two parts: 'Jackson Junior' and 'The Lost Lambs'). ('Tales of Wrykyn' ran in *The Captain* in 1905, but never achieved book publication.) *Mike* was a superlative and much longer than average school story – probably one of the best and most entertaining ever written – and was additionally notable for the fact that the latter half introduced the sophisticated and hilariously witty character Psmith, who went a long way in setting the pattern for Wodehouse's future career. More Psmith books which followed were *Psmith in the City* (1910; serialised in *The Captain* as 'The New Fold', 1908–9), *Psmith, Journalist* (1915; serialised in *The Captain*, 1909–10) and *Leave It To Psmith* (1923). The second half of *Mike* was published as *Enter Psmith* in 1935; *Mike* was published in two separate volumes in 1953 as *Mike at Wrykyn* and *Mike and Psmith*, slightly edited and up-dated. Wodehouse's final serial for *The Captain*, which had done so much for his early career, was 'The Eighteen-Carat Kid' (1912–13), told from the point of view of a master at a small preparatory school and published in book form as *The Little Nugget* in 1913. Before leaving his 'juvenile' career it is worth mentioning that he wrote (with an 'assist' from his author-friend W. Townend) a school and mystery serial called 'The Luck Stone' for the boys' paper *Chums* in 1908–9, under the pseudonym 'BASIL WINDHAM'. It never appeared between hard covers. After leaving the Hong Kong and Shanghai Bank, Wodehouse joined the staff of the *Globe* (then a London evening newspaper) and wrote the 'By the Way' column for it for eight years, with the exception of one year, 1909, which he spent in America. He sold two short stories in New York for 300 dollars apiece and decided to stay there. Eventually he sold a serial to the *Saturday Evening Post* and for the next twenty-five years almost all his books appeared first in this magazine. He also wrote lyrics to music by Jerome Kern and other composers and, a few years later, formed a partnership with Guy Bolton, which resulted in a number of musical shows and plays (one of his most famous lyrics was that for the show-stopping song 'Bill' in *Showboat*). He also wrote screenplays in Hollywood. Today he is famous as the creator of such immortal humorous characters as Jeeves, Bertie Wooster, Mr Mulliner, Lord Emsworth, Ukridge, Uncle Fred and the aforementioned Psmith. His 'Blandings Castle' is one of the best-known fictional spots in Britain and his place as the world's Number One Humorist has been assured for over forty years. He has written nearly 100 books, close on forty shows and plays and over twenty films. He still produces a new book every year or so and, at a hearty eighty-seven, lives in New York.

Wood, Lorna

Born 1913, at Pex Hill, Lancashire, and educated at the Convent of Notre Dame, Liverpool. Was a concert pianist 1935–38 and worked for the BBC's Monitoring Service in the early 1940s. In 1954 she published the first of her diverting series of children's humorous fantasies featuring Hag Dowsabel, the witch, *The People in the Garden*. Others in this series include: *Rescue by Broomstick* (1956), *The Hag Calls for Help* (1957), *Seven-League Ballet Shoes* (1959), *Hags on Holiday* (1960) and *Hag in the Castle* (1962). She has written several other children's books as well as three adult novels.

Woolsey, Sarah Chauncey

See: Coolidge, Susan

Wyss, Johann David and Johann Rudolf

Johann David Wyss was born in 1743 in Berne, Switzerland, and became a well-known pastor there. He originally told the famous *Swiss Family Robinson* as a story to his four sons for their instruction and amusement, continuing it from day to day. The tale was based on a Russian sea-captain's report of his discovery of a Swiss pastor and his family who had been shipwrecked on an island near New Guinea. Eventually Johann David wrote it down, but with no idea of publication in his mind. At this stage it was for reading aloud to the family only. One of his four sons was Johann Rudolf Wyss, born in Berne in 1781. He became a brilliant scholar, studied philosophy and theology, and was appointed Professor of Philosophy at the Berne Academy in 1805, when he was only twenty-four. A few years later he came across his father's manuscript of *Swiss Family Robinson* and, after revising it to some extent, submitted it to a Zurich publisher. So it was that the first volume was published in 1812 under the title *Der Schweizerische Robinson, Oder der Schiffbruchige Schweizerprediger und Seine Familie*. In English: *The Swiss Family Robinson, or The Shipwreck of the Swiss Minister and His Family*. The second and final volume appeared in 1813. The name of the author given on the title-page was that of Johann Rudolf Wyss, but in a preface he pointed out that 'the book . . . is an adaptation of my father's work and all that is original, instructive and best in this book is due to my father'. (Johann David Wyss died in 1818.) In this original version, the family was rescued after only ten years and returned home. But some years after its first appearance the Baroness de Montolieu, a French writer, translated it into French and subsequently obtained Professor Wyss's permission to extend and enlarge the story. Her new and much-lengthened version was published in Paris in 1824, being, in turn, translated back into German again. The story made its first English appearance in 1814, published by William Godwin. The most widely-known translations have been those of Mrs H. B. Paull (1868) and of W. H. G. Kingston (1879), who enlarged the story still further. Another notable translation was that of H. Frith (1878). The story of a Swiss pastor, his wife and their four young sons (Fritz, Franz, Ernest and Jack) shipwrecked on a tropical island, with day-to-day accounts of their adventures and discoveries, has since been translated into numerous languages and been perennially popular with young readers all over the world. Over 200 versions have been published in England and America alone. Children usually accept the story wholeheartedly, complete with the enormous amount of errors in the matters of natural history, geography, flora and fauna and navigation which mar the tale for adult readers. Pastor Robinson took advantage of the convenient situation whereby practically every type of vegetation, animal, bird and fish appeared to exist in one spot, and lectured his captive audience on everything in sight. Religion was naturally not forgotten. But the story, for all its absurdities, has exuberance and colour and succeeding generations have taken it to their hearts. Johann Rudolf Wyss also published collections of Swiss folk songs, legends and historical subjects. He was responsible, too, for the words of the Swiss national anthem. He died in Berne in 1830 – and *Swiss Family Robinson* lived on to give inspiration for a host of imitations, good and bad. They included Marryat's *Masterman Ready* (1841), Mayne Reid's *English Family Robinson* (1851), Ballantyne's *Coral Island* (1857), Catharine Traill's *Canadian Family Robinson* (1852), Percy St John's *Arctic Crusoe* (1854) and Kingston's *Rival Crusoes* (1878). Jules Verne – who admitted his debt to both Defoe and Wyss – wrote a long sequel to *Swiss Family Robinson* which appeared originally in France under the title *Second Fatherland* and in English translation the same year (1900) in two volumes: *Their Island Home* and *The Castaways of the 'Flag'*. *Willis the Pilot; a sequel to the Swiss Family Robinson*, by Adrien Paul, was published in Paris in 1855, appearing in London two years later.

Yonge, Charlotte Mary

Born on 13th August 1823, at Otterbourne, near Winchester, Hampshire, the daughter of a retired army officer who had fought at Waterloo. She was educated at home by her parents and had a very strict and lonely childhood; her diet consisted largely of bread and milk and her playfellows were her dolls. She maintained in later life, however, that her childhood had been a happy one. There was a strong religious element in her home life (both her parents were descended from clergymen) and she taught regularly at the village Sunday school from the age of seven until her death. At an early age she came under the influence of John Keble, the theologian and one of the founders of the High Church Oxford Movement, when he held a local church post. From then onwards the major interest in her life was religion. She had won something of a reputation as a storyteller during periodic visits to her cousins, and had translated little stories from their original French in the course of her studies. When she and her family were trying to think of ideas to raise funds for the local girls' school it was suggested that Charlotte might weave the tales into one longer story and publish it privately, the proceeds from any sales to benefit the school. This transpired and *Le Château de Melville* appeared in 1838, when Charlotte was fifteen. In 1842 she began to write stories and articles for a Sunday school magazine, *Magazine for the Young*, and in 1844 came her first properly published novel *Abbeychurch*. Several more followed, but met with small success.

In 1851 Charlotte was invited by the publishers of *Magazine for the Young* to become editor of their new publication, *The Monthly Packet*, which was intended for young ladies aged between fifteen and twenty-five. The successful periodical was to remain under her editorship until 1890 and published early works by Mrs Ewing among many others. In 1853 she published *The Heir of Redclyffe*, which received a remakable popular reception and became one of the most widely read novels of the nineteenth century. It was a 'modern romance', had the Oxford Movement figuring prominently and provided in its hero, Sir Guy Morville, the ideal model for young men of the time to copy in every way they were able. Young girls of every class cried over it and it was even said to have influenced more than one famous poet and painter in his work. *The Little Duke* (1854) was a historical story and told of Richard the Fearless, a young Norman who was held captive throughout his childhood as hostage at the French Court. It had originally run as the first serial in the opening numbers of Miss Yonge's *The Monthly Packet*. After another social novel, *Heartsease* (1854), came a story of the Black Prince, *The Lances of Lynwood* (1855), another fine historical novel for young readers. In 1856 came another famous and best-selling book, *The Daisy Chain*. This was the first of Miss Yonge's long series of detailed stories of family life in Victorian times and recounted the fortunes and misfortunes of Dr May and his large family of children and how they all fared after the death of Mrs May in an accident. On this occasion it was the book's heroine – thin, clumsy, rather plain, but exceedingly virtuous and good-hearted – who became the idol of every girl reader in the country. Her name was Ethel May and her huge success reflected that of her shy, quiet creator, Charlotte Yonge. She went on to publish more than 150 further titles, most of the novels being either long family chronicles or historical subjects. The better-known include: *Dynevor Terrace* (1857), *Countess Kate* (1862), *The Prince and the Page* (1865), *The Dove in the Eagle's Nest* (1866), *The Chaplet of Pearls* (1868), *The Caged Lion* (1870) and *The Pillars of the House* (1873). Her non-fiction titles include: *Landmarks of History* (1852–57), *History of Christian Names* (1863) and *A Book of Golden Deeds* (1864). She also wrote a long series of *Aunt Charlotte's History Stories* (1873–93). Charlotte Yonge was rather prim and prudish in her outlook and opinions and viewed her outstanding literary success diffidently. She was essentially a good and generous woman and the proceeds from her books invariably went towards church and missionary causes. Profits from *The Daisy Chain* established a missionary college in Auckland, New Zealand, and those from *The Heir of Redclyffe* fitted out and financed a missionary schooner for work in the South Seas. She believed passionately in self-denial and the inferiority of women. Her family sagas today seem gratuitously sentimental and pathetic; yet they have humour and a great deal of excellent characterisation. She never married, and lived in the village of Otterbourne throughout her entire life and died there (still at work on three books) on 24th March 1901.

The Illustrators

Ambrus, Victor G.

Born during the early 1930s in Budapest, Hungary, the son of an engineer. He studied graphic design at the Hungarian Academy of Fine Arts. During his third year at the Academy, in 1956, came the Hungarian uprising and he eventually escaped and made his way to England. He continued his studies at the Farnham School of Art, Surrey, and at the Royal College of Art in London and began illustration work in 1960 with A. C. Jenkins' *White Horses and Black Bulls*. He has illustrated a large number of books since then, including: René Guillot's *The Master of the Elephants* (1961), *The Changeling* by William Mayne (1961), *Hills and Hollows* by Sheena Porter (1962), *The Heron Ride* by Mary Treadgold (1962), *The Cossacks* by B. Bartos-Hoppner (1962), *Castors Away!* by Hester Burton (1962), *Time of Trial* by Hester Burton (1963), *Camerons in the Hills* by Jane Duncan (1963), *The Hound of Ulster* by Rosemary Sutcliff (1963), *The British Army* by Edward Fitzgerald (1964) and *The Royal Navy*, by Peter Dawlish (1964). Ambrus won the Kate Greenaway Medal in 1965 for his *The Three Poor Tailors*, a picture book based on an old Hungarian tale, and for his other work during the year, including his illustrations to *The Royal Air Force* by John W. R. Taylor. His subsequent assignments include *The Challenge of the Green Knight* by Ian Serraillier (1966), *The Merchant Navy* by Peter Dawlish (1966), *The Wild Horse of Santander* by Helen Griffiths (1966) and Ambrus's own picture book *Brave Soldier Janosh* (1967). Ambrus is among the most versatile of modern illustrators and can turn his talented hand to most types of story. He particularly enjoys depicting battle scenes and is at pains to present these as authentically as possible. He reads history avidly and collects old weapons and swords. He enjoys fencing and horse riding too. Since 1962 he has taught at the Farnham School of Art.

Ardizzone, Edward

Born on 16th October 1900, in China, of a French Italian father and a Scots mother. Went with his parents to settle in England at the age of five and lived in Ipswich for much of his childhood. Educated at Clayesmore School and on leaving took up office work in the City of London. But he really wanted to become an artist (an ambition fired by a copy of Bunyan's *The Pilgrim's Progress*, given to him while a schoolboy, and illustrated by an unnamed artist) and attended regular evening classes at the Westminster School of Art. At twenty-six – and with some financial help from his father – the frustrated artist was able to leave his desk job and take up painting full-time. His first exhibition of pictures came in 1928 and his first book illustrations were for Sheridan Le Fanu's *In a Glass Darkly* in 1929. His first two children's books were written and illustrated in 1935 solely for the amusement of his two children, then aged six and four. In 1936 the first of them was published: *Little Tim and the Brave Sea Captain* (it was re-drawn and revised in 1955). The enchanting story of a small boy who runs away to sea and has all kinds of exciting adventures was illustrated in Ardizzone's own unique way – sensitive, subtle and charming – and made a big impact on the children's picture-book field of the mid-'thirties. In 1937 came *Lucy Brown and Mr Grimes*, which he again wrote and illustrated, and the illustrations for H. J. Kaeser's children's book *Mimff* (he later illustrated the three further titles in the series). In 1939 he illustrated two adult books: H. E. Bates' *My Uncle Silas* and Maurice Gorham's *The Local*. During the Second World War Ardizzone served first as a Gunner then, from 1940, as an official war artist, seeing action in France, Italy, Libya, Sicily, Normandy and Germany; there are 300 of his paintings in the Imperial War Museum in London. In 1946 he returned to book illustration with Walter de la Mare's *Peacock Pie* (he was later to illustrate the new edition of this author's *Stories from the Bible*). He continued with his own illustrated stories, which have included, in addition to the first two titles: *Tim and Lucy Go to Sea* (1938, revised and re-drawn 1958), *Paul, the Hero of the Fire* (1948), *Nicholas and the Fast-Moving Diesel* (1948), *Tim to the Rescue* (1949), *Tim and Charlotte* (1951), *Tim in Danger* (1953), *Tim All Alone* (1956) (this title won for Ardizzone the first Kate Greenaway Medal, presented by the Library Association for the year's most distinguished contribution to children's book illustration in Britain), *Johnny the Clockmaker* (1960), *Tim's Friend Towser* (1962), *Peter the Wanderer* (1963) and *Tim and Ginger* (1965). In 1966 came *The Little Girl and the Tiny Doll*, illustrated by Ardizzone and

305

written by his daughter Aingelda. He has also illustrated around 100 books by other authors; titles showing the range of his talents include: Bunyan's *The Pilgrim's Progress* (1947), C. Day Lewis's *The Otterbury Incident* (1948), *The Charles Dickens Birthday Book* (1949), Trollope's *The Warden* (1952) and *Barchester Towers* (1953), Eleanor Farjeon's *The Little Bookroom* (1955) (this book won for the author the Carnegie Medal as the Best Children's Book of the Year, also the Hans Christian Andersen Medal), A. Philippa Pearce's *Minnow on the Say* (1955), Surtees' *Hunting With Mr Jorrocks* (1956), Cervantes' *Don Quixote* (1959), Barrie's *Peter Pan* (retold by Eleanor Graham) (1962), Dana Faralla's *The Singing Cupboard* (1962), Farjeon's *Kalaeidoscope* (1963), Christianna Brand's *Nurse Matilda* (1964) (and its sequel *Nurse Matilda Goes to Town* [1967]), and Noel Streatfeild's *The Growing Summer* (1966). He has also painted many pictures, chiefly in water-colour, and as well as having held several one-man shows in London, has also exhibited at the Tate Gallery (which has also officially purchased his work), various English provincial galleries, Paris, and the New York World's Fair. He is a Fellow of the Society of Industrial Artists. His own three children are now grown-up and he is a grandfather. He lives in London and is probably generally regarded as the *doyen* of contemporary illustrators of children's books in Britain.

Attwell, Mabel Lucie

Born on 4th June 1879, in London, and educated at Cooper's Company School and privately. She studied painting and drawing at the Regent Street Art School and Heatherley's Art School, in London. At sixteen she was drawing imaginative sketches of small children, animals and fairies. When she presented her first folder of pictures to a leading London artists' agency, she – and her work – were received unenthusiastically and she was told to leave the pictures for a few days but not to hope for any results, since young girls' work was not in demand. She left depressed and upset. But a few days later the agency informed her that all her drawings had been sold and asked for more. Soon afterwards her drawings were selling for twenty guineas each. It was the start of a remarkably successful and consistent career which lasted for nearly seventy years. Miss Attwell soon became famous throughout Britain and many other parts of the world for her pictures of small children; they were all cherubic and 'lovable', with big blue eyes, chubby rosy cheeks, stubby legs and arms, plump tummies, button noses and sturdy shoes. They appeared in magazines (both children's and adults'), coloured picture postcards (particularly popular during the First World War and sent in their hundreds of thousands to cheer up troops in the trenches) and children's books and annuals, especially her own *Mabel Lucie Attwell's Annual* which is still appearing today after over forty years. Her most famous creation was probably 'Diddums' who, as well as appearing in drawings, was also a boy-doll in typical Attwell style, with especially large shoes. Thousands of children grew up with him and it was said that he could be found in nurseries all over the world. She also illustrated many famous children's books including *Alice in Wonderland, The Water Babies, Peter Pan and Wendy, Hans Andersen's Fairy Tales* and *Grimm's Fairy Tales*. Queen Marie of Rumania invited her to illustrate her own book of fairy stories and also to stay with her at the Royal Palace in Bucharest. Mabel Lucie Attwell's chubby creations appeared on china, pottery, textiles, handkerchiefs, nursery curtains, linen, framed pictures and countless toys. She designed many posters too, including one of the first for London Transport's underground railway. It was said that the young Prince of Wales even insisted upon using his own set of Attwell cups and plates! Mabel Lucie Attwell was probably at the height of her popularity and success in the 1915–30 period, but her work is still in demand today and her particularly cosy, sentimental appeal seems to be timeless. She was once quoted as saying: 'I see the child in the adult, then I draw the adult as a child. . . .' She married artist Harold Earnshaw in 1908 (he died in 1937) and had two children: Peter and Peggy, the latter also becoming an artist. Mabel Lucie Attwell died at the age of eighty-five, on 13th November 1964, at her home in Fowey, Cornwall, where she had lived and worked for many years.

Baynes, Pauline Diana

Born on 9th September 1922, in Brighton, Sussex, then spent

the first five years of her childhood in India, where her father worked. Then returned to England and was educated at Hillside Convent, Farnborough, Hampshire, and at Beaufront School, Camberley, Surrey. She studied at the Farnham School of Art and the Slade School, London. An early achievement was her election to the Women's International Art Club at sixteen (though she later resigned her membership in 1946). She returned to her old school, Beaufront, for a time to teach art before working for both the army and the Admiralty during the Second World War (in a civilian capacity), engaged mainly on camouflage and charting assignments. She subsequently began illustrating books, one of her early successes being Tolkien's *Farmer Giles of Ham* in 1949. In 1950 she illustrated the first of C. S. Lewis's now-famous 'Narnia' books, *The Lion, the Witch and the Wardrobe*, going on to illustrate the entire series of seven titles, ending with *The Last Battle* in 1956. Among the many other books she has illustrated are: *A Treasury of French Tales* (Henri Pourrat) (1953), *The Arabian Nights* (Amabel Williams-Ellis) (1957), *Fairy Tales from the British Isles* (Amabel Williams-Ellis) (1960), *The Unicorn Window* (Lynette Muir) (1961), *The Little Knife That Did All the Work* (Alison Uttley) (1962) and *The Puffin Book of Nursery Rhymes* (Iona and Peter Opie) (1963). She has also illustrated a series of educational history books ('The Pilgrim Way' Series, Vols 1–4). Miss Baynes' work is formal, elegant and delicate and often shows signs of oriental influences. She has admitted that she has been deeply influenced by mediaeval and Persian paintings. Her knowledge of costume and its history makes her historical drawings authentically alive. She is at her best in fairy and fantasy tales and her *Arabian Nights* is particularly memorable. Miss Baynes is a Member of the Society of Industrial Artists and lives at Farnham, Surrey.

Bedford, Francis Donkin

Born 21st May 1864, in London, and educated at Westminster. Studied at the Royal College of Art and Royal Academy Architectural Schools, London, originally intending to become an architect. He gradually gravitated towards painting and illustration work, though his pictures often included a finely-drawn building or design in them. His earliest work included illustrations for children's picture books, but his first notable book illustrations were for S. Baring-Gould's *Old Country Life* (1890), followed by other titles including *The Battle of the Frogs and Mice* (1894), S. Baring-Gould's *Old English Fairy Tales* (1897) and *A Book of Nursery Rhymes* (1897). Around this time E. V. Lucas invited Bedford to illustrate *A Book of Verses for Children*, which he had just edited. The book was a success and Bedford was subsequently associated with Lucas in a beautifully designed series of titles, including *A Book of Shops* (1899), *Four and Twenty Toilers* (1900), *Old-Fashioned Tales* (1905), *Forgotten Tales of Long Ago* (1906), *Another Book of Verses for Children* (1907) and *Runaways and Castaways* (1908). In 1911 came what is probably Bedford's best-known work, his illustrations to J. M. Barrie's story of his famous stage success *Peter Pan* and titled *Peter and Wendy*. Later titles included *The Magic Fishbone* by Charles Dickens (1922), Dickens' *A Christmas Carol* (1923), *Billy Barnicoat* by Greville MacDonald (1923), *At the Back of the North Wind* by George MacDonald (1924), *The Princess and the Goblin* by the same author (1926) and *Through Merrie England* by Frank Leonard Stevens (1928). Perhaps Bedford's most perfect pictures, in colour and black-and-white, were for *The 'Original Poems' and Others* by Ann and Jane Taylor and Adelaide O'Keeffe (1903). His drawings and water colours depicting small children at work, at play and at rest were ideally matched to the text of these old poems and moral verse tales. Bedford was at his best, in fact, with pictures of children; they were always pretty and winsome, it is true, but they could be mischievous and naughty too and had a great deal of appeal. Bedford did many paintings in tempera and water-colours and exhibited at various galleries in London. He lived in Wimbledon, London, for many years. He died *c.* 1950.

Bewick, Thomas

Born 1753 at Cherryburn, near Newcastle-upon-Tyne, Northumberland, the son of a colliery-owner, and educated at nearby Ovingham. In 1767 he was apprenticed to a Newcastle engraver, Ralph Beilby, having shown a marked aptitude for art from an early age. While working on woodcuts for chapbooks and broadside sheets, he experimented with a new technique of wood-engraving and gradually came to specialise in the use of the end-grain of box-wood, which was tougher than the side-grain and gave him considerably more control in his highly intricate work. He also worked in the 'white line' process of engraving. By the early 1770s Bewick was supplying illustrations to several children's stories. One of the first important books he illustrated was *Select Fables of Aesop and Others* in 1774. *The New Lottery Book of Birds and Beasts* had already appeared in 1771. In 1779 – by which time he had been made a partner in Beilby's firm – Bewick illustrated *A Pretty Book of Pictures for Little Masters and Misses: or, Tommy Trip's History of Beasts and Birds*, with verses said to have been written by Goldsmith. Bewick's later work was prolific and a major influence on the whole field of book illustration; it was due to his success that the woodcut became popular again. He was a great nature lover and a keen observer of all forms of wild life. Among his many works in this field were *A General History of Quadrupeds* (1790) and *A Natural History of British Birds* (1797–1804), which are generally regarded as his masterpieces. His vignettes, chapter-headings and tail-pieces for these and many other volumes were especially delightful, with much beautifully observed detail. By the turn of the century Bewick was in complete control of the Newcastle engraving firm; also with the firm, until his death in 1795, was his younger brother, John, another illustrator of note. By the time he died, in 1828, Thomas Bewick had become responsible for developing a whole new school of English illustration whose influence was felt for many years afterwards. He can be truly described as one of the great book illustrators and artistic pioneers of all time.

Briggs, Raymond

Born 1934 in London, the son of a milkman. Studied at the Wimbledon School of Art and the Slade School in London. Began both writing and illustrating children's books in 1957 and has since become a leading illustrator in the field. Among the books he has written and illustrated are *The Secret House* (1960), *The Strange House* (1961), *Midnight Adventure* (1961), *The Big Rocket* (1962) and *Sledges to the Rescue* (1963). *Ring-a-Ring*

O'Roses (1962), *The White Land* (1963) and *Fee Fi Fo Fum* (1964) are illustrated collections of nursery and traditional rhymes, showing his imaginative and effective use of colour. He illustrated James Aldridge's *The Flying 19* (a story about a flying bus) in 1966. In the same year he produced his magnificent *The Mother Goose Treasury*, which contained 408 rhymes and no less than 897 illustrations in colour and black-and-white. This collection – one of the most definitive and superb books of nursery rhymes for children ever published – won Briggs the Kate Greenaway Medal for 1966. The rich, detailed drawings were full of humour and life and truly established Briggs' reputation as one of the foremost illustrators of modern times. In 1968 he inaugurated 'the Briggs Books', published by Hamish Hamilton, in which he illustrated great modern exploits of courage and daring. The first titles were *Lindbergh Flies the Atlantic, Nuvolari and the Alfa Romeo, Richthofen the Red Baron,* and *Jimmy Murphy and the White Duesenberg*. He is married to an artist and lives in Burgess Hill, Sussex.

Brock, Charles Edmond and Henry Matthew

Two members of a well-known and large artistic family. C. E. was the eldest of a family of four artist-brothers while H. M. was the youngest. Their father was an artist too and the whole family worked together for much of the time, in a large, old-world studio in their home town of Cambridge. The two best-known and most prolific brothers – C. E. and H. M. – turned out an incredible amount of first-class illustration work for books and magazines, also exhibiting paintings at the Royal Academy and elsewhere. Both excelled at 'costume' illustrations, revelling in ladies in poke-bonnets, prim little girls in patterns, dashing young rakes of the Regency period and jovial, wine-bibbing old cronies. Their styles were very similar but always good to look at and they both come high in the long list of illustrators at their peak around the turn of the century and just after.

Charles Edmond Brock was born in Holloway, London, on 5th February 1870, and educated at the Higher Grade School, Cambridge. He received his art education primarily from the noted sculptor, Henry Wiles, also in Cambridge. His first important illustrations were for Thomas Hood's *Comic Poems*, in 1893, followed by those for *English Fairy and Folk Tales* the same year. Subsequently came his work for *Gulliver's Travels* (1894), *Westward Ho!* (1896), *Ivanhoe* (1897), *The Vicar of Wakefield* (1898), *Robinson Crusoe* (1898), Fenimore Cooper's *The Pathfinder* and *The Prairie* (1900), Lamb's *Essays and Sketches* (1903) and *Mrs Leicester's School* (1904), Mrs Mitford's *Our Village* (1904), Mrs Gaskell's *Cranford* (1904), Dickens' *The Cricket on the Hearth* (1905), E. Nesbit's *Oswald Bastable and Others* (1905) (with H. R. Millar), Eliot's *Silas Marner* (1905), Irving's *Christmas at Bracebridge Hall* (1906), E. Nesbit's *The Railway Children* (1908), Blackmore's *Lorna Doone* (1910), Farnol's *The Broad Highway* (1912) and *The Amateur Gentleman* (1914), Mrs Burnett's *Little Lord Fauntleroy* (1925), Eleanor Farjeon's *Martin Pippin in the Apple Orchard* (1921) and Louey Chisholm's anthology *The Golden Staircase* (1928) (with H. M. Brock). C. E. combined with brother H. M. to illustrate an edition of Jane Austen's novels in the early 1900s too. He also contributed work to many magazines, including *Punch* and *The Graphic* and various juvenile publications including *The Captain*, for which he illustrated Herbert Strang's three best serials. He exhibited at the Royal Academy and became a member of the Royal Institute of Painters in Water-Colours in 1908. He died on 28th February 1938.

Henry Matthew Brock was born in Cambridge on 11th July 1875, and was also educated at the Higher Grade School, Cambridge. He later studied at the Cambridge School of Art. His style was almost indistinguishable from his brother's and he did much the same sort of work as C. E., though he did seem to specialise more in the juvenile market. He illustrated a large number of school stories for boys, for example, including thirteen serials in *The Captain* and many more in hard covers by such well-known authors in the *genre* as Hylton Cleaver, Gunby Hadath, Desmond Coke and Jeffrey Havilton. He also did many fine colour plates, again mainly for school tales, in such 'bumper' publications as *Herbert Strang's Annual*, *The Oxford Annual for Boys*, etc., and seemed to be very much at home in depicting the public schoolboy, his masters and the school buildings and playing fields with delightful realism and character. He sold his first professional illustrations at eighteen and then, in 1895, illustrated Marryat's *Japhet in Search of a Father* and *Jacob Faithful*. His subsequent illustrations included those to Mrs Gaskell's *Cranford* (1897), Scott's *Waverley* (1898), Bunyan's *The Pilgrim's Progress* (1900), Fenimore Cooper's *The Deerslayer*, *The Last of the Mohicans* and *The Pioneers* (all 1900), Dickens' *The Old Curiosity Shop* (1901), Thackeray's *Henry Esmond* (1904), Louisa M. Alcott's *Little Women* (1904), Hans Andersen's *Fairy Tales* (1905), *The Book of Fairy Tales* (1914), Mrs Ewing's *Jackanapes and Other Stories* (1916), John Drinkwater's *All About Me* (1928) and its sequel *More About Me* (1929), Stevenson's *Treasure Island* (1928), Kingsley's *The Heroes* (1928), *The Book of Nursery Tales* (1934), Dickens' *A Christmas Carol* (1935), and *The Children's Omnibus* (*c.* 1946) in which his illustrations to *Alice in Wonderland* appeared. He contributed to many magazines and juvenile periodicals, including *Little Folks*, *Boy's Own Paper*, the aforementioned *The Captain* (to which he was a prolific illustrator from 1911 to 1924), *Punch* and *The Strand*. It was for the latter magazine that he illustrated one Sherlock Holmes story (with Joseph Simpson) in 1911 – *The Adventure of the Red Circle*. He exhibited at the Royal Academy and became a member of the Royal Institute of Painters in Water-Colours in 1906. He died on 21st July 1960.

Brooke, Leonard Leslie

Born on 24th September 1862, in Birkenhead, Cheshire, of Irish descent. He studied art at the Royal Academy Schools in London and became a serious professional painter, particularly noted for his fine portraits, before he turned to the illustrating work for which he is today best remembered. After some early minor work he illustrated a series of children's books by Mrs Molesworth, in succession to Walter Crane who had been her most regular illustrator until the early 1890s. Brooke began his association with Mrs Molesworth with *Nurse Heatherdale's Story* in 1891, continuing with *The Girls and I* (1892), *Mary* (1893), *My New Home* (1894), *The Carved Lions* (1895), *The Oriel Window* (1896) and ending with her *Miss Mouse and Her Boys* (1897). In 1897, too, he established his reputation with his black-and-white and coloured illustrations to *The Nursery Rhyme Book*, edited by Andrew Lang. This work also began his thirty-year association with the publishing house of Warne's, for which he drew practically exclusively from then onwards. Brooke's illustrated edition of Edward Lear's *Nonsense Songs* appeared in 1900 in two parts: *The Pelican Chorus* and *The Jumblies*; they were also issued in one volume. In 1903 came what many consider Brooke's most perfect work: *Johnny Crow's Garden*. He had originally heard rhymes about Johnny Crow – who had a little garden which was visited by a succession of unlikely animals – from his father. Brooke's wife (he had married a distant cousin, Sybil Brooke, in 1894) urged him to write and illustrate the story for their two sons, Leonard and Henry. He did – and the result was the supreme example of Brooke's gentle, humorous, detailed animal drawing; his animals and birds wore clothes, as often as not, but these did not, could not, disguise the creatures' natural characteristics. If he tended to humanise the animals' expressions rather, this just added to the general, cosy sense of fun and companionship. Children love to search out the minor touches of detail in his drawings and can pore over a single picture for long minutes on end. Another 'Crow' book, *Johnny Crow's Party*, was published in 1907, but was preceded in 1905 by *The Golden Goose Book*, in which he illustrated *The Three Little Pigs*, *Tom Thumb*, *The Golden Goose* and *The Story of the Three Bears* (the titles were also available separately). Next came *The House in the Wood and Other Old Fairy Stories* (*from the Brothers Grimm*) (1909), *The Truth About Old King Cole* (1910) and *The Tailor and the Crow* (1911). In 1922 came *Ring O'Roses*, in which Brooke illustrated in his own unique and warmly humorous way many old nursery rhymes (these were also available in slim, separate volumes too). He illustrated R. H. Charles' story in verse *A Roundabout Turn* (which had originally appeared in *Punch*) in 1930; it told the story of a toad who wanted to see the world. Brooke's last book was *Johnny Crow's New Garden* (1935) which was delightfully like the first 'Crow' title – thirty years had not dimmed the artist's sense of style and fun. During his career, Brooke had lived at Harwell; St John's Wood, London; Cumnor, near Oxford; and, finally, close to Church Row, Hampstead, London, where he died on 1st May 1940. His work is still popular today, though it is probably loved more in the United States than in Brooke's native England.

314

Browne, Gordon

Born on 15th April 1858, at Banstead, Surrey, the son of Hablot Knight Browne, better known as 'Phiz', the famed illustrator of several of Charles Dickens' novels. He studied art at South Kensington and at Heatherley's Art School, London. His first book illustrations were for a school story by Ascott R. Hope, *The Day After the Holidays* (1875), when he was only seventeen. This led to illustration work for *Aunt Judy's Magazine* (edited by Mrs Ewing). He next designed and drew several Christmas cards for the de la Rue Company, before undergoing a course of instruction in drawing on wood. His tutor, James Cooper, introduced him to Blackie's, the London publishers, for whom he began to illustrate juvenile books. He also began his long association with the *Boy's Own Paper* around this time, when he was called in to provide illustrations to Talbot Baines Reed's serial *The Adventures of a Three Guinea Watch* in 1881; Browne's brother had originally been commissioned to do the job but had had to give it up for various reasons, so Gordon Browne was invited to complete the assignment. Later that same year he illustrated Gordon Stables' *The Cruise of the 'Snow-Bird'* in the same paper, following it with T. B. Reed's famous *The Fifth Form at St Dominic's*. From then on, Browne continued to draw for *BOP*, *Chums* (for which he designed the original cover picture and the one used on the annual bound volume for many years), *The Captain* and many other boys' papers and magazines, in addition to his book work. He also drew for many adult magazines, such as *Strand*, *Good Words*, *Leisure Hour*, *Sunday at Home*, *Black and White*, *The Graphic* and the *Illustrated London News* (for which he illustrated R. L. Stevenson's *The Beach of Falesa*). He became one of Britain's most brilliant and prolific illustrators, averaging around six or more books a year, in addition to his magazine work, paintings, etc. Some of the many titles which he illustrated were *Robinson Crusoe* (1885), Mrs Ewing's *Mary's Meadow* (1886), *Melchior's Dream* (1886) (and several further titles by Mrs Ewing), *Gulliver's Travels* (1886), *Rip Van Winkle* (1887), *Devon Boys* by George Manville Fenn (1887), *Fairy Tales by the Countess d'Aulnoy* (1888), *My Friend Smith* by Talbot Baines Reed (1889), *Prince Prigio* by Andrew Lang (1889), *A Apple Pie* (1890), Mrs Molesworth's

The Red Grange (1891), *Fairy Tales from Grimm* (1895), *Prince Boohoo and Little Smuts* by Harry Jones (1896), *Sintram and his Companions* and *Undine* by de la Motte Fouqué (1896), *The Surprising Adventures of Sir Toady Lion* (1897), *National Rhymes for the Nursery* (1895), Crockett's *Sweetheart Travellers* (1895), *Paleface and Redskin and Other Stories* by F. Anstey (1898), *Dr Jollyboy's ABC* (1898), E. Nesbit's *The Story of the Treasure Seekers* (with Lewis Baumer) (1899), Farrar's *Eric, or Little by Little* (1899) and *St Winifred's* (1900), Andersen's *Fairy Tales* (1902), Crockett's *Sir Toady Crusoe* (1905), Thackeray's *The Rose and the Ring* (1909), *Lorna Doone* (1911), John Masefield's *Book of Discoveries* (1910), Charles Reade's *The Cloister and the Hearth* (with others) (1912) and *Don Quixote* (1921). He also illustrated several volumes by Sir Walter Scott (undated). Perhaps his greatest achievement was his *The Henry Irving Shakespeare* (1895), in eight volumes, for which he did over 550 illustrations. He illustrated many books by G. A. Henty too. In a rather different guise, Browne assumed the pseudonym of 'A. NOBODY' when he both wrote and illustrated two books of nonsense pictures and rhymes: *Nonsense for Somebody, Anybody and Everybody, Particularly the Baby-Body* (1895) and *Some More Nonsense for the Same Bodies as Before* (1896). Gordon Browne's work over the years was so varied and full, so skilled, and of such a consistently high standard that praise would seem invidious. He was equally at home with character-drawing, action scenes or placid landscapes. His animals were as convincing as his people and his children were realistic and vigorous. In matters of detail he was extremely painstaking and ensured that drawings of historical dress, weapons, etc. were absolutely authentic by keeping a large collection of armour, helmets, swords, pistols, daggers, saddles and uniforms to which he constantly referred (he most enjoyed depicting the period of the Roundheads and Cavaliers). He exhibited in oils and watercolours many times at the Royal Academy, the Royal Institute and the Grosvenor Gallery in London. He became a member of the Royal Society of British Artists and also of the Royal Institute of Painters in Water-Colours. He spent his later years living at a house in the Upper Richmond Road, Barnes, Surrey (now outer London). Gordon Browne died in 1932.

Browne, Tom

Born 1872 in Nottingham, and educated at St Mary's National School there, leaving when he was only eleven to work as an errand-boy for a local firm. He did several similar jobs until he was fifteen, when he was apprenticed to a lithographic company in Nottingham. He began his artistic career by designing cigar-box labels, then, at seventeen, he had his first humorous black-and-white sketches accepted by the magazine *Scraps*. He received thirty shillings for them and, since this sum represented three months' wages, began to think seriously of trying to make his living at illustration work. He subsequently moved to London and began doing a vast amount of comic drawing and illustration. His first major success came in 1896 when he created a pair of the most famous and best-loved comic paper characters of all time, Weary Willie and Tired Tim, the blissfully idle tramps who made their bow on the front page of *Chips* in 1896. They remained there until the paper's demise in 1953 (subsequently drawn, of course, by other hands). It is said that Browne eventually gave up drawing the Weary Willie and Tired Tim strip because he started to dream of the characters and they began to play on his nerves. Other pens willingly took them up. There was a time when Browne was turning out seven sets of six drawings apiece weekly for various comic papers in the 1890s. His drawings appeared on postcards and in numerous magazines and papers, both juvenile and adult, including *Punch*. He visited America twice during the early 1900s and his work appeared with enormous success in papers such as the *New York Herald*, the *New York Times* and the *Chicago Tribune*. He also developed a great love for Holland and his paintings and drawings of the people and places in that country enjoyed a tremendous vogue at one time. In 1897 he exhibited at the Royal Academy for the first time and later had many further pictures hung there. He became a member of the Royal Society of British Artists in 1898 and of the Royal Institute of Painters in Water-Colours in 1901. He died in 1910.

Burningham, John

Born in 1935. In 1953, as an alternative to National Service, he joined the Friends' Ambulance Unit, also working at farming, slum-clearance, forestry and school-building in Italy and at demolition in Israel. He had always been keenly interested in drawing and, on his return to England in 1955, he began his studies at the Central School of Arts and Crafts in London. Upon leaving he concentrated on commercial art and gradually won a name for himself with his striking and colourful posters, especially those for London Transport and the British Transport Commission. His posters, often seen on the London Underground, frequently featured dogs, horses and little men, and his bold designs were also seen in magazine advertisements (including *Vogue*) and even on corn-flake packets. In 1963 he wrote and illustrated his first children's book: *Borka: the Adventures of a Goose With No Feathers*. Burningham's vivid, bold, poster-like coloured pictures won him the Kate Greenaway Medal for 1963. *Trubloff: the Mouse Who Wanted to Play the Balalaika* followed in 1964, again both written and illustrated by Burningham. In 1964–65 he illustrated the late Ian Fleming's humorous fantasy for children, *Chitty-Chitty Bang-Bang*, which told of the adventures of a magical car and was issued in three volumes. Also in 1964 came *John Burningham's A.B.C.*, supplying strong, highly-coloured images to the letters of the alphabet. *Humbert, Mr Firkin and the Lord Mayor of London* (1965) was another Burningham solo which told the delightful story of a scrap-iron merchant's horse who comes to draw the Lord Mayor's coach through the streets of London. In 1966 Burningham tried his hand at something new – colourful wall-friezes for children's rooms. There were three of them, measuring 8 ft by 1 ft, and the titles were *Storyland, Birdland* and *Lionland*. Another picture-story book, *Cannonball Simp* – about an ugly but appealing little dog in a circus – was also published in 1966. After that came *Harquin: the Fox Who Went Down to the Valley* (1967).

Caldecott, Randolph

Born on 22nd March 1846, in Chester, Cheshire, the son of an accountant and educated at King's School, Chester, where he became Head Boy. At fifteen he was working in a bank at Whitchurch, Shropshire, where he remained for six years. During this period he lived in an old farm-house, went fishing and shooting, watched the local Hunts, attended cattle markets and fairs and generally acquired a deep knowledge of and liking for country life – all of which was to be useful in his later illustrations. In 1867 he was transferred to a bank in Manchester, where he stayed for a further five years. He had been interested in sketching since childhood and now studied in his spare time at the Manchester School of Art, also joining the Brasenose Club and meeting (and learning from) a host of new artistic friends. His first drawings appeared in a paper called *Will o' the Wisp* in July 1868, and the following year another paper, *The Sphinx*, ran several pages of his work. In 1871 Caldecott's drawings began to appear in *London Society* and in 1872 he resigned his job at the bank in Manchester and went to London to earn his living as an artist. His work began to appear regularly in several London magazines, including *Punch*, and he made several important friendships with leading artists, including George du Maurier and Charles Keene. The first book he illustrated was *The Harz Mountains; a Tour in the Toy Country*, written by Henry Blackburn, in 1872. He also began to contribute regularly to the London *Graphic* and the American *Harper's Monthly Magazine*. The London *Pictorial World* also used regular drawings. Caldecott's illustrations to Washington Irving's *Old Christmas* and *Bracebridge Hall* (both published in 1876) established his reputation and achieved enormous success. In 1878 Edmund Evans, who was looking for someone to illustrate a new series of toy picture books for publishers Routledge (following on the success of Walter Crane's work in this field), invited Caldecott to illustrate a pair of children's books in colour. Thus it was that, in 1878, the first of Randolph Caldecott's now famous picture books appeared: *The House That Jack Built* and William Cowper's ballad *John Gilpin*. He continued to produce two titles in the colourful toy books series each year until shortly before his death – a total of sixteen in all. They include (in addition to the first pair) Oliver Goldsmith's *Elegy on a Mad Dog* and *The Babes in the Wood* (1879), *Three Jovial Huntsmen* and *Sing a Song of Sixpence* (1880), *The Queen of Hearts* and *The Farmer's Boy* (1881), *The Milkmaid* and *Hey-Diddle-Diddle* (and *Baby Bunting*) (1882), *The Fox Jumps Over the Parson's Gate* and *A Frog He Would A-Wooing Go* (1883), *Come Lasses and Lads* and *Ride a Cock*

Horse to Banbury Cross (and *A Farmer Went Trotting*) (1884) and Goldsmith's *Mrs Mary Blaize* and Samuel Foote's *The Great Panjandrum* (1885). The whole series has sold well over a million copies and comprises Caldecott's best-known and most-loved work. His illustrations to the toy books are full of life and action and humour, with animals and country scenes being particularly well depicted. They are all still in print today. Originally appearing separately in paper covers, the toy books were later issued in four volumes (each containing four titles): *Picture Books 1* and *2*, *Hey-Diddle-Diddle Picture Book* and *The Panjandrum Picture Book*. Later still they appeared in two volumes (with eight titles in each) as *Collection of Pictures and Songs 1* (upright shape) and *2* (oblong shape). In 1879 Caldecott met popular children's author Mrs Ewing, who was a great admirer of his work. At her invitation he illustrated *Jackanapes* (1884) and *Daddy Darwin's Dovecot* (1884), also re-illustrating *Lob-Lie-By-the-Fire* (originally published 1874). He also designed the cover for *Aunt Judy's Magazine* (in its later period) in which many of Mrs Ewing's tales first appeared. In 1883 Caldecott's version of Aesop's Fables (brought up-to-date) was regarded as a disappointment, even by the artist himself. He illustrated other books, and further collections of his sketches, etc. were published, but his work for children really ended with *The Great Panjandrum*. Never robust, he went to America in 1886 in search of health – but on 12th February of that same year he died in St Augustine, Florida, at the early age of forty. In 1938 the first Caldecott Medal Award was presented in America; this was – and is – given to the artist responsible for the most distinguished American picture book for children chosen from those first published in the United States during the previous year. Its British equivalent is the Kate Greenaway Medal.

Chapman, Charles Henry

Born on 1st April 1879, in Thetford, Norfolk, and educated at Kendrick School, Reading, Berkshire. He showed an aptitude for art at school and, on leaving, studied drawing under the late Allen W. Seaby, Professor of Fine Art at Reading University. He was later apprenticed to an architect at Basingstoke, but found he enjoyed turning out humorous drawings and cartoons more than applying himself to draughtsmanship and design. He began sending his work to London editors and, in 1900, celebrated his twenty-first birthday by having a drawing accepted by the boys' magazine *The Captain*. Over the next few years his drawings appeared in numerous boys' papers and comic papers until, in 1911, Chapman joined the staff of *The Magnet*, which ran Frank Richards' popular stories about Greyfriars School, Billy Bunter, Harry Wharton and Co, and the rest. He took over the illustrating work from an artist named Arthur Clarke, who had died suddenly. Chapman did so well that his association with *The Magnet* continued until the paper's demise in 1940. For nearly thirty years he drew Billy Bunter and the rest of the ever popular Greyfriars characters, so helping to immortalise one of juvenile literature's most famous schoolboys. He also illustrated the long series of Bunter books from 1955 until they ended in 1965. Today, in his late eighties, Chapman is still drawing Bunter (his privately published *The Billy Bunter Picture Book* in 1967 was a magnificent achievement, depicting the 'fat owl of the Remove' in a hundred-and-one moods and guises) and maintains that he keeps fit by cycling, walking and taking a daily cold bath! He lives at Tokers Green, near Reading in Berkshire.

Crane, Walter

Born 1845 in Liverpool, the son of Thomas Crane, a well-known painter of portraits, from whom he derived his love of art. At fourteen he drew a set of coloured page designs for Tennyson's *Lady of Shalott*, which were shown to John Ruskin and to W. J. Linton, the London wood-engraver. They enthused and Crane joined Linton in London as an apprentice for a period of three years from 1859. He also studied in evening classes at Heatherley's Art School. He illustrated his first book, J. R. Wise's *The New Forest, Its History and Scenery*, in 1862, at the age of seventeen, and the following year did his first illustrations for a children's book, *The True, Pathetic History of Poor Match*, a dog story by Holme Lee. He also designed many of the yellow-hued paper-covered railway-bookstall popular novels and this led to meetings with pioneer colour printer and engraver Edmund Evans, with whom he (and later Randolph Caldecott and Kate

Greenaway) was to become closely associated. Evans, who was starting his epoch-making campaign to persuade publishers that the public would buy good, well designed picture books if given the chance instead of the crude, coarsely printed works then so prevalent, invited Crane to illustrate a series of children's toy picture books. Crane readily agreed and in 1865 the first titles appeared, including *The Railroad Alphabet, The Farmyard ABC, The House That Jack Built, The History of Cock Robin, Dame Trot and Her Comical Cat* and *Sing a Song of Sixpence*. Others in the first 6*d*. series included *This Little Pig, One, Two, Buckle My Shoe, The Fairy Ship, Annie and Jack in London, Multiplication in Verse, Grammar in Rhyme* and *King Luckieboy's Party*. The 6*d*. titles (all undated and difficult to place accurately in year of publication) ran between 1865 and 1873. In 1873 a new series of 1*s*. toy picture books began, ending in 1876. Titles included *Blue-Beard, Cinderella, Little Red Riding-Hood, Puss-in-Boots* (all 1873), *Jack and the Beanstalk* (1874), *Goody Two-Shoes* (1874), *Beauty and the Beast* (1875) and *The Sleeping Beauty* (1876). His later picture books and indeed much of his later work generally show the effects of two major influences, Japanese prints and Italy. A naval friend presented him with a collection of Japanese prints during the mid-1860s and they excited him enormously; he loved the definite black outline and flat, brilliant yet delicate colours, allied to the vivid, dramatic and decorative effect. In 1871, following his marriage, he went to Italy for a long stay and later admitted that the trip had something of an 'Italianising' influence on his work. It was, incidentally, his older sister, Lucy Crane, who wrote most of the rhymed versions of the old nursery and fairy stories for his picture books. They numbered about forty and were best-sellers in their day. They were also published in various omnibus collections, including *King Luckieboy's Picture Book* (1871) (containing four titles), *Walter Crane's New Toy Book* (1873) (containing eight titles) and *Goody Two-Shoes' Picture Book* (1875) (containing four titles). In the 'seventies Crane's work began to become more intricate and decorative, a mixture of his own sophisticated style added to Pre-Raphaelite, Japanese, and William Morris. Not content to make his picture a mere illustration, it had to be a design too, and where possible an integral part of the design of the book in which it appeared. He loved decorative borders on his pages and did them brilliantly. His work generally (and with notable exceptions) was perhaps confusing and complicated to the average child who might have preferred something simpler. Adult readers could appreciate the beauty of his designs but only perhaps a minority of children would find them absorbing. Crane nevertheless played an invaluable and key part in the development of children's book illustration and, with Caldecott and Greenaway, makes up a trio of artists who stand in a class by themselves in nineteenth-century children's literature. Crane, in fact, collaborated with Kate Greenaway in *The Quiver of Love: a Collection of Valentines, Ancient and Modern* (1876). A trio of Crane's most popular children's books comprised *The Baby's Opera* (1877), a collection of old English nursery rhymes and songs complete with music, coloured pictures and decorative borders, *The Baby's Bouquet* (1878), a similar anthology including French and German songs as well as English ones, and *The Baby's Own Aesop* (1886). The rhymes and tunes for the first two titles were collected and arranged by Lucy Crane. The text of Aesop was by Crane's old employer and teacher, W. J. Linton, by then living in America. In 1882 came Crane's illustrations to his sister Lucy's translation of *Household Tales from Grimm*. Crane's illustrations to Mrs Molesworth's *Tell Me a Story* in 1875 marked the beginning of a long association with that popular and prolific children's writer. He went on to illustrate about fifteen further books by Mrs Molesworth including *Carrots* (1876), *The Cuckoo Clock* (1877), *The Tapestry Room* (1879), *A Christmas Child* (1880), *Herr Baby* (1881) and *Four Winds Farm* (1887). Crane's other illustration work was versatile and varied. Among the many other books he illustrated were: *The Head of the Family* by Mrs Craik (1875), *The Necklace of Princess Fiorimonde* by Mary de Morgan (1880), *The First of May: a Fairy Masque* by J. R. Wise (1881) (this was probably Crane's most beautiful – and expensive – book), *Pan Pipes: a Book of Old Songs* by Theo Marzials (1883), *Slateandpencilvania* (1886); *Little Queen Anne* (1886), *Pothooks and Perseverance* (1886), *The Golden Primer* by J. M. D. Meiklejohn (1885), *The Sirens Three* (1886), *The Happy Prince and other Tales* by Oscar Wilde (1888), *Flora's Feast: a Masque of Flowers* (1889), *A Wonder Book for Boys and Girls* by Nathaniel Hawthorne (1892), *Queen Summer* (1892), *The Tempest* by William Shakespeare (1893), *The Old Garden* by Margaret

Deland (1893), *The Two Gentlemen of Verona* by Shakespeare (1894), *The Story of the Glittering Plain* by William Morris (1894), *The Merry Wives of Windsor* by Shakespeare (1894), *The Faerie Queen* ed. by Thomas J. Wise (1895), *The Walter Crane Readers* by Nelle Dale (1898), *A Floral Fantasy in An Old English Garden* (1899), *Don Quixote* retold from Cervantes by Judge Parry (1900) and *A Flower Wedding* (1905). Apart from his illustration work, Crane did a large number of paintings, both in oil and water-colour, and murals, exhibiting at the Dudley and Grosvenor Galleries in London and in several galleries in the United States, which he visited in 1891–2. Several private and public buildings in Britain contain his friezes, mosaics, panels, wallpapers, etc. and some of his tapestry designs are at the Victoria and Albert Museum in London. He and William Morris were largely responsible for the revival of decorative arts and crafts in England. Crane was the first president of the Arts and Crafts Society, which he helped to found in 1888. He was also an ardent and active Socialist and a member of the Fabian Society. From 1893–96 he was Director of Design at the Manchester School of Art and lectured widely (two of his lecture courses were later published as books). For a time he was Principal at the Royal College of Art in Kensington, London. Walter Crane, one of the most significant and influential book illustrators and designers of the nineteenth century, died in 1915.

Dulac, Edmund

Born 1882, in Toulouse, France. Studied at Toulouse University, Toulouse Art School, and Académie Julian, Paris. He was originally intended for a law career but loved painting and decided to make this his livelihood instead. He had annual shows at the Leicester Galleries, London, from 1907 to 1918 and in 1912 became a British citizen. Among his first book illustration commissions were editions of *Jane Eyre* (1905) and *Wuthering Heights* (1905), followed by the *Arabian Nights Entertainments* (1907), *The Tempest* (1908), *The Sleeping Beauty* (1910), *Stories from Hans Andersen* (1912), Hawthorne's *Tanglewood Tales* (1918) and Stevenson's *Treasure Island* (1927). In 1916 he published *Edmund Dulac's Fairy Book* and also around this period came *Edmund Dulac's Picture Book*. His de luxe illustrated gift books were almost as popular and sought-after as those of Arthur Rackham, his contemporary. Dulac enjoyed a versatile career during which he painted portraits and drew caricatures of notables of the day, designed stage sets and costumes, designed several British and French postage stamps (including the British Coronation stamp of 1937), and made the King's Poetry Prize Medal. He died in 1953.

Duvoisin, Roger

Born 1904 in Geneva, Switzerland, the son of an architect. He studied in Geneva at École Professionelle, École des Arts et Métiers, and École des Beaux Arts. On leaving art school he did mural painting, stage scenery, posters, illustration work and pottery design. Then he went to Lyons and Paris to design textiles. His textile work took him to America in the late 1920s and he has lived and worked there ever since. His first book was *A Little Boy Was Drawing* (1932), which he originally wrote for his own small son. Later came illustrations to *Mother Goose* (1936), *The Pied Piper of Hamelin* (1936), his own *Christmas Whale* (1945) and Stevenson's *A Child's Garden of Verses* (1944). In 1948 he was awarded the Caldecott Medal for *White Snow, Bright Snow*, written by Alvin Tresselt. He is probably best known for his gay, colourful pictures to the series written by his wife, Louise Fatio, about *The Happy Lion* (1955), with later titles including *The Happy Lion Roars* (1959), *The Three Happy Lions* (1960), *The Happy Lion's Quest* (1962), *The Happy Lion in Africa* (1963) and *The Happy Lion and the Bear* (1965). Duvoisin has also written and illustrated series of books about a goose, 'Petunia' (first title in 1958) and a hippopotamus, 'Veronica' (first title in 1962). He has illustrated many other children's books, written by himself and by others. He wrote and illustrated *The Missing Milkman* in 1968.

Folkard, Charles James

Born 1878 in Lewisham, London, and educated at Colfe's Grammar School there. Studied art at Goldsmith's College and the Blackheath and Sidcup Schools of Art. Did many fine colour and black-and-white illustrations for editions of Grimm,

Andersen, Aesop, the *Arabian Nights*, *Alice's Adventures in Wonderland* and also for many other books for children, chiefly during the first thirty years of the century. Folkard's main claim to fame, however, is as the creator of 'Teddy Tail', an adventurous mouse whose adventures comprised the first British newspaper picture-strip, making its bow in the *Daily Mail* in 1915 and continuing until a few years ago. Folkard did the illustrations for the popular *Teddy Tail Annuals* too. He died in 1963.

Furniss, Harry

Born 26th March 1854, in Wexford, Ireland, and educated at Wesleyan College, St Stephen's Green, Dublin, where he edited a magazine called *The Schoolboys' 'Punch'* and contributed many of his first cartoons to it. At seventeen he had left school and was drawing cartoons and illustrations for a wide range of publications, from *Zozimus* (the Irish equivalent of *Punch* at that time) to religious works. He left Dublin at nineteen and went to try his luck in London, where he began contributing to such magazines as *London Society*, *Illustrated London News* and *Cornhill*. In 1880 he joined the staff of *Punch* and became one of its most talented and popular artists. He specialised in the parliamentary scene and came to know most of the leading political personalities of the day. With a famous political cartoon of Gladstone he 'invented' the Gladstone collar. With another cartoon – showing a tramp writing a 'testimonial' reading 'Two years ago I used your soap, since when I have used no other' – he won fame as the creator of one of the most celebrated advertisements (for Pear's soap) of all time. His early book illustration work included drawings for Thackeray's *Ballads* and *The Rose and the Ring* (with Du Maurier, Thackeray, etc.) in 1879. In 1885–86 he illustrated a series of four picture books called *Holiday Romps*. He is probably best known in the field of children's books by his illustrations to Lewis Carroll's *Sylvie and Bruno* (1889) and *Sylvie and Bruno Concluded* (1893), and also for his pictures to G. E. Farrow's nonsense classic *The Wallypug of Why* (which was 'co-illustrated' by his daughter Dorothy) (1895). Father and daughter also collaborated on Farrow's *The Missing Prince* (1896). (Later 'Wallypug' books were illustrated by Alan Wright.) Furniss illustrated many other books, most of them humorous or sporting, and also wrote and illustrated two autobiographical works: *Confessions of a Caricaturist* (1901) and *Harry Furniss at Home* (1903). In 1912 he executed 500 full-page illustrations for a new eighteen-volume edition of the works of Charles Dickens. He was one of the great social personalities of his time and a celebrated lecturer, raconteur and clubman; he even wrote and appeared in two early motion pictures. He died in 1925.

Greenaway, Kate

Born on 17th March 1846, at No. 1, Cavendish Street, Hoxton, London, the daughter of John Greenaway, a noted wood-engraver and draughtsman, and his wife, Elizabeth Jones. She spent much of her early childhood on a farm at Rolleston, near Newark, Nottinghamshire, enjoying protracted holidays there and gaining her great love of country life. After a move to Islington her family settled down at Highbury, in North London, where Mrs Greenaway ran a successful shop, selling children's dresses, lace and fancy goods. Kate's education was spasmodic and mostly comprised private lessons, but she had been a keen artist from her earliest days and by the time she was twelve she was attending art classes at Miss Springet's School at Canonbury House. Here she won many prizes and awards for her work and subsequently studied at Heatherley's and at the newly opened Slade School in London. At twenty-two she was exhibiting a water-colour and a series of drawings on wood at the Dudley Gallery, where her work was seen and purchased by the editor of the *People's Magazine*. Her drawings appeared in this publication and were followed by early, unsigned work for Kronheim and Company, the colour printers; among her commissions for this firm was an illustrated picture book, *Diamonds and Toads*, in the *Aunt Louisa's London Toy Books* series, published by Warne's. In 1871 she did illustrations for a group of toy books, including *Babes in the Wood*, *Tom Thumb*, *Red Riding Hood* and *Puss in Boots*. She also designed a series of Christmas and birthday cards, as well as several Valentine cards (later published in a book *The Quiver of Love* in 1876). Her work was appearing in such diverse magazines as *Little Folks* and the *Illustrated London News* too. Other early book illustrations were for *Fairy Gifts* (1874), *Poor Nelly* (1878) and *Topo* (1878). In 1877 she had a picture accepted for exhibition at the Royal Academy. Kate Greenaway's first major success was *Under the Window: Pictures and Rhymes for Children* (1878), which she both wrote and illustrated in colour. The book was a masterpiece (for that period) of colour printing and was carried out by the brilliant Edmund Evans, who was also closely associated with illustrators Crane and Caldecott, among others. It was a sensation – in Europe and America as well as in Britain – and sold 100,000 copies in its first editions. Kate Greenaway's verses were charming enough, but it was her illustrations that really attracted people. They generally depicted delightful little children, usually girls, wearing enchanting frilly, be-ribboned dresses, sun-bonnets and cloaks, engaged in pretty pastimes such as taking tea on the lawn, picking flowers or fruit, playing or dancing. Her characters were always shown in beautiful idyllic settings, in entrancing colours, with flowers usually much in evidence, either in the pictures or in decorative borders, or both. *Under the Window* became one of the most influential children's picture books ever published, and almost at once Kate Greenaway became a household name throughout Britain, America, and many other parts of the world. Other illustrators soon began to copy her style, almost exactly – but there was nothing quite like the original Greenaway. *Under the Window* was published by George Routledge and Sons, who subsequently published most of her later major titles. A word on the now famous Kate Greenaway costumes worn by the children in her books: she did not copy the styles from an old book. Rather she thought back to the late eighteenth century (to the characters of Jane Austen, perhaps) and also to the type of clothes worn by the country children around Rolleston when she was a child, and 'adapted' them to her own use. She would design and make the dresses herself and put them on real-life child models or lay figures to obtain the most realistic and satisfactory effect. Her mob-capped and high-waisted, be-muffed and demure little girls had probably never really existed in real life – but they did soon after Kate Greenaway's books achieved popular success and a new fashion was born. An early encourager, admirer and friend was John Ruskin, who even lectured on her work at Oxford. In 1880 came *Kate*

Greenaway's Birthday Book for Children, with 382 illustrations by Kate Greenaway and verses by Mrs Sale Barker. The following year appeared *A Day in a Child's Life*, a book of songs with music by Myles B. Foster, and *Mother Goose, or the Old Nursery Rhymes*. As a child she had enjoyed the verses of Jane and Ann Taylor and in 1882 she illustrated *Little Ann and Other Poems* by that pair of writers. In 1883 came the first of her ever-popular *Almanacks*; an *Almanack* was to appear for each subsequent year (with the exception of 1896) until 1897 – a series of fourteen in all. Among her many other books are: *Language of Flowers* (1884); *Dame Wiggins of Lee and Her Seven Wonderful Cats* (1885) (a new edition of the old rhyme with extra verses by John Ruskin); *Marigold Garden* (1885); *A Apple Pie* (1886); *The Queen of the Pirate Isle* (1886) (by Bret Harte); *The Pied Piper of Hamelin* (1888) (by Robert Browning); *Kate Greenaway's Book of Games* (1889) and – her last work – *The April Baby's Book of Tunes* (1900) (by the author of *Elizabeth and Her German Garden*). She also contributed to many magazines, including *The Girls' Own Paper* and *St Nicholas*. She exhibited at several leading galleries and was elected a member of the Royal Institute of Painters in Water-Colours in 1889. By 1900 her great friend Ruskin had died, to her sadness, and she was suffering from continual ill-health. She was planning to illustrate a new edition of William Blake's *Songs of Innocence* when she died, at her home at Frognal, Hampstead, on 6th November 1901. She was buried in Hampstead Cemetery and many tributes were paid to her throughout the world. To this day she remains probably the best-loved illustrator of children's books – and especially children – of all. In 1955 the Library Association of Great Britain established the 'Kate Greenaway Medal', to be awarded annually to the artist who has produced the most distinguished work in the illustration of children's books during the year (the artist has to be domiciled in Britain and the book published there).

Henry, Thomas

Born 1879, in Eastwood, Nottinghamshire, under his real name of Thomas Henry Fisher, in the house opposite that of D. H. Lawrence. He was the son of an engineer and educated at

Hollygirt School, Nottingham, later studying at Nottingham School of Art. At the age of fourteen he was apprenticed to Messrs Forman and Sons, newspaper proprietors and printers, in Nottingham. One of his first jobs was on the lithographic work for the original colour production of the famous 'Sailor' trade-mark of Player's Cigarettes. He later became a showcard and poster designer and regular newspaper cartoonist for the *Nottingham Guardian*. His cartoons and humorous illustrations appeared in practically every leading magazine and humorous weekly, including *Punch*. He did countless drawings for such periodicals as *The Captain, Chums, Home Magazine, Crusoe* and *Happy*. He became most famous for his inimitable illustrations to Richmal Crompton's ever-popular 'William' books, from the first, *Just William*, in 1922, to the thirty-fourth, *William and the Witch*, in 1964 (also part-illustrated by his successor, Henry Ford). His first pictures of 'William' appeared, together with the original stories, in the pages of *Home Magazine* in 1920 and subsequently in *Happy Magazine*. An interesting point is that, despite their long and successful association, it was not until 1954 that Thomas Henry and Richmal Crompton actually met; the occasion was a dinner held during the Nottingham Book Festival. Henry used a seemingly casual but witty technique and, apart from his 'William' work, was at his best in illustrating humorous stories and boys' school tales. He exhibited his work at the Walker Art Gallery, London, and at Nottingham Castle. He died suddenly on 15th October 1962, while working on a 'William' drawing.

Hilder, Rowland

Born on 28th June 1905, in Long Island, New York, of British parents. His spent his childhood and received his early education in Morristown, New Jersey, before going to live in London in 1916. His education was completed at Aske's, Hatcham, New Cross, London. He had crossed the Atlantic several times as a boy and it was through these trips that he developed his love of the sea and ships. It was also in his youth that he made regular voyages in coasters and sailing ships, often sailing to the Continent. He had always enjoyed drawing and had ambitions to illustrate books from an early age. He studied under E. J. Sullivan at Goldsmith's College School of Art, London, between 1922–25 (subsequently teaching there himself for several years until 1939) and exhibited his first painting at the Royal Academy when he was only eighteen. He later became one of Britain's most accomplished and successful painters and illustrators, with the main emphasis of his best work being upon maritime and country scenes. His paintings have been widely exhibited and he is represented in several leading English art galleries as well as in the National Gallery at Sydney, New South Wales. His first major book illustrations were to an edition of Melville's *Moby Dick* in 1926. His subsequent illustrations include those to John Masefield's *The Midnight Folk* (1927), Stevenson's *Treasure Island* (1929), Harold Avery's *No Surrender* (1933), Monica Redlich's *Five Farthings* (1939), and *The Shell Guide to Flowers of the Countryside* (1955) (in collaboration with his wife, Edith Hilder). He also illustrated a modern edition of the Bible and several volumes by Mary Webb. Rowland Hilder is President of the Royal Institute of Painters in Water-Colours and a Member of the Society of Marine Artists and of the Wapping Group. He lives at Blackheath, London, and maintains a twenty-six-foot cabin-cruiser in which he makes frequent sea trips.

Hodges, Cyril Walter

Born on 18th March 1909, in Beckenham, Kent, and educated at Dulwich College. On leaving school he studied under Edmund J. Sullivan at Goldsmith's College School of Art, London. While there he developed a deep love for stage and costume designing, becoming especially interested in the theatre and dress of Shakespeare's time. On leaving art school he worked on a number of productions at the Everyman Theatre, in Hampstead, designing both costumes and scenery. He only earned around thirty shillings a week, however, and decided to take a job in an advertising agency which paid considerably more. He found the work dull and uninspiring and left after a short period, deciding to concentrate on free-lance illustration and commercial art work. His first published drawing appeared in the BBC's *Radio Times* in 1931 and he contributed regularly to that magazine for many years afterwards. The first book he illustrated was L. A. G. Strong's *King Richard's Land* in 1934. It was followed by *Treasures of English Verse* (edited by Herbert Strang) (1934), Gerald Bullett's *The Happy Mariners* (1935), L. A. G. Strong's *Mr Sheridan's Umbrella* (1935), Leslie Barringer's *Know Ye Not Agincourt* (1936), Sir William Beach Thomas's *The Squirrel's Granary* (1936) (later re-issued as *A Countryman's Anthology*), and C. Fox Smith's *The Ship Aground* (1940). In 1939 C. Walter Hodges (as he always signs himself) wrote and illustrated *Columbus Sails*, which quickly established itself as a classic of juvenile literature. It described, in vivid prose and beautiful pictures, the story of Columbus's first voyage to the New World. He went on to illustrate over fifty more books and to write a further seven, including: G. B. Harrison's *New Tales from Shakespeare* (1938), Elizabeth Goudge's *Sister of the Angels* and *Smoky House* (both 1940), Ursula Hourihane's *Adventures of Buttons and Mac* (1946), Elizabeth Goudge's Carnegie Award-winning *The Little White Horse* (1946), Hodges' own humorous fantasy *The Flying House* (which he wrote and illustrated) (1947), re-issues of E. Nesbit's *The Treasure Seekers*, *The Would-Be-Goods* and *The New Treasure Seekers* (all 1947), Ian Serraillier's *They Raced for Treasure*, C. Fox Smith's *Painted Ports* (1948), Elizabeth Goudge's *Make Believe* (1949), Wyss's *The Swiss Family Robinson* (1949), Rosemary Sutcliff's *The Queen Elizabeth Story* and *The Chronicles of Robin Hood* (both 1950), Ralph Hammond's *Cocos Gold* (1950), Rosemary Sutcliff's *Brother Dusty-Feet* (1952), *The Eagle of the Ninth* (1954) and *The Shield Ring* (1956), William Mayne's trio of stories set in the Canterbury Cathedral Choir School – *A Swarm in May* (1955), *Chorister's Cake* (1956) and *Cathedral Wednesday* (1960), *Red Indian Folk and Fairy Tales* (edited by Ruth Manning-Sanders) (1960), Robert Graves' *The Siege and Fall of Troy* (1962), Hodges' own distinguished historical novel about King Alfred, *The Namesake* (1964), again his own *Shakespeare's Theatre* (1964) (the magnificent book about theatrical life and people in Shakespeare's time which won him the Kate Greenaway Medal for producing the best illustrations for a children's work in 1964), his own *The Norman Conquest* and *Magna Carta* (both 1966) and a new edition of Geoffrey Trease's *Bows Against the Barons* (1966). C. Walter Hodges served in the armed forces throughout the Second World War and took part in the landings on the Normandy beaches. In 1951 he designed (with Michael Stringer) the stage for the original Mermaid Theatre in St John's Wood; Hodges and Stringer also designed the stage for the present Mermaid Theatre in London, which opened in 1959. Hodges' deep interest in Elizabethan and Shakespearian matters is reflected in two major adult books he wrote and illustrated: *Shakespeare and the Players* (1948) and *The Globe Restored* (1953). He has also contributed to the annual Shakespeare Survey. In 1934 he designed a mural ninety feet in length for the Museum of the Chartered Insurance Institute of London; he also executed a mural painting for the United Kingdom Provident Institute in 1957. Hodges has been one of Britain's most accomplished illustrators for more than a quarter of a century and he is particularly at home in depicting Tudor, Elizabethan, Shakespearean, country and maritime scenes. His historical details are always absolutely authentic and are the result of considerable research and knowledge. He is a Member of the Society of Industrial Artists. He is married, with two sons in their early twenties, and lives at Seaford, on the Sussex coast.

Horrabin, James Francis

Born 1884 and educated at Stamford Grammar School, Lincolnshire, subsequently studying at Sheffield Technical School of Art. Became well known for his superlative map-drawing, diagrams and atlas work, illustrating many books including H. G. Wells' *Outline of History* and Lancelot Hogben's *Mathematics for the Million*. Later appeared in and drew maps for many BBC TV programmes in the late 1940s, including television news programmes. Also broadcast as member of the BBC radio Brains Trust team, 1942–46. He is probably best known, however, for his popular newspaper strip-cartoon series featuring *Happy and Japhet*, which ran in the London *News Chronicle* from 1919 until 1950. This entertaining and humorous strip recounted the daily adventures of Mr and Mrs Noah, their bespectacled son, Japhet, and a whole host of resident animals, notably a small and resourceful brown bear named Happy. A thriving juvenile club – the Arkubs – grew up around the characters and boasted a membership of many thousands. A series of *Happy and Japhet Annuals* appeared between 1921–51 too and are today collectors' items. Horrabin also created the *Dot and Carrie* strip which appeared in the London evening newspaper *The Star* for nearly forty years. Was a Member of the Society of Industrial Artists. He died in 1962.

Hughes, Arthur

Born in London, in 1832, and studied art at Somerset House and at the Royal Academy Schools in London, being a fellow-student of both Holman Hunt and Rossetti and also a member of the Pre-Raphaelite movement. With others, he decorated the Oxford University Union, with frescoes, in 1858. Among his several famous oil-paintings are 'April Love' and 'Eve of St Agnes', revered during Victorian times and still highly regarded today. He was also a fine water-colourist. But he excelled in black-and-white drawings. His first book illustrations appeared in William Allingham's *Music Master* (which also included one drawing each by Millais and Rossetti) in 1855. In 1867 he began his distinguished association with George MacDonald, when he illustrated the latter's *Dealings With Fairies*, a collection of stories. In 1868 he illustrated MacDonald's *At the Back of the North Wind*, when it originally ran as a serial in the magazine *Good Words for the Young*; the story and pictures eventually appeared in book form in 1871. Hughes subsequently illustrated nearly all MacDonald's later children's stories, including *Ranald Bannerman's Boyhood* (1871), *The Princess and the Goblin* (1872), *The Princess and Curdie* (1883) and *Gutta Percha Willie* (1873). MacDonald's *Phantastes: a Faerie Romance*, originally appeared in 1858, without illustrations; when an illustrated edition later appeared – without the author's sanction – Greville MacDonald (his son) was so distressed that he later persuaded Hughes to supply the drawings for a new edition in 1905. And when Greville published two children's books of his own – *The Magic Crook* (1911) and *Jack and Jill* (1913) – Hughes, then around eighty, illustrated them too. Apart from his association with MacDonald, Hughes illustrated many other books, including (with Sydney Prior Hall) the first illustrated edition of Thomas Hughes' *Tom Brown's Schooldays*. Others included

334

Mother Goose's National Nursery Rhymes (with others) (1870), *Christmas Carols* (with others) (1871), Christina Rossetti's *Sing-Song* (1872) and *Speaking Likenesses* (1874), and *Babies' Classics* (1904). Hughes' illustrations – especially those for MacDonald's fantasies – usually had a rather beautiful, serious, graceful, almost spiritual quality. Dream-like, out-of-this-world, magical and flowing, they are at once haunting and memorable, while being very much of their period. When the occasion called for it, however, he could throw off his dream-like air and depict sturdy, laughing boys and girls, and country life and animals with superb artistry. And, as Tenniel is for ever linked with Carroll, so Hughes will always be associated with MacDonald; in both instances, the writer discovered an artist who could make his characters live as no one else ever could. Arthur Hughes died in 1915.

Jacques, Robin

Born 1920 in Chelsea, London, and educated at the Royal Masonic Schools, Bushey, Hertfordshire. Received no formal art training, but worked from the age of sixteen and practised his drawing in the evenings and at week-ends. Served with the Royal Engineers during the Second World War and began illustrating books soon after the war ended. Within a few years he had illustrated such titles as *Don Quixote*, Hans Andersen's *Fairy Tales*, *Gulliver's Travels* and *The Arabian Nights*. He was art editor of the *Strand Magazine*, 1948–50, and principal art editor for the Central Office of Information, 1950–51. He has also worked for advertising agencies. Over the years, Jacques has established himself as one of Britain's foremost illustrators and his elegant style and wealth of character and detail have come to be immediately recognisable. He has illustrated many children's books, one of the most outstanding being Walter de la Mare's *Collected Stories for Children*, in 1957. More recently he has won high praise for his drawings to Ruth Manning-Sanders' 'Book of . . .' series, including: *The Book of Giants* (1962), *The Book of Dwarfs* (1963), *The Book of Dragons* (1964), *The Book of Witches* (1965), *The Book of Wizards* (1966) and *The Book of Mermaids* (1967).

Jones, Harold

Born on 22nd February 1904, in London, and educated at St Dunstan's College, Catford, South London. He originally intended to make farming his career but, after working on a farm near Stratford-upon-Avon for a year, he decided that his true vocation lay in the field of art, which he had always loved. He returned to London and studied at Camberwell School of Arts and Crafts. From there he went to the Royal College of Art, in South Kensington, and studied under Sir William Rothenstein (who subsequently painted Jones' portrait, which today hangs in the National Gallery of Canada, in Toronto). His studies at the R.C.A. led to an intense interest in lithography, which later had a direct influence on his work. On leaving the College he taught art and began his illustration work. His earliest pictures were for M. E. Atkinson's *August Adventure* in 1936, followed by the same author's *Mystery Manor* in 1937. In 1937 the late Walter de la Mare happened to see a series of coloured lithographs Jones had made depicting the various phases of a year as remembered in a child's mind. Jones had originally intended to write his own verses for the pictures, but when de la Mare said he would very much like to write them Jones readily agreed. The resulting partnership between poet and artist produced *This Year, Next Year* (1937), generally agreed to be one of the loveliest children's books ever published and a minor classic in its own right. De la Mare was so delighted with the work that he wrote a special tribute in verse to Jones, whose original lithographs for the book can today be seen in London's Victoria and Albert Museum. Next, Jones renewed his association with M. E. Atkinson, illustrating her *The Compass Points North* (1938), *Smugglers' Gap* (1939), *Going Gangster* (1940) and *Crusoe Island* (1941). By now he had two small daughters and decided to write and illustrate a book for each of them. The first was *The Visit to the Farm* (1941). Then came the Second World War, during which he served in the army, in the Royal Engineers (one of his tasks was to help draw the D-Day maps for the invasion of Europe). After the war his first job was to write and illustrate the long-delayed book for his other little girl – *The Enchanted Night* (1947). In the same year he illustrated John Pudney's *Selected Poems*. In 1954

336

came his big triumph when he illustrated *Lavender's Blue*, a sumptuous collection of old nursery rhymes compiled by Kathleen Lines. His achievement in colour, design, detail and delightful characterisation was hailed throughout the world and the book has gone into many editions. Harold Jones has a disarming and deceptively easy simplicity in his work which has an immediate appeal, and his use of colour is impressively effective. Among his more recent illustrations have been those for *Bless This Day: a Book of Prayer for Children* compiled by Elfrida Vipont (1958), Donald Suddaby's *Prisoners of Saturn* (1957), *A Ring of Tales* (1958), *Once in Royal David's City* (1959), *Jack and the Beanstalk* (1960) (all three compiled by Kathleen Lines), *Noah and the Ark* by Kathleen Lines (1961), Robert Browning's *The Pied Piper of Hamelin* (1962) and *The Complete Greek Stories of Nathaniel Hawthorne* (1963). He is an Associate of the Royal College of Art and his work has been purchased by the Tate Gallery, the Victoria and Albert Museum, and the London County Council. He has lived for many years in Putney, London.

Kiddell-Monroe, Joan

Born on 9th August 1908, in Essex, of Scots-Welsh parents. Brought up and educated in Essex, Cheshire and London. Her love of drawing, as a child, subsequently led to her deciding to become an artist and she studied at Willesden and Chelsea Schools of Art. She worked in an advertising agency for several years before becoming a free-lance illustrator. She was inspired to write and illustrate her first book by the baby giant panda in the London Zoo and it was published, under the title *In His Little Black Waistcoat*, in 1939. In the same year she married the Canadian artist Webster Murray. During the Second World War she worked for the Women's Voluntary Service and did other war work. In 1947 three more books about the baby giant panda appeared and she went on to illustrate well over 200 books, writing a few of them too. She is probably best known for her outstanding illustrations to the seventeen volumes (so far) of the 'Oxford Myths and Legends' Series, which began in 1954 with *English Fables and Fairy Stories*, re-told by James Reeves. It has continued over the past few years, building up a

337

unique library of volumes containing folk tales and fairy stories from many different countries, some translated into English for the first time and all superlatively illustrated by Miss Kiddell-Monroe in black-and-white and in colour. Her style is almost classical and well suited to these ancient legends and heroic characters. She makes great use of plain white space and is very selective in what she puts into a picture, preferring to use too little rather than too much. Her illustrations and designs are exquisite, versatile and striking. She has illustrated several of René Guillot's children's stories, including *Sama* (1952), *Sirga* (1953), *Oworo* (1954) and *Kpo the Leopard* (1955). Another of her series has been Lorna Wood's 'Hag Dowsabel' stories, starting with *The People in the Garden* (1954). Again in classical mood she has illustrated the *Iliad of Homer* (1960), the *Odyssey of Homer* (1952), and the *Aeneid of Virgil*. Other titles include *Tam the Untamed* by M. E. Patchett (1954), *Orla of Burren* by Patricia Lynch (1954), *The Secret of the Sandhills* by Kitty Barne (1955), *Fury, Son of the Wilds* by Hazel M. Peel (1959), *The Great Gale* by Hester Burton (1960) and *The Moving Finger* by Frederick Grice (1962). In recent years Joan Kiddell-Monroe – who is a Fellow of the Royal Zoological Society of London – has lived in Mallorca, Spain.

Millar, Harold Robert

Born 1869 in Thornhill, Dumfriesshire, Scotland. Originally began studying to become a civil engineer, but gave it up to concentrate on art, which he had always really loved best. He travelled south to study at the Birmingham Municipal School of Art and, by the time he was forty, was one of Britain's most brilliant and distinguished illustrators. He became a regular illustrator to the famous *Strand Magazine* during the early 1890s and particularly excelled at fairy tales and folk stories from all parts of the world. More than 350 of these drawings were reproduced in a quartet of collections of stories: *The Golden Fairy Book* (1894), *The Silver Fairy Book* (1895), *The Diamond Fairy Book* (1897) and *The Ruby Fairy Book* (1898). A similar collection was *Fairy Tales Far and Near* (1895). Other early books he illustrated were *The Humour of Spain* (1894), *The Adventures of Hajji Baba of Ispahan* (1895), Marryat's *The*

Phantom Ship (1896), Thomas Love Peacock's *Headlong Hall* and *Nightmare Abbey* (1896), and Marryat's *Frank Mildmay* (1897) and *Snarleyyow* (1897). In 1899 Millar began his long and successful association with E. Nesbit, when he illustrated her series of magical tales in the *Strand Magazine*, subsequently collected and published in book form in 1900 as *The Book of Dragons*. He went on to illustrate most of Nesbit's best-known children's books, the majority making their original appearance in the pages of the *Strand*. They were: *Nine Unlikely Tales for Children* (1901), *Five Children and It* (1902), *The Phoenix and the Carpet* (1904), *Oswald Bastable and Others* (1905) (with C. E. Brock), *The Story of the Amulet* (1906), *The Enchanted Castle* (1907), *The House of Arden* (1908), *Harding's Luck* (1909), *The Magic City* (1910), *The Wonderful Garden* (1911), *The Magic World* (1912) (with Spencer Pryse) and *Wet Magic* (1913). Millar caught the magical half-world of Nesbit completely successfully and the author-artist combination is one of the most memorable in the world of children's books. Millar depicted the children, the enchanted, historical and everyday settings, and the strange creatures (especially the Psammead, the Phoenix, the Mouldi-warp and the Ugly-Wuglies) with equal brilliance and technical flair. His delicate black-and-white line and his sympathetic craftsmanship gave his drawings their own special touch of magic and made him an outstanding illustrator of the late nineteenth/early twentieth centuries. He contributed to many other periodicals besides the *Strand*, including *Pearson's*, *Chatterbox*, *Little Folks* and *Chums*. Among the other books he illustrated were Mrs Molesworth's *Wood-Pigeons and Mary* (1901), F. Anstey's *Only Toys!* (1903) and Kipling's *Puck of Pook's Hill* (1906). His last drawings appeared in Geoffrey Mure's *The Boots and Josephine* (1939) and he died soon afterwards.

Morton-Sale, John and Isobel

This husband-and-wife team has produced some of the loveliest drawings of children in all their moods ever to appear in books for and about children. John Morton-Sale was born in 1901 in Kensington, London, and he used to see his future wife, Isobel, at a local church they both attended. He studied at Putney

School of Art, London, and later at the Central School of Arts, London. Isobel Morton-Sale was born in 1904 in Chelsea, London, and studied at Ramsgate School of Art, Kent, and the Central School of Arts, London. Husband and wife have each illustrated books individually, but their best-known work is as a partnership. One of their first major successes was Eleanor Farjeon's *Martin Pippin in the Daisy Field* in 1937. It was also the first of several collaborations with that fine children's writer. In 1938 the Morton-Sales illustrated Farjeon's *Sing for Your Supper*, subsequently combining with the writer on a trilogy of books which comprised verse and pictures – *Cherrystones* (1942), *The Mulberry Bush* (1945) and *The Starry Floor* (1949) (these three titles later appeared between one set of covers as *Then There Were Three* in 1958). In 1945 they illustrated Beverley Nichols' *The Tree That Sat Down*. Probably their finest pictures appeared in *Something Particular* (1955), a book about music, movement and drama work with young children. Both together and individually the Morton-Sales have also done a great deal of magazine illustration work.

Parker, Eric R.

Born *c.* 1897 and educated at Northwold Road School, Stoke Newington, London. At school he showed such artistic promise that the London County Council awarded him a special art scholarship plus a maintenance grant. His first commission – a series of comic postcards – came in 1915. His early work appeared in such magazines as *Boy's Own Paper*, the *Strand* and *Corner*. His career was interrupted when he served with the Bucks Hussars in the First World War. He later resumed his artistic career and became one of the most brilliant and successful illustrators in Britain. His chief claim to fame lies in his role as the definitive illustrator of the popular fictional detective, Sexton Blake (whose adventures have appeared since 1893 and are still going strong today). Parker first began illustrating the Blake stories in the *Union Jack* magazine in the 1920s and he soon became the most popular and regular Blake artist. He continued his Blake illustrations in the *Union Jack's* successor, *Detective Weekly*, throughout the 1930s, also drawing the 'Sexton Blake Library' series cover-pictures from

1930 until 1953. He also drew the Sexton Blake picture-strip stories in the popular *Knockout Comic* for many years, as well as designing a bust of Sexton Blake which is now rarely seen. He did a prolific amount of illustration work for other juvenile papers, magazines, annuals and books and is still kept busy to-day. He has a particular liking for historical stories, especially of a military nature. He can draw a Napoleonic soldier with every button authentically reproduced and much painstaking research goes into his work.

Peake, Mervyn

Born on 9th July 1911, in Kuling, Central China, and spent his childhood there (attending Tientsin Grammar School), going to England at the age of twelve to complete his education at Eltham College, London. After studying painting and drawing at the Royal Academy Schools in London he spent over a year living and painting in Sark, in the Channel Islands. He returned to England and taught at the Westminster School of Art until the outbreak of the Second World War in 1939. He joined the army and, upon being invalided out after three years' service, worked for the Ministry of Information. In 1945 he was officially assigned to visit Belsen Concentration Camp and do drawings of the scenes there. Peake went on to gain a high reputation as artist, illustrator, novelist and poet. One of his first successes as an illustrator came in 1942 with his drawings for Lewis Carroll's *The Hunting of the Snark*. In 1945 he wrote and illustrated an amusing children's book, *Captain Slaughterboard Drops Anchor* (reissued in 1967), having in the previous year provided pictures for a collection of his poems for children, *Rhymes Without Reason*. He subsequently illustrated editions of *Grimm's Household Tales* (1946), *Treasure Island* (1949) and *Alice's Adventures in Wonderland and Through the Looking-Glass* (1954). He has also published a striking trilogy of novels: *Titus Groan* (1946), *Gormenghast* (1950) and *Titus Alone* (1962). He won the Heinemann Award for Literature in 1950. He has written two books of poetry and also a play, *The Wit To Woo*, which has been produced at the Arts Theatre in London. His paintings have been exhibited in London (where he has had five one-man shows), New York, Paris, Madrid and Dublin,

341

and have been bought by the Tate Gallery, the Victoria and Albert Museum, the Imperial War Museum and many provincial galleries. His illustrations are usually striking, grotesque, macabre – and touched with genius. His work has been compared with that of Hieronymus Bosch, Gustave Doré and Richard Doyle, but he has, in fact, his own very distinctive and immediately recognisable style. His powerful, often malevolent drawings are not, perhaps, ideally suited to children's tastes, since his work is the exact opposite of the 'pretty, charming and colourful' school. Once seen, his work is rarely forgotten. He has not been able to produce much work in recent years since he has been unfortunately dogged by illness.

Provensen, Alice and Martin

American husband-and-wife illustrating team responsible for some of the most outstanding children's books of recent years. Alice Provensen was born in 1918 and spent her childhood in Chicago. She studied at the School of the Art Institute of Chicago, the University of California at Los Angeles, and the Art Students' League in New York. Martin Provensen was born in 1916 and spent his childhood in Chicago. He studied at the School of the Art Institute of Chicago, and the University of California at Los Angeles. Despite the fact that they grew up in Chicago and attended the same art school and university, it wasn't until they had completed their education that they first met. They first collaborated on a collection of folk songs and have since illustrated many fine children's books, including the *Iliad* and the *Odyssey* (1956), *The Golden Treasury of Myths and Legends* (1959), *Aesop's Fables* (1965) and *The Giant Golden Mother Goose* (1966). They wrote, as well as illustrated, *Animal Fair*, in the late 'fifties. Their versatile pictures – sometimes brilliantly formalised, sometimes hilariously funny – are superbly executed and a delight to all ages. The Provensens' working method is to pass a drawing back and forth between one another, adding and deleting until the finished page has the approval of both artists.

Rackham, Arthur

Born in London, on 19th September 1867, and studied at the

Lambeth and Slade Schools of Art, and also in Paris. Many of his early drawings appeared in various magazines of the early 'nineties, especially the *Westminster Gazette*. His first book illustrations were for Anthony Hope's *The Dolly Dialogues*, in 1894, followed by Mrs Alfred Berlyn's *Sunrise-Land* that same year. He first came into prominence with his remarkable illustrations to Barham's *Ingoldsby Legends* (1898, with a much larger and improved edition appearing in 1907). His reputation was quickly consolidated with his work for Lamb's *Tales from Shakespeare* (1899), *Grimm's Fairy Tales* (1900) and *Gulliver's Travels* (1900). He subsequently illustrated very many books, including: Irving's *Rip Van Winkle* (1905), Barrie's *Peter Pan in Kensington Gardens* (1906), Lewis Carroll's *Alice's Adventures in Wonderland* (1907), Shakespeare's *A Midsummer Night's Dream* (1908), *Aesop's Fables* (1912), *Mother Goose: The Old Nursery Rhymes* (1913), *Arthur Rackham's Book of Pictures* (1913), Dickens' *A Christmas Carol* (1915), Malory's *King Arthur and His Knights of the Round Table* (1917), *English Fairy Tales* (1918), *Cinderella* (1919), *Irish Fairy Tales* (1920), Hawthorne's *A Wonder Book* (1922), Shakespeare's *The Tempest* (1926), *Andersen's Fairy Tales* (1932), *The Arthur Rackham Fairy Book* (1933) and Kenneth Grahame's *The Wind in the Willows* (1940 – published posthumously). Rackham was, without doubt, one of the finest illustrators of the century. His drawings and water-colours had an eerie, haunting quality all their own and he was unsurpassed at gaunt trees, shadowy woods, goblins, witches, evil spirits, fairies, gnarled old men and women, and animals. He liked browns and greys as predominant colours and his pictures nearly always seemed to be set in the autumn or winter seasons, with a cold nip in the air that one could almost feel. It was once said that his pictures were 'lyric poems in line'. His main works were often presented in big, heavy, handsome, lavish gift-book style and sold at an expensive price. Rackham editions during the first thirty years of the century were either given by adults to adults – or, more rarely perhaps, by adults to children with an indication that the book was to be kept 'for best' and looked at with clean hands only. . . . These opulent Rackham editions were the equivalent of the 'coffee-table books' of today, in a sense. They were certainly first-class pieces of book production and are collectors' items now. Rackham was a member of the Royal Institute of Painters in Water-Colours and also of the Royal Water-Colour Society. His paintings were exhibited at the Royal Academy, London, in Paris, Barcelona, Vienna, Luxembourg and Melbourne. His wife, Edyth Starkie Rackham, was a noted painter too. Arthur Rackham lived in Hampstead, London, for some years. He died in September 1939, while still working on his illustrations for *The Wind in the Willows*.

Robinson, Thomas Heath, Charles, and William Heath

The very talented Robinson brothers rate high in the list of accomplished colour and black-and-white illustrators of children's books and each worked through from the 1890s to the 1920s, 1930s and (in W. Heath's case) the 1940s. They were all born and brought up in North London, the sons of Thomas Robinson, himself a well-known artist and wood-engraver. The eldest brother, Thomas Heath Robinson, was born in Islington in 1869. He was educated at Islington High School and studied at the Islington School of Art and at Westminster Art School. His first published illustrations were to Frank Rinder's *Old World Japan* in 1895, followed in 1896 by those to Mrs Gaskell's *Cranford*. His subsequent commissions included Thackeray's *History of Henry Esmond* (1896), Hawthorne's *The Scarlet Letter* (1897), William Canton's *A Child's Book of Saints* (1898), Kingsley's *The Heroes* (1899), *Four Tales from the Arabian Nights* (1899), Wyss's *Swiss Family Robinson* (1913) and Wilson's *Story of Cortes* (1933). During the 1920s and 1930s he worked extensively for several boys' magazines, particularly *Chums*, for which he illustrated many of the fine public school stories of Gunby Hadath, Hylton Cleaver and St John Pearce. Although his work was nearly as decorative as his brothers', T. H. tended to be slightly more 'down to earth' in his approach and took great pains to ensure accuracy in the matters of dress, place, historical detail, etc. He died in 1950.

Charles Robinson was born in Islington in 1870. He was educated at Islington High School and, on leaving, was apprenticed to a lithographer, also studying art in the evenings at Islington School of Art. He made an immediate impression with his illustrations to *Aesop's Fables* in 1895, following this

344

with those for H. O. Lowry's *Make-Believe* (1896), Stevenson's *A Child's Garden of Verses* (1896) (an outstanding achievement which established his high reputation), Setoun's *Child World* (1896) and Eugene Field's *Lullaby Land* (1898). His subsequent illustrations appeared in *The True Annals of Fairyland* (three volumes, 1900–3), Jerrold's *Big Book of Fairy Tales* (1910), Lewis Carroll's *Alice's Adventures in Wonderland* (1910), Mrs Burnett's *The Secret Garden* (1911), *The Big Book of Nursery Rhymes* (1911), Blake's *Songs of Innocence* (1912), Jerrold's *Big Book of Fables* (1912), Perrault's *Fairy Tales* (1913), Wilde's *The Happy Prince* (1913) and *Mother Goose's Nursery Rhymes* (1928). Charles Robinson was the decorative artist *par excellence* and no one has excelled his intricate flower- and baby-entwined title-pages, chapter-headings and illustrations. He was at his best in these and in depicting the wistful innocence of babyhood and childhood, not forgetting fairies and enchanted woodland glades. His pictures and decorations for *A Child's Garden of Verses* and the three-volumed *True Annals of Fairyland* were *tours de force*, exquisitely imagined and designed. It was also Charles Robinson who designed the double-page title-spread used in all children's works included in the early Everyman Series. He died in 1937.

William Heath Robinson, the youngest of the brothers, was born in 1872, in Hornsey, North London, and educated at Islington High School, later studying at the Islington Art School and the Royal Academy Schools. He sold his first professional illustration to the juvenile magazine *Little Folks* and this led to other similar commissions. In 1897 came his first major work, when he illustrated *Don Quixote* and *The Pilgrim's Progress*; also that year he illustrated two children's books: Rouse's *The Giant Crab and Other Tales from Old India* and Andersen's *Danish Fairy Tales and Legends*. His subsequent illustrations included those to *The Arabian Nights Entertainments* (1899) (with others), *The Poems of Edgar Allan Poe* (1900), Lamb's *Tales from Shakespeare* (1901), Shakespeare's *Twelfth Night* (1908), Kipling's *Song of the English* (1909) and *Collected Poems* (1910), Shakespeare's *A Midsummer Night's Dream* (1914), Kingsley's *The Water Babies* (1915), de la Mare's *Peacock Pie* (1917) Perrault's *Old-Time Stories* (1921) and *Andersen's Fairy Tales* (1924). In 1913 he illustrated an edition of Rabelais'

345

Pantagruel and Gargantua. He wrote, as well as illustrated, two children's fantasies: *Uncle Lubin* (1902) and *Bill the Minder* (1912). In 1933 Heath Robinson memorably illustrated Norman Hunter's *The Incredible Adventures of Professor Branestawm.* In 1934 came Heath Robinson's *Book of Goblins*, a collection of folk and fairy tales, illustrated profusely by himself. His reputation as one of the foremost humorous artists of his period began around the First World War, when he began to pin-point the absurdities of man and his inventions. He became a regular contributor to such magazines as *The Sketch*, the *Strand* and *Punch*, and many of his comic drawings were reproduced in such books as *The Humour of Golf* (1923), *Absurdities* (1934), *Railway Ribaldry* (1935), *How to Live in a Flat* (1936) and *Heath Robinson at War* (1942). His humorous drawings depicted many ingenious and crazy – but logical – mechanical inventions and gadgets and he became so famous for these elaborate and detailed imaginings that his name gave birth to a new descriptive phrase – 'Heath Robinsonian' – used to describe a complicated and slightly weird piece of machinery or invention. Many of his later pictures also showed the pitfalls, etc. of living in a modern flat, being married, fighting a war, building a railway, playing games, and so on. Some of his later humorous books were written in collaboration with Kenneth R. G. Browne, son of Gordon Browne, the nineteenth-century illustrator. His autobiography, *My Line of Life*, was published in 1938. His paintings were exhibited at the Royal Academy. William Heath Robinson died in September 1944, his last illustrations having been for Liliane Clopet's *Once Upon a Time*. It should be added that all three Robinson brothers collaborated memorably in 1899 to illustrate *Fairy Tales from Hans Christian Andersen*, containing well over 100 drawings.

Rojankovsky, Feodor Stepanovich

Born 1891 in Mitava, Russia, and spent his childhood in Reval (now Tallin) and St Petersburg (now Leningrad). Educated at Reval High School and Moscow Academy of Fine Arts. After army service during the 1914–17 campaign he began illustrating Ukrainian children's books during the period of the Revolution. After a series of varied occupations and wide travel he began working in Paris and his first book to be published there (and also in the USA) was Esther Averill's *Daniel Boone* (1931). He subsequently illustrated many children's picture books for the famous French publisher, Père Castor, between 1932–42, a typical title being Lida's *Plouf, the Little Wild Duck* (1936). In 1941, Rojankovsky went to America, where he has lived and worked ever since, becoming one of the country's most popular children's illustrators. In 1956 he was awarded the Caldecott Medal for his illustrations to John Langstaff's *A Frog Went a-Courtin'*. He has illustrated more than 100 books, among the best-known being *The Tall Book of Mother Goose* (1942) and *The Tall Book of Nursery Tales* (1944), which became best-sellers. In 1942 he illustrated a series of four picture books based on Kipling's *Just So stories*. Rojankovsky's vivid colours, rich textures and humorous characterisation appeal enormously to children, who love the life and vigour evident in all his work.

Rountree, Harry

Born 1878, in Auckland, New Zealand, the son of a banker, and educated at Queen's College there. He arrived in London in 1901, armed with a bundle of drawings and one editorial introduction. The editor, having inspected the drawings, asked Rountree how much money he had. The surprised artist told him – and the editor promptly advised him to spend it on a return ticket to New Zealand. Rountree fortunately decided to disregard this advice and forged ahead to make a unique reputation for himself as a superlative animal artist. His animal drawings, both in colour and black-and-white, were sometimes serious, but more often than not were humorous in content. He was an expert on all aspects of animal, bird and fish life and spent hours at the London Zoo watching his 'subjects'. He was a witty, mercurial, bubbling character, 'as chirpy', someone once said, 'as the sparrows he draws so well'. He contributed to numerous magazines and papers, including *Punch*, *The Sketch* and *The Graphic*. He drew many coloured covers and inside colour plates for the juvenile magazine *Little Folks*, as well as countless pictures for all kinds of children's annuals. He did much of his best work in the coloured comic paper *Playtime*

(1919–29); as well as being the regular cover-artist, he contributed a double-page strip called *Coral Island, or Jill and Her Jungle Friends*, rather reminiscent of Mrs Bruin and the Bruin Boys. He also illustrated many children's books, including Dumas' *Fairy Tales* (1904), Wyss' *Swiss Family Robinson* (1907), *My Book of Best Fairy Tales* (*c.* 1914), *Aesop's Fables* (1924), and Lewis Carroll's *Alice's Adventures in Wonderland and Through the Looking-Glass* (1928). His distinctive and appealing rabbits and mice were made famous in a long-running series of advertisements for Mansion Polish and Cherry Blossom Boot Polish. Rountree served as a Captain in the Royal Engineers during the First World War and was at one time president of the London Sketch Club. He lived for some years in St Ives, Cornwall, and died in September 1950.

Shepard, Ernest Howard

Born in St John's Wood, London, on 10th December 1879, the son of an architect, and educated at St Paul's School, London. He began drawing as a small child and by the time he was seven was turning out excellent portraits of members of his family. He studied art at Heatherley's, London (1896–97), and at the Royal Academy Schools (1897–1902), where he was a Landseer Scholar in 1899 and a British Institute Scholar in 1900. He exhibited his first picture at the Royal Academy in 1901 and, in 1907, began his fifty-year association with *Punch*, when the magazine accepted one of his drawings. (He was elected to the famous '*Punch* Round Table' in 1921.) Much of his early work appeared in such magazines as *The Sketch* and *Illustrated London News*, as well as in *Punch*. He served in the Royal Artillery in France, Belgium and Italy, 1915–18, and won the Military Cross. He first won prominence as a book illustrator with his drawings for A. A. Milne's ever-popular quartet about Christopher Robin, Winnie-the-Pooh *et al.*: *When We Were Very Young* (1924), *Winnie-the-Pooh* (1926), *Now We Are Six* (1927) and *The House at Pooh Corner* (1928), when his enchanting work contributed in no small measure to the huge success of the stories and verses. His drawings were reproduced in *The Christopher Robin Birthday Book* (1930). After illustrating another book of children's verses (by Georgette Agnew) in 1927, he illustrated new editions of Kenneth Grahame's *The Golden Age* (1928) and *Dream Days* (1930). In 1931 came his superb and definitive illustrations to Grahame's classic *The Wind in the Willows*, and in 1932 he did similar outstanding work for a new edition of Richard Jefferies' *Bevis*. That same year he matched drawings to Jan Struther's collection of children's verses, *Sycamore Square*. Among his other superlative work in the 'thirties were his pictures for *Everybody's Pepys*, *Everybody's Lamb* and *Everybody's Boswell*, and for Houseman's *Victoria Regina*, etc. He has illustrated many other works over the years, chiefly children's books, and they include: Roland Pertwee's *The Islanders* (1950) and *Rough Water* (1951), Eleanor Farjeon's *The Silver Curlew* (1953) and *The Glass Slipper* (1955), Mrs Ewing's *The Brownies and Other Stories* (1954), *Modern Fairy Stories* (1955), several of Malcolm Saville's '*Susan and Bill*' books (1954–56) and new editions of Mrs Burnett's *The Secret Garden* (1956) and George MacDonald's *At the Back of the North Wind* (1956). It was not until 1965 that he wrote, as well as illustrated, his own children's book – the result was *Ben and Brock*; it was followed by another, *Betsy and Joe*, in 1966. In 1967 Shepard supplied four of the original Pooh stories with several new illustrations (both colour and black-and-white) which, combined with many of his old pictures, made up *The Pooh Story Book*, issued in picture-book format. In 1957 he wrote and illustrated his childhood autobiography, *Drawn from Memory*; he described his life through his art student days and up to his marriage in a sequel, *Drawn from Life*, in 1961. E. H. Shepard is one of the most delightful and memorable illustrators of children's books who ever put pencil to paper. He is best known, of course, for his Pooh books and his *Wind in the Willows*, But he has done an enormous amount of good work throughout his entire career (which is close on seventy years), some of the best being in the pages of *Punch*. He was at his peak during the 'twenties and 'thirties and catches the atmosphere and manners of those days perfectly in his exquisite drawings of the period. His daughter is Mary Shepard, who illustrated the *Mary Poppins* books.

Shepard, Mary Eleanor

Born 1909 in England and educated at St Monica's School,

Tadworth, Surrey, and Villa Ste Monique, Auteuil, Paris. She studied at the Slade School of Fine Art, London. Her parents were Florence Eleanor Chaplin and Ernest H. Shepard, both artists too. Her first illustrations were for P. L. Travers' *Mary Poppins* in 1934. She went on to illustrate the subsequent books in the popular series: *Mary Poppins Comes Back* (1935), *Mary Poppins Opens the Door* (1944), *Mary Poppins in the Park* (1952) and *Mary Poppins from A to Z* (1963). In 1937 she illustrated the American edition of Arthur Ransome's *Pigeon Post*. A. A. Milne's *Prince Rabbit and The Princess Who Could Not Laugh* (1966) contained her most recent illustrations. She has exhibited her work at two London art galleries. In 1937 she married E. V. Knox, then editor of *Punch*. She lives in London.

Smythe, J. Louis

Born in the 1880s in Ireland. Was a prolific illustrator for countless stories and serials in many boys' and girls' magazines during the period 1910–20, including *Fun and Fiction*, *Bullseye*, *Young Britain* and *Girls' Home*. He finds a place here because, although he never drew the character for actual publication, Smythe was the very first artist to draw *Tiger Tim*, one of the most famous and popular figures ever to grace the pages of a juvenile comic paper or annual. Smythe was called upon to picture an incident from a story. The passage chosen was one in which the heroine stepped from her carriage and entered a house . . . 'followed by her tiger, Tim.' And Smythe, unaware of the fact that in this instance a 'tiger' signified a page-boy or youthful attendant, drew instead a small striped tiger promenading serenely upright upon his hind legs! The editor who had commissioned Smythe's drawings gasped, laughed, and mentally noted for future use a new and attractive character . . . a character named *Tiger Tim*, later of Mrs Bruin's School and 'star' of his own comic paper for many years.

Stanley, Diana

Born 1909 in London and educated at Cheltenham Ladies' College, Gloucestershire. Studied at the Byam Shaw School of Art, under F. Ernest Jackson, 1929–34. For a time, during her early career, she worked as an engineering draughtsman in a London factory. She later taught drawing at the Byam Shaw School of Art from 1934 until 1938, when it closed, returning to teaching for a further two years in 1946. Following an injury sustained during an air raid on London in 1944, she could draw and paint only with her left hand for a long period. Her paintings have been exhibited at the Royal Academy and in 1945 she held a one-man show at the Batsford Gallery in London. Her memorable achievement in the children's book world has been her illustration work for Mary Norton's now-classic *The Borrowers* series. She has illustrated all four titles in the series: *The Borrowers* (1952), *The Borrowers Afield* (1955), *The Borrowers Afloat* (1959) and *The Borrowers Aloft* (1961). Her exquisite drawings have brought Mary Norton's miniature characters to life with perfection. In 1954 Miss Stanley produced a set of eight Tenniel drawings for a new edition of the Alice books, re-drawing them in full colour. She wrote and illustrated *Anatomy for Art Students* in 1951.

Steadman, Ralph

Born 1936 in Wallasey, Cheshire, and educated at Abergele Grammar School, in North Wales. Worked in an advertising agency for a year before doing his National Service in the RAF. Decided he would try his hand at cartooning and drawing and studied at the East Ham Technical College and, part-time, at the London School of Printing and Graphic Arts. He joined Kemsley Newspapers as a cartoonist, staying for three years before turning free-lance. Since then his work – ranging from light-hearted sketches to satirical and political cartoons – has appeared in many papers and magazines, especially *Punch*, *Private Eye* and the *Daily Telegraph*. He illustrated his first children's book – Frank Dickens' *Fly Away, Peter* – in 1964, when his highly-coloured, poster-like and amusing pictures drew wide praise. In 1965 he illustrated a new edition of Daisy Ashford's story *Love and Marriage*, to great and hilarious effect, following it in 1966 with another Ashford book, *Where Love Lies Deepest*. In the same year he supplied the pictures to Richard Ingrams' *The Tale of Driver Grope* – a semi-political satire for children dealing with rail travel versus road travel. In

351

1967 came his controversial illustrated edition of Lewis Carroll's *Alice in Wonderland*, which people tended to either love or loathe. Steadman used a satirical approach and depicted many of the classic characters as grotesques. Many bookshops and libraries stocked it in their adult section, saying the work was too frightening for youthful eyes. Also in 1967 there appeared *Ralph Steadman's Jelly Book*, an amusing and highly-coloured picture book about 'the cultivation and distribution of jelly'. Steadman is very adaptable in his work and varies his technique and materials according to the type and theme of his current assignment. He does this deliberately, not wishing to become identified with one particular style. He lives by the River Thames at Putney, London, with his wife and their three children.

Stobbs, William

Born 27th June 1914, in South Shields, County Durham, and educated at Durham University, where he gained his M.A. degree. He subsequently studied at the King Edward VI School of Art, before becoming an artist, illustrator and art teacher. He was Head of the Design Department at the London School of Printing and Graphic Arts, 1950–58. His book illustrations first gained prominence in the early 1950s, when one of his first notable assignments was Hilda Lewis's *The Gentle Falcon* (1952). In 1954 he illustrated the Carnegie Award-winning book for that year: Ronald Welch's *Knight Crusader* (later illustrating many other historical stories by this author). Among his subsequent illustration work has been that for: Lois Lamplugh's *Nine Bright Shiners* (1955), Tyler Whittle's *Spades and Feathers* (1955), R. F. Delderfield's *The Adventures of Ben Gunn* (1956), Elizabeth Grove's *Wintercut* (1957), Ronald Syme's *River of No Return* (1958) and David Scott Daniell's *The Boy They Made King* (1959). He won the 1959 Kate Greenaway Medal for his illustrations to two books: Chekov's *Kashtanka* and Ruth Manning-Sanders' compilation *A Bundle of Ballads*. Later titles include Frederick Grice's *Aidan and the Strollers* (1960), *Here Comes Harry* by Hilda Lewis (1960), William Mayne's *Summer Visitors* (1961), Henry Treece's *The Golden One* (1961), *The Gorgon's Head* by Ian Serraillier (1961), *The Cat Thief* by Joan

Cass (1961), *The Smugglers* by Ruth Manning-Sanders (1962) René Guillot's *Rex and Mistigri* (1963), Amabel Williams-Ellis's *Round the World Fairy Tales* (1963), *Jack and the Beanstalk* (1965), *The Story of the Three Little Pigs* (1965), *The Golden Goose* (1966), Amabel Williams-Ellis's *Old World and New World Fairy Tales* (1966), Audrey Erskine Lindop's *The Adventures of the Wuffle* (1966) and *The Three Billy Goats Gruff* (1967). Stobbs is particularly at home with historical subjects and maritime themes. His male characters are usually immediately recognisable for their square, tough, almost wood-hewn features and his drawings are noted for their vigour and strength. Over the past two years he has produced some excellent picture books based on well-known nursery stories. He admits to having been influenced by Renaissance drawing and also admires Caravaggio, Picasso and Rembrandt. He is a Member of the Society of Industrial Artists. For several years he has held the position of Principal of Maidstone College of Art, in Kent, where he also lives.

Tenniel, Sir John

Born 28th February 1820, in Kensington, London, the son of John Baptist Tenniel, who came of Huguenot stock. He taught himself to draw at an early age and later studied for a short time at the Royal Academy Schools, soon leaving when he became dissatisfied with the teaching methods there. He joined a leading London art society, sketched live models (for the only time in his career), and paid regular visits to the British Museum. His earliest work was in oils and at sixteen he was exhibiting a painting at the Suffolk Street Galleries in London. Less than a year later he had an oil painting at the Royal Academy. This was in 1837 and he exhibited regularly at the Academy for the next five years. In 1845 he was commissioned to paint a fresco portraying Dryden's St Cecilia in the House of Lords. Tenniel's first book illustrations appeared in *The Book of British Ballads*, in 1842. His illustrations for *Undine* appeared in 1845 and those for Thomas James's edition of *Aesop's Fables* in 1848. He was working, like most of his contemporary book-illustrators, on wood blocks. In 1850, Mark Lemon, then editor of *Punch*, invited Tenniel to join the magazine as joint leading cartoonist (with John Leech). So began Tenniel's fifty-year association with *Punch*, during which period he became one of the magazine's greatest artists. The whole social and political history of England can be pungently traced through his cartoons and caricatures spanning the entire second half of the nineteenth century. He was, of course, a member of the famous '*Punch* Round Table'. In April 1864 Tenniel accepted Charles L. Dodgson's (Lewis Carroll, as he later became known and revered) invitation to supply illustrations to his *Alice's Adventures in Wonderland*. The working relationship between the two Victorian gentlemen was a trifle stormy – though always scrupulously polite. Tenniel would submit a drawing to Carroll, who would then proceed to criticise it in practically every detail and request the artist to re-draw it. It was reported that out of the ninety-odd drawings Tenniel did for both Alice books, Carroll only really accepted one happily – and that was his depiction of Humpty Dumpty. When eventually Alice appeared in July 1865, Tenniel objected so vehemently to the poor reproduction of his drawings that Carroll (also dissatisfied) recalled the entire edition (all but a dozen or so copies, which 'got away'). In December 1865 (dated 1866) Macmillan's issued the second edition, which was approved by both author and artist. In December 1871 (dated 1872) came *Through the Looking Glass and What Alice Found There*, again illustrated by Tenniel (though he had originally refused the commission). The two Alice books came to be regarded as the perfect combination between author and artist and, indeed, it is difficult to separate text and pictures in one's mind when thinking of Alice and her adventures. The original of Carroll's 'Alice' was, as is generally known, Alice Liddell, but the original of Tenniel's Alice was almost certainly one Mary Hilton Badcock (afterwards Mrs Carwardine Probert), one of Carroll's little girl friends. Carroll sent a photograph of Mary to Tenniel with the suggestion that she might make a good model for Alice. It is unlikely that Tenniel copied the girl feature-for-feature, but it was reported that his depiction of Alice certainly resembled little Mary Hilton Badcock. There were some who said that Tenniel had drawn Alice from his own niece, but this can safely be refuted by the fact that Tenniel staunchly refused ever to use a life-model. Whoever she was – and quite a lot of her came from his own original interpretation – Tenniel's Alice is once-seen, never-forgotten. With her grave, prim and interested demeanour, her long, straight hair, pinafore-covered dress and striped stockings, and her delightful acceptance of the most amazing people and events, Alice is unique – as is Carroll's and Tenniel's Wonderland. Alice has been illustrated very many times since the copyright expired in 1907 – but Tenniel remains the master, good though some of his successors have been. Tenniel illustrated only eleven books solely (including those already mentioned), but his drawings appeared in many other books, including *The Juvenile Verse and Picture Book* (1848), Mrs Gatty's *Parables from Nature* (1861), *The Ingoldsby Legends* (1864) and Dalziel's *Arabian Nights' Entertainments* (1865). He was also a prolific contributor to such periodicals as *Once a Week* and *Good Words*, in addition to his amazing output for *Punch*. He was knighted in 1893 and died in London on 25th February 1914.

Wain, Louis

Born 5th August 1860. Probably the most famous and popular cat artist of all time. He drew other animals too, but specialised chiefly in cats of all breeds, shapes, colours and sizes, usually depicted in semi-human situations and walking on their hind legs. They invariably had large eyes, expressive faces and varied interests. Wain normally drew his cats in humorous pictures but also produced some fine serious studies too. His pictures first found popular favour when they began to appear in various adult and juvenile publications in the 1880s. Coloured prints of Wain paintings were soon hanging on the walls of almost every home in the country – and his calendars were in evidence in every office. He had his own *Louis Wain's Annual* for many years (copies of which are rare and much sought-after today). One of Wain's staunchest admirers was H. G. Wells, who once penned a eulogy to his work. Wain died in 1939, having spent the last twenty-five years of his life, tragically, in a mental institution, following injuries received in a bus accident in Bond Street, London – terrible repayment for a man who had brought so much happiness and laughter to so many people.

Wildsmith, Brian

Born 1930 in Penistone, near Sheffield, Yorkshire, and brought up in this small mining village. He studied at the Barnsley School of Art and then won a scholarship to the Slade School in London. Here he studied drawing and painting under William Coldstream from 1949–52. Then he spent two years undergoing his National Service in the army, devoting much of this period to teaching music at the Royal Military School of Music, since he loves music and is an accomplished pianist. On leaving the army in 1954 he became an art teacher and soon afterwards began to do book illustrations. One of his early successes was his work for Eleanor Graham's widely praised *The Story of Jesus* (1959) and some of his other commissions around this time included Eileen O'Faoláin's *High Sang the Sword* (1959), Nan Chauncy's *Tangara* (1960), Frederick Grice's *The Bonny Pit Laddie* (1960), Veronique Day's *Landslide!* (France 1958, England 1961), Madeleine Polland's *The Town Across the Water* (1961) and Roger Lancelyn Green's *Myths of the Norsemen* (1962). It was in 1962 that the turning-point in his career came when he published his *A.B.C. – Brian Wildsmith's A.B.C.*, as it came to be called. This outstanding children's picture book glowed with rich colour and inventive ideas and won the Kate Greenaway Medal for 1962. Wildsmith had by this time given up art teaching and was a full-time illustrator and painter. His subsequent work includes that to La Fontaine's fable *The Lion and the Rat* (1963), Charlotte Morrow's *The Watchers* (1963), Geoffrey Trease's *Follow My Black Plume* (1963), the *Oxford Book of Poetry for Children* (edited by Edward Blishen, 1963), La Fontaine's *The North Wind and the Sun* (1964), *Brian Wildsmith's Mother Goose* (1964) – another big success – *One, Two, Three* (1965) (a series of abstracts and designs incorporating numbers), La Fontaine's *The Rich Man and the Shoemaker* (1965), Robert Louis Stevenson's *A Child's Garden of Verses* (1966), La Fontaine's *The Hare and the Tortoise* (1966), *Birds* (1967) and *Wild Animals* (1967). He has illustrated well over thirty books in all and is today one of Britain's most famous and widely hailed younger illustrators. He is probably best known for his exuberant colour pictures (which are often enjoyed as much by adults as by children) but he is also an accomplished pen-and-ink artist too and has produced some fine work in this field. He has four young children himself and usually tries out his work on them before producing the final picture. He lives in south-west London.

Principal annual awards in British and American children's literature

Britain has two principal awards in the field of children's books, both presented annually by the Library Association.

The Carnegie Medal has been awarded annually since 1936, for an outstanding book for children published during the preceding year and written by a British subject living in the United Kingdom. The recipients have been:

1936 Arthur Ransome. *Pigeon Post.*
Illustrated by the author.
1937 Eve Garnett. *The Family From One End Street.*
Illustrated by the author.
1938 Noel Streatfeild. *The Circus is Coming.*
Illustrated by Clarke Hutton.
1939 Eleanor Doorly. *Radium Woman.*
Illustrated by Robert Gibbings.
1940 Kitty Barne. *Visitors from London.*
Illustrated by Ruth Gervis.
1941 Mary Treadgold. *We Couldn't Leave Dinah.*
Illustrated by Stuart Tresilian.
1942 B.B. (D. J. Watkins-Pitchford). *The Little Grey Men.*
Illustrated by the author.
1943 Prize withheld as no book considered suitable.
1944 Eric Linklater. *The Wind on the Moon.*
Illustrated by Nicolas Bentley.
1945 Prize withheld as no book considered suitable.

1946   Elizabeth Goudge. *The Little White Horse.*
       Illustrated by C. Walter Hodges.
1947   Walter de la Mare. *Collected Stories for Children.*
       Illustrated by Irene Hawkins.
1948   Richard Armstrong. *Sea Change.*
       Illustrated by M. Leszczynski.
1949   Agnes Allen. *The Story of Your Home.*
       Illustrated by Agnes and Jack Allen.
1950   Elfrida Vipont. *The Lark on the Wing.*
       Illustrated by T. R. Freeman.
1951   Cynthia Harnett. *The Wool-Pack.*
       Illustrated by the author.
1952   Mary Norton. *The Borrowers.*
       Illustrated by Diana Stanley.
1953   Edward Osmond. *A Valley Grows Up.*
       Illustrated by the author.
1954   Ronald Welch. *Knight Crusader.*
       Illustrated by William Stobbs.
1955   Eleanor Farjeon. *The Little Bookroom.*
       Illustrated by Edward Ardizzone.
1956   C. S. Lewis. *The Last Battle.*
       Illustrated by Pauline Baynes.
1957   William Mayne. *A Grass Rope.*
       Illustrated by Lynton Lamb.
1958   Philippa Pearce. *Tom's Midnight Garden.*
       Illustrated by Susan Einzig.
1959   Rosemary Sutcliff. *The Lantern Bearers.*
       Illustrated by Charles Keeping.
1960   I. W. Cornwall. *The Making of Man.*
       Illustrated by M. Maitland Howard.
1961   Lucy Boston. *A Stranger at Green Knowe.*
       Illustrated by Peter Boston.
1962   Pauline Clarke. *The Twelve and the Genii.*
       Illustrated by Cecil Leslie.
1963   Hester Burton. *Time of Trial.*
       Illustrated by Victor Ambrus.
1964   Sheena Porter. *Nordy Bank.*
       Illustrated by Annette Macarthur-Onslow.
1965   Philip Turner. *The Grange at High Force.*
       Illustrated by William Papas.
1966   Prize withheld as no book considered suitable.
       (Highly Commended, however, was *The Bayeux Tapestry,*
       by Norman Denny and Josephine Filmer-Sankey).
1967   Alan Garner. *The Owl Service.*

The Kate Greenaway Medal, inaugurated in 1955, is intended to recognise the importance of illustrations in children's books. It is awarded to the artist who, in the opinion of the Library Association, has produced the most distinguished work in the illustration of children's books during the preceding year. The artist has to be a British subject living in the United Kingdom. Those so far honoured are:

1955   Prize withheld as no book considered suitable.
1956   Edward Ardizzone. *Tim All Alone.*
1957   V. H. Drummond. *Mrs Easter and the Storks.*
1958   Prize withheld as no book considered suitable.
1959   William Stobbs. *Kashtanka,* and *A Bundle of Ballads.*
1960   Gerald Rose. *Old Winkle and the Seagulls.*
1961   Antony Maitland. *Mrs Cockle's Cat.*
1962   Brian Wildsmith. *A.B.C.*
1963   John Burningham. *Borka.*
1964   C. Walter Hodges. *Shakespeare's Theatre.*
1965   Victor C. Ambrus. *The Three Poor Tailors,* and for illustrations to other books, including *The Royal Air Force.*
1966   Raymond Briggs. *The Mother Goose Treasury.*
1967   Charles Keeping. *Charley, Charlotte and the Golden Canary.*

America has several annual awards to children's books, the most important being the Newbery and Caldecott Medals.
The Newbery Medal is awarded annually to the author (who has to be a citizen or resident of the United States) of the most distinguished contribution to American literature for children, published during the previous year. The recipients have been:

1922   Hendrik Willem van Loon. *The Story of Mankind.*
1923   Hugh Lofting. *The Voyages of Dr Dolittle.*
1924   Charles Hawes. *The Dark Frigate.*
1925   Charles Finger. *Tales from Silver Lands.*
1926   Arthur Bowie Chrisman. *Shen of the Sea.*
1927   Will James. *Smoky, the Cowhorse.*
1928   Dhan Gopal Mukerji. *Gayneck, the Story of a Pigeon.*
1929   Eric P. Kelly. *The Trumpeter of Krakow.*
1930   Rachel Field. *Hitty, Her First Hundred Years.*
1931   Elizabeth Coatsworth. *The Cat Who Went to Heaven.*
1932   Laura Adams. *Waterless Mountain.*
1933   Elizabeth Lewis. *Young Fu of the Upper Yangtze.*
1934   Cornelia Meigs. *Invincible Louisa.*

1935 Monica Shannon. *Dobry.*
1936 Carol Brink. *Caddie Woodlawn.*
1937 Ruth Sawyer. *Roller Skates.*
1938 Kate Seredy. *The White Stag.*
1939 Elizabeth Enright. *Thimble Summer.*
1940 James Daugherty. *Daniel Boone.*
1941 Armstrong Sperry. *Call It Courage.*
1942 Walter D. Edmonds. *The Matchlock Gun.*
1943 Elizabeth Janet Gray. *Adam of the Road.*
1944 Esther Forbes. *Johnny Tremain.*
1945 Robert Lawson. *Rabbit Hill.*
1946 Lois Lenski. *Strawberry Girl.*
1947 Carolyn Sherwin Bailey. *Miss Hickory.*
1948 William Pène du Bois. *The Twenty-One Balloons.*
1949 Marguerite Henry. *King of the Wind.*
1950 Marguerite de Angeli. *The Door in the Wall.*
1951 Elizabeth Yates. *Amos Fortune, Free Man.*
1952 Eleanor Estes. *Ginger Pye.*
1953 Ann Nolan Clark. *Secret of the Andes.*
1954 Joseph Krumgold. *. . . and now Miguel.*
1955 Meindert DeJong. *The Wheel on the School.*
1956 Jean Lee Latham. *Carry On, Mr Bowditch.*
1957 Virginia Sorensen. *Miracles on Maple Hill.*
1958 Harold Keith. *Rifles for Watie.*
1959 Elizabeth George Speare. *The Witch of Blackbird Pond.*
1960 Joseph Krumgold. *Onion John.*
1961 Scott O'Dell. *Island of the Blue Dolphins.*
1962 Elizabeth George Speare. *The Bronze Bow.*
1963 Madeleine l'Engle. *A Wrinkle in Time.*
1964 Emily Neville. *It's Like This, Cat.*
1965 Maia Wojciechowska. *Shadow of a Bull.*
1966 Elizabeth Borton de Trevino. *I, Juan de Pareja.*
1967 Irene Hunt. *Up a Road Slowly.*

The Caldecott Medal is awarded annually to the most distinguished American picture book for children, first published in the United States during the previous year. Those honoured to date have been:

1938 *Animals of the Bible.* Illustrated by Dorothy P. Lathrop. Text selected by Helen Dean Fish.
1939 *Mei Li.* Written and illustrated by Thomas Handforth.
1940 *Abraham Lincoln.* Written and illustrated by Ingri and Edgar d'Aulaire.

1941   *They Were Strong and Good.* Written and illustrated by Robert Lawson.

1942   *Make Way for Ducklings.* Written and illustrated by Robert McCloskey.

1943   *The Little House.* Written and illustrated by Virginia Lee Burton.

1944   *Many Moons.* Illustrated by Louis Slobodkin. Written by James Thurber.

1945   *Prayer for a Child.* Illustrated by Elizabeth Orton Jones. Written by Rachel Field.

1946   *The Rooster Crows.* . . . Illustrated by Maud and Miska Petersham.

1947   *The Little Island.* Illustrated by Leonard Weisgard. Written by Golden MacDonald (Margaret Wise Brown).

1948   *White Snow, Bright Snow.* Illustrated by Roger Duvoisin. Written by Alvin Tresselt.

1949   *The Big Snow.* Written and illustrated by Berta and Elmer Hader.

1950   *Song of the Swallows.* Written and illustrated by Leo Politi.

1951   *The Egg Tree.* Written and illustrated by Katherine Milhous.

1952   *Finders Keepers.* Illustrated by Nicolas (Nicolas Mordvinoff). Written by Will (William Lipkind).

1953   *The Biggest Bear.* Written and illustrated by Lynd Ward.

1954   *Madeline's Rescue.* Written and illustrated by Ludwig Bemelmans.

1955   *Cinderella, or the Little Glass Slipper.* Illustrated and translated from Perrault by Marcia Brown.

1956   *A Frog Went A'Courtin'.* Illustrated by Feodor Rojankovsky. Text retold by John Langstaff.

1957   *A Tree Is Nice.* Illustrated by Marc Simont. Written by Janice May Udry.

1958   *Time of Wonder.* Written and illustrated by Robert McCloskey.

1959   *Chanticleer and the Fox.* Adapted from Chaucer's *The Canterbury Tales* and illustrated by Barbara Cooney.

1960   *Nine Days to Christmas.* Illustrated by Marie Hall Ets. Written by Marie Hall Ets and Aurora Labastida.

1961   *Baboushka and the Three Kings.* Illustrated by Nicolas Sidjakov. Written by Ruth Robbins.

1962   *Once a Mouse.* Retold and illustrated by Marcia Brown.

1963   *The Snowy Day.* Story and pictures by Ezra Jack Keats.

1964   *Where the Wild Things Are.* Written and illustrated by Maurice Sendak.

1965 *May I Bring a Friend?* Illustrated by Beni Montresor. Written by Beatrice Schenk de Regniers.
1966 *Always Room for One More.* Written and illustrated by Nonny Hogrogian.
1967 *Sam, Bangs and Moonshine.* Written and illustrated by Evaline Ness.

Bibliography

In the following pages are listed brief details of books likely to be useful for following up certain individual authors and illustrators, past and present, and for gaining a general knowledge of children's literature. (For an excellent and more comprehensive list, readers are referred to *Books About Children's Literature*, edited by Marcus Crouch and published by the Library Association, London, revised edition 1966.) I gratefully acknowledge my own indebtedness to several of these titles whilst compiling the present work. Another important source of information has been my own personal collection of children's books and magazines of all periods, in addition to many thousands of notes and newspaper and magazine cuttings accumulated over the years with the idea of an eventual book such as this in mind.

General

ARBUTHNOT, MAY HILL, *Children and Books*, Scott, Foresman and Co, Chicago, USA, 1947.

AVERY, GILLIAN, with ANGELA BULL, *Nineteenth Century Children: heroes and heroines in English children's stories, 1780–1900*, Hodder and Stoughton, London, 1965.

CROUCH, MARCUS, *Treasure Seekers and Borrowers; children's books in Britain, 1900–1960*, Library Association, London, 1962.

CROUCH, MARCUS (ed.), *Chosen for Children: an account of the books which have been awarded the Library Association Carnegie Medal, 1936–65*, revised edition, Library Association, London, 1967.

DARTON, F. J. HARVEY, *Children's Books in England; five centuries of social life*, Cambridge University Press, London, 1932. Second edition, 1958.

DE VRIES, LEONARD, *Flowers of Delight . . . culled from the Osborne collection of early children's books*, Dennis Dobson, London, 1965.

EYRE, FRANK, *Twentieth Century Children's Books*, Longmans (for the British Council), London, 1952.

ELLIS, ALEC, *How To Find Out About Children's Literature*, Pergamon Press, London, 1966.

FIELD, E. M., *The Child and His Book*, Wells Gardner, London, 1891.

FISHER, MARGERY, *Intent Upon Reading: a critical appraisal of modern fiction for children*, Brockhampton Press, Leicester, 1961. Revised edition, 1964.

GREEN, ROGER LANCELYN, *Tellers of Tales*, Edmund Ward, Leicester, 1946. Re-written and enlarged edition, 1965.

— *Authors and Places: a literary pilgrimage*, Batsford, London, 1963.

HAZARD, PAUL, *Books, Children and Men*, translated from the French by Marguerite Mitchell, Horn Book, Boston, USA, 1944. (Original edition published by Boivin, Paris, 1932.)

HOLLOWELL, LILLIAN, *A Book of Children's Literature*, third edition, Holt, Rinehart and Winston, New York, 1966.

HÜRLIMANN, BETTINA, *Three Centuries of Children's Books in Europe*, translated and edited by Brian W. Alderson, Oxford University Press, London, 1967. (Original edition published by Atlantis Verlag, Zurich, 1959.)

JORDAN, ALICE, M., *From Rollo to Tom Sawyer*, Horn Book, Boston, USA, 1948.

KAMM, ANTHONY, and TAYLOR, BOSWELL, *Books and the Teacher*, University of London Press, 1966.

KING, ARTHUR, and STUART, A. F., *The House of Warne: one hundred years of publishing*, Warne, London, 1966.

LEWIS, NAOMI, *The Best Children's Books of 1963; 1964; 1965; 1966; 1967*, etc, published annually by Hamish Hamilton, London.

LEYLAND, ERIC, *Meet Your Authors*, Harrap, London, 1963.

LINES, KATHLEEN, *Four to Fourteen: a library of books for children*, second edition, Cambridge University Press for the National Book League, 1956.

MEIGS, CORNELIA, and others, *A Critical History of Children's Literature*, Macmillan, New York, 1953.

MUIR, PERCY H., *English Children's Books, 1600–1900*, Batsford, London, 1954.

NATIONAL BOOK LEAGUE, *Children's Books of Yesterday: a catalogue of an exhibition*, National Book League, London, 1946.

NEUBURG, VICTOR E., *The Penny Histories*, Oxford University Press, London, 1968.

OPIE, PETER AND IONA, *The Oxford Dictionary of Nursery Rhymes*, Oxford University Press, London, 1951.

PICKARD, P. M., *I Could a Tale Unfold: violence, horror and sensationalism in stories for children*, Tavistock Publications, London, 1961.

ST. JOHN, JUDITH (ed.), catalogue of the *Osborne Collection of Early Children's Books, 1566–1910*, Toronto Public Library, Canada, 1958.

SMITH, LENA, *A History of the Newbery and Caldecott Medals*, Viking Press, New York, 1957.

SMITH, JAMES S., *A Critical Approach to Children's Literature*, McGraw-Hill, New York, 1967.

TARG, WILLIAM (ed.), *Bibliophile in the Nursery: a bookman's treasury of collec-*

tors' lore on old and rare children's books, World Publishing Co, Cleveland, USA, 1957.

THWAITE, M. F., *From Primer to Pleasure*, Library Association, London, 1963.

TOWNSEND, JOHN ROWE, *Written for Children: an outline of English children's literature*, Garnet Miller, London, 1965.

TREASE, GEOFFREY, *Tales Out of School*, Heinemann, London, 1948. Revised edition, 1964.

TUER, ANDREW, C. W., *History of the Horn Book*, Leadenhall Press, London, 1897.

— *Pages and Pictures from Forgotten Children's Books*, Leadenhall Press, London, 1898–9.

— *Stories from Old-Fashioned Children's Books*, Leadenhall Press, London, 1899–1900.

The following magazines, published on a regular basis, will also be of interest to anyone who follows the world of children's books, past and present.

The Horn Book Magazine, Horn Book, Boston, USA. (Six issues a year.)

Junior Bookshelf, Marsh Hall, Thurstonland, Huddersfield, Yorkshire. (Six issues a year.)

The School Librarian and School Library Review, School Library Association, 150 Southampton Row, London, WC1. (Three issues a year.)

The Times Literary Supplement, Printing House Square, London, EC4. (Two special *Children's Books Supplements* a year.)

Growing Point, Mrs Margery Fisher, Ashton Manor, Northampton. (Nine issues a year.)

Children's Book News, Children's Book Centre Ltd, 140 Kensington Church Street, London, W8. (Six issues a year.)

Illustration

BLAND, DAVID, *A History of Book Illustration*, Faber, London, 1958.

— *The Illustration of Books*, third edition, Faber, London, 1962.

CLIVE, MARY, *The Day of Reckoning*, Macmillan, London, 1964.

DARTON, F. J. HARVEY, *Modern Book Illustration in Great Britain and America*, Studio, London, 1931. (Special Winter Number of *The Studio*.)

HÜRLIMANN, BETTINA, *Picture-Book World*, translated and edited by Brian W. Alderson, Oxford University Press, London, 1968.

JACQUES, ROBIN, *Illustrators at Work*, Studio, London, 1963.

JAMES, PHILIP, *Children's Books of Yesterday*, Studio, London, 1933. (Special Autumn Number of *The Studio*.)

— *English Book Illustration, 1800–1900*, a 'King Penguin', published by Penguin Books, Harmondsworth, Middlesex, 1947.

MAHONY, BERTHA, and others (compilers), *Illustrators of Children's Books, 1744–1945*, Horn Book, Boston, USA, 1947.

MORRIS, CHARLES H., *The Illustration of Children's Books*, Library Association, London, 1957.

PITZ, HENRY C., *Illustrating Children's Books: history-technique-production*, Watson-Guptill, New York, 1963.
RYDER, JOHN, *Artists of a Certain Line: a selection of illustrators for children's books*, Bodley Head, London, 1960.
SKETCHLEY, R. E. D., *English Book Illustration of Today*, Kegan Paul, London, 1903.
SMITH, JANET ADAM, *Children's Illustrated Books*, Collins, London, 1948.
VIGUERS, RUTH HILL, and others, *Illustrators of Children's Books, 1946–1956* (a supplement to *Illustrators of Children's Books, 1744–1945*), Horn Book, Boston, USA, 1958.
WHITE, GLEESON, *Children's Books and Their Illustrators*, Studio, London, 1898. (Special Winter Number of *The Studio*.)
WHO'S WHO IN ART, Art Trade Press, London, 1927 and subsequent editions.

Books etc. relating to juvenile periodicals
BECKER, STEPHEN, *Comic Art in America*, Simon and Schuster, New York, 1959.
DOYLE, BRIAN, *The Who's Who of Boys' Writers and Illustrators*, limited edition published by the author, London, 1964.
— *More Next Week: a survey of British old boys' papers and their authors*, included in *Boys' World Annual, 1966*, Odhams, London, 1965.
— *Tons of 'Tecs: the facts and fantasies of detective fiction in British old boys' papers*, included in *Boys' World Annual, 1967*, Odhams, London, 1966.
EGOFF, SHEILA A., *Children's Periodicals of the Nineteenth Century: a survey and bibliography*, Library Association, London, 1951.
PERRY, GEORGE, and ALDRIDGE, ALAN, *The Penguin Book of Comics*, Penguin Books, Harmondsworth, Middlesex, 1967.
PUMPHREY, GEORGE H., *What Children Think of Their Comics*, Epworth Press, London, 1964.
TURNER, E. S., *Boys Will Be Boys: the story of Sweeney Todd, Deadwood Dick, Sexton Blake, Dick Barton et al.*, Michael Joseph, London, 1948. Revised edition, 1957.
WERTHAM, FREDERIC, *Seduction of the Innocent* (a detailed study of horrific and erotic comic-books and their effect upon young readers), Museum Press, London, 1955. (Original American edition published in 1954.)

Anyone interested in the history and content of old boys' and girls' papers, children's comics, etc will find the undermentioned 'amateur' magazines invaluable. They include details of authors, illustrators, editors, publishers and stories in a wide range of British juvenile periodicals, from *Boy's Own Paper, Chums, Captain, Union Jack* and *Boy's Friend* to *Magnet, Gem, Nelson Lee, Sexton Blake Library, Chips, Rainbow* and *Scout*.

COLLECTOR'S DIGEST (Founded 1946), edited by Eric Fayne and published at Excelsior House, Grove Road, Surbiton, Surrey (monthly).
COLLECTOR'S DIGEST ANNUAL (Founded 1947), as above.
THE STORY PAPER COLLECTOR (Founded 1941), edited by the late W. H. Gander, in Manitoba, Canada. It ceased publication on his death in 1966 (quarterly).

General biographical guides

AUTHORS AND WRITERS WHO'S WHO, Shaw, London, 1934 and subsequent editions.

— Burke's Peerage, London, 1960 and subsequent editions.

BROWNING, D. C. (compiler), *Everyman's Dictionary of Literary Biography*, Dent, London, revised edition, 1962.

BURKE, W. J., and HOWE, WILL D. (augmented and revised by IRVING R. WEISS), *American Authors and Books: 1640 to the Present Day*, Gramercy, USA, 1943. Revised edition, Crown, 1962. Nicholas Vane, London, 1963.

KUNITZ, STANLEY J. and HAYCRAFT, HOWARD (editors), *British Authors of the Nineteenth Century*. Wilson, New York, 1936.

— *British Authors of the Twentieth Century*. Wilson, New York, 1942.

Biographies of individual authors and illustrators

Alcott, Louisa May

TICKNER, C., *May Alcott: a memoir*, Little, Brown, Boston, USA, 1928.

MEIGS, CORNELIA, *Invincible Louisa*, Little, Brown, Boston, USA, 1933. (Published under the title *The Life of Louisa Alcott* by Harrap, London, 1936.)

ANTHONY, KATHERINE, *Louisa May Alcott*, Cresset Press, London, 1939.

SALYER, SANDFORD, *Marmee, the Mother of Little Women*, Oklahoma University Press, 1949.

STERN, MADELEINE, *Louisa May Alcott*, Peter Nevill, London, 1952.

Alger, Horatio

MAYES, HERBERT R., *Alger: a biography without a hero*, Macy-Masius, New York, 1948.

'A.L.O.E.' – see *Tucker, Charlotte Maria*.

Andersen, Hans Christian

ANDERSEN, HANS CHRISTIAN, *The Fairy Tale of My Life*, Copenhagen, 1855. Translated into English, with additional material, Riverside Press, Cambridge, Mass., USA, 1871. Abridged edition, published under the title *The Mermaid Man*, Barker, London, 1955.

BAIN, R. N., *Hans Christian Andersen*, Lawrence and Bullen, London, 1895.

TOKSVIG, SIGNE, *The Life of Hans Christian Andersen*, Macmillan, London, 1933.

BURNETT, CONSTANCE BUEL, *The Shoemaker's Son: the life of Hans Christian Andersen*, Harrap, London, 1943.

MANNING-SANDERS, RUTH, *Swan of Denmark: the story of Hans Christian Andersen*, Heinemann, London, 1949.

MEYNELL, ESTHER, *The Story of Hans Christian Andersen*, Methuen, London, 1949.

NATIONAL BOOK LEAGUE, *Hans Christian Andersen, 1805–1955*, catalogue of a Jubilee Exhibition held at the National Book League, London, 1955.

GODDEN, RUMER, *Hans Christian Andersen*, Hutchinson, London, 1955.

LARSEN, SVEND, *Hans Christian Andersen*, translated into English by Mabel Dyrup, Odense, Denmark, 1961.
STIRLING, MONICA, *The Wild Swan*, Collins, London, 1965.

Anstey, F.
ANSTEY, F., *A Long Retrospect*, Oxford University Press, London, 1936.

Baden-Powell, Lord Robert
HILLCOURT, WILLIAM, with OLAVE, LADY BADEN-POWELL, *Baden-Powell: the two lives of a hero*, Heinemann, London, 1964.

Ballantyne, R. M.
BALLANTYNE, R. M., *Personal Reminiscences in Book-making*, Nisbet, London, 1893.
QUAYLE, ERIC, *Ballantyne the Brave*, Rupert Hart-Davis, London, 1967.

Barrie, J. M.
MOULT, THOMAS, *Barrie*, Cape, London, 1928.
HAMMERTON, J. A., *Barrie: the story of a genius*, Sampson Low, London, 1929.
DARTON, F. J. HARVEY, *J. M. Barrie*, Nisbet, London, 1929.
DARLINGTON, W. A., *J. M. Barrie*, Blackie, London, 1938.
MACKAIL, DENIS, *The Story of J.M.B.: a biography*, Peter Davies, London, 1941.
MEYNELL, VIOLA (ed.), *Letters of J. M. Barrie*, Peter Davies, London, 1942.
GREEN, ROGER LANCELYN, *Fifty Years of Peter Pan*, Peter Davies, London, 1954.
ASQUITH, CYNTHIA, *Portrait of Barrie*, James Barrie, London, 1954.
GREEN, ROGER LANCELYN, *J. M. Barrie*, Bodley Head, London, 1960 (a 'Bodley Head Monograph').

Bewick, Thomas
DOBSON, AUSTIN, *Thomas Bewick and His Pupils*, Chatto and Windus, London, 1884.
BEWICK, THOMAS, *Memoir of Thomas Bewick, written by himself*, Centaur Press, Arundel, Sussex, 1961.

Blyton, Enid
Enid Blyton: A Complete List of Books, an illustrated catalogue (with a foreword by Enid Blyton) of her books in print, issued by John Menzies, Edinburgh, Scotland, 1956.
ENID BLYTON, *The Story of My Life*, Pitkins, London, n.d. (c. 1957).

Boston, Lucy M.
ROSE, JASPER, *Lucy Boston*, Bodley Head, London, 1965 (a 'Bodley Head Monograph').

Brazil, Angela
BRAZIL, ANGELA, *My Own Schooldays*, Blackie, London, 1935.

369

Bridges, T. C.
BRIDGES, T. C., *From Florida to Fleet Street*, Hutchinson, London, 1928.

Browne, Tom
JOHNSON, A. E., *Tom Browne, R. I.*, A. and C. Black, London, 1909.

Burnett, Frances Hodgson
BURNETT, FRANCES HODGSON, *The One I Knew the Best of All*, Warne, London, 1893.
BURNETT, VIVIAN, *The Romantick Lady: the life story of an imagination*, Scribners, New York, 1927.
LASKI, MARGHANITA, *Mrs Ewing, Mrs Molesworth and Mrs Hodgson Burnett*, Barker, London, 1950.

Caldecott, Randolph
BLACKBURN, HENRY, *Randolph Caldecott: a personal memoir of his early art career*, Sampson Low, London, 1886.
DAVIS, MAY GOULD, *Randolph Caldecott*, Lippincott, New York, 1946.

Carroll, Lewis (and the Alice books)
COLLINGWOOD, STUART DODGSON, *The Life and Letters of Lewis Carroll*, T. Fisher Unwin, London, 1898.
BOWMAN, ISA, *The Story of Lewis Carroll, told for young people by the real Alice in Wonderland*, Dent, London, 1899.
WILLIAMS, SIDNEY HERBERT, and MADAN, FALCONER, *The Handbook of the Literature of the Rev. C. L. Dodgson*, Oxford University Press, London, 1931. New edition, revised by Roger Lancelyn Green, published under the title *The Lewis Carroll Handbook*, 1962.
REED, LANGFORD, *Life of Lewis Carroll*, Foyle, London, 1932.
DE LA MARE, WALTER, *Lewis Carroll*, Faber, London, 1932.
MADAN, FALCONER, *The Lewis Carroll Centenary in London, 1932*, Bumpus, London, 1932.
CARROLL, LEWIS, *A Selection from the Letters of Lewis Carroll to His Child Friends*, Macmillan, London, 1933.
LENNON, FLORENCE BECKER, *Lewis Carroll*, Cassell, London, 1947.
GREEN, ROGER LANCELYN, *The Story of Lewis Carroll*, Methuen, London, 1949.
TAYLOR, A. L., *The White Knight*, Oliver and Boyd, London, 1952.
GREEN, ROGER LANCELYN (ed.), *The Diaries of Lewis Carroll*, 2 volumes, Cassell, London, 1953.
HUDSON, DEREK, *Lewis Carroll*, Constable, London, 1954.
— *Lewis Carroll*, Longmans, for the British Council and the National Book League, London, 1958.
GREEN, ROGER, LANCELYN, *Lewis Carroll*, Bodley Head, London, 1960 (a 'Bodley Head Monograph').
GARDNER, MARTIN (ed.), *The Annotated Alice*, Clarkson N. Potter, New York, 1960. Blond, London, 1964. Penguin Books, Harmondsworth, Middlesex, 1965.

370

WEAVER, WARREN, *Alice in Many Tongues: the translations of Alice in Wonderland,* University of Wisconsin Press, USA, 1964.
Alice One Hundred: a catalogue in celebration of the 100th birthday of Alice's Adventures in Wonderland, Adelphi Bookshop, Victoria, B.C., Canada, 1966.

Chapman, C. H.
CHAPMAN, C. H., *The Billy Bunter Picture Book,* Charles Hamilton Museum, Maidstone, Kent, 1967.

Collodi, C.
MARCHETTI, ITALIANO, *Carlo Collodi,* Le Monnier, Florence, 1959.
SANTUCCHI, LUIGI, *Collodi,* La Scuola, Brescia, Italy, 1961.

Church, Richard
CHURCH, RICHARD, *Over the Bridge,* Heinemann, London, 1955.
— *The Golden Sovereign,* Heinemann, London, 1957.
— *The Voyage Home,* Heinemann, London, 1964.

Cooper, James Fenimore
DEKKER, GEORGE, *James Fenimore Cooper, the Novelist,* Routledge and Kegan Paul, London, 1967.
GROSSMAN, JAMES, *James Fenimore Cooper,* Methuen, London, 1950.

Crane, Walter
KONODY, P. G., *The Art of Walter Crane,* Bell, London, 1902.
CRANE, WALTER, *An Artist's Reminiscences,* Methuen, London, 1907.
MASSÉ, GERTRUDE, *A Bibliography of First Editions of Books Illustrated by Walter Crane,* Chelsea Publishing Co, London, 1933.

Cross, John Keir
CROSS, JOHN KEIR, *Aspect of Life: an autobiography of youth,* Selwyn and Blount, London, 1937.

Day, Thomas
GIGILLAT, G. W., *The Author of Sandford and Merton: a life of Thomas Day Esq.,* Columbia University Press, USA, 1932.
SCOTT, SIR S. H., *The Exemplary Mr Day, 1748–1789, Author of Sandford and Merton,* Faber, London, 1935.

Defoe, Daniel
DOTTIN, P., *The Life and Strange and Surprising Adventure of Daniel Defoe,* Stanley Paul, London, 1928.
WATSON, F., *Daniel Defoe,* Longmans, London, 1952.

De La Mare, Walter
MEGROZ, R. L., *Walter de la Mare: a biographical and critical sketch,* Hodder and Stoughton, London, 1924.

371

REID, FORREST, *Walter de la Mare: a critical study*, Faber, London, 1929.
HOPKINS, KENNETH, *Walter de la Mare*, Longmans, London, 1953.
CLARK, LEONARD, *Walter de la Mare*, Bodley Head, London, 1960 (a 'Bodley Head Monograph').

Disney, Walt
FEILD, ROBERT, D., *The Art of Walt Disney*, Collins, London, 1944. (Original US edition, 1942.)
MILLER, DIANE DISNEY, *Walt Disney: an intimate biography*, Curtis, USA, 1956. Odhams, London, 1958.

Dodge, Mary Mapes
HOWARD, ALICE B., *Mary Mapes Dodge of St Nicholas*, Messner, New York, 1943.

Doyle, Sir Arthur Conan
DOYLE, SIR ARTHUR CONAN, *Memories and Adventures*, Hodder and Stoughton, London, 1924.
LAMOND, REV JOHN, *Arthur Conan Doyle: a memoir*, Murray, London, 1931.
PEARSON, HESKETH, *Conan Doyle: his life and art*, Methuen, London, 1943.
CARR, JOHN DICKSON, *The Life of Sir Arthur Conan Doyle*, Murray, London, 1949.
HARDWICKE, MICHAEL and MOLLIE, *The Man Who Was Sherlock Holmes*, Murray, London, 1964.
NORDON, PIERRE, *Conan Doyle*, trans. by Frances Partridge, Murray, London, 1966.
(Also numerous books, pamphlets and magazines dealing with aspects of the Sherlock Holmes canon.)

Edgeworth, Maria
EDGEWORTH, MARIA, *Life and Letters*, Edward Arnold, London, 1894.
CLARKE, I. C., *Maria Edgeworth, her family and friends*, Hutchinson, London, 1950.
NEWBY, P. H., *Maria Edgeworth*, Barker, London, 1950.
INGLIS-JONES, ELIZABETH, *The Great Maria*, Faber, London, 1959.

Edwards, Monica
EDWARDS, MONICA, *The Unsought Farm*, Michael Joseph, London, 1954.

Evens, G. Bramwell ('Romany')
EVENS, EUNICE, *Through the Years With Romany*, University of London Press, 1946.

Ewing, Juliana Horatia, Mrs
GATTY, HORATIA K. F., *Juliana Horatia Ewing and Her Books*, SPCK, London, 1885.
MARSHALL, MRS, *A.L.O.E. and Mrs Ewing*, London, 1897.
MAXWELL, CHRISTABEL, *Mrs Gatty and Mrs Ewing*, Constable, London, 1949.

LASKI, MARGHANITA, *Mrs Ewing, Mrs Molesworth and Mrs Hodgson Burnett*, Barker, London, 1950.
AVERY, GILLIAN, *Mrs Ewing*, Bodley Head, London, 1961 (a 'Bodley Head Monograph').

Farjeon, Eleanor
FARJEON, ELEANOR, *A Nursery in the Nineties*, Gollancz, London, 1935. Second edition, Oxford University Press, London, 1960.
COLWELL, EILEEN H., *Eleanor Farjeon*, Bodley Head, London, 1961 (a 'Bodley Head Monograph').
BLAKELOCK, DENYS, *Eleanor: portrait of a Farjeon*, Gollancz, London, 1966.
The Eleanor Farjeon Book (with an introductory essay by Naomi Lewis and a personal recollection by Rumer Godden), Hamish Hamilton, London, 1966.

Farrar, Frederick W.
FARRAR, REGINALD F., *The Life of F. W. Farrar*, Nisbet, London, 1904.

Furniss, Harry
FURNISS, HARRY, *Confessions of a Caricaturist*, 2 volumes, Fisher Unwin, London, 1901.
— *Harry Furniss at Home*, Fisher Unwin, London, 1903.

Gatty, Horatia K. F., Mrs
MAXWELL, CHRISTABEL, *Mrs Gatty and Mrs Ewing*, Constable, London, 1949.

Gilson, Charles
GILSON, CHARLES, *Chances and Mischances*, Jarrolds, London, n.d. (*c.* 1930s).

Goodrich, S. G. ('Peter Parley')
GOODRICH, S. G., *Recollections of a Lifetime*, 2 volumes, Miller, Orton and Mulligan, USA, 1856.

Grahame, Kenneth
CHALMERS, PATRICK, *Kenneth Grahame: life, letters and unpublished work*, Methuen, London, 1933.
GRAHAME, ELSPETH (ed.), *First Whisper of The Wind in the Willows*, Methuen, London, 1944.
GREEN, PETER, *Kenneth Grahame, 1859–1932: a study of his life, work and times*, Murray, London, 1959.
GRAHAM, ELEANOR, *Kenneth Grahame*, Bodley Head, London, 1963 (a 'Bodley Head Monograph').

Greenaway, Kate
SPIELMANN, M. H., and LAYARD, G. S., *Kate Greenaway*, A. and C. Black, London, 1905.
MOORE, ANNE CARROLL, *A Century of Kate Greenaway*, Warne, London, 1946.

373

NEWCOMB, CORELLE, *The Secret Door: the story of Kate Greenaway*, Dodd, Mead, New York, 1946.

Grimm, Jacob and Wilhelm
HAMMOND, MURIEL E., *Jacob and Wilhelm Grimm: the fairy tale brothers*, Dobson, London, 1968.
GRIMM, JACOB and WILHELM, *Grimm's Fairy Tales*, trans. and ed. Margaret Hunt, revised by James Stern, Routledge, London, 1948. (Contains excellent short biographies of the Grimm Brothers and a history of the Tales, by Joseph Campbell.)

Haggard, Sir H. Rider
HAGGARD, SIR HENRY RIDER, *The Days of My Life*, ed. C. J. Longman, 2 volumes, Longmans, London, 1926.
HAGGARD, LILIAS RIDER, *The Cloak That I Left*, Hodder and Stoughton, London, 1951.
COHEN, MORTON, *Rider Haggard: his life and works*, Hutchinson, London, 1960.
COHEN, MORTON (ed.), *Rudyard Kipling to Rider Haggard: the record of a friendship*, Hutchinson, London, 1965.

Hamilton, Charles ('Frank Richards', etc.)
RICHARDS, FRANK, *The Autobiography of Frank Richards*, Skilton, London, 1952. Revised Memorial edition, 1962.
BUTCHER, J. S., *Greyfriars School: a prospectus*, Cassell, London, 1965.
The Charles Hamilton Museum, Old Boys' Book Club (London Section), Maidstone, Kent, 1966.
(Also numerous articles in *Collector's Digest Magazine* [1946–], *Collector's Digest Annual* [1947–] [Surbiton, Surrey] and *The Story Paper Collector* [1941–66, Manitoba, Canada—ceased publication in 1966].

Harris, Joel Chandler
HARLOW, ALVIN F., *Joel Chandler Harris: plantation story-teller*, Messner, New York, 1941.

Hawthorne, Nathaniel
VAN DOREN, MARK, *Nathaniel Hawthorne*, Methuen, London, 1948.

Henty, G. A.
FENN, GEORGE MANVILLE, *George Alfred Henty: the story of an active life*, Blackie, London, 1907.

Hope, Anthony
HOPE, ANTHONY, *Memories and Notes*, London, 1927.
MALLET, CHARLES, *Anthony Hope and His Books*, London, 1935.

Hughes, Thomas
MACK, E. C., and ARMYTAGE, W. H. G., *Thomas Hughes: the life of the author of Tom Brown's Schooldays*, Benn, London, 1952.

Kingsley, Charles
KINGSLEY, F. E. G. (ed.), *Charles Kingsley: His Letters and Memories of His Life,* edited by His Wife, Kegan Paul, London, 1883.
KENDALL, GUY, *Charles Kingsley and His Ideas,* Hutchinson, London, 1947.
POPE-HENNESSY, UNA, *Canon Charles Kingsley: a biography,* Chatto and Windus, London, 1948.
MARTIN, ROBERT BERNARD, *The Dust of Combat: a life of Charles Kingsley,* Faber, London, 1960.

Kipling, Rudyard
HOPKINS, R. THURSTON, *Rudyard Kipling: a character study,* Simpkin Marshall, London, 1915.
DUNSTERVILLE, L. C., *Stalky's Reminiscences,* Cape, London, 1928.
BERESFORD, G. C., *Schooldays With Kipling,* Gollancz, London, 1936.
KIPLING, RUDYARD, *Something of Myself: for my friends known and unknown,* Macmillan, London, 1937.
SHANKS, EDWARD, *Rudyard Kipling: a study in literature and political ideas,* Doubleday, Doran, New York, 1940.
BROWN, HILTON, *Rudyard Kipling: a new appreciation,* Hamish Hamilton, London, 1945.
CARRINGTON, CHARLES, *Rudyard Kipling: his life and work,* Macmillan, London, 1955.
TOMPKINS, J. M. S., *The Art of Rudyard Kipling,* Methuen, London, 1959.
SUTCLIFF, ROSEMARY, *Rudyard Kipling,* Bodley Head, London, 1960 (a 'Bodley Head Monograph').
GREEN, ROGER LANCELYN, *Kipling and the Children,* Elek, London, 1965.
COHEN, MORTON (ed.) *Rudyard Kipling to Rider Haggard: the record of a friendship,* Hutchinson, London, 1965.

Lagerlöf, Selma
BERENDSOHN, W. A., *Selma Lagerlöf: her life and work,* adapted from the German by George F. Timpson, Nicholson and Watson, London, 1931.

Lang, Andrew
GREEN, ROGER LANCELYN, *Andrew Lang: a critical biography,* Edmund Ward, Leicester, 1946.
— *Andrew Lang,* Bodley Head, London, 1962 (a 'Bodley Head Monograph').

Lear, Edward
DAVIDSON, ANGUS, *Edward Lear: landscape painter and nonsense poet,* Murray, London, 1933. New edition, 1968.

Lewis, C. S.
LEWIS, C. S., *Surprised by Joy: the shape of my early life,* Bles, London, 1955.
GREEN, ROGER LANCELYN, *C. S. Lewis,* Bodley Head, London, 1963 (a 'Bodley Head Monograph').

Lucas, E. V.
LUCAS, E. V., *Reading, Writing and Remembering,* Methuen, London, 1932.

LUCAS, AUDREY, *E. V. Lucas: a portrait*, Methuen, London, 1939.

Lynch, Patricia
LYNCH, PATRICIA, *A Storyteller's Childhood*, Dent, London, 1947.

MacDonald, George
MACDONALD, GREVILLE, *George MacDonald and His Wife*, Allen and Unwin, London, 1924.
WOLFF, R. I., *The Golden Key: a study of the fiction of George MacDonald*, Yale University Press, USA, 1961.

Marryat, Frederick
MARRYAT, FLORENCE, *Life and Letters of Captain Marryat*, 2 volumes, London, 1872.
HANNAY, DAVID, *Captain Marryat*, London, 1889.
CONRAD, JOSEPH, *Notes on Life and Letters*, Dent, London, 1921.
LLOYD, CHRISTOPHER, *Captain Marryat and the Old Navy*, London, 1939.
WARNER, OLIVER, *Captain Marryat: a rediscovery*, Constable, London, 1953.

Martineau, Harriet
MARTINEAU, HARRIET, *Autobiography*, Smith Elder, London, 1877.
MILLER, F. FENWICK, MRS, *Harriet Martineau*, Allen, London, 1884.
WHEATLEY, VERA, *The Life and Work of Harriet Martineau*, Secker and Warburg, London, 1957.

Masefield, John
MASEFIELD, JOHN, *In the Mill*, Heinemann, London, 1941.
— *New Chum*, Heinemann, London, 1944.
— *So Long to Learn: chapters of an autobiography*, Heinemann, London, 1952.
STRONG, L. A. G., *John Masefield*, Longmans, London, 1952.
SPARK, MURIEL, *John Masefield*, Peter Nevill, London, 1953.
FISHER, MARGERY, *John Masefield*, Bodley Head, London, 1963 (a 'Bodley Head Monograph').

Mee, Arthur
HAMMERTON, SIR JOHN, *Child of Wonder: an intimate biography of Arthur Mee*, Hodder and Stoughton, London, 1946.

Milne, A. A.
MILNE, A. A., *It's Too Late Now: the autobiography of a writer*, Methuen, London, 1939.

Molesworth, Mary Louisa, Mrs
LASKI, MARGHANITA, *Mrs Ewing, Mrs Molesworth and Mrs Hodgson Burnett*, Barker, London, 1950.
GREEN, ROGER LANCELYN, *Mrs Molesworth*, Bodley Head, London, 1961 (a 'Bodley Head Monograph').

Nesbit, E.
MOORE, DORIS LANGLEY, *E. Nesbit: a biography*, Benn, London, 1933. New edition, with added material, 1967.
STREATFEILD, NOEL, *Magic and the Magician: E. Nesbit and her children's books*, Benn, London, 1958.
BELL, ANTHEA, *E. Nesbit*, Bodley Head, London, 1960 (a 'Bodley Head Monograph').
NESBIT, E., *Long Ago When I Was Young*, Whiting and Wheaton, London, 1966.

Newbery, John
WELSH, CHARLES, *A Bookseller of the Last Century: being some account of the life of John Newbery*, Griffith Farran, London, 1885.
NEWBERY, JOHN, *A Little Pretty Pocket-book*, a facsimile, with an introductory essay and bibliography by M. F. Thwaite, Oxford University Press, London, 1966.

Pemberton, Sir Max
PEMBERTON, SIR MAX, *Sixty Years Ago and After*, Hutchinson, London, 1936.

Phillpotts, Eden
PHILLPOTTS, EDEN, *From the Angle of 88*, Hutchinson, London, 1951.

Porter, Gene Stratton
MEEHAN, JEANETTE PORTER, *The Lady of the Limberlost: the life and letters of Gene Stratton Porter*, USA, 1928.

Potter, Beatrix
LANE, MARGARET, *The Tale of Beatrix Potter: a biography*, Warne, London, 1946.
POTTER, BEATRIX. *The Art of Beatrix Potter*, with an appreciation by Anne Carroll Moore and reproductions selected and arranged by Leslie Linder, Warne, London, 1955.
CROUCH, MARCUS, *Beatrix Potter*, Bodley Head, London, 1960 (a 'Bodley Head Monograph').
POTTER, BEATRIX, *The Journal of Beatrix Potter from 1881 to 1897*, transcribed from her code writings by Leslie Linder, Warne, London, 1966.
NATIONAL BOOK LEAGUE, *Beatrix Potter, 1866–1943*, Catalogue of a Centenary Exhibition held at the National Book League, London, 1966.

Pyle, Howard
ABBOTT, CHARLES D., *Howard Pyle: a chronicle*, Harper, New York, 1925.
NESBITT, ELIZABETH, *Howard Pyle*, Bodley Head, London, 1966 (a 'Bodley Head Monograph').

Rackham, Arthur
HUDSON, DEREK, *Arthur Rackham: his life and work*, Heinemann, London, 1960.

Ransome, Arthur
SHELLEY, HUGH, *Arthur Ransome*, Bodley Head, London, 1960 (a 'Bodley Head Monograph').

Reed, Talbot Baines
HUTCHISON, GEORGE ANDREW, *Talbot Baines Reed as Boy and Man*, an appreciation by the Editor of the *Boy's Own Paper*, contained in Nos. 789 and 790 (February 24 and March 3, 1894), Volume 16 of the *Boy's Own Paper*. Religious Tract Society, London, 1894.
SIME, JOHN, *Talbot Baines Reed: a memoir*, included in *Kilgorman*, Nelson, London, 1895.
MORISON, STANLEY, *Talbot Baines Reed: author, bibliographer, typefounder*, Cambridge University Press (privately printed), 1960.

Reid, Mayne
REID, ELIZABETH, *Captain Mayne Reid: his life and adventures*, Greening, London, 1900.

Robinson, William Heath
JOHNSON, A. E., *William Heath Robinson*, A. and C. Black, London, 1913.
ROBINSON, WILLIAM HEATH, *My Line of Life*, Blackie, London, 1938.
DAY, LANGSTON, *The Life and Art of William Heath Robinson*, Herbert Joseph, London, 1947.
ROBINSON, WILLIAM HEATH, *The Penguin W. Heath Robinson*, introduction by R. Furneaux Jordan, Penguin Books, Harmondsworth, Middlesex, 1966.

Seton, Ernest Thompson
SETON, ERNEST THOMPSON, *Trail of an Artist-Naturalist*, Hodder and Stoughton, London, 1951.

Sewell, Anna
BAKER, MARGARET J., *Anna Sewell and Black Beauty*, Harrap, London, 1956.

Shepard, E. H.
SHEPARD, E. H., *Drawn from Memory*, Methuen, London, 1957.
— *Drawn from Life*, Methuen, London, 1961.

Sherwood, Mary Martha, Mrs
SHERWOOD, MARY MARTHA, MRS, *The Life of Mrs Sherwood . . . edited by her daughter, Sophia Kelly*, Darton, London, 1857.
SMITH, NAOMI ROYDE, *The State of Mind of Mrs Sherwood*, Macmillan, London, 1946.

Spyri, Johanna
PAUR-ULRICH, MARGUERITE, *Johanna Spyri*, Waldmann, Zurich (n.d.).

Stevenson, Robert Louis
BALFOUR, GRAHAM, *The Life of Robert Louis Stevenson*, 2 volumes, Methuen, London, 1901.

378

FURNESS, J. C., *Voyage to Windward: the life of Robert Louis Stevenson*, Faber, London, 1952.
STERN, G. B., *He Wrote Treasure Island: the story of Robert Louis Stevenson*, Heinemann, London, 1954.
ALDINGTON, RICHARD, *Portrait of a Rebel: the life and work of Robert Louis Stevenson*, Evans, London, 1957.
BUTTS, DENNIS, *Robert Louis Stevenson*, Bodley Head, London, 1966 (a 'Bodley Head Monograph').
– plus many more.

Stowe, Harriet Beecher
STOWE, C. E., *Life of Harriet Beecher Stowe*, USA, 1889.
FIELD, A. A., *Life and Letters of Harriet Beecher Stowe*, USA, 1897.
WILSON, FORREST, *Crusader in Crinoline*, USA, 1941.

Streatfeild, Noel
WILSON, BARBARA KER, *Noel Streatfeild*, Bodley Head, London, 1961 (a 'Bodley Head Monograph').

Sutcliff, Rosemary
MEEK, MARGARET, *Rosemary Sutcliff*, Bodley Head, London, 1962 (a 'Bodley Head Monograph').

Tarkington, Booth
TARKINGTON, BOOTH, *Gentleman from Indiana*, USA, 1955.

Taylor, Ann and Jane
ARMITAGE, DORIS MARY, *The Taylors of Ongar*, Heffer, Cambridge, 1939.

Tenniel, Sir John
SARZANO, FRANK, *Sir John Tenniel*, Art and Technics, London, 1948.

Trease, Geoffrey
MEEK, MARGARET, *Geoffrey Trease*, Bodley Head, London, 1960 (a 'Bodley Head Monograph').

Tucker, Charlotte Maria ('A.L.O.E.')
MARSHALL, MRS, *A.L.O.E. and Mrs Ewing*, London, 1897.

Twain, Mark
HOWELLS, WILLIAM DEAN, *My Mark Twain*, Harper, New York, 1910.
PAINE, ALBERT BIGELOW, *Mark Twain: a biography*, Harper, New York, 1912.
TWAIN, MARK, *Mark Twain's Autobiography*, ed. Albert Bigelow Paine, Harper, New York, 1924.
CLEMENS, SARA, *My Father, Mark Twain*, Harper, New York, 1931.
ALLEN, JERRY, *The Adventures of Mark Twain*, Weidenfeld and Nicolson, London, 1954.

MELTZER, MILTON, *Mark Twain Himself: a pictorial biography*, Crowell, New York, 1960.
— plus many more.

Upton, Florence K.
LYTTELTON, EDITH, *Florence Upton, Painter*, Longmans, London, 1926.

Verne, Jules
DE LA FUYE, MARGUERITE ALLOTTE, *Jules Verne*, Paris, 1925. Staples Press, London, 1954.
ALLOTT, KENNETH, *Jules Verne*, Macmillan, New York, 1941.
WALTZ, GEORGE H., JR., *Jules Verne: the biography of an imagination*, Holt, New York, 1943.
EVANS, I. O. (ed.), *Jules Verne: master of science fiction*, Sidgwick and Jackson, London, 1956.
PEARE, CATHERINE O., *Jules Verne*, Dobson, London, 1961.
EVANS, I. O., *Jules Verne and His Work*, Arco, London, 1965.

'Wetherell, Elizabeth' *(Susan Warner)*
WARNER, ANNA B., *Susan Warner*, USA, 1909.

White, T. H.
WARNER, SYLVIA TOWNSEND, *T. H. White*, Cape with Chatto and Windus, London, 1967.

Wiggin, Kate Douglas
SMITH, NORA A., *Kate Douglas Wiggin As Her Sister Knew Her*, USA, 1925.

Wodehouse, P. G.
WODEHOUSE, P. G., *Performing Flea: a self-portrait in letters*, Jenkins, London, 1953.
— *Over Seventy*, Jenkins, London, 1957.
USBORNE, RICHARD, *Wodehouse at Work*, Jenkins, London, 1961.
FRENCH, R. B. D., *P. G. Wodehouse*, Oliver and Boyd, London, 1966.

Yonge, Charlotte Mary
COLERIDGE, CHRISTABEL, *Charlotte Mary Yonge: her life and letters*, Macmillan, London, 1903.
BATTISCOMBE, GEORGINA, *Charlotte Mary Yonge: the story of an uneventful life*, Constable, London, 1943.
MARE, MARGARET, and PERCIVAL, ALICIA C., *Victorian Best-seller*, Harrap, London, 1947.
BATTISCOMBE, GEORGINA, and LASKI, MARGHANITA, *A Chaplet for Charlotte Yonge*, Cresset, London, 1965.

380